A REVIEW
of the
GREEK INSCRIPTIONS AND PAPYRI
Published 1984–85

NEW DOCUMENTS ILLUSTRATING EARLY CHRISTIANITY

• *Volume 8* •

A REVIEW
of the
GREEK INSCRIPTIONS
AND PAPYRI
Published 1984–85

S. R. Llewelyn

ANCIENT HISTORY DOCUMENTARY RESEARCH CENTRE
MACQUARIE UNIVERSITY, N.S.W. AUSTRALIA

WILLIAM B. EERDMANS PUBLISHING COMPANY
GRAND RAPIDS, MICHIGAN / CAMBRIDGE, U.K.

© 1998 Macquarie University

Published 1997 by Wm. B. Eerdmans Publishing Co.
255 Jefferson Ave. S.E., Grand Rapids, Michigan 49503 /
P.O. Box 163, Cambridge CB3 9PU U.K.
in association with
The Ancient History Documentary Research Centre,
Macquarie University, NSW 2109, Australia

All rights reserved

04 03 02 01 00 99 98   5 4 3 2 1

ISBN 0-8028-4518-5

The Ancient History Documentary Research Centre (Director: Emeritus Professor E. A. Judge) within the School of History, Philosophy and Politics at Macquarie University fosters research and professional development in association with other organizations interested in the documentation of the ancient world.

Committee for NEW DOCUMENTS ILLUSTRATING EARLY CHRISTIANITY
P. W. Barnett (Chairman), P. Geidans, E. A. Judge, A. McComb, J. A. Shepherd

Editorial Consultants

G. W. Clarke	Director, Humanities Research Centre, Australian National University
G. H. R. Horsley	Professor of Classics and Ancient History, University of New England
M. Lattke	Professor of Studies in Religion, University of Queensland
J. A. L. Lee	Senior Lecturer in Greek, University of Sydney
K. L. McKay	Formerly Reader in Classics, Australian National University
S. R. Pickering	Research Fellow, Macquarie University
G. R. Stanton	Associate Professor in Classics and Ancient History, University of New England
M. Wilcox	Hon. Professorial Fellow, Macquarie University

This volume has been produced with the support of a Macquarie University Research Grant. It has also been partially subsidized by a grant from the Greek Publications Fund, which seeks to support the publication of scholarly research in Australia in the field of ancient Greek studies.

Editorial correspondence should be addressed to
Dr. S. R. Llewelyn, School of History, Philosophy and Politics
Macquarie University, NSW 2109, Australia.

TABLE OF CONTENTS

INTRODUCTION

    Abbreviations

    Textual Sigla

    Acknowledgements

SLAVERY

1	The Crucifixion of a Slave	1
2	A Curse against a Fugitive Slave?	4
3	The Government's Pursuit of Runaway Slaves	9

TAXATION

4	Tax Collection and the τελῶναι of the New Testament	47
5	Taxes on Donkeys: An Illustration of Indirect Taxation at Work in Roman Egypt	77
6	Flight from Personal Obligations to the State	97

PUBLIC COURTESIES AND CONVENTIONS

7	Benefaction Ideology and Christian Responsibility for Widows by *J.R. Harrison*	106
8	The Epitaph of a Student Who Died Away from Home	117
9	Prescripts and Addresses in Ancient Letters	122
10	A Rescript to the Victors of Sacred Games	129

JUDAICA

11	A Hebrew Congregational Prayer from Egypt by *Mark Harding*	145
12	An Association of Samaritans in Delos	148
13	The Career of T. Mucius Clemens and its Jewish Connections	152

TABLE OF CONTENTS

ECCLESIASTICA

14	The Christian Symbol ΧΜΓ, an Acrostic or an Isopsephism?	156
15	Christian Letters of Recommendation	169
16	A Confessional Inscription	173
17	Baptism and Salvation	176

INDEXES

Subjects	181
Words Greek	189
Latin	190
Hebrew	191
Greek and Roman Writers	191
Patristic Writers	192
Inscriptions	193
Papyri	194
Ostraca	196
Old Testament	196
Apocrypha and Pseudepigrapha	197
Qumran Texts	197
Rabbinical Text	197
New Testament	197

INTRODUCTION

The eighth volume in the *New Documents Illustrating Early Christianity* series continues the format of the preceding two volumes. The documentary evidence is gouped under five larger headings (Slavery, Taxation, Public Coutesies and Conventions, Judaica and Ecclesiastica) each dealing with a topic of interest to the study of the New Testament and the history of the early church. *New Docs* seeks to elucidate these topics by better understanding their historical and social milieus. The intended reader is the researcher, teacher or student in biblical studies and other related fields. The series is offered as a tool to broaden the context of studies in these fields.

In order to assist the reading of the Greek text, the translation has attempted to reflect as far as practicable the formal structure of the document. This means that the translation is line-by-line, with doubtful and restored readings marked by *sigla* in the English translation. Naturally, one cannot translate the Greek document into flowing English if at the same time one pays strict regard to formal structures. Thus something of a compromise has resulted. For example, the indication of doubtful and restored readings can only be approximate. Again not all documents can be rigidly translated line-by-line. Words and expressions may need to appear on different lines in the Greek and English texts for syntactic reasons. Where this occurs to a significant degree the reader will be alerted to the fact by the translation's continued indentation. Resumption of line-by-line translation is indicated by the cessation of indentation. It is hoped that all these devices will help the non-Greek reader to use the documents in a more critical fashion, knowing what the text actually says and what the editor has restored to it.

Most quotations from other ancient texts or secondary sources are also translated to assist the English reader. Exceptions exist. For example, where the reader's access to an adequate translation can be assumed or when the quotation is paraphrased in the preceding sentence, translation may be omitted. If I have used the translation of another author, this is acknowledged in the text. My own translations, however, are those not otherwise acknowledged.

New Docs 8 covers documents which were first published or significantly re-edited in the years 1984-85. As already flagged in the preceding volume, it also contains documents held over from the years 1982-83.

New Docs 8 marks the end of my period of my sole editorship of the series. Contact will be maintained with the project, however, by the contribution of entries and the supervision of the publication of the series.

Future volumes, it is hoped, will adopt a different format. The in-depth discussion will be replaced by shorter entries with the secondary literature and debates largely covered by bibliographies rather than discussion in the pages of each entry. The entries will thus function as pointers to the interested reader. To this end, experts in various aspects of the ancient world will be invited to contribute entries to future volumes. These changes should make possible the annual publication of the series, as well as presenting the reader with a greater range of documents for consideration.

Abbreviations

Abbreviations follow standard conventions, except where altered for clarity.
> Journals - as in *L'Année philologique*.
> Papyrological works - as in S.R. Pickering, *Papyrus Editions held in Australian Libraries* (North Ryde 1984); ibid., *Papyrus Editions: Supplement* (North Ryde 1985).
> Epigraphical works according to generally used conventions (see LSJ), preceded where necessary by *I*. (e.g. *I. Ephesos*).
> Ancient authors, biblical and patristic works - generally as in LSJ, BAGD, and Lampe (see below).

Textual sigla used are as follows:

αβ̣	—	letters not completely legible
. . . .	—	4 letters missing
...	—	indeterminate number of letters missing
[αβ]	—	letters lost from document and restored by editor
[±8 letters]	—	about 8 letters lost
‹αβ›	—	letters omitted by scribe and added by editor
«αβ»	—	editorial correction of wrong letters in the text
(αβ)	—	editor has resolved an abbreviation in the text
{αβ}	—	letters wrongly added by scribe and cancelled by editor
⟦αβ⟧	—	a (still legible) erasure made by scribe
`αβ´	—	letters written above line
ā	—	letter stands for a numerical equivalent
v., vv., vac.	—	one, two, several letter spaces left blank (*vacat*) on document
m.1, m.2	—	first hand (*manus*), second hand

Acknowledgements

Mr J.R. Harrison and Dr Mark Harding have each contributed an entry in the present volume. Appreciation is expressed to E.A. Judge for reading each entry and offering many constructive ideas and criticisms. He has also directed me to relevant secondary literature. Thanks are also extended to E.A. Judge, C.B. Forbes and M. Wilcox who were the successful applicants for a Macquarie University Research Fellowship from which the project has been funded. I am also indebted to E.A. Lewis whose careful typing of the Greek documents and assistance in the typesetting of the volume have been much appreciated. I would like to express my thanks to R. Cook and P. Geidans of the Ancient History Documentary Research Centre, who have helped in various ways in the production of this volume. Finally, I wish to thank my wife Susie for her moral support and love. This volume is dedicated to her.

S.R. Llewelyn

Slavery

§1 The Crucifixion of a Slave

Amyzon   Not later than second century BC

Ed. — J. and L. Robert, *Fouilles d'Amyzon en Carie I. Exploration, histoire, monnaies et inscriptions* (Paris 1983) 259-263.

Δημήτριος Παγκράτου.	Demetrios son of Pankrates.
Πᾶσιν δακρυτὸς Δημήτριος, ὃγ γλυκὺς ὕπνος	Demetrios, mourned by all, whom sweet sleep
εἶχεν καὶ Βρομίου νεκτάρεαι προπόσεις·	held and the nectarous drink of Bromios;
δούλου δ' ἐκ χειρῶν [σ]φαγισθεὶς καὶ πυρὶ πολλῶι	slain by the hands of a slave and in a great conflagration
5 φλεχθεὶς σὺμ μελάθροις ἤλυθον εἰς Ἀίδην,	burnt together with the house, I came to Hades,
ὄφρα πατὴρ καὶ ὅμαιμοι ἐμοὶ καὶ πρέσβεα μήτηρ	whilst my father, siblings and elderly mother
δέξαντ' εἰς κόλπους ὄστεα καὶ σποδιήν·	received to their bosoms bones and ashes;
ἀλλὰ πολῖται ἐμοὶ τὸν ἐμὲ ῥέξαντα τοιαῦτα	but the one who did such things to me my fellow-citizens
θηρσὶ καὶ οἰωνοῖς ζωὸν ἀνεκρέμασαν.	crucified alive for the wild beasts and birds.

J. and L. Robert observe that the epitaph is quite unique in the story it tells of the master-slave relationship. The slave, apparently availing himself of the deep sleep which had overtaken his master after a banquet, killed him and then tried to conceal the crime by setting the whole house alight. As such the document stands as a counter-balance to the numerous (and no doubt biased) epitaphs commemorating a good relationship between master and slave. On this topic see *New Docs* 6 (1992) 51-2 and 57 n.67.

The epitaph also records the punishment meted out to the culprit. The citizens of Amyzon (i.e. the βουλή) crucified the slave alive for the wild beasts and birds of prey to eat. J. and L. Robert draw attention to the adjective ζωόν (*l*.9) arguing that the crucified slave may have been placed in the mountains or forests of Latmos where birds of prey and wild animals still roamed. Execution was by crucifixion. In other words, the fate described here was not that of a person who had been executed by some other means and whose corpse had been put up for display.[1] Interpretation is made difficult, however, by the presence of a literary motif[2] and the evident desire of the epitaph's writer to accentuate the plight of the culprit. The document surely serves as a sober warning to both masters and slaves, but most especially to slaves. A

---

[1] M. Hengel, *Crucifixion* (ET: London 1977) 24, notes that the 'distinction between the crucifixion of the victim while he is still alive and the display of the corpse of someone who has been executed in a different fashion' was not always clearly made.

[2] On the motif of being eaten by wild beasts and birds of prey see Aristophanes, *Thesm.* 1029, Pseudo-Manetho, *Apostelesmatica* 4.198-200, and Hengel, *Crucifixion* 87.

number of observations on the text bear this out. The epitaph is composed of four sense units of two lines each (*ll*.2-3, 4-5, 5-6, 7-8). *Ll*.2-3 contrast with *ll*.4-5 as do *ll*.6-7 with *ll*.8-9. The convivial and contented picture of sweet sleep induced by the nectarous drink is shattered by the slave's vicious attack thus acccentuating the heinous nature of the crime (cf. also πᾶσιν δακρυτός). Then the fond care of the master's next of kin for his remains stands in sharp contrast with the fate meted out to the criminal. Such is the penalty of one who commits so vile a crime. Note must also be taken of the emphatic position of πᾶσιν (*l*.2) and the reference to the πολῖται (*l*.8). The crime is such as to cause all to mourn. Moreover, the (entire) citizen body stands behind the deceased master and in an act of solidarity against any slave who might think to take such action in the future it punishes the slave by crucifixion (an execution without burial for all to see) and no doubt also attended to the erection of the epitaph (a permanent witness to their resolve).

The epitaph raises the question of crucifixion and its use by the Greeks. Latte[3] observes concerning the inscription that 'here in (this) half-barbarian region the penalty had survived under Eastern influence until late into the Hellenistic period'. J. and L. Robert counter: 'Indeed, the Amyzonians had lived under Persian rule and influence. However, at this date they were certainly not semi-barbarous, but Hellenised Carians as all those of the province.'[4] Hengel's chapter on the use of crucifixion in the Greek-speaking world confirms the objection.[5] But Hengel also argues that the use of crucifixion for the punishment of slaves (i.e. *servile supplicium*) was more prevalent under Roman rule. Crucifixion in the Hellenistic world was used to punish crimes of treason and acts of war. It was a political and military punishment and tended not to be used as a civil punishment against slaves and violent criminals. A further distinction in the use of crucifixion is also noted with the Romans employing it as a punishment against the lower classes of society and slaves in particular: maiores nostri in omni supplicio severius servos quam liberos, famosos quam integrae famae homines punierunt — *Our ancestors used to punish slaves more severely than freemen, the notorious than persons of uncorrupted repute in every punishment* (*Dig.* 48.19.28.16). Hengel[6] connects this distinction in types of punishment with the growth in slave numbers in Italy and the fear of rebellion. Cf. Seneca, *Epist.*, 47.5: *totidem hostes esse quot servos*. By a *senatus consultum* all slaves and freedmen under a master's roof were to receive the same penalty if the master was assassinated by one of his slaves (*Dig.* 29.5.1 and Tacitus, *Ann.* 13.32). The measure was apparently introduced and maintained (a) because the complicity of fellow household slaves and freedmen was assumed and (b) because fear of one's own death would coerce a slave to protect his master (Tacitus, *Ann.* 14.42-45).[7]

Hengel, in consideration of the evidence and his dating of the epitaph, understands the document to show Roman influence: 'It dates from the second or first century BC. Roman influence may already be evident here, since in 133 BC Attalus III had made over his kingdom

---

[3] K. Latte, *RE* s.v. 'Todesstrafe' 1606 (cited by Robert, *Fouilles d'Amyzon en Carie* 263 n.23).

[4] Robert, *Fouilles d'Amyzon en Carie* 263. On the Hellenisation of the area see also A.H.M. Jones, *The Greek City from Alexander to Justinian* (Oxford, repr. 1971) 28; cf. also pp.1, 25, 42, 161, 281 and 289.

[5] Hengel, *Crucifixion* 69-83.

[6] Hengel, *Crucifixion* 56.

[7] On the *senatus consultum Silanianum* see further A. Watson, *Roman Slave Law* (Baltimore 1987) 134-8. Cf. also P. Garnsey, *Social Status and Legal Privilege in the Roman Empire* (Oxford 1970) 26. The murder of a master by his slave was traditionally regarded by Romans 'as an outrage which threatened the existence of the Roman social order'. It was accordingly cruelly punished, e.g. the retaliatory execution of all slaves under the same roof.

to the Romans.'[8] But the earlier dating of the epitaph by J. and L. Robert[9] presents a problem for this interpretation. It should also be noted that Caria (i.e. the territory in which Amyzon was located) did not form part of the kingdom of Attalus III and thus could not have formed part of his bequest.[10] With the battle of Magnesia and the subsequent treaty of Apamea (189/188 BC) Caria south of the Maeander river transferred from Seleucid to Rhodian rule; however, some twenty years later after the Rhodians' lukewarm support of Rome during the Third Macedonian War the territory was made free (168 BC). This was its political status in 133 BC when Attalus made his bequest. The freedom was revoked as a result of Carian support for the Aristonicus's revolt and attempt to frustrate Attalus's legacy (133-130 BC).

S.R.L.

---

[8] Hengel, *Crucifixion* 76.

[9] Robert, *Fouilles d' Amyzon en Carie* 263 n.22. They date the epitaph palaeographically to the Hellenistic period and not later than the second century BC.

[10] See further Robert, *Fouilles d' Amyzon en Carie* 209 and 249, and Jones, *The Greek Cities* 54 and 115-6 (data on p.44 seems confused).

§2 A Curse against a Fugitive Slave?

Provenance unknown   5.9 x 4.9 cm   Fifth to sixth century AD

Ed. pr. — H. Harrauer, 'Strafaufschub', *ZPE* 30 (1978) 209-210 (= *SB* XIV 12184).

The text is written on the verso of a papyrus which had been cut from a larger and already used sheet. The dating of the text is according to the dating of the hand on the recto. The script is unskilled both in the formation of letters (unligatured block letters) and the maintenance of the line (sloping down from left to right). However, Lukaszewicz comments that the language and spelling is faultless.

Bibliography: A. Lukaszewicz, 'Christlicher Fluchtext', *ZPE* 73 (1988) 61-2.

Chi-rho	
χμγ	
πρὸ μὲν πάν-	Before all,
των κακὸς και-	evil times
5 ρὸς τοῦ κολα-	for the obnoxious
σίμου Θεοδώ-	Theodoros,
ρου. Κακὸς	for he is
γάρ ἐστιν.	evil.

Harrauer conjectures that the text represents a letter forming part of the 'criminal procedure' against Theodoros. As such it does not speak against punishment, only that the present moment was unfavourable. From the absence of the names of addressee and sender Harrauer suggests that the two stood in a close relationship. They also knew the nature of the unnamed offence committed by Theodoros. The following translation is offered:

> Vor allem ist es ein schlechter Augenblick für die Bestrafung des Theodoros. Er is wirklich schlecht.

From the opening monograms it is clear that the text is Christian. Harrauer suggests perhaps a monastic milieu; however, in so far as this is based on the reconstruction of a word on the recto (παν[ήγυριν), little can be based on the conjecture.

Lukaszewicz offers a quite different interpretation of the text. He suggests that the text be understood as a wish for harm against Theodoros. The suggestion is based on the similarity between the expressions κακὸς καιρὸς τοῦ + name and the formula κακὰ τὰ ἔτη τοῦ + name, found in a number of acclamations.[1] The following translation (cf. English above) is offered:

> Vor allem schlechte Zeiten für den zu bestrafenden Theodoros, weil er böse ist.

Three texts are given in support of the interpretation. All concern acclamations of circus factions of the late Roman period.

Circus Factions

The factions, originally four in number (Blues, Greens, Reds and Whites), were responsible for the organization of circus games at Rome. At first they were run by private businessmen

---

[1] Lukaszewicz cites Z. Borkowski, *Alexandrie II. Inscriptions des factions à Alexandrie* (Warsaw 1982) no. 47, p.87, and A. Cameron, *Circus Factions: Blues and Green at Rome and Byzantium* (Oxford 1976) 315.

but from the fourth century they became organizations with their own officials paid by the emperor. At the same time the circus games and their organizing factions appear to have spread to many of the cities of the eastern provinces. Each faction had its own band of supporters or partisans who identified themselves under the colour of their faction. At public games the partisans would make their acclamations of praise or blame against the governor and from AD 331 these were reported to the emperor. Cameron[2] considers this a witness to the breakdown in the traditional government of the Greek city. From the fourth century the Roman governor exercised more direct control over the cities in his province and the authority of the traditional organs of civil government, the councils, was weakened. The acclamation became a check against the increased power of the governor and an alternative avenue to influence imperial opinion.

Acclamation continued a long established practice of audiences at theatre and circus where as Tacitus states the crowd had the greatest licence (*ubi plurima vulgi licentia*, Tac. *Hist*. 1.72), attempting to influence imperial policy by their cries. In a society where people held opinions but had little political power these venues offered them the opportunity to express their views and to influence policy. There was strength in numbers and the people were emboldened to speak en masse.[3] Here one thinks of two scenes recounted in the New Testament, the influence exercised by the crowd on Pilate at the trial of Jesus (Mark 15.6-15 et par.) and the attempt by the Ephesian crowd to influence the city's magistrates at the instigation of the goldsmiths (Acts 19.23-41). Both incidents also illustrate the way in which the crowd could be or was often thought to have been manipulated by interested parties, i.e. the high priests and the goldsmiths respectively.

Be that as it may, at some time in the fifth century the factions appear to have amalgamated with the theatre claques adopting the latters' custom of antiphonal chanting. At the same time the factions acquired responsibility for the organization of public entertainment more generally, and two colours, the Blues and the Green, appear as the dominant organizations. From the late sixth to early seventh centuries the Blues and Greens increasingly took on a ceremonial role as the rivalry of the two factions was sublimated to the desires of the imperial court. In this regard cf. (C) below with (A) and (B).

(A)
Alexandria   AD 608-610

Ed. pr. — Z. Borkowski, *Alexandrie II. Inscriptions des factions à Alexandrie* (Warsaw 1982) no. 47, p.87 (= *SEG* XXXI 1494).

Νικᾷ ἡ τύχη	The fortune
Εὐτοκίου	of Eutokios
κὲ Βενέτων·	and the Blues triumphs.
κακὰ τὰ ἔτη	Bad years
5 τοῦ Λαχανᾶ.	for Lachanas.

---

[2] Cameron, *Circus Factions*, 241-3.
[3] See further R. MacMullen, *Enemies of the Roman Order. Treason, Unrest, and Alienation in the Empire* (Cambridge Mass., 1966) 168-173, on the circus and threatre. On the role of guilds as centres of unrest see pp.173-8.

The graffito is one of thirty-two graffiti inscribed on seats in the Alexandrian circus. This text and most other graffiti are acclamations expressing the propaganda of their respective circus factions, i.e. the Greens and the Blues. The texts bear formulae found in other acclamations dated to the sixth and seventh centuries, a time when such factions were active in the politics of the day. On the basis of his no. 39, Borkowski[4] dates the texts more precisely to the rebellion of Heraclius against Phocas (AD 608-610) and postulates that the period of civil war saw a proliferation of inter-factional struggles, the Greens supporting Heraclius and the Blues Phocas. As no. 39 speaks of the complete fall of the Blues, Borkowski suggests that the above text (no. 47) which acclaims the triumph of the Blues was perhaps inscribed before the others and the defeat of their faction.

No. 47 is the sole graffito honouring the Blues. The text also contains a malediction against Λαχανᾶς, a name not attested in the papyri. If Eutokios was the leader of the Blues, then it might be supposed that Lachanas was the leader of the Greens, their factional opponents. Tentative support for this assumption might be found if the name were coined with reference to λάχανον (vegetable) so that there was a play between the name and the colour of his faction. Borkowski, noting that the name was also a synonym for λαχανοπώλης/-πράτης (vegetable merchant) in late Greek, suggests a pejorative sense, e.g. 'peddler of greens' or 'vegetable-grubber'. In view of the difficulty in deciding the sense of the name he concludes:

> Incontestablement, l'auteur Bleu remplaça le terme courant <<Vert>> par un épithète injurieux qui pouvait comporter, à ce qu'on sache, des allusions aussi bien à la couleur qu'à l'origine médiocre et à la conduite douteuse de l'ennemi.

(B)
Aphrodisias   Mid-fifth to late sixth
                                            or early seventh centuries

Ed. — C. Roueché, *Aphrodisias in Late Antiquity* (London 1989) 223 (= *IAphrodChr* §181 ii).

κακὰ τὰ ἔτη   Bad years
τῶν Πρασίνων.   for the Greens.

The text is one of a number informally inscribed on seats in the theatre of Aphrodisias. The inscriptions date from all periods of the theatre's use with some cut on top of earlier ones. Though the texts are not easily dated, those referring to the circus factions are assigned to the late Roman period (mid-fifth to late sixth or early seventh centuries) because of their mention of the circus factions. From the position of the seats the editor suggests that the Greens and Blues were located in specific locations: The Greens 'in the *cunei* to the north, opposite the stage room apparently used by Green performers' and the Blues 'in the *cunei* to the south'. Oddly, the seat containing the above inscription was found on the Green side of the theatre and the editor suggests that it 'was perhaps inserted surreptitiously to annoy the Greens'. This may explain the attempt to erase the first line of the text.

(C)
The third text is an acclamation found in the *Book of Ceremonies*. It forms part of the antiphonal chanting in preparation for the circus. Chanting preceded the emperor's mounting of the *charisma*. This included orthodox declarations and doxologies, prayers for the emperor

---

[4] Z. Borkowski, *Alexandrie II. Inscriptions des factions à Alexandrie* (Warsaw 1982) 77 and 85-6.

and requests for the victory of the chanters' factions. On mounting the *charisma* the emperor blessed the people. Antiphonal chanting continued during the blessing, celebrating both the emperor and his orthodoxy. After the call of the Blues or Greens (the faction was determined by its precedence at the time) to members of the senate or of the guard to arise and make their vows to the emperor, the chanters declare (Constantinus VII Porphyrogenitus, *De caer.* 318):

τῶν φιλούντων ἡμᾶς πολλὰ τὰ ἔτη, καὶ πάλιν, τῶν δὲ μισούντων ἡμᾶς κακὰ τὰ ἔτη.
"Many years[5] for those loving us", and again, "bad years for those hating us".

The declaration was then repeated thrice by the people.

A fourth, though incomplete, example can be added to those cited above. *IGC* 1156[6] (= *I. Magn.* 239, sixth century) is described as the scribble of a Christian. It was inscribed on the back of a pillar marking the site of the attendants of the builders under Pollion, the high-priest and scribe: τόπος ὑπηρετῶν οἰκοδόμων | ἐπὶ Πωλλίωνος | τοῦ ἀρχιερέος | καὶ γραμματέος. The pillar was found *in situ* in the southern part of the agora of Magnesia. The text reads:

+ κακὰ τὰ ἔτι <<ἔτη>> τοῦ - - -   *Bad years for N.*

Conclusion

Returning to *SB* 12184, Lukaszewicz offers the suggestion that Theodoros was a run-away slave. The suggestion is possible but support for it is slender.

(a) The name Theodoros could belong to a slave but this was not necessarily the case. For example, Solin[6] gives the following break-up of the 89 persons with the name Theodoros in Rome: 7 of senatorial status, 1 of equestrian status, 4 free-born, 61 of uncertain status, 13 slaves and freedmen and 1 peregrine.

(b) κολάσιμος (derived from κολάζω / κόλασις), an adjective not otherwise attested, is understood to refer to the urgency or necessity of punishment. Again, this might suggest that Theodoros was a slave. But it need not.

(c) As Lukaszewicz recognises, κακὸς καιρός is not attested as an expression associated with servile flight. The only collocation that I have been able to find is Georgius Monachus, *Chronicon.* 5.795 (*MPG* vol. 110 col. 1124). Leo VI appointed his brother Alexander as emperor entreating him to protect his own son Constantine VII. On seeing Alexander approach on one occasion it was reported that Leo with prescience of the future had stated: "Ἴδε, ὁ κακὸς καιρὸς μετὰ τοὺς ιγ μῆνας *Beware, the evil time after 13 months.* Alexander reigned one year and twenty-nine days (May AD 912 till June AD 913) with Constantine before he died of over-indulgence, struck down by a divinely sent sword (ῥομφαίᾳ θεηλάτῳ πληγείς). There is in this collocation no association with the notion of flight.

---

[5] For the acclamation πολλὰ τὰ ἔτη see Peterson, ΕΙΣ ΘΕΟΣ (Göttingen 1926) 167-8 (non vidi). The expression is widely attested in time and place. It is found from the fourth century AD (*I. Nikaia* 1005: Bithynia, AD 337-340) to the fourteenth century (Constantinople). It is found widely dispersed in the East, e.g. Crete, Cyprus, Asia Minor, Greece, Macedonia, Syria, Palestine and Egypt.

[6] See H. Solin, *Die griechischen Personennamen in Rom* I (Berlin 1982) 76.

Ambiguity thus surrounds the status of Theodoros and the nature of his relationship to the writer. The three texts cited as parallels are circus texts and do not concern runaway slaves. Be that as it may, the function of the papyrus is magical. It seeks to impose a curse that evil befall Theodoros. A magical significance must also be ascribed to the Christian symbols of chi-rho and χμγ at the top of the text. The significance of these symbols is discussed below (*New Docs* 8 [1997] §14).

S.R.L.

§3 The Government's Pursuit of Runaway Slaves

Oxyrhynchus   16 x 9.5 cm   Third century AD?
Ed. pr. — J.R. Rea, *P. Oxy.* LI 3616 (London 1984) 39-41.

The editor describes the text as 'written in a good clear documentary hand without any pretension to calligraphy'; it is dated by its hand 'probably in the second half of the third century, and possibly in the early part of the fourth'. There is a lower margin of approx. 3 cm. The foot of the sheet and last(?) line of the text are worn. The back is blank.

 εἴ [τι]ς [ε]ὗρεν δοῦλον ὀνόματι   If anyone finds a slave by the name of
  Φίλιππον, ... ν,   Philippos [nationality/trade?],
 ὡς ἐτῶν ῑδ, λευκόχροον, ψελλόν,   about 14 years of age, of pale complexion,
  πλατύρυγχον,   faltering in speech, broad-nosed,
 μ.[.].[.] . . αε . . ν, ἐνδεδυμένον   [...] wearing a thick
  στιχάριον
 ἐρεο[ῦ]ν παχὺ(ν) καὶ βάλτιον ἀπὸ   woollen tunic and a used belt
  χρήσεως
5 [. . . ε]νεγκάτω ἐν τοῖς σίγνοις   let him deliver [him] / report [it] to the army
  λαμβάνων   post, taking
 [. . . . .] (vac.?)   [...]

Oxyrhynchus   Third century AD
Ed. pr. — J.R. Rea, *P. Oxy.* LI 3617 (London 1984) 41-2.

The handwriting is described as 'a good round official cursive of the third century'. The back is blank. The right side of the text is lost; words and letters have been supplied from the commentary of the *editio princeps*.

 [Παῖς ᾧ ὄνομα Ὧ]ρος Αἰγύπτιος ἀπ[ὸ   [Slave by the name of Ho]ros, Egyptian
  κώμης]   from [the village of]
 Χενρῆς τοῦ Ἀθρειβίτου νομοῦ τὸ   Chenres of the Athribite nome,
  [καθ' ὅλον]   [altogether]
 Ἑλληνιστὶ μὴ εἰδώς, μακρός,   ignorant of Greek, tall,
  λεπτ[ός],   thin,
 ψειλόκουρος, ἐπὶ τοῦ ἀριστεροῦ [μέ-]   smooth-shaven, on the left side
5 ρους τῆς κεφαλῆς ἔχων τραῦ[μα μικ-]   of his head having a [small] wound,
 ρον, μελίχρους, ὑπόχλωρος,   honey-complexion, pale, with scanty
  σπ[ανοπώ-]   beard
 γων—τὸ καθ' ὅλον τρίχας μὴ ἔχ[ων]   — altogether not having hair
 ἐπὶ τοῦ πώγωνος, λεῖος, στε[νὸς]   on his chin, smooth-skinned, narrow
 ἐκ τῶν γνάθων, ἐπίριν (vac.) [ὢν δὲ]   in the jaws, with a long nose, [being]
10 τέχνην γέρδιος, περιπατ[εῖ σκαι-]   a weaver by trade, he walks awkwardly
 ὦς σαλακάτος ὀξείᾳ φωνῇ   speaking with the shrill voice of a
  [κατα-]   pretentious person.
 λαλῶν. ἔστιν δὲ ὡς (ἐτῶν) λ̄β. [τριβω-]   He is about 32 years of age.
 νάρια δὲ φορεῖ ἰδιόχρωμα ῥά[κινα.]   He wears a ragged undyed coat.

ἔχει [δ]ὲ ἐπὶ τω[   ]   He has on his [...]
15   [. . . . .] . [   ]   [...]
‾‾‾‾‾‾‾‾‾‾‾‾‾‾‾‾‾‾‾‾‾‾‾‾‾‾
2. 'Αθριβίτου   4. ψιλόκουρος   9. ἐπίρριν

P. Oxy. 3616 is a notice seeking the apprehension of a runaway slave. The editor argues, apparently on the basis of the hand, that the papyrus was posted.[1] The notice has the form of a protasis followed by a command: 'If anyone has seen a slave (description), let him report/deliver him to (place) and receive (reward)'. On the basis of the parallel offered Lucian, *Fugitivi* 27 (εἴ τις εἶδεν ἀνδράποδον (description of slave) μηνύειν ἐπὶ ῥητῷ αὐτόν[2]), the editor suggests that the wording was formulaic.[3] In P. Oxy. 3616 one is either to deliver or to report the slave to an army post[4] for which he would presumably receive a reward. The last line of the text is worn and cannot be read. The editor assumes that it specified the reward; cf. Lucian, *Fugitivi* 27, 29 and UPZ I 121 for the payment of rewards, μήνυτρα. From the extant portions of P. Oxy. 3617 it is unclear whether the text concerns a fugitive slave or for that matter a slave at all. The editor, however, assumes from the unflattering nature of the description and from the declaration of an ethnic (l.1) that the person was a slave. It is further suggested that the damaged area of l.1 or the lost end of the papyrus may have contained explicit reference to the person's status as a slave. If so, both attest the making of a public notice in order to recover a fugitive.

Pursuit of Fugitive Slaves in the Ptolemaic Period

UPZ I 121 (= *P. Par.* 10, dated 13 August 156 BC) is perhaps the best known example of a public notice declaring runaway slaves and attests an official involvement both in the posting of details relevant to their apprehension (i.e. descriptions and rewards) and in the receiving of information about them. From the papyrus we learn that two slaves had escaped from their masters in Alexandria. The common flight, search, reward and its subsequent increase indicate that the named individuals, both slaves and masters, were probably known to each other, presumably through the Alexandrian court. Wilcken conjectures that the slaves escaped together from Alexandria and fled to the large city of Memphis where they might disappear amongst its mixed population or where they might find asylum in its renowned Serapeum. The public notice has been corrected later (but in the same year)[5] by a second hand. As the corrections comprise in part increased rewards (from 2 to 3, 1 to 2 and 3 to 5 talents respectively), it is assumed that they were made to the original notice after such time as it had become evident that the first publication had failed to produce a result. Scholl[6] reckons with

---

[1] The editor does not express as strong a view with regard to *P. Oxy.* 3617. He states: 'Neither (the handwriting) nor the format specially suggests that the sheet was intended to be posted in public, but it may have been.'

[2] U. Wilcken, *UPZ* I p.576, suggests reading τῷ ἀστυνόμῳ instead of αὐτόν.

[3] Cf. *P. Lond.* VII 2052 — ἐάν τις παραβάληι, συνσχεῖν καὶ ἡμῖν γράψαι; *P. Heid.* 212 — [ἐὰν μὲν ἐ]πισκεψάμενος εὑρίσκη⟨ι⟩ς ... ἀνάπεμ[ψ]ο[ν ἡ]μ[ῖ]ν; *BGU* VIII 1774 — ἐὰν ἐντετευχότες παραδιδῶσι τὴν σημαινομένην δούλην, παραλαβόντες καταστῆσατ' ἐφ' ἡμᾶς.

[4] On the role of the army in the search and apprehension of fugitive slaves see H. Bellen, *Studien zur Sklavenflucht im römischen Kaiserreich* (Wiesbaden 1971) 11-13.

[5] Cf. the date placed on the upper margin of the papyrus.

[6] R. Scholl, *Corpus der ptolemäischen Sklaventexte* (Stuttgart 1990) 286-7.

only a short period, perhaps a little more than one month. He reasons that the longer the slaves remained on the run the greater their chances of not being found.

There is some disagreement concerning the origin of *UPZ* 121. Meyer suggests that the actual extant document originated in Alexandria with both the prepositional phrase ἐν 'Αλεξανδρείᾳ (*l*.3) and the increased rewards being added to the document in the *chora*.[7] Alternatively, Wilcken argues that our document is a copy made in a police station or in the bureau of the agents of the *strategos* (*ll*.15-16 and 26) at Memphis. The notice was then probably attached to the wall of the same station or bureau. However, the wording of the notice, it is argued, originated from Alexandria (cf. the later addition of ἐν 'Αλεξανδρείαι, *l*.3, which would have been absent from the original text sent from the capital) and like other notices was probably prepared in the bureau of ὁ ἐπὶ τῆς πόλεως for dispatch to officials in the *chora*. If so, it is of interest to note that as information was to be declared to the agents of the *strategos*, a nome official, the notices were composed with the provincial reader in mind. Wilcken further surmises that the subsequent increase in the rewards was communicated by police officials from Alexandria to the authorities in Memphis who made the necessary changes to the notice.

Anubieion district in Memphis?   31 x 14 cm   13 August 156 BC

Ed. — U. Wilcken, *UPZ* I 121 (Berlin and Leipzig 1922-27) 566-76 (= *P. Par.* 10, Meyer, *Jur. Pap.* §50, *Sel. Pap.* §234, Scholl, *Corpus* §81).

```
(m.2) ⟦E . . . . αι . . . . ⟧              ⟦ ... ⟧
      ⟦("Ετους) κ̄ε̄⟧                        ⟦ Year 25 ⟧
```

(m.1) Τοῦ κ̄ε̄ 'Επεὶφ ῑς̄ 'Αριστογένου	On 16 Epeiph (year) 25, a slave of
τοῦ Χρυσίππου	Aristogenes, son of Chrysippos,
'Αλαβανδέως πρεσβευτοῦ παῖς ἀναχεχώ-	from Alabanda, envoy, fled
ρηκεν (m.2) ˋἐν 'Αλεξανδρείαι ˊ, (m.1) ᾧι ὄνομα Ἕρμων, ὃς καὶ Νεῖλος	ˋin Alexandriaˊ by the name of Hermon, also called Neilos,
καλεῖται, τὸ γένος Σύρος ἀπὸ Βαμβύκης	Syrian by birth from Bambyke,
5 ὡς ἐτῶν ῑη̄, μεγέθει μέσος, ἀγένειος,	about 18 years of age, medium height, beardless,
εὔκνημος, κοιλογένειος φακὸς παρὰ ῥῖνα	with strong calfs, dimple in chin, mole on nose
ἐξ ἀριστερῶν, οὐλὴ ὑπὲρ χαλινὸν ἐξ ἀριστερῶν,	on the left, scar above corner of mouth on the left,
ἐστιγμένος τὸν δεξιὸν καρπὸν γράμμασι	tattooed on right wrist with two
βαρβαρικοῖς δυσίν, ἔχων χρυσίου ἐπισήμου	foreign letters, having of coined gold
10 μναιεῖα γ̄, πίνας ῑ, κρίκον σιδηροῦν,	3 minae, 10 pearls, an iron ring

---

[7] P.M. Meyer, *Jur. Pap.* p.165.

ἐν ὧι λήκυθος καὶ ξύστραι. καὶ περὶ τὸ σῶμα	on which an oil-bottle and strigils (are represented) and about his body
χλαμύδα καὶ περίζωμα. Τοῦτον ὃς ἂν ἀνα-	a cloak and loin-cloth.[8] Whoever brings this (slave) back
γάγη, λήψεται χαλκοῦ (τάλαντα) β̄ (m.2) ‵γ̄′, (m.1) ἐφ' ἱεροῦ δείξας (τάλ.) ᾱ (m.2) ‵β̄′,	will receive (2) 3 bronze talents, showing (him) at the temple (1) 2 talent,
(m.1) παρ' ἀνδρὶ ἀξιοχρείωι καὶ δωσιδίκωι (τάλ.) γ̄ (m.2) ‵ε̄′.	with a man of substance and legally actionable (3) 5 talents.
15 (m.1) Μηνύειν δὲ τὸν βουλόμενον τοῖς παρὰ τοῦ στρατηγοῦ.	He who wishes should disclose information to the agents of the *strategos*.
Ἔστιν δὲ καὶ ὁ συναποδεδρακὼς αὐτῶι	There is also the one who ran away with him,
Βίων δοῦλος Καλλικράτου τῶν περὶ αὐλὴν	Bion, the slave of Kallikrates, one of the court
ἀρχυπηρετῶν, μεγέθει βραχύς, πλατὺς	head-assistants, short in height, broad
20 ἀπὸ τῶν ὤμων, κατάκνημος, χαροπός,	in the shoulders, with thin calfs, bright-eyed,
ὃς καὶ ἔχων ἀνακεχώρηκεν ἱμάτιον καὶ	who also fled having a cloak,
ἱματίδιον παιδαρίου καὶ σεβίτιον γυναι-	the mantle of a slave,[9] a woman's box
κεῖον ἄξιον (ταλάντων) ϛ̄ καὶ χαλκοῦ ⟦ . ⟧ Ē.	worth 6 talents and 5000 bronze (drachmae?).
Τοῦτον ὃς ἂν ἀναγ⟨άγ⟩η, λήψεται ὅσα καὶ ὑπὲρ τοῦ	Whoever brings this one back will receive as much as for the
25 προγεγραμμένου. Μηνύειν δὲ καὶ ὑπὲρ	aforementioned. One should disclose also information concerning this
τούτου τοῖς παρὰ τοῦ στρατηγοῦ.	one to the agents of the *strategos*.

The description of the slaves and what they took with them is of interest, for such information naturally assisted in their identification and subsequent apprehension. It is for this reason that the following details were noted:

(a) tattoo — possibly the Aramaic letters indicated that the slave had given himself to the deities, Hadad and Atargatis, of Bambyke, i.e. Hierapolis in Syria;[10]

---

[8] The περίζωμα was the clothing of a slave. The χλαμύς is assumed to have belonged to the runaway's master, presumably the cloak given to the slave by his master as he entered the bath. See Scholl, *Corpus* 283.

[9] The cloak is assumed to have covered the slave's mantel thus disguising his identity. See Scholl, *Corpus* 286.

[10] Letronne in the *ed. pr.* had assumed that the letters marked the slave as a runaway. However, branding of runaway slaves was infrequently practised in the Greek world. W.L. Westermann, *The Slave Systems of Greek and Roman Antiquity* (Philadelphia 1955) 23, considers the economic factor to be an important disincentive as

(b) coined gold and pearls — a young person trying to exchange such goods might easily be identified;
(c) iron ring — possibly fixed to the slave's arm or neck and identifying him as the envoy's personal valet, to guess from the engraved representations;[11] and
(d) expensive box — Bion might be identified when he attempted to sell the object.[12]

Theft of valuable property was quite usual in cases of flight.[13] More often that not the slave hoped to be able to support himself from the property or its sale.[14] It is of interest to note that the stolen property became an identifying item associated closely with the description of the fugitive. On attempting to exchange a stolen item for cash the slave might be discovered and apprehended. Of interest also is the naming of the slaves' owners and their position. As this was unnecessary for the search, Scholl[15] surmises that such information was added to encourage persons, knowing that the reward would be paid, to assist. The reward promised in the first instance (i.e. two talents) was approximately a year's wages for an ordinary worker.

There is uncertainty as to the meaning of *ll.*12-14. Does the notice attest two alternative approaches, namely the actual return of the slave and the mere disclosure of his whereabouts? Wilcken disputes this on syntactic grounds (i.e. the want of parallel between the relative clause ὃς ἂν ἀναγάγῃ and the participial expression δείξας) and on the basis of the abbreviated repetition in *ll.*24-5.[16] In all cases payment of the reward was conditional upon the return of the slave. Wilcken argues that ἀνάγειν does not refer only to the actual physical return of the slave but also to its accomplishment through the laying of information.[17] In either case, if the

---

such a practice would have made the resale of the slave difficult. Instead, it is suggested that *UPZ* 121 attests the use of an iron ring to designate servile status.

[11] Westermann, *The Slave Systems* 39, notes the find of a statuette attesting the wearing by a slave of a metal neck-ring with an oil flask and bath strigils in relief. On evidence for the use of slave collars see Westermann, *The Slave Systems* 77. Of particular interest is the collar (Dessau, *ILS* §8731) bearing the inscription: Fugi; tene me; cum revocaveris me d(omino) m(eo) Zonino, accipis solidum — 'I have run away; stop me; when you bring me back to my master Zoninus, you receive a solidus.' For other examples of neck-collars see J.G. Nordling, 'Onesimus Fugitivus: A Defence of the Runaway Slave Hypothesis in Philemon', *JSNT* 41 (1991) 104. I. Bieżuńska-Małowist, *L'esclavage dans l'Égypte gréco-romaine*, vol. 1 (Warsaw 1974) 75, and eadem , 'Les esclaves fugitifs dans l'Égypte gréco-romaine', *Studi in onore di Edoardo Volterra* vol. 4 (Milan 1971) 77-8, sees in the valet evidence for the ownership of large numbers of slaves in the great houses of Alexandria and for the specialisation in functions of the slaves within these households.

[12] Note that the worth of the box exceeds the value of the reward. The possibility of its recovery does not appear to have been taken into account when calculating the latter.

[13] A.I. Pavlovskaja, 'Die Sklaverei im hellenistischen Ägypten', *Die Sklaverei in hellenistischen Staaten im 3.-1. Jh. v. Chr.*, edd. T.V. Blavatskaja, E.S. Golubcova and A.I. Pavlovskaja (Wiesbaden 1972, trans. from Russian) 271, Bieżuńska-Małowist, 'Les esclaves fugitifs' 80, and Scholl, *Corpus* 300. *PSI* 329 (258-7 BC), *P. Cair. Zen.* 59213 (254 BC) and *P. Cair. Zen.* 59613, and *UPZ* 121 (156 BC) are cited as evidence. For the Roman period see *P. Cair. Preis.* I (second century), *P. Turner* 41 (third century), and *P. Oxy.* 1423 (fourth century).

[14] It might be thought that the theft and fear of detection prompted a slave's decision to flee, e.g. Cicero, *Epist. ad fam.* 13.77.3. Scholl, however, argues that theft was only a means to an end, namely flight, and that there is no indication that flight resulted from fear of detection and punishment. See R. Scholl, *Sklaverei in den Zenonpapyri. Eine Untersuchung zu den Sklaventermini, zum Sklavenerwerb und zur Sklavenflucht* (Trier 1983) 221-2, and idem, *Corpus* 300. Similarly, Bieżuńska-Małowist, 'Les esclaves fugitifs' 80, holds that the purpose of the theft was to supply the immediate needs created by the escape.

[15] Scholl, *Corpus* 282 and 285-6. See also p.301.

[16] The imperatival infinitive μηνύειν (*ll.*15 and 25) is construed to refer to all three cases in which a reward was paid.

[17] The argument rests on Wilcken's interpretation of *P. Cair. Zen.* 59015 (verso). The relevant passage reads:

slave was regained, a reward was paid. Special cases prevailed if the slave was declared ἐφ' ἱεροῦ or to be παρ' ἀνδρὶ ἀξιοχρείωι καὶ δωσιδίκωι. Wilcken understands the first expression to refer not only to the right of asylum as originally thought,[18] a privilege which was conferred on a limited number of temples only, but also to a more general protection, which all temples offered to suppliants. Indeed, it would appear that there was an assimilation between the degrees of protection offered to slaves by both types of temple. This arose from a limitation placed on the right of asylum for slaves in comparison with that offered to suppliants of free status. Westermann[19] holds that even in temples with a right of asylum the authority of its priests was circumscribed in the case of suppliant slaves, for the slave was either to be reconciled with his master or sold to a new master. In *UPZ* 121 only the return of the slave to his master is contemplated. Nothing is said about sale to another master, a right under both

---

ὅτι οἱ παῖδες οἱ ἀποδράντες μηνυτρίζοιντο εἶναι παρὰ τῶι Κολλοχούτωι καὶ τῶι Ζαιδήλωι τῶι ἀδελφῶι καὶ αἰτοίησαν ἐφ' ὧι ἀνάξουσιν, ἀργυρίου (δραχμὰς) ρ̄ —
'the runaway slaves are reported to be with Kollochoutos and his brother Zaidelos and that they have demanded 100 silver drachmae for returning (them)'.
The argument runs as follows:
  (a) As μηνυτρίζειν means 'to inform for a reward (μήνυτρον)', then the μηνυτρίζοντες and the αἰτοῦντες for the reward are one and the same.
  (b) As it would be highly audacious of Zaidelos (and his brother) to demand payment for giving information concerning the slaves' whereabouts and as Zenon would be unlikely to pay the reward, then those laying the informing must be unnamed persons.
  (c) Though Pasikles, Epikrates and others were to effect the slaves' apprehension and Straton their return to Zenon, in the second letter (*l*.24) it is stated: [ὃ δ' ἂν ἀνηλώσηις τοῖς ἀ]ναγαγοῦσιν (the remaining lines in the column are fragmentary) — 'Whatever you spend on those returning (them)'. In other words, those who had laid information and sought a reward are in the second letter described as the ἀναγαγοῦντες.
Bieżuńska-Małowist, *L'esclavage* I 129-130, and Scholl, *Sklaverei* 41, follow this interpretation. However, difficulties in Wilcken's argument can be suggested. First, the correction of *l*.4 from παρὰ τῶι Κολλοχ⟦ . . ι⟧ τῶι Ζαιδήλ⟦ου⟧ ἀδελφῶι to παρὰ τῶι Κολλοχούτωι καὶ τῶι Ζαιδήλωι τῶι ἀδελφῶι, if it occurred after the writing of the plural in *l*.5, implies that the writer assumed the two brothers to have been the subject of the verb αἰτοίησαν. Moreover, Kollochoutos and Zaidelos are grammatically the most natural antecedents of the verb. Wilcken must assume a more distant and unstated antecedent. Second, the two brothers may well have acted audaciously if they thought that they might be able to get away with their demand. C. Orrieux, *Les papyrus de Zenon* (Paris 1983) 48-9, suggests that Kollochoutos and Zaidelos were nomads living on the borders of the Ptolemaic territories. No doubt, the brothers were aware of the difficulty which anyone seeking recovery of the lost slaves would face and thus might have sought to take advantage of the situation, demanding 100 drachmae to bring them in. The very fact that Zenon sought the help of several contacts and friends to effect recovery further confirms this impression. Third, it is unclear whether the payment of expenses referred to at *ll*.10 and 24 was actually made to the persons who had disclosed the slaves' whereabouts. Indeed, the expenses may relate to costs incurred in despatching persons to apprehend the slaves and to hand them over to Straton. In other words, the ἀναγαγοῦντες may not have been the same persons as those who disclosed the slaves' whereabouts. Fourth, as the reading of *l*.24 is largely restored, it is unclear what was intended here.

[18] Meyer, *Jur. Pap.* p.165, follows the interpretation of Letronne in the *ed. pr.*

[19] Westermann, *The Slave Systems* 40-41; cf. also p.108. On slavery and the right of asylum see also Scholl, *Corpus* 301-3. Scholl argues that explicit evidence for the right of asylum is wanting. *UPZ* 121 and *P. Cair. Zen.* 59620 only indicate a temporary right. However, as the latter papyrus attests a self-imposed limitation (i.e. Eutychos presumably only intended to stay in the Serapeum in Memphis until the ownership of the house, which was a matter of dispute between his master and freeborn wife, was resolved), its value as evidence is rather circumscribed. See Scholl, *Corpus* 284, for evidence that asylum did not always in practice offer protection.

§3 The Government's Pursuit of Runaway Slaves

Attic and Roman law.[20] Scholl concludes that on the basis of this text it can be neither verified nor refuted whether slaves who fled to a temple had the right to demand sale to another master or whether the right of asylum guaranteed only an incomplete protection. However, such evidence as *UPZ* I 3, 4[21] and 121, *P. Hamb.* 91[22] and *P. Cair. Zen.* 59620, it is argued, points to a limited right of asylum for slaves in practice. In the case of *UPZ* 121 a reduced reward was made to the informant. Wilcken contends that the reduced payment took into account a contribution required by the priesthood or temple, which may have been half that of the normal reward or an amount fixed by special arrangement.[23]

A more substantial payment of 3 (later corrected to 5) talents was to be paid if the slave was 'with a man of substance and legally actionable'. Wilcken understands the larger amount to reflect the fact that such a person in addition to returning the runaway had to pay both compensation and a penalty to the master.[24] Further, from the fact that only one amount was

---

[20] See Justinian, *Institutes* 1.8.1. If asylum was sought because of the master's cruelty or severity, the slave was to be sold and the price paid to the master. The reason for the intervention is given, namely that it was in the state's interest that no one use his property badly.

[21] *UPZ* I 3 and 4 are drafts of a petition to the king from Ptolemaios accusing Zoilos, a temple functionary, of accepting a διάφορον (bribe?) and forcibly seizing the slave, Herakleia. The slave had earlier fled to the Serapeum and been adopted by Ptolemaios for services rendered. Wilcken, *UPZ* I pp.121 and 126, holds that it is unclear whether Zoilos had actually breached the right of asylum — for if he had, this charge is not mentioned — or whether through adoption Herakleia had replaced the protection of asylum with the protection offered by the adopter. If so, then there was no breach. The legal status of the adoption is questioned by Scholl, *Corpus* 292-3. He holds that Herakleia's flight might have been prompted by her sale to the soldier to whom she was later handed over by Zoilos. Without means and in need of support (cf. *P. Cair. Zen.* 59620) she had sought and found a helper in Ptolemaios. Scholl concludes that the papyrus shows that asylum offered no sure haven for the runaway. Moreover, by drawing attention to a possible connection between the διάφορον paid to Zoilos and the reward offered in *UPZ* 121 for a person shown ἐφ' ἱεροῦ, he implies that the reduction in the latter may have taken into account such payments.

[22] *P. Hamb.* 91 (167 BC) is a petition by a soldier named Herakleides and concerns the flight of four female prisoners of war allotted to him as booty. When Herakleides found that one of the women had been resold, she promised to pay him her ransom and to deliver the three others if she herself was restored. Accordingly she was sent to her father, but the ransom was not paid. The text continues: ἐνθ'[ἡ αἰχμάλ]ωτος ψυχαγωγηθεῖσα ὑπὸ τῶν ἐκ τῆς κώμης ἱερείων ... — 'where the prisoner of war being deluded by the village priests ...'. The text makes no explicit mention that the woman had sought asylum in the temple. The soldier merely writes in order that he might regain his booty and that a decision be made concerning those complicit in the deed, no doubt the father and priests. The petition is addressed by Herakleides to the *strategos* of the Herakleopolite nome. Bieżuńska-Małowist, *L'esclavage* I 104, sees in this and the request made of the *strategos* to write to the ἐπιστάτης to effect the return of the booty evidence that the state was involved in the pursuit of runaways.

[23] R. Taubenschlag, *The Law of Greco-Roman Egypt in the Light of the Papyri* (Warsaw 1955) 84, follows Wilcken's interpretation in thinking that the priest handed over the slave for a reward. Wilcken surmises that 1 talent was paid to the temple, i.e. 1 + 1 = 2 talents (the reward offered in the first instance). The difficulty is to explain the later increase to 2 talents. It is assumed that the temple's reward remained constant at 1 talent, i.e. 1 + 2 = 3.

[24] Evidence for the payment of compensation and a penalty in Greek law is found in an inscription from Andania, Ditt., *Syll.*³ 736 *ll.*81-2 (92 BC). Here Wilcken argues that if the person harbouring (i.e. receiving, feeding or providing work to) the slave did not return the runaway, he had to pay twice the value of the slave plus the 500 dr. penalty. On the other hand, if he returned the slave, the simple worth was paid plus the 500 dr. penalty. According to Wilcken's interpretation of *UPZ* 121 a reward was only paid if the runaway was recovered. It is not explained why a reward was not paid in the case where the slave was not recovered but where presumably the owner had a right of action for both compensation and a penalty against the person harbouring his slave. If one accepts the legal analogy between harbouring a runaway and wrongful *assertio in libertatem* (i.e. wrongly claiming a slave as free, Demosthenes, *Contra Theoc.* 19-21), the payment of a penalty to the

specified, Mitteis, whom Wilcken followed, concluded that as distinct from Roman law[25] no distinction was drawn between whether the person had knowingly received the runaway or had acted in ignorance. Scholl[26] further notes that if there was no legal distinction, then it was up to the individual to assure himself of the status of any person to whom he might show hospitality or offer employment. If such was the case, then it can be assumed that people would have been reluctant to help persons of uncertain status. In turn, this would have made escape difficult for any runaway and explains the prevalence of theft associated with flight. However, the suggestion that there was no legal distinction is problematic as there is no necessary connection between the payments of compensation/penalty and reward, as the later increase in the reward demonstrates. The evidence of *UPZ* 121 alone is insufficient to establish whether Hellenistic law differentiated in this matter.

A number of other papyri from the Ptolemaic period also declare information about persons who actually were or who may have been runaway slaves. *P. Lond.* VII 1950 and two papyri identical with it (*P. Cair. Zen.* 59070 and *P. Lond.* VII 1949), it is alleged, contain information about a runaway slave.

Philadelphia   3.6 x 10.2 cm   29th May 257 BC

Ed. — T.C. Skeat, *P. Lond.* VII 1950 (London 1974) 38 (= Scholl, *Sklaverei* § 17 and *Corpus* §63).

(ἔτους) κ̄θ̄, Ξανδικοῦ κ̄ς̄.	Year 29 Xandikos 26.
Θώρ[α]ξ Κίλιξ τετα(νὸς)	Thorax, Cilician, with long straight
μελί(χρους)	hair, honey complexion,
στρογγυλοπρ(όσωπος), οὐ(λὴ) ὑπ'	round face, scar under
ὀφρ(ὺν) ἀρ(ιστερᾶι) καὶ δε(ξιᾶι) καὶ	eyebrow on left and right and
ὑπ' ὀφθαλ-	under eye,
μόν, (ἐτῶν) τη	18 years of age.
Verso	
[ ] Θώρακος	[ ] of Thorax

The above text is extant in three copies, each in a different hand. The text's significance has been disputed. Edgar[27], who was already aware of the existence of the two other copies, tentatively postulated that it represented an εἰκών (personal description) of a runaway slave. Wilcken[28] doubted the suggestion. He argued that such descriptions were more detailed and mentioned also clothing and goods taken with the runaways. In support of this Wilcken cited the example of *UPZ* 121. In publishing the second and third copies (*P. Lond.* 1949 and 1950)

---

state may also arise as an issue. On this see Wilcken, *UPZ* I p.572, and Westermann, *The Slave Systems* 39. However, such a payment is attested as a penalty neither at Andania nor in *UPZ* 121.

[25] In Roman law it was considered theft (*furtum*) to aid a fugitive and a penalty was imposed on the implicated person. Constantine, however, recognised the possibility that assistance might be given in ignorance of a fugitive's true status. In such cases the person was freed from the heavy penalty which would otherwise have applied.

[26] Scholl, *Corpus* 285.
[27] Edgar, *P. Cair. Zen.* I p.93.
[28] Wilcken, *AFP* 8 (1927) 277-8.

Skeat supported Wilcken's interpretation and offered as additional evidence *P. Lond.* 2052 and *P. Cair. Zen.* 59613. More recently Scholl has argued again for Edgar's postulation. He notes that the additional evidence cited by Skeat undermines rather than supports his interpretation; *P. Lond.* 2052 only records the slaves' names, ages, professions and distinguishing features. Moreover, Scholl[29] argues that the existence of three identical copies in different hands supports the interpretation of the text as a personal description of a runaway slave. It can hardly, however, make the text an arrest warrant (*Streckbrief*), as Scholl suggests, for nothing is mentioned in the text regarding either the laying of information or the apprehension of Thorax. It has been noted that a slave by the name of Thorax is mentioned in a later papyrus from the Zenon archive, i.e. *P. Col. Zen.* 75 (248/246 BC). If the names refer to the one individual, then it follows that the earlier escape was unsuccessful. However, the identity is not assured.

A better example of the declaration of information about runaway slaves is provided by *P. Lond.* 2052, dated *ca* 241 BC.[30] The papyrus is a memorandum[31] concerning runaways and was found in the Zenon archive. The text gives a full description of the slaves but differs in two important respects from *UPZ* 121: (a) it is not a public notice but a private memorandum; and (b) no reward is offered. The relationships between the persons named in the document are not altogether certain. Sosikrates is presumably the ἐπὶ τῆς οἰκίας or agent of Paideas. He may also have been at an earlier date an employee of Apollonios.[32] Sosikrates writes to Zenon describing four runaway slaves. The first two slaves, it would appear, formerly belonged to Apollonios and the second two formerly to Alexandros.[33] At the time of writing they presumably belonged to Paideas. Why then mention earlier masters? Scholl[34] suggests that Paideas had only just recently acquired the four slaves. This might explain (a) why they ran away (i.e. they were unhappy about the change of masters) and (b) why their former masters were named (i.e. they were still generally known as the slaves' masters). Sosikrates thus writes to Zenon requesting that if the slaves are found, he should arrest them and inform the writer.

Philadelphia   26.5 x 12.6 cm   *ca* 241 BC

Ed. pr. — T.C. Skeat, *P. Lond.* VII 2052 (London 1974) 198-201 (= Scholl, *Sklaverei* §32 and *Corpus* §78).

ὑπόμνημα Ζήνωνι παρὰ	Memorandum to Zenon from
Σωσικράτους τῶν πρότερον	Sosikrates (concerning) those formerly

---

[29] Scholl, *Sklaverei* 143-4, and idem, *Corpus* 245-6.

[30] The editor of *P. Lond.* 2052, T.C. Skeat, tentatively assigns the papyrus to *ca* 241 BC in view of the mention of a hostage (Alexandros) possessing a Babylonian and a Median slave (*ll*.16-24). It is assumed that the hostage was a prominent Seleucid who had been sent as a guarantee under the terms of peace at the end of the Third Syrian War. It is further assumed that he sold his slaves on release. Scholl offers a more open dating after 245 BC, i.e. the death of Apollonios.

[31] A second memorandum addressed to Zenon dealing with runaway slaves is *BGU* 1993. See below for the text of this papyrus.

[32] Scholl, *Sklaverei* 201 and 205. The possibility that Sosikrates was a former employee of Apollonios would explain his acquaintance with Zenon and why he would write to him for help.

[33] It is not agreed by all that two slaves formerly belonged to Apollonios and two to Alexandros. For example, Bieżuńska-Małowist, 'Les esclaves fugitifs' 78, follows Rostovtzeff in arguing that all four slaves formerly belonged to Apollonios and were bought by Paideas after the liquidation of the latter's assets.

[34] Scholl, *Sklaverei* 203.

ὄντων Ἀπολλωνίου τοῦ ⟦διοι⟧	belonging to Apollonios, the
γενομένου διοικητοῦ νῦν δ' ὄν-	ex-*dioiketes*, but now belonging to
5 των Παιδέου. ἐάν τις παραβάληι,	Paideas. If anyone encounters (them)
συνσχεῖν καὶ ἡμῖν γράψαι.	let him arrest (them) and write to us.[35]
Πίνδαρον Λύκιον διάκονον	Pindaros, Lycian, servant,
ὡς (ἐτῶν) κ̄θ̄ μέσον	about 29 years of age, medium height,
μελίχρουν	honey-complexion,
σύνοφρυν ἐπίγρυπον, οὐλὴ	with meeting eyebrows, hook-nosed, scar
10 ὑπὸ γόνυ ἀριστερόν.	under left knee.
καὶ Φιλωνίδην ὃς καὶ Βελτε-	And Philonides who is also called
νοῦρις καλεῖται, ὡς (ἐτῶν) κ̄δ̄	Beltenouris,[36] about 24 years of age,
μέσος [με]λίχρους, οὐλὴ ἐπ' ὀφρύι	medium height, honey-complexion, scar on
ἀριστερᾶι καὶ ὑπὸ χεῖλος	left eyebrow and under lip
15 ἐγ δεξιῶν.	on right.
καὶ τῶν Ἀλεξάνδρου τοῦ	And of those (belonging to) Alexandros the
ὁμη-	ex-
ρεύσαντος Φιλῖνον Βαβυλώνιον	hostage, Philinos, Babylonian,
τριβέα ὡς (ἐτῶν) μ̄δ̄ βραχὺν	shampooer, about 44 years of age, short,
μελαν-	black-skinned,
χρῆ ἐπίγρυπον σύνοφρυν, φακὸν	hook-nosed, with meeting eyebrows,
20 ἔχοντα παρὰ τὸν ἀριστερὸν	having a mole on the left
κρόταφον.	temple.
καὶ Ἀμύνταν Μῆδον συνωριστὴν	And Amyntas, Mede, coachman,
ὡς (ἐτῶν) λ̄δ̄ μέσον	about 34 years of age, medium height,
μελανχρῆ, οὐλὴ	black-skinned, scar
μετώπωι καὶ ῥινί.	to forehead and nose.

The profile of the four runaways agrees with other evidence for the types of slaves who ran away, for they were predominantly adult males holding domestic functions.[37] From the text it would appear that the slaves planned and executed their escape together. Their point of escape was probably Alexandria and their destination the *chora* (Zenon resided in the Fayum). As four fled at the same time, the financial loss would have been great. Scholl[38] suggests that

---

[35] The infinitives are understood as imperatives. This alleviates the need to supply κελεύεται.

[36] Beltenouris is a Babylonian name. Skeat assumes a mix-up between Philonides and Philinos, who is declared to be Babylonian.

[37] Scholl, *Sklaverei* 224. Scholl admits the slave's employment or function as a possible bias. Since the functions and values of slaves were probably correlated, the search for valued slaves would have been more extensive.

[38] Scholl, *Sklaverei* 204-5.

§3 The Government's Pursuit of Runaway Slaves

Paideas probably sought their recovery by public notice and the offering of rewards as in *UPZ* 121. In the present papyrus, however, Paideas appears to have prevailed upon Sosikrates, an employee, to write to his friend or acquaintance, Zenon, seeking his help in their recovery, evidence Scholl[39] suggests for the extensive nature of the association of Greeks living in Egypt. But in what capacity was Zenon addressed? Was it as the person in charge of the *phylakitai*, as the memorandum *BGU* X 1993 and the letter *PSI* VI 570 might suggest? But even in these two papyri it is not clear whether Zenon held such an office or was merely asked to intervene as a person of some influence in the region where the slaves where thought to be hiding. And even if he did hold the post, it would not necessarily follow that it was a duty of office to undertake a search for the fugitives. Sosikrates's request might equally be construed as a personal favour asked of an office holder, e.g. see *P. Cair. Zen.* 59015 (verso) and the discussion of it in *New Docs* 6 (1992) 101-5. The discussion gives rise to the question of state involvement in the pursuit of runaways. For the purposes of the present study a distinction between passive involvement (posting and receipt of information) and active involvement (search and apprehension) will be made.

UPZ 121 attests the Ptolemaic government's involvement in the posting of public notices and in the receipt of information about runaways. But how extensive was official involvement in the active pursuit of slaves? Pavlovskaja[40] and Westermann[41] note that the Ptolemaic government only assisted in the posting of a public notice describing the runaways; an active search by government officials was unknown. As *P. Cair. Zen.* 59015 (verso), for example, shows, the owner with whatever means he had at his disposal (e.g. friends and official contacts) carried out the actual search, apprehension and return of the runaway. Alternatively, Scholl holds that the government's involvement extended to the search itself. Pasikles, mentioned in *P. Cair. Zen.* 59015 (verso), may have possibly been the ἐπιστάτης τῶν φυλακίτων, who after posting a notice of reward had received information about the runaways' whereabouts.[42] Zenon now writes to him to effect their apprehension and to hand them over to Straton, whom he was sending. State involvement in the actual apprehension of runaways, it is argued,[43] is further shown by *BGU* 1993 (Zenon is requested to write to the gendarmes in order that they should look for the two runaways in company with persons sent by the owner) and by *PSI* 570 (Zenon is requested to send (?) the gendarmes to the village where the slave is hiding in order to secure his dispatch). Bieżuńska-Małowist[44] also argues for a more active, official involvement in the pursuit of runaway slaves. However, the question must be whether such help was generally available to all owners or whether it was only available to those of position and influence.

---

[39] Scholl, *Sklaverei* 205.
[40] A.I. Pavlovskaja, 'Die Sklaverei im hellenistischen Ägypten' 271.
[41] Westermann, *The Slave Systems* 39.
[42] Scholl, *Sklaverei* 37.
[43] Scholl, *Sklaverei* 171 and 180.
[44] Bieżuńska-Małowist, *L'esclavage* I 103-5, eadem, *L'esclavage dans l'Égypte gréco-romaine*, vol. 2 (Wrocław 1977) 68-71, and eadem, 'Les esclaves fugitifs' 86-7. The involvement is perceived as one aspect of the protection offered to the rights and interests of masters, i.e. the control of title. The protection was a by-product of the state's attempt to guarantee revenues derived from slaves and the transactions involving them and to control status in society as a whole.

| Philadelphia | 12.5 x 11.3 cm | After 256 BC |

Ed. pr. — W. Müller, *JJP* 13 (1961) 75-6 (= *BGU* X 1993, *P. Ibscher* 11, *SB* VIII 9779, *P. L. Bat.* XX 43, Scholl, *Sklaverei* §26 and *Corpus* §72).

Writing is on the recto and parallel to the fibres in large, clear letters. Margins on the top, right and left sides are complete; the bottom of the text is broken leaving only the tops of the letters on the last line. There is a *kollema* running from the top to the bottom of the papyrus and located at the beginning of the lines.

Ὑπόμνημα Ζήνωνι	Memorandum to Zenon
παρὰ Σωσιτίμου. παῖδες	from Sositimos. My two
ἀποκεχωρήκα`σι΄ μου δύο,	slaves have run off
τυγχάνουσι δὲ ἀναστρε-	and happen to be residing
5 φόμενοι ἐν τῶι Ἀρσινοίτηι	in the Arsinoite
νομῶι καὶ ἐν τῶι Ἡρακλεο-	nome and in the Herakleo-
πολίτηι. καλῶς ἂν οὖμ	polite (nome). Therefore you would
ποιήσαις γράψας πρὸς τοὺς	do well writing to the
ἐκεῖ φυλακίτας, ὅπως ἂν	*phylakitai* there, that
10 μετὰ τῶν παρ' ἐμοῦ ἀπεσ-	together with those sent by me
ταλμένων συζητήσουσιν	they will search for
αὐ[τοὺ]ς.	them.

In the above papyrus Sositimos[45] (otherwise unknown but possibly a friend or acquaintance of Zenon)[46] writes to Zenon concerning two of his slaves who had turned to flight. As has already been noted above, two or three slaves often ran away together. For other examples from the Ptolemaic period see *P. Cair. Zen.* 59015 (verso), *P. Lond.* 2052, *UPZ* 121 and *P. Hamb.* 91, and from the Roman period *P. Harr.* 62 and *P. Berl. Leihg.* 15. Bieżuńska-Małowist[47] suggests that the reason for this was the increased sense of security gained by companions and the greater ease of organisation, especially if the slaves were from the same household. Here, however, they appear to have parted company and fled to different nomes. The general whereabouts of the slaves is known (from informants?) and Zenon is asked to write to the gendarmes in the respective nomes to assist in the search for them. The persons despatched by Sositimos will have known or at least carried the personal descriptions, if these should be required for the apprehension of the slaves.[48] Scholl[49] assumes that a public notice with the description of the slaves would have been posted as well as a description of the them handed to the relevant gendarmes. We have here, it is argued, evidence for both personal and official involvement in the search. But the evidence is not unproblematic for it is unclear in what capacity Zenon was to act. Was he to write to the *phylakitai* in some official capacity or

---

[45] Müller, *JJP* 13 (1961) 75 and *BGU* 1993, suggests that Sositimos resided in the Memphite nome. The latter nome bordered the Arsinoite and Herakleopolite nomes and was where Apollonios also possessed a δωρεά. The suggestion is questioned by M. Muszynski in *P.L. Bat.* XX p.174.

[46] Scholl, *Sklaverei* 180.

[47] Bieżuńska-Małowist, *L'esclavage* I 131, and eadem, 'Les esclaves fugitifs' 78.

[48] Scholl, *Corpus* 261.

[49] Scholl, *Sklaverei* 181. Müller, *JJP* 13 (1961) 76, thinks that in this instance a warrant like *UPZ* 121 was unnecessary, as Sositimos had despatched some of his own people for the search (*l*.10). However, I do not see how the sending of his own people necessarily precluded the posting of a warrant.

did Sositimos seek his help merely as a person of influence who could ask and gain a favour from the local officials.[50]

Philadelphia   12 x 14.5 cm   13 June 252 BC

Ed. — G. Vitelli, M. Norsa, V. Bartoletti et al., *PSI* VI 570 (Florence 1920) (= Scholl, *Sklaverei* §23 and *Corpus* §69).

['Ο δεῖνα Ζήνωνι χαίρειν. Ε]ἰ
ἔρρωσαι καὶ ἐν τοῖς λοιποῖς
ἀπαλλάσσεις κατὰ λόγον,
[εἴη ἂν τὸ δέον· ὑγίαινον δὲ καὶ]
αὐτός. Μένανδρος, ὁ φέρων σοι
τὰ γράμματα,
[ἐστὶν ἡμῖν ἐν γνώσει· στρατε]ύεται
δὲ ἐν τοῖς Ἀλκίπ‹π›ου ἱππεῦσιν.
Ἀπο-
[δέδρακεν δ᾿ αὐτοῦ παῖς ὃς ἔ]στι ἐν
τῆι Λίμνηι. κα[λῶ]ς οὖν ποιήσεις
5 [ἀποστείλας τοὺς ἐκεῖ φυλ]ακίτας εἰς
ἣν ἂν κώμην ἦι ὁ παῖς, ὅπως
[ἀποστάληι μετ᾿ ἀσφ]αλείας. ἔτι δὲ
καὶ προπεμψάτωσαν αὐτὸν
[   ]ο σπουδήν ποιεῖσθαι
τῶν πολιτικῶν
[   ]ων.
Ἔρρωσο. (ἔτους) λ̄δ̄ Ξανδικοῦ ζ̄.

Verso
10 Ζήνωνι.

[N. to Zenon greeting. If] you are well and otherwise fare as expected, [it would be fitting. I] myself [also am well.] Menandros who brings you this letter [is known to us. He is a soldier] in the cavalry of Alkippos. [His slave has runaway and] is in the Limne. Therefore you would do well to [send the local] gendarmes to whatever village the slave is now in that [he might be dispatched] securely. Yet also let them escort him [...] to make haste [...]
[...].
Farewell. (Year) 34 Xandikos 7.

To Zenon.

The writer, whose name is lost at the beginning of the papyrus, writes to Zenon to seek his help in the apprehension of a runaway slave now residing in his district (the Limne is situated in the Arsinoite nome). The role played by Zenon is uncertain in this papyrus and *BGU* 1993 (cf. also *P. Lond.* 2052). Is the request made to him in an administrative capacity (i.e. as chief of police in his region) or merely personally in the knowledge that by virtue of his position he might be able to exert influence? Some indication of his capacity might have been implicit in the actual request made of him in *PSI* 570. Unfortunately, it is uncertain how to reconstruct the beginning of *l*.5. Following *BGU* 1993 *l*.8 one is tempted to restore γράψας; however, this restoration is not consistent with the remainder of the line, i.e. εἰς ἣν ἂν κώμην ἦι ὁ παῖς, which seems to require a verb of sending. In either case it follows that Zenon was thought by the writers of *BGU* 1993 and *PSI* 570 to exert an authority over the gendarmes. He appears able to order the *phylakitai* to investigate and apprehend runaways. Bieżuńska-Małowist[51] observes that the *phylakitai* appear to have been the instrument of pursuit and

---

[50] So Muszynski in *P.L. Bat.* XX p.174.
[51] Bieżuńska-Małowist, *L'esclavage* I 104.

Zenon to act as their chief. As tentative support for the last suggestion she cites *P. Hib.* I 54. But the evidential value of this last document may be questioned.[52]

Returning to *PSI* 570, Scholl[53] merely notes that it is unclear in what capacity Zenon was informed, reading the evidence instead as an indication of how the flight of slaves was an everyday occurrence. The editor of *P.L. Bat.* XX 43 (= *BGU* 1993) suggests that Zenon was probably informed of the escape because he was the most influential person known to the writer in the region where the slaves had fled. In other words, Zenon was not requested to write to the gendarmes in any official capacity but was to exert only his influence in the matter. But there is a slight difficulty in accepting this interpretation. One might use it to explain the fact that Zenon was written to about runaways if this occurred once or twice. However, as *P. Lond.* 2052 and perhaps also 1950 show, this may well have been a more frequent occurrence. If so, the possibility that Zenon held some official post with the *phylakitai* becomes more attractive.

Was the assistance attested in *UPZ* 121 (i.e. public notification of a runaway slave) available to all owners of runaways? In view of the high rank of the two masters in the papyrus Bieżuńska-Małowist[54] holds that the text by itself is insufficient to prove the case for masters generally. This, it is argued, is proved by two further papyri, namely *BGU* VIII 1774 and *P. Heid.* 212.

Herakleopolis	11 x 29 cm	Reign of Auletes (59/58 - 50/49 BC)

Ed — W. Schubart and D. Schäfer, *BGU* VIII 1774 (Berlin 1933) 59-60 (= Scholl, *Corpus* §85).

Τοῖς ἐπὶ χρειῶν τεταγμένοις.	To those appointed to service.
Ἀπολλωνίου καὶ Ἡρακλείδου	As Apollonios and Herakleides,
ἀμφοτέρων Ἡρακλείδου	both (sons) of Herakleides,
[ἐ]νκαλεσάντων τῆι ἑαυτῶν	have brought charges against
5 μητρὶ καὶ τῆι ταύτης	their mother and her
[δ]ούληι Ζωσίμηι περὶ ἐκφο-	slave Zosime concerning the
ρήσεως σκευῶν τε καὶ	removal of both utensils and
βιβλίων ʽπατρικῶνʼ καὶ ἑτέρων	patrimonal documents as well as other
ἀδικη-	wrongs,
[μ]άτων συνετάξαμ[ε]ν	we gave orders
10 παραγγεῖλαι, τῶν δὲ πρὸς	to summons (them). Since those attending
τούτοις	to these matters

---

[52] See Scholl, *Corpus* 296. The papyrus is a letter (*ca* 245 BC) from Demophon to Ptolemaios and is mainly concerned with the provision of performers for a private religious celebration. In passing, as it were, the writer requests that should the slave be apprehended, Ptolemaios hand him over to Semphtheus to bring back. One surmises that the escape had been the subject of an earlier piece of correspondence (cf. the use of the definite article with σῶμα, *l.*20) and that Semphtheus was employed by Demophon to locate and return the runaway. However, there is nothing in the letter to indicate that Ptolemaios was a φυλακίτης. Indeed, the request may be better understood as a personal favour asked of a friend. See Scholl, *Corpus* 296.

[53] Scholl, *Sklaverei* 181 (*BGU* 1993), 197 (*P. Cair. Zen.* 59613), and idem, *Corpus* 261 (*BGU* 1993).

[54] Bieżuńska-Małowist, *L'esclavage* I 105.

ἀνενηνοχότων πεποιῆσθαι	have reported that the summons
τὰ τῆς παραγγελία[ς] καὶ διὰ	had been issued and, though by
προγράμματος δὲ προσκεκλη-	public notice they have been summoned,
μένων [μ]ηδ' οὕτως ἀπην-	not even so did they appear
15 τηκυιῶν, ἐὰν οἱ ἐντετευχότες	in court, if those finding (her)
παραδιδῶσι τὴν σημαινο-	deliver the indicated
μένην δούλην, παραλαβόντες	slave (to you), taking charge (of her)
καταστήσατ' ἐφ' ἡμᾶς.	bring (her) before us.

BGU 1774 belongs to an archive (*BGU* VIII 1730 and 1756-1890) coming from the bureau of the *strategos* of the Herakleopolite nome. No doubt its provenance is accounted for by the fact that the *strategos* and his bureau were involved in the procedures of παράγγελμα and πρόγραμμα. The text is an order for the apprehension and delivery to the court of a missing slave-woman, Zosime. The order had arisen from a private suit. Apparently a dispute had occurred over a paternal inheritance with the sons bringing a charge against their mother, who remains unnamed in the text, and her slave. They had removed certain property and documents possibly relevant to the dispute. From their subsequent failure to appear Scholl[55] concludes that they were probably guilty of the charge. The court (*chrematistai*?) had issued a summons which was disregarded by the defendants (*ll*.9-12). As a next step, a public notice of the summons was issued but again without effect (*ll*.12-15). The usual procedure was for a second direct summons to be issued to the defendants. If again they did not appear, a judgement-in-default was issued against them.[56] *BGU* 1774 gives no indication that a second direct summons was issued. However, such a step was evidently difficult given the situation that the accused persons were in hiding. The editor assumes that a judgement-in-default was given against the mother and orders issued for the apprehension of the slave. Those who find Zosime are to hand her over to the authorities, who in turn are to bring her to the court (*ll*.15-18). To achieve this a circular notice was issued to all relevant authorities and officials (*l*.1). But why was Zosime being sought in the first place? Was it because she was to be a witness[57] or because she was a fellow-accused? The wording of the order (*ll*.4-9) indicates the latter.[58] In either case Zosime was not technically a runaway, for she was with her mistress. I assume together with Scholl that she formed part of the widow's property lying outside the dowry.[59] *BGU* 1774 is thus not relevant evidence to prove that official involvement was available to all owners.

---

[55] Scholl, *Corpus* 299. Scholl appears to believe that the *strategos* rather than the court issued the order for the apprehension of the slave-woman. That the order was issued by the court is preferable for two reasons: (a) the apparent use of the first person plural συνετάξαμ[ε]ν (*l*.9); and (b) the otherwise unnecessary account of the charge and procedures already undertaken.

[56] Wilcken, *UPZ* I pp.552-3, summarised in *New Docs* 7 (1994) 213.

[57] Bieżuńska-Małowist, 'Les esclaves fugitifs' 84, suggests that the slave woman was sought as a witness. On a slave's capacity as witness and the use of torture in this regard see *New Docs* 7 (1994) 176-7. Cf. also *P. Oxy*. 283 *ll*.13-14 (AD 45).

[58] On the legislation of Ptolemaic cities dealing with actions against slaves see *New Docs* 7 (1994) 168-188.

[59] Scholl, *Corpus* 299. Zosime presumably formed part of her mistress's προσφορά. Items belonging to the προσφορά (i.e. land and slaves) remained the property of the wife or her parents. See G. Häge, *Ehegüterrechtliche Verhältnisse in den griechischen Papyri Ägyptens bis Diokletian* (Köln-Graz 1968) 250ff.

Provenance unknown	18.2 x 9.3 cm	67-66 or 38-37 or 16-15 BC

Ed. pr. — J. Seyfarth, *APF* 16 (1958) 148-9 (= *P. Heid*. 212, *SB* 9532, Scholl, *Corpus* §82).

In the *ed. pr.* the papyrus was dated by script to the second century AD. This dating was revised by E.G. Turner, *APF* 18 (1960) 106, to the first century BC in view of the script and the nature of the opening and closing greetings. The papyrus is written on the recto. The back is blank. There is a *kollema* in the right margin. The letter was folded perpendicular to the writing with a fold missing on the left (1-8 letters).

["Ε]ρμης Ἔρωτι τῶ[ι] ἀδελφῶι χαίρειν	Hermes to Eros, his brother, greetings
[καὶ] ὑγιαίνειν· δοῦλος ἐμοῦ	and good health. My slave
Ἡρακλείδης	Herakleides
[με]τὰ τὸν σὸν χωρισμὸν ἀφανὴς	after your departure has
γέγονεν·	absconded.
[ἐ]πεὶ δὲ πᾶσι τοῖς σοῖς συνήθης	Since he is familiar to all
ἐστίν,	yours
5 .(.).].ὑπονοῶ[[ι]] μὴ σὺν αὐτοῖς	[...] I suspect that he has taken off with
διῆρκεν·	them.
[εἰδὼς δέ] σου τὸ φιλότειμον καὶ τὸ	[Knowing] your love of honour and
ἀκρι-	strictness
[βὲς ἔκρ]ινα σε διὰ γραπτοῦ	[I decided] to beseech you
παρακαλέσαι·	in writing.
[ἐὰν μὲν ἐ]πισκεψάμενος εὑρίσκη⟨ι⟩ς	If after investigation you find
τοῦ-	this [slave,]
[τον.(.). δ]ήσας χερσὶ καὶ ποσὶ	[binding (him)] hand and foot
ἀνάπεμ-	send (him)
10 [ψ]ο[ν ἡ]μ[ῖ]ν· ἐὰν δὲ ἀφανὴς ἦι	to us. If his whereabouts is
συνπρόσ-	unknown,
[εσ]ται τις παρ' ἐμοῦ μέχρι οὗ	one of my people will be present until
διὰ προ-	by
[γρ]άμματος ἐκθεματισθῆι ὡς καθήκει·	placard public notice is given as is proper.
ἐπίδος δὲ καὶ ἑτέροις φίλο[ις] καὶ τοῖς	Deliver also (this letter?) to other friends and
οἰκε[ίοις]· τ[ὸ] δὲ σὸν ἀκριβὲς καὶ	relatives. Your strictness,
ἄγρυπνον	vigilance
15 καὶ ἀκάματον προτ[έτρ]απταί με	and tirelessness has urged me to write to
σοι	you.
γραφ[εῖν] παράπαντα χαριῆι	Altogether you gratify (us)
σεαυτ⟨οῦ⟩ ἐπιμελόμενος, ἵν'	taking care of yourself that
ὑγιαίνη⟨ι⟩ς·	you are well.
(m.2) ἔρ[ρω]σο (ἔτους) ιε Παχὼν β̅.	Farewell. Year 15 Pachon 2.

Seyfarth[60] sees the papyrus as a private letter authorizing Eros to apprehend the runaway slave. He further suggests that only when this simpler means failed (or where the apprehension was complicated in some way or other) did a master take the more public step of posting a notice. *P. Heid*. 212 confirms the procedure of a public posting of descriptions of runaway slaves. In

---

[60] J. Seyfarth, *APF* 16 (1958) 149.

particular the text states that if the recipient is unable to find the slave, then a public notice of the fugitive will be posted. In *UPZ* 121 we have one such notice.

In the view of Bieżuńska-Małowist[61] *P. Heid.* 212 offers 'definitive proof of the practice of the official pursuit of fugitive slaves'. It was not only persons of high social standing who by virtue of their influence benefited from state assistance in the search for and apprehension of runaway slaves. But some caution is called for as the rank or status of the correspondents is unknown. The high style together with the final greeting in a second hand (*l*.18) suggests to Scholl[62] that the main text was prepared by a scribe and that the letter may have been between officials. However, there is no other indication of the official status of the correspondents; indeed the letter concerns a purely personal matter and it is on this basis that the request for help was made. Only a passive, official involvement (i.e. the posting of a public notice) is contemplated in *P. Heid.* 212, for it is unclear in what capacity Eros's and Hermes's agent (*l*.11) were to act.

The above evidence shows the various means available to masters to find and apprehend their runaways. These include: the posting of public notices and the use of officials as recipients of information, the offering of rewards, the hiring of a professional searcher, the prevailing on friends and acquaintances for help and the seeking of help from individuals able to exert influence on official personnel. Official involvement extended to the posting of public notices and the use of officials as recipients of information. Evidence of an active involvement of the same officials and their assistants for all owners is open to question. Persons of position and influence might gain such assistance, but it might be argued that it was not available to all. A decision in this matter will dependent on one's view of (a) the role played by Zenon in *P. Lond.* 2052, *BGU* 1993 and *PSI* 570 and (b) of the Ptolemaic government and the control it exercised over both the population and the status of its subjects. Would the government be content to take only a passive role in the pursuit of runaways? Scholl and Bieżuńska-Małowist believe that it did adopt an active stance, and they find corroboration for their position in the activities of Zenon and the *phylakitai* in *BGU* 1993 and *PSI* 570. Their position is accepted in the present discussion and finds indirect confirmation from *P. Harr.* 62, a papyrus from the time of Antoninus Pius (see below). The possible effect of flight on fiscal revenue and/or its distribution is also a relevant consideration which is likely to have prompted a more active involvement by the state. Though coming from the Roman period, *P. Gen.* I 5 (AD 138-161) illustrates the point.[63] In this papyrus the *komogrammateus* of the village of Dionysias informs the *strategos* of his nome that the name of a slave belonging to Aphrodisios, a former *komogrammateus*, had been added to the finance department's list of fugitives (ἡ τῶν ἀφ[αν]ῶν γραφὴ τῆς διοικήσεως). And as we learn from other documents, flight or ἀναχώρησις in this period caused a redistribution of the tax burden in the fugitive's ἰδία or fiscal domicile.[64] Evidence that individuals continued to use their own personnel to find

---

[61] Bieżuńska-Małowist, *L'esclavage* I 105. So also Seyfarth, *APF* 16 (1958) 149. In conclusion Bieżuńska-Małowist observes: 'The participation of authorities in the pursuit of fugitive slaves indicates that the protection of private property extended to slaves as to all other immovable goods.'

[62] Scholl, *Corpus* 288.

[63] See J.A. Straus, 'Pour une autre interprétation du *P. Gen.* 5', *CE* 60 (1985) 298-300. Straus suggests that the slave in the instance of *P. Gen.* 5 might have turned to flight as a result of an action against his master's property, of which he himself was part. The action was to cover a loss which had accrued to his master when he had held the liturgy of *komogrammateus*. Against Taubenschlag, Westermann and Bieżuńska-Małowist it is argued that the property referred to (see *l*.8) was not that belonging to the slave but that of his master.

[64] See the discussion in *New Docs* 6 (1992) 113-4, and *New Docs* 8 (1997) §6.

runaways might be construed as an indication that the government was not actively engaged. However, it might equally indicate that, though officials were actively involved in the pursuit, owners placed little trust in the efficiency of these official channels, preferring instead to supplement this from their own resources.

Pursuit of Fugitive Slaves in the Roman Period

Roman authorities did not originally offer help to a master in the search and apprehension of his fugitive slave. It was left to the owner to do this. There were, of course, areas of exception. For example, in the case of Roman conquests from second century BC, the senate followed a policy of returning runaways to their former masters when possible. Westermann[65] argues that the policy was based on the sanctity of private property and served to enlist the support of the propertied class. But there was no elaborate state intervention during the Republican period in the finding, apprehension and return of fugitive slaves. It was left to the owner to find the runaway himself, to seek the help of friends or to use what influence he could bring to bear on magistrates or provincial officials, e.g. Cicero, *Ad fam.* 13.77.3, 5.9.2 and 10.1. Bellen[66] lists a number of ways in which masters sought assistance in their pursuit of runaways: public notice and the offering of a reward; the calling on friends and acquaintances to assist; and the employment of a *fugitivarius* or professional searcher (usually enlisted when regaining the slave was considered difficult). If all else failed, a master might avail himself of an oracle or the interpreter of dreams to learn the whereabouts of the fugitive or the likelihood of his being found. But at the same time the state did afford some protection to masters of newly acquired slaves. The aediles' edict required the vendor to declare besides any disease, defect or noxal liability adhering to a slave whether he/she was inclined to run away or a loiterer on errands, *Dig.* 21.1.1.1.[67] If not declared, the purchaser had a right to rescind the sale. Unless otherwise indicated in the sale by having the slave wear the *pilleus*, it was immaterial whether the vendor was aware of the fact or not.[68]

Bellen[69] offers a picture of the gradual engagement of the offices of government in the search for fugitives during the course of the first two centuries of the principate. The original occasion for intervention was provided by the need to search for fugitives thought to be hiding on another's property. In Rome the praetor provided a *servus publicus* to act as *conquistor* of the fugitive. He was authorized to use force, if necessary. In Italy, on grounds of the *lex Fabia* and a *senatus consultum* issued from the late first to the first half of the second century AD a master could be issued with a certificate entitling him to search for the fugitive and prescribing a penalty of 10,000 sesterces both for magistrates who did not give their assistance and for property owners who resisted (*Dig.* 11.4.1.2). By a *senatus consultum* (*Dig.* 11.4.1.1) possibly moved by Antoninus Pius the earlier *lex Fabia* and *senatus consultum* was reaffirmed. The same *senatus consultum* also appears to have prescribed a penalty for failure to hand over a fugitive to his master or to the magistrates within 20 days, if found on one's

---

[65] Westermann, *The Slave Systems* 64.

[66] H. Bellen, *Studien zur Sklavenflucht im römischen Kaiserreich* (Wiesbaden 1971) 7-9. Slaves also used various ways to guarantee the success of their flight ranging from the superstitious (e.g the interpretation of dreams, the asking of an oracle and the use of magical amulets) to the more practical (e.g. covering of distinguishing features, changing name and buying the silence of confidants).

[67] See also Aulus Gellius, *Noctae Atticae* 4.2

[68] B. Nicholas, *An Introduction to Roman Law* (Oxford 1962, repr. 1972) 181-2, and A. Watson, *Roman Slave Law* (Baltimore 1987) 49-50.

[69] Bellen, *Studien zur Sklavenflucht* 9-16.

property (*Dig.* 11.4.1.1). By a rescript of Antoninus Pius (*Dig.* 11.4.3) the procedure was extended to all provinces.[70] Governors were to provide a letter authorizing the master or his representative to enter the property of another and search for the fugitive. If required, an *apparitor* or attendant was provided by the governor. How effective these procedures were remains unclear. No doubt, governors and magistrates may have been on occasion reluctant to act and owners of property may have resisted entry. Marcus Aurelius issued a general letter declaring that officials (governors, magistrates and *milites stationarii*) should assist the owner in his search and punish those who might conceal fugitives. Bellen[71] notes in this same period a change in the position of the state with the latter now taking greater initiative in the search. Anyone could apprehend a fugitive and hand him over to a magistrate (*Dig.* 11.4.1.3). The latter was to guard the slave until his master should appear (*Dig.* 11.4.1.4). If the master failed to appear, the slave was to be sent to either the *praefectus vigilum* in Rome or the provincial governor (*Dig.* 11.4.1.8). No doubt, if the slave remained unclaimed, after a sufficient interval he was sold.[72] This new procedure extended beyond the mere offer of assistance to the master in search of his slave. The state's role had become more active. This is further implied by the fact that magistrates were now to be informed of a fugitive's name, distinguishing features including scars and the name of his master (*Dig.* 11.4.1.8a). Such information would assist them in the search for a runaway. Bellen[73] argues that Septimius Severus still further strengthened the engagement of the state and its offices. In a rescript to the *praefectus vigilum* he advised that the official should seek out fugitives and return them to their masters (*Dig.* 1.15.4). It is also assumed that the same obligation was placed on all provincial governors implicitly in their *mandata*.[74] It is at this stage that Bellen[75] sees the state as fully engaged in the pursuit of fugitives; it was not only acting to help a master in search of his slave but also taking the initiative in the search and apprehension of the fugitive. The effectiveness of the procedures is questioned by Bellen. If initially successful, they enjoyed only a short-lived success, for by the end of the third century it appears that once again the search was mostly left to the master.

To what extent were the developments in Roman law concerned with slavery reflected in the administrative practices of Egypt? Did government involvement in the search and apprehension of runaway slaves lapse with the coming of Roman rule only to be gradually reimposed in the course of time? Or was there a continuity of practice spanning the Ptolemaic and Roman periods? In other words, did the practice in Egypt pre-empt the developments which were introduced into Roman law especially from the time of Antoninus Pius? The paucity of relevant documents makes it difficult to give a definite answer. Bieżuńska-Małowist[76] argues

---

[70] Bellen, *Studien zur Sklavenflucht* 10-11.

[71] Bellen, *Studien zur Sklavenflucht* 12.

[72] An unclaimed fugitive might be sold by the *fiscus*. The *fiscus* guaranteed to restore the purchase price to the buyer in case of a later eviction by the owner. On the legal status of runaways and the benefits and liabilities which might accrue to a master by the actions of his fugitive slave see W.W. Buckland, *The Roman Law of Slavery* (Cambridge 1908, reprinted 1970) 269-274.

[73] Bellen, *Studien zur Sklavenflucht* 13.

[74] Bellen, *Studien zur Sklavenflucht* 13-14.

[75] Bellen, *Studien zur Sklavenflucht* 14.

[76] Bieżuńska-Małowist, 'Les esclaves fugitifs' 87 ff. See also Taubenschlag, *Law* 83-5. *P. Heid.* 212 (*SB* VI 9532 — see text above) might be cited as further evidence for the continued involvement of the state in the pursuit of fugitives after the establishment of Roman rule. The evidential value of the papyrus is, of course, conditional on accepting (a) that its date is 16-15 BC rather than the other possible dates of 77-6 and 38-7 BC and (b) that the posting of a public notice does not necessarily entail a more active involvement by the state.

for the continuity of practice and points in particular to *P. Oxy.* XII 1422 and *P. Harr.* 62. By way of caution it should be note that the earliest direct evidence, i.e. *P. Harr.* 62, is dated to the reign of Antoninus Pius. However, in so far as Ptolemaic practice was consistent with the tendency of Roman administrative practice and law it may reasonably be assumed that an official engagement continued after 30 BC. A continuance would also be consistent with Roman policy which largely adopted the administrative systems already in place in newly acquired provinces.

Oxyrhynchus   16.2 x 6.4 cm   *ca* AD 128

Ed. pr. — B.P. Grenfell and A.S. Hunt, *P. Oxy.* XII 1422 (London 1916) 74-5.

```
     [      ] ἐλ(άβομεν) Μεχ(εὶρ) ιδ̅. (m.2)        [ ... ] (we) have rec(eived) Mecheir 14.  87.
     π̅ζ̅.
     (m.3)[....Δ]ημήτριος στρατηγὸς               [ ... ] Demetrios, strategos of the
     [Γυναι?]κοπολείτου Ἀγαθῷ Δαίμον[ι]           [Gynae]kopolite nome, to dearest Agatho-
     [στρατη]γῶι Ὀξυρυγχείτου τῶι                 daimon, [strate]gos of the Oxyrynchite
5    [      ] φιλτάτωι χαίρει[ν.]                  nome [ ... ] greeting.
     [......] Ἀχιλλεὺς ὃν ἐδήλωσας [ἐν-]          [ ... ] Achilleus whom you indicated
     [κεκλῆσθαι] ὑπὲρ ὑποδοχῆς δού[- ]            [to have been accused] of harbouring a slave
     [λου.... ἐδη]λώθη καὶ ὑπὸ τῶν [ ]            [of name?] has been indicated by the
     [κωμογρα]μματέων τοῦ ν[ομοῦ]                 [komogra]mmateis of the n[ome]
10   [καὶ τῶν τῆς μη]τροπόλεως γραμ-              [and the] scribes of [the me]tropolis
     [ματέων ἀφανὴ?]ς εἶναι. (m.4)                to have [absconded].
           ἐρρῶσθαί σε                             Farewell
     [εὔχομαι.........]ταμιο( ) γρ κ( ).          [I pray ... ]
     (m.3)[(ἔτους) ιβ̅ ? Αὐτοκράτορος              [Year 12? of Imperator
        Κα]ίσ[α]ρος Τραιανοῦ                      Ca]esar Trajanus
     [Ἀδριανοῦ Σεβαστοῦ Τ]ῦβι κ̅.                 [Hadrianus Augustus T]ybi 20
15   (m.5?) [      Τῦβι ?] κδ̅.                   [Tybi?] 24.
```

The document is a letter from the *strategos* of the Gynaekopolite (?) nome to the *strategos* of the Oxyrhynchite nome. The letter appears to have been prepared and dated by a scribe working in the bureau of the *strategos* (*ll*.2-11, 13-14, 3rd hand). Enough space was left between *ll*.11 and 13 for the *strategos* to add a farewell in his own hand (4th hand). He may have also added the later date, if that is the meaning of *l*.15, at the time of his signing the letter (5th hand?). The letter was docketed as received some 20 days later (*l*.1, 1st hand) and registered in the correspondence received by the *strategos* of the Oxyrhynchite nome (*l*.1, 2nd hand). The letter is dated by the office of Agathodaimon.

If a reconstruction of the letter's context were to be offered, it would appear that the slave of a master living in the Oxyrhynchite nome had fled and was found in hiding with Achilleus in the Gynaekopolite nome. The fate of the fugitive is unknown; however, the state is shown in *P. Oxy.* 1422 to be involved in the prosecution of the person who had assisted him. In this instance it appears that Achilleus had received news of the impending action against him and had turned to flight. The papyrus does not offer direct evidence for state involvement in the pursuit of fugitives; however, the fact that the *strategoi* were involved in the prosecution of a

§3 The Government's Pursuit of Runaway Slaves

person assisting the fugitive suggests that the state may well have been involved in the pursuit itself. Accordingly, Bieżuńska-Małowist[77] believes that the investigation described in the papyrus was conducted by the authorities in keeping with the practice of pursuing fugitive slaves.

Provenance unknown   33 x 30 cm   AD 151
Ed. pr. — J.E. Powell, *P.Harr.* 62 (Cambridge 1936) 42-3.

θ̄   9

Παρὰ Σαραπίωνος στρατηγοῦ 'Οάσεως
    ζ̄ Νομ[ῶν ...]
τυπι, ὁμοίως προγράμματα π[ερὶ]
    ζητήσεως[...]
δουλικῶν σωμάτων προ[.......]
    γραφείσας[...]
στρατηγῶν ἄλλω⟨ν⟩ νομῶν τοῦ
    ἐνεστῶτος ῑδ̄ (ἔτους)[...]
5   Ἀντωνίνου Καίσαρος τοῦ κυρίου.
    ἐστὶ δέ·
Ἑρμαῖος ὁ καὶ Δρύτων στρατηγὸς
    Β[ο]υσιρίτου μια[...]
περὶ διαζη⟨τή⟩σεως τῶ[ν
    ὑ]πογεγραμμένων δου[λικῶν]
σωμάτων ὡς ἐγ μέ[ρο]υς ὑπαρχόντων
    Ἀραβίωνι[ ]
10   τῷ καὶ Ἰσχυρίωνι Ἀχιλλέως ἀπὸ
    κώ[μης ......]
ἐκείνου τοῦ νομοῦ αρεσταιμεν . [...]
οντων . ασι . . . ν προέγραψα[...]
καὶ οιδε . . . μεν . ων . [...]
διὰ τρει . . τα προσελθόντες μὴ οὑτωσί.
    παράγγε[λλεται δὲ]
15   καὶ τοῖς πρὸς τῇ παραφυλακῇ
    τεταγμένοις καὶ τοῖς [ἄλλοις]
δημοσίοις πᾶσαν ἀναζήτησιν αὐτῶν
    ποιήσασθαι, καὶ τὸ[ν ἐν-]
τυχόντα προσαγαγεῖν μοι.
[...]′′   Θώθ δ̄
[...] Ἀρτεμίδωρος (ἐτῶν) κ̄ϛ̄
20   Ἰσίδωρο(ς) (ἐτῶν) κ̄β̄   Μάρτιλλα
    (ἐτῶν) λ̄η̄

From Sarapion, *strategos* of the Oasis of
    the Heptanomis [...]
[...], likewise public notices concerning
    the search [...]
for slaves [...]
    written [by the ?]
strategoi of other nomes in the
    present year 14 [...]
of Antoninus Caesar, the lord.
It is:
I, Hermaios, also called Dryton, *strategos*
    of the Busirite nome [...]
concerning the search for the
    undermentioned slaves
belonging in part to
    Arabion [...]
also called Ischyrion, son of Achilleus from
    the village [of ...]
of that nome [...]
[...] I have given public notice ...
[...]
through [...] coming not thus.
    It is announced
also to those appointed to garrison-duty and
    the [other]
officials to make every search for them and
    the person who
finds (them) to bring (them) to me.
[...] Thoth 4
[...] Artemidoros, 26 years of age;
Isidoros, 22 years of age; Martilla,
    38 years of age.

---

[77] Bieżuńska-Małowist, 'Les esclaves fugitifs' 87.

(m.2) Σύρος ὑπηρέτης διὰ ʽΗρακλήου υἱοῦ τοῦ ὑπογράφοντο[ς] αὐτοῦ προτέθειμαι δημοσίᾳ καὶ κατεχώρισα.	I, Syrus, assistant, through Herakleos, son of the person undersigning himself, have posted publicly and have recorded (it).

Marginal notes

(m.3) γ̄λ̄ .[ ]αλειτω μετὰ του . . ( ) . . ( ) κατὰ τὸν [. . . . .]	[...] [...] [...]

....

2. *Editio princeps* reads προγραμμάτων 11. The personal name ʼΑρεστᾶι Μενω[νος has been suggested, *JEA* 24 (1938) 142 14. *APF* 12 (1937) 235; the *editio princeps* reads παράγγε[ιλον. 15. τοῖς [ἄλλοις, Bell, *JEA* 24 (1938) 142.

In the *editio princeps* the papyrus is described as a 'fragment from a τόμος συγκολλήσιμος, probably of a strategus'. There is evidence of letters on the right-hand side of the preceding column; they were not reproduced in *P. Harr.* 62. The text as it stands consists of a document concerning runaway slaves (*ll.*1-20), an endorsement by the assistant (3rd hand) who entered the document in the τόμος συγκολλήσιμος (*ll.*21-22 and presumably the number θ at the top of the page) and marginal notes (2nd hand — the hand is misleadingly described as the 'third hand' in the editor's introductory description of the letter).

Bieżuńska-Małowist[78] offers the following interpretation of the text. Arabion, a resident in a village of the Busirite nome, gave notice of the flight to the nome *strategos*, who in turn issued a circular arrest warrant (cf. *BGU* 1774 above) for the four[79] runaways (*ll.*7-20). The present papyrus represents a copy of the arrest warrant which was transmitted or passed on by the *strategos* of the Oasis in the Heptanomis (*ll.*1-6), presumably to the *strategos* of the Oxyrhynchite nome.[80] The final two lines (*ll.*21-2) are described as the annotation of a functionary declaring that the document had been registered and posted. The document thus attests an active official involvement in the pursuit and apprehension of fugitive slaves in Egypt already before this had become practice under Roman law. Here one can see the *strategoi* of various nomes active in the notification of fugitives and their details, in the ordering of underlings to search for them and in the receipt and guarding of the same. The implication of *P. Harr.* 62 must be that the Romans were here continuing an older practice. If so, it is probable that in the Ptolemaic period official involvement extended to the search and apprehension of fugitives and that on assuming control of Egypt the Romans continued this practice.

As a later example of the state's engagement in the pursuit and apprehension of fugitives two further documents may be cited. *P. Turner* 41 (AD 250-271) is a petition of a woman named Sarapias possibly living in Antinoopolis to the *strategos* of the Oxyrhynchite nome. The papyrus with translation and comments are to be found in *New Docs* 6 (1992) 55-60, and will not be reproduced here. The text concerns a trusted slave who had run away. It is

---

[78] Bieżuńska-Małowist, *L'esclavage* II 127 and 141, and idem, 'Les esclaves fugitifs' 76 n.6, 87-8.

[79] It is assumed that the name of a fourth fugitive is lost from the beginning of *l.*19.

[80] *P. Harr.* 137, a copy of a lease agreement for three vineyards, is on the verso of our document. 'It is a reasonable assumption that *P. Harr.* 137 is the later document and, since it names villages in the Oxyrhynchite nome, its provenance was that nome. If so, the copy of the arrest warrant was transmitted by the *strategos* of the Oasis in the Heptanomis to the *strategos* of the Oxyrhynchite nome.

§3 The Government's Pursuit of Runaway Slaves

suggested that after having learned of his whereabouts by a privately commissioned search, Sarapias had at first taken steps to engage the relevant authorities (*ll*.20-1) but without success. The editor argues that is improbable that Sarapias learned of his whereabouts by chance as the fugitive (a) was probably living in another nome and (b) was living in the countryside and not the *metropolis*.[81] The possibility that Sarapias learned of the slave's whereabouts after the posting of his description and the promise of a reward has not been entertained to date. Unfortunately, the end of the petition is lost and it is no longer clear what exactly was asked of the *strategos*. The editor assumes either the arrest and return of the runaway or the prosecution of those individuals who had hindered the execution of her earlier request (cf. *P. Oxy.* 1422 above).

The second document is *P. Beatty Panop.* 1 *ll*.149-152, a draft letter of a *strategos*.

Πομπονίῳ Δόμνῳ. Ἀμμώνιος ὁ καὶ Ἀμπέλιος κράτιστος δι᾽ ὧν ἐπέστειλεν [ἐμοὶ καὶ Πλουτογέ]νει ἠθέλησεν Ἀργέντιον καὶ οἰκέτην ῥεμβὸν
150 καταλημφθέντα καὶ παραδοθέντα αὐτῷ δι᾽ ἐπιστολῆς τοῦ κυρ[ίου τοῦ διασημο]τάτου ἡγουμένου Θηβαίδος Ἰουλίου Ἀθηνοδώρου παραπεμφθῆναι πρὸς τὴν σὴν τοῦ ἐμοῦ κυρίου τάξιν· ὅνπερ απ[. . . .]. καὶ ἵν᾽ εἰδέναι ἔχοι σου τὸ μεγαλεῖον γράφω, κύριέ μου. (ἔτους) τε καὶ (ἔτους) ιδ καὶ (ἔτους) ζ, Θὼθ [.]

To Pomponius Domnus. Ammonius, also called Ampelius, *vir egregius*, through what he has written [to me and Plutoge]nes wished Argentius and a runaway slave, who had been apprehended and handed over to him by letter of the lord *perfectissimus* governor of the Thebaid, Julius Athenodorus, to be escorted to your office of my lord. Whom [...] and that your highness may know I write, my lord. Year 15 and year 14 and year 7, Thoth ...

P. Beatty Panop. 1, dated AD 298, is a register of official outgoing correspondence of the *strategos* of the Panopolite nome. Two individuals, one of whom was a slave, had been handed over by letter of the Roman governor of the Thebaid to Ammonius, an official who was apparently a subordinate of the *magister privatae* and possessed a policing function.[82] The latter official then handed them over to the *strategos* (Apolinarius) and Plutogenes (president of the senate of Panopolis) with orders that the individuals be escorted to Pomponius Domnus, the *magister privatae*.[83] At the same time the papyrus illustrates a dilemma already perceived and discussed above in relation to the Ptolemaic papyri . In *P. Beatty Panop.* 1 *ll*.149-152 we have an example of the state's engagement in the apprehension of a fugitive; however, at the same time it is difficult to determine whether the procedure illustrated by the letter was at all typical of a general procedure. The conveyance of a slave in the company of an apparently free

---

[81] U. Hagedorn, *P. Turner* p.169.
[82] See *P. Beatty Panop.* 1 *ll*.192-201, 225-9 and 338-341; also A.H.M. Jones, J.R. Martindale and J. Morris, *The Prosopography of the Later Roman Empire*, vol. 1 (Cambridge 1975).
[83] On the role of the *magister privatae* see J. Lallemand, *L'administration civile de l'Égypte de l'avènement de Dioclétien à la création du diocèse, 284-382* (Paris 1964) 88-9.

person and the involvement of fiscal officials might well imply that the former's apprehension was motivated by a concern for public revenue.

In the long term the effectiveness of the state's engagement may be questioned. Two papyri (*P. Oxy.* XIV 1643 and *P.Oxy.* XII 1423) illustrate how owners did not entrust the search for and apprehension of fugitives to the machinery of government; in each case they took the initiative themselves. However, some caution is required in interpreting the evidence. U. Hagedorn argues that though the evidence of *P. Harr.* 62, *P. Turner* 41, *P. Oxy.* 1643 and *P.Oxy.* 1423 might incline one to assume a gradual decline in the efficiency of the official machinery, the amount of evidence is too small to justify such a conclusion. Indeed, she thinks it likely that a master would avail himself of whatever means, whether private or official, he could to apprehend his runaway. Conversely, in the light of evidence from Roman law Bellen questions the effectiveness of the official machinery. If initially successful, this was only short-lived, for by the end of the third century the search was once again left largely to the master.

Oxyrhynchus   25.5 x 11.3 cm   AD 298

Ed. pr. — B.P. Grenfell and A.S. Hunt, *P. Oxy.* XIV 1643 (London 1920) 70-2.

[Αὐρήλ(ιος) Σαραπ]άμμων ὁ καὶ	Aurelius Sarapammon, also called
[Δ]ίδυμος Ὀξυρυγχεί-	Didymus, a citizen of Oxyrhynchus,
[της ......] καὶ Ἀθηναῖος	[...] and Athenaeus, victor in all the great
π[ερι]οδονίκης κράτιστος	games, *vir egregius*,
[ξυστάρχης δ]ιὰ βίου καὶ ὡ[ς]	*xystarches* for life, and as
χρημα(τίζω)	I am styled
[Αὐρηλ(ίῳ) ....]ῳ καὶ ὡς χρημα(τίζεις)	[to Aurelius ...] and as you are styled from
ἀπὸ τῆς αὐτῆς Ὀξυρυγ-	the same city of the
5 [χειτῶν πόλε]ως χαίρειν.	Oxyrhynchites, greeting.
ἀποσ[υ]νίστημί σε κατὰ τόδε τὸ	I appoint you as my representative by
[ἐπίσταλμα ὥσ]τε σε ἀποδημοῦντα εἰς	this [letter] so that you will travel to
τὴν λαμπροτά-	the illustrious
[την Ἀλεξάνδρια]ν ἀναζητῆσαι δοῦλόν	Alexandria and search for my slave by the
μου ὀνόμα-	name of
[τι ....]ν ὡς (ἐτῶν) λε, ὃν καὶ	[...] about 35 years of age, whom you
σὺ αὐτὸς γνωρίζεις	yourself also know
[..........], ὅνπερ ἀνευρὼν	[...] whom finding you will
παραδώσεις,	hand over,
10 [ἐξουσίας σοι] οὔσης ὅσα κἀμοὶ	[the authority] being yours as much as is
παρόντι ἔξεστιν	mine, if I were present,
[.........]ασθαι καὶ εἴργιν καὶ	to [...], to imprison,
μαστιγοῖν καὶ ἐνα-	to whip,
[γωγὴν ποιεῖν? ἐ]φ' ὧν δέον ἐστὶν	[to bring a suit] before those whom it is
πρὸς τοὺς ὑποδεξα-	proper against those
[μένους αὐτὸν] καὶ αἰτεῖσθαι	harbour[ing him] and to seek
ἐκδικείαν. τὸ δὲ ἐπί-	satisfaction. This

§3 The Government's Pursuit of Runaway Slaves

[σταλμα τοῦτο] μοναχόν σοι ἐξεδόμην, ὅπερ κύ-	letter in single copy I have given to you;
15 [ριον ἔστω] πανταχοῦ ἐπιφερόμενον, καὶ ἐπερωτη-	[let it be] valid wherever it is produced; being asked
[θεὶς ὡμολό]γησα. (ἔτους) ιδ καὶ (ἔτους) ιγ τῶν κυρίων	I acknowledged. Year 14 and year 13 of [our] lords
[ἡμῶν Διοκλ]ητιανοῦ καὶ Μαξιμιανοῦ Σεβαστῶν καὶ (ἔτους) ϛ	[Diocl]etianus and Maximianus Augusti and year 6
[τῶν κυρίων ἡμ]ῶν Κωνσταντίου καὶ Μαξιμιανοῦ τῶν	[of our lords] Constantius and Maximianus the
[ἐπιφανεστάτω]ν Καισάρων Παχὼν ιϛ, ὑπατίας Φαύστου	[most illustrious] Caesars, Pachon 16, of the consulship of Festus
20 [καὶ Γάλλου.]	[and Gallus.]
(m.2)[Αὐρήλιο]ς Σαραπάμμων ὁ καὶ Δίδυμος	I, [Aurelius] Sarapammon, also called Didymus,
[κράτιστο]ς ξυστάρχης διὰ βίου ἐπέστει-	[vir egregius,] xystarches for life, have enjoined
[λα πάν]τα τὰ προκείμενα ὡς πρό- [κειται.]	[all] the aforesaid as [set] forth.

The above papyrus describes itself as an ἐπίσταλμα and was issued by Sarapammon to a person whose name is now lost. It authorized this person to travel to Alexandria in search of a fugitive (name lost) who was already known to him. It further vests in this person the authority to imprison and to whip the fugitive and to lodge an action against any person found harbouring him. The document presupposes at most only a passive role for the state. The search is conducted by a private individual authorized by the owner of the fugitive. The state involved itself, if at all, in guarding the apprehended slave. As usual any action against another person, in this case for harbouring the fugitive, was to be initiated by the injured party or his representative.

Oxyrhynchus   27.3 x 11.4 cm   Fourth century AD

Ed. pr. — B.P. Grenfell and A.S. Hunt, *P.Oxy.* XII 1423 (London 1916) 75-6.

Φλαού[ιος] Ἀμμωνᾶς ὀφφικιάλιος τά[ξ]εως ἐπάρχου Αἰγύπτου Φλαουίῳ Δωροθέῳ ὀφφικιαλίῳ χαίρειν. ἐντέλλομαί σοι	Flavius Ammonas *officialis* of the bureau of the prefect of Egypt to Flavius Dorotheus *officialis*, greeting. I command
5 καὶ ἐπιτρέπω δοῦλόν μου Μάγνον κ[α]λούμενον δράσαν- τα καὶ ἐν Ἑρμοῦ πόλι διατρίβοντα καί τινά μου εἴδη ἀφελόμενον δι[α]δήσας δέσμιον ἀγαγεῖν	and entrust to you my slave called Magnus who has run away and is residing in Hermopolis and (who) has stolen some things of mine to bind and bring (him) back prisoner
10 με[τ]ὰ τοῦ ἐπὶ τῆς Σέσφθα. κυρία ἡ ἐντολὴ καὶ ἐπερωτηθὶς	with the person in charge of Sesphtha. The command is valid and being asked

ὁμολόγησα. Φλαούιος Ἀμμω- νᾶς ὀφφικιάλιος τάξεως ἐπάρχου Αἰγύπτου πεποίημαι 15 τήνδε τὴ[ν ἐν]τολήν.	I acknowledged. I, Flavius Ammonas, *officialis* of the bureau of the prefect of Egypt, have made this command.

....

9. δι[α]δήσαντι   11. ἐπερωτηθείς   12. ὡμολόγησα

The papyrus is a letter addressed by one *officialis* to another and authorizes the apprehension and return of the writer's slave. The two *officiales* are not acting in any official capacity here but as private individuals. The slave had taken with him certain objects which are not specified in the letter. Above we have seen that theft of property often accompanied flight and was used to finance the escape. It has also been noted that the property was often described as it might assist in the identification of the fugitive, no doubt when he attempted to exchange it. The omission of details of the stolen property might be explained in this instance by the fact that the writer already knew the whereabouts of his slave. But this only introduces a new problem, for the letter gives no information to its recipient concerning the precise location of the slave. Are we to assume that the recipient already knew? Perhaps he had located the runaway, informed the owner and awaited authorization. Furthermore, it is not clear why the person in charge of Sesphtha (the *comarches* ?) was also to be arrested. Had he assisted the fugitive? This would appear to be the most reasonable suggestion.

Nordling[84] evinces the view that *P.Oxy.* 1423 and 1643 'may be interpreted as evidence that outside agents induced slaves to steal from their masters and then abscond'. He entertains the possibility of collusion between a *fugitivarius* and the slave to defraud the latter's master of his property, namely of the slave himself and whatever stolen goods he had taken with him on his escape. In support a comment by Daube is cited:[85]

> Your slave would run away to a *fugitivarius* [slave-catcher]. The latter would approach you, tell you that with much effort he might perhaps discover the fugitive, and declare himself prepared to buy him right now at a low figure. You had no choice but to accept, whereupon the slave-catcher could resell or manumit the slave.

From his understanding of ἀνδρὶ ἀξιοχρείωι καὶ δωσιδίκωι (*UPZ* 121 *l*.14) as a reference to a slave-catcher Nordling concludes that the practice of collusion had a long history, not being legislated against until the third century AD (thereafter a slave bought by a slave-catcher could not be manumitted without the consent of his former owner for a period of ten years) and even then without much effect to judge by the evidence of *P.Oxy.* 1423 and 1643. But there are a number of difficulties with Nordling's suggestion.

First, there is no indication in the two papyri that the third party had acted in collusion with the slave to defraud his master. The suggestion is possible but evidence for it is lacking in the documents. More probably the actions referred to in *P.Oxy.* 1423 and 1643 concern suits against persons found harbouring fugitives. Such actions were available under both Hellenistic and Roman law. For its availability under Hellenistic law see the above discussion on *UPZ* 121 *l*.14 (cf. also *P. Oxy.* 1422, ca AD 128, reproduced above) and Ditt., *Syll.*³ 736 *ll*.81-2. The relevant paragraph of the latter document reads:

> That there be an asylum for slave — Let the temple be an asylum for slaves according as the priests will show the place, and let no one harbour runaways nor feed nor provide them with work. Let the person who

---

[84] Nordling, *JSNT* 41 (1991) 104-5.
[85] On the practice see also Watson, *Roman Slave Law* 64-66.

acts against what has been written be liable to the master for double the worth of the slave and for a penalty of five hundred drachmae. And let the priest decide concerning the runaways as many as are from our city and as many as he deems at fault, let him hand them over to their masters. If he does not hand (them) over, let it be permitted to the master to take (his slave) and depart.

At the same time that the privilege of asylum was conferred on the temple, a suit for compensation and penalty was instituted against any private individual who should either help or harbour a runaway. Flight of slaves was an issue to be regulated. Private individuals were to be legally discouraged from offering assistance and an alternative course of action was to be offered to the slave, i.e. the seeking of asylum. The latter institution rests on the assumption that the runaway could trust himself to the integrity of the priesthood.

The prosecution of persons either for persuading a slave to run away, concealing his whereabouts, or seizing, selling or purchasing him was known to Roman law from the second century BC. Under the *lex Fabia* the delict of *plagium*, which covered the wrongs listed above, was heard by a *iudicium publicum*.[86] The delict was perceived as a public offence and tried accordingly. If found guilty, a penalty of 50,000 sesterces was exacted and paid to the state. There were also actions which might be brought under private law (*actio servi corrupti* and *actio furti*). Bellen[87] argues that such actions were themselves in time influenced by the formulation of the *lex Fabia*. The later application of the *lex Fabia* is also considered. By the time of Hadrian, it appears to have applied to peregrines and their slaves.[88] Certain of its concepts also appear to have required clarification, e.g. what exactly constituted concealment and sale/purchase.[89] Of course, the delict was increasingly being tried under the principate by *cognitio*, under Septimius Severus by the *praefectus urbi*, *praefectus praetorio*, provincial governors and especially appointed procurators. This drew in its wake a change in the nature of the delict. It became a *crimen capitale* no longer punished necessarily (depending on the category of the delict) by a monetary penalty but also by banishment to the mines or crucifixion for *humiliores* and *relegatio in perpetuum* for *honestiores*.[90]

Second, it is not the case that the legal systems of antiquity were ignorant of the possibility of collusion between slaves and third parties to defraud masters and that the practice was not legislated against before the third century AD. Laws seldom give explicit reason for their creation. As a case in point one might consider *P. Lille* I 29 col.1 *l*.27 - col.2 *l*.39 (third century BC), which concerns the bringing of a suit for injury against a slave's master where the master was alleged to be either the instigator of his slave's delict or an accessory to it. If the master was found to be neither an instigator of nor accessory to the delict, he was still held liable for his slave's action, but could free himself from that liability by handing the slave over to the plaintiff before the relevant official. The new owner was then obliged to scourge and/or brand the slave or hand him over, possibly to one of the officials overseeing the execution of private debts, for sale overseas. The harsh provisions envisaged for the slave were probably instituted to stop any collusion between slave and plaintiff to deceive a master and thus deprive him of his property.[91]

---

[86] Bellen, *Studien zur Sklavenflucht* 45-6.
[87] Bellen, *Studien zur Sklavenflucht* 46-50.
[88] Bellen, *Studien zur Sklavenflucht* 50.
[89] Bellen, *Studien zur Sklavenflucht* 52-3.
[90] Bellen, *Studien zur Sklavenflucht* 53-4. On the distinction between *humiliores* and *relegatio in perpetuum* for *honestiores* see P. Garnsey, *Social Status and Legal Privilege in the Roman Empire* (Oxford 1970).
[91] *P. Hal.* 1 p.113 n.1; see also Scholl, *Corpus* 11.

Third, it is improbable that the phrase ἀνδρὶ ἀξιοχρείωι καὶ δωσιδίκωι in *UPZ* 121 *l.*14 refers to a slave-catcher. The choice of adjectives is inappropriate, nor does the suggestion by itself explain why the highest reward was paid in this case. Wilcken's interpretation of the expression (see above), which entails a less specific reference, is to be preferred.

Finally, the papyrological evidence bearing on the issues of reason for theft and the choice of hiding-place gives no indication that flight was undertaken in collusion with a third party and with the intention to defraud. Slaves stole to support themselves in hiding; descriptions of stolen goods were provided as the slave might be caught whilst attempting to trade them; slaves fled to regions of former residence where they might find help, to populous regions and cities where they might gain work and where it would be difficult to find them amongst the masses, or to temples offering some form of asylum. The frequency of multiple escape (i.e. two or more fugitives) also undermines Nordling's suggestion.

Why did slaves flee?

In their analyses of the evidence Bieżuńska-Małowist[92] and Scholl[93] adduce a number of reasons for a slave's flight. Sale and transport away from home were occasions which appear to have prompted slaves to escape, e.g. *P. Cair. Zen.* 59804,[94] 59015 (verso) and 59537. *P. Lond.* 2052 might also be considered here, if Paideas had only recently acquired the slaves. No doubt, the fear associated with having a new master and place of residence as well as the mere opportunities for escape offered by the transfer were underlying factors here. Another opportunity for flight was also provided by periods of civil disturbance and upheaval. Recent reduction to servile status was another occasion, e.g. *P. Hamb.* 91 (167 BC). In this instance, four women, who had only recently been given as booty, escaped from their new master. Slaves might also escape to avoid giving evidence in a legal dispute, e.g. *P. Cair. Zen.* 59620-1, or to avoid possible legal action, e.g. *P. Grenf.* 47 (AD 148); cf. also *P. Oxy.* III 472 (ca AD 130). If none of these conditions pertain, then it may be assumed that the escape was prompted by some difficulty in the household such as cruel treatment or fear of punishment, e.g. *PSI* VI 667 (after 256 BC) and *P. Cair. Zen.* 59537.[95] The assumption rests on the premise that, as escape was seldom rewarded with success, it is unlikely that a slave would turn to flight without some compelling reason.

Philadelphia   13 x 11 cm   After 256 BC

Ed. pr. — G. Vitelli, M. Norsa, V. Bartoletti et al., *PSI* VI 667 (Florence 1920) 85.

[τ]ουτ[έ]στιν	[...] this is [...]
ὀχ[ληρ]ῶν κεκ[μηκυῖ]α ξυλοφο-	of the irksome things having laboured
ροῦσα καὶ ἀλί[ζουσα, κα]ὶ οὐ θέλουσα	carrying wood and piling it up and not
ἀναχωρῆσαι [ἀπὸ] σοῦ, ὥσπερ αἱ	wanting to flee from you, just as the
5 λοι[π]αὶ παιδίσκ[αι ἀ]δικεθῖσαι ἀνα-	rest of the maidservants do when wronged,

---

[92] Bieżuńska-Małowist, *L'esclavage* II 142, and idem, 'Les esclaves fugitifs' 81.

[93] Scholl, *Sklaverei* 222, and idem, *Corpus* 300.

[94] With regard to *P. Cair. Zen.* 59804, Scholl, *Corpus* 152, notes that as the slaves had to be guarded at the port of Gaza before conveyance to Egypt, their flight was already anticipated.

[95] On the interpretation of *PSI* 667, *P. Cair. Zen.* 59537, see Scholl, *Corpus* 158 and 263. See also idem, *Sklaverei* 43-5 and 182-5.

χωροῦσειν, ἐγὼ δέ γε εἰδυῖα τοὺς	but I at least knowing
σου τρόπους [ὅ]τι μισοπόνερος εἶ	your ways, that you hate evil,
οὐ ποιῶ αὐτό.	do not do it.
Εὐτύχει.	Farewell.

....

5. ἀδικεθεῖσαι   5-6. ἀναχωροῦσιν   7. μισοπόνηρος

PSI 667 is the fragment of a memorandum written by a slave woman and addressed possibly to Zenon. The text illustrates from the slave's perspective that cruelty or unjust handling was an important motive behind flight; cf. the generalising force of present tense ἀναχωροῦσιν (*ll*.5-6) and the adjective λοιπαί. The slave woman writes knowing that the recipient of the memorandum is μισοπόνηρος, and is confident that he/she will remedy the situation by removing the injustice.

A similar motive for flight is alleged in the fragmentary text of the letter *P. Cair. Zen.* 59537 *ll*.3-4: [... τὰ ἀγορασθέντα σώματα] ὑπὸ σοῦ ἐν Μαρίσηι κακῶς διατεθέντα [...] — 'the slaves bought by you in Marisa having been badly treated'. If as seems likely the lines concern the same slaves as those mentioned in *P. Cair. Zen.* 59804 and 59015 (verso), it would appear that the reason for their escape was ill-treatment. In view of the absence of information about the slaves, such as their number, ages and sex, Scholl[96] believes that Zenon, the supposed addressee of the letter, had already been informed of the flight and that the purpose of the present correspondence was to explain the reason for it.

P. Berl. Leihg. 15 is often cited as further evidence of flight due to cruelty; however, the interpretation depends on reading between the lines. The document is a duplicate of a house-by-house census declaration by a mistress, Isidora, acting with her *kyrios*. She declares both paternally and maternally acquired property in which she registers herself and five female slaves together with their offspring. A number of features mark the document as a duplicate. They are: (a) the multiple addressees (the document names all officials with whom a declaration was lodged, i.e. *strategos*, *basilikogrammateus*, *komogrammateus* and the collectors of the poll-tax); (b) lack of the declarant's signature and oath; and (c) the addition of an official's subscription *ll*.25-6. The subscription functioned either as a receipt of registration returned to the declarant or as the official's mark that he had seen the declaration in its administrative travels. Duplicates were circulated to other relevant officials who would make a check or ἐξέτασις of the details contained in the declaration.

Tebtynis	23-21 x 15.5 cm	AD 189

Ed. pr. — T. Kalén, *P. Berl. Leihg.* 15 (Uppsala 1932) 171-3.

Ἥρωνι στρα(τηγῷ) Ἀρσι(νοΐτου)	To Heron, *strategos* of the Arsinoite nome,
Θεμίστ(ου) καὶ [Πολ]έ(μωνος)	of the Themistos and Polemon divisions
μερίδω(ν) καὶ Διονυσάμμωνι	and to Dionysammon,
βασιλ(ικῷ) γραμματῖ Ἀρσι(νοΐτου)	*basilikogrammateus* of the Arsinoite nome,
Πολέ(μωνος) μερίδο(ς) καὶ	of the Polemon division and to
Πανεσνε[ῦ]τι κωμω-	Panesneus *komogrammateus*

---

[96] Scholl, *Corpus* 158.

γραμματ(εῖ) Τεπτύνεως καὶ Διδύμῳ καὶ Δίῳ λα[ογ]ρά(φοις) [τ]ῆς αὐτῆς κώμης	of Tebtynis and to Didymos and Dios, collectors of the poll-tax of the same village
5 παρὰ Ἰσιδώρας Ὀρσέως πρεσβυτέρου Ὀρσέως μ[ητ]ρὸς Ἡσᾶτο[ς]	from Isidora, daughter of Orseus, son of the elder Orseus, her mother being Esas,
τῆς Παεῦτος ἀπὸ κώμης Τεπτύνεως μετὰ κυρίου [Π]ακήβκε- ως Αὐνείου τοῦ Ὀρνόφρεως.	daughter of Paeus, from the village of Tebtynis with her *kyrios*, Pakebkis, son of Aunes, son of Ornophris.
Ὑπάρχει μοι ἐν τῇ αὐτῇ «αὐτῇ» κώμῃ	There belong to me in the same village of
Τεπτύνει πατρικὰ καὶ μητρικὰ οἰκόπεδα· πατρικὰ μ[ὲ]ν οἰκίαι δύο, ἐν αἷς καμάραι καὶ αἴθριον καὶ αὐλαὶ καὶ ἕτερα χρηστήρια	Tebtynis paternally and maternally inherited buildings — paternally inherited two houses in which there are vaulted chambers, an atrium, courtyards, other appurtenances,
10 καὶ εἴσ[ο]δος καὶ ἔξοδος, καὶ ἀπὸ βορρᾶ τούτων ἑτέρα οἰκία καὶ αὐλὴ καὶ ἕτερα χρηστήρια καὶ εἴσοδος καὶ ἔξοδος· μητρ[ι]- κὰ δὲ ἐν ἄλλῳ τόπῳ καμάρας δύο σὺν τοῖς ἐπάνω καὶ αἰθρί- ου καὶ αὐλῆς καὶ ψειλοὺς τόπους, ἐν ᾧ οἰκίδιον καὶ εἴσοδος καὶ ἔξοδος· ἐν οἷς ἀπογράφομα[ι] εἰς τὴν τοῦ διεληλυθότος κ̄η̄ (ἔτους)	an entrance and exit, and to the south of these another house, courtyard, other appurtenances, and an entrance and exit; maternally inherited in another location two vaulted chambers together with an upper level consisting of an atrium, courtyard and vacant land in which there is a hut, and an entry and exit — in which I register in the house-by-house census of the past 28th year
15 Αὐρηλίου Κομμ[ό]δου Ἀντωνείνου Καίσαρος τοῦ κυρίου κατ᾽ οἰκίαν ἀπογραφὴν ἐπὶ τῆς προκιμένης κώμης.	of Aurelius Commodus Antoninus Caesar, the lord, in the aforementioned village.
Καί εἰμι Ἰσιδώρα (ἐτῶν) ξ̄[.], καὶ δουλικά μου σώματα· Φι- λουμένην (ἐτῶν) μ̄ε̄ καὶ ταύτης ἔγγονα Διοσκοροῦν	I am Isidora, 6[?] years of age, and my slaves: Philomene, 45 years, and her issue, Dioskorous,
(ἐτῶν) η̄ [καὶ] Ἀθηνάριον (ἐτῶν) δ̄, καὶ ἑτέραν δούλην Ἐλεφαντίνην	8 years, [and] Athenarion, 4 years, and another slave Elephantine,
20 ἔγγονον Δημητ[ρί]ας (ἐτῶν) κ̄ καὶ ἔγγονον Εὐδαιμονίδα (ἐτῶν) ε̄	issue of Demetria, 20 years, and (her) issue Eudaimonis, 5 years,
καὶ Ἰσαροῦς (ἔτους) ᾱ, [κα]ὶ ἄλλην δούλην Ἑλένην οὖσαν ἐν δρασ- μῷ (ἐτῶν) ξ̄η̄ καὶ Ἀμ[μ]ωνάριον (ἐτῶν) μ̄β̄ καὶ Ἡράκλειαν (ἐτῶν) λ̄η̄ ὁμοίως ἐν δρα[σμ]ῷ. Διὸ ἐπιδίδωμει.	and Isarous, 1 year, and another slave Helene being in flight, 68 years of age, and Ammonarion, 42 years, and Herakleia, 38 years, likewise in flight. Wherefore I declare.
(Ἔτους) κ̄θ̄ Αὐρηλίου	Year 29 of Aurelius

«Αὐρηλίου» Κομ[μό]δου Ἀντωνείνου	Commodus Antoninus
Καίσαρος τοῦ κυρίου	Caesar, the lord,
25 Μεσορὴ κ̄θ̄. (m.2) Δ[ί]δυμος καὶ	Mesore 29. Didymos and
Δεῖος λαογρά(φοι) δι᾽ ἐμοῦ	Dios, collectors of the poll-tax through
Διδύμου	me Didymos
ἔσχον τούτου τὸ ἴ[σο]ν ἄχρι	have held the copy of this till
(ἐξ)ετάσεως.	examination.
Verso: Traces of the address	

....

2. γραμματεῖ

The editor of *P. Berl. Leihg.* 15 draws attention to the interesting fact that of the five declared slaves the three who were without children were in flight. The age and sex of the fugitives is unusual. Apparently, the burden and responsibility of children had hindered the remaining two from attempting to escape. The editor observes that the impression gained from the papyrus is not favourable and indicates poor treatment. Bieżuńska-Małowist[97] notes that the registration of five female slaves together in the one house also raises suspicions regarding the nature of their employment, implying that the house was a brothel. The ages of the women might give cause to doubt.

Bieżuńska-Małowist notes the apparent higher incidence of escape by slaves in the earlier Ptolemaic period. Why was this not the case in the later Ptolemaic and the Roman periods? A number of reasons can be suggested:

(a) Ownership of large numbers of slaves was more prevalent in the earlier period. This made the preparation for escape easier as: (i) most escapes involved more than one slave and it was easier to organise this within a single household; (ii) the escape could be hidden in a large household; (iii) resources were often more plentiful and more easily stolen without detection in a large household. It is also assumed that treatment was harsher in larger households as masters and slaves were less likely to be in intimate contact.

(b) In the later periods there was a higher incidence of ownership of slaves in small households. Here one or two slaves appear to have been the norm. In such circumstances there was less opportunity for escape and presumably less reason as slaves, it is assumed, were treated more humanely.[98] More often than not the same household was also the slave's place of birth and residence during his or her growing years.[99] As well, the chance of purchasing manumission offered in most cases a less risky means of obtaining freedom.[100]

(c) By the later periods the registration of the population, including slaves,[101] was firmly established and the movement of peoples better controlled. Accordingly, the chance of a successful escape was much

---

[97] Bieżuńska-Małowist, 'Les esclaves fugitifs' 78.

[98] Bieżuńska-Małowist, *L'esclavage* II 93, 116-7. Bieżuńska-Małowist argues that the role of slaves in Egypt was largely domestic (p.107) and that slavery extended to smaller households due to development of the private ownership of land (pp.108-9). Even so, slaves might still be treated brutally which itself is a sign that there was no legal protection offered to them as persons (p.139).

[99] In Egypt slave numbers were in time increasingly supplied by birth to a slave mother or by the raising of foundlings. For the Roman period see Bieżuńska-Małowist, *L'esclavage* II 13-42, esp. 21-4, 29-30 and 42.

[100] Bieżuńska-Małowist, *L'esclavage* II 149.

[101] On the registration of slaves see Bieżuńska-Małowist, 'Les esclaves fugitifs' 82-4, and idem, *L'esclavage* II 43-72. From the first half of the second century BC and perhaps earlier the registration and control of the possession of slaves was instituted by the Ptolemaic government and this included also the noting of distinguishing features. On the latter see also Bieżuńska-Małowist, *L'esclavage* I 93. In the Roman period Bieżuńska-Małowist argues for an even tighter regulation and control of slavery through (a) the registration of

reduced.[102] Success was further reduced by the state's involvement in the pursuit of runaways and the punishment of those who assisted in the escape.[103]

As the above conditions were largely peculiar to Egypt, it is somewhat risky to use the evidence of this province to draw conclusions about the practice of flight elsewhere in the Graeco-Roman world. One must proceed with caution allowing the evidence to raise questions rather than to supply answers.

The New Testament and the Flight of Slaves

Slavery and the master/slave relationship are dealt with in various places in the New Testament. Of particular importance are the *Haustafeln* of Ephesians (6.5-9) and Colossians (3.22-4.1), and the advice of 1 Timothy (6.1-2) and 1 Peter (2.18-20) which have already been treated in previous volumes in the *New Documents* series and will not be revisited here.[104] The above evidence raises interesting points of consideration for the study of Paul's letter to Philemon and the situation which must be supposed to underlie it. An interpretation of the letter very much turns on two issues: (a) whether Onesimus committed a theft or not (v.18); and (b) whether Onesimus was a fugitive or not. The issues will be discussed in the light of the evidence adduced in the preceding pages.

The language Paul uses to describe the wrong committed by Onesimus is vague: εἰ δέ τι ἠδίκησέν σε ἢ ὀφείλει, τοῦτο ἐμοὶ ἐλλόγα (v.18). What was the nature of the wrong? Some have supposed a theft. If so, the above evidence would lead one to ask whether the theft was committed to finance the flight. Under this hypothesis it is reasonable to assume that as Paul guaranteed repayment, if required (v.19), Onesimus had already exhausted whatever financial resources he had once had at his disposal. This may well have occurred already before his encounter with the apostle and it was perhaps the resulting destitution or the threat thereof that prompted Onesimus to turn to Paul. But v.18 may equally imply that Onesimus either by an act of commission or omission had caused his master some loss. Under this scenario Onesimus fled either as a result of punishment or in fear of the loss being discovered and of his being punished. If so, the letter indicates that in Onesimus's perception the new belief of his master was likely to affect minimally how he treated his slave. The same conclusion can be drawn from Eph. 6.9 and Col. 4.1. Masters are told to give up threatening their slaves (there is no reason to suppose that Paul is only thinking of empty threats) and to treat them justly and fairly.

As we are not fully informed of the circumstances of Onesimus's departure, we cannot be sure whether Onesimus fled alone or with others. I assume that Onesimus fled rather than that he had sought Paul out to act as a mediator between himself and Philemon. Be that as it may, it has been noted above that it was usual for two or more slaves to escape at the same time.

---

the births of slaves (οἰκογένεια), (b) the registration of deeds of sale, (c) census and property declarations, (d) ἐπίκρισις and (e) the verification of servile status at the time of their first sale (ἀνάκρισις). Bieżuńska-Małowist, *L'esclavage* II 68-9, argues that the registration was also associated with a precise description of the slave which assisted in the pursuit of a slave, should he turn to flight.

[102] The moderating influence of government regulation and control explains why the flight of slaves was a frequent occurrence in periods of social upheaval, i.e. war or civil disturbance. See Westermann, *The Slave Systems* 39.

[103] Scholl also thinks that a slave's prospects for a successful escape were small. This, however, he does not ascribe so much to the efficiency of official involvement in the pursuit as to the control and regulation exercised over all the population of Egypt by the Ptolemies.

[104] *New Docs* 6 (1992) 53-5, and *New Docs* 7 (1994) 194-5.

Various reasons have been alleged to explain the phenomenon. Of these the sense of security in numbers and the importance of companionship when undertaking a risky enterprise are important considerations. If from the silence of Paul's letter one concludes that Onesimus escaped alone, implications follow bearing on the character either of the master and/or of his slave. Either Onesimus was forced to accept the risk of flight by an actual or anticipated punishment at the hands of his master or the escape may indicate the independence and self-assertiveness of the runaway.

In his article 'Keine »Sklavenflucht« des Onesimus', *ZNTW* 76 (1985) 135-7, P. Lampe has argued that Onesimus was not a fugitive. His argument rests on Ulpian's citation of Vivianus who reported the legal opinion of Proculus (first century AD), an opinion which does not appear to have been contradicted by an opposing view and which as such was widely accepted: *fugitivum non esse, sicuti ne eum quidem, qui cum dominum animadverteret verberibus se adficere velle, praeripuisset se ad amicum, quem ad precandum perduceret* — 'that he (i.e. the slave who hid until his master's anger abated) is not a fugitive just as he is not who, when he perceived that his master wished to punish him with lashes, took himself off to a friend, whom he induced to plead (on his behalf)', *Dig.* 21.1.17.4. The definition of *fugitivus* rests on the intention of the slave at the time of his hiding or fleeing from his master. If his intention was to continue in the service of his master, then he was not a *fugitivus*. Thus also the slave who fled to his mother that she might plead with his master for him (Vivianus cited by Ulpian, *Dig.* 21.1.17.5) and the slave who sought asylum at a temple or the statue of the emperor (Labeo and Caelius cited by Ulpian, *Dig.* 21.1.17.12) were not by definition fugitives. It is precisely this intention that Lampe wishes to ascribe to Onesimus. In support he observes that if Onesimus had sought to disappear, there would have been more appropriate refuges than the apostle's Roman prison cell.

Lampe further cites *Dig.* 21.1.43.1 (the opinion of Paulus) and Pliny, *Epist.* 9.21 and 24 as evidence that the slave might betake himself to a friend of his master. By analogy it is suggested that Onesimus sought the help of the Christian teacher Paul in the hope that he would have influence over his Christian master, Philemon. The wrong mentioned in vv.18-19 was not a theft committed to finance his escape, but rather the cause of his master's anger and the reason for his seeking the mediation of the apostle. Paul's request that Philemon forgive his slave and not punish him relates to this wrong that he had committed. Paul offers to make good the loss himself.

There are a number of difficulties with Lampe's interpretation of the text. First, the example of the practice sought in Pliny's letters raises a number of questions over the difference between them and Paul's letter to Philemon. I leave aside the issue of difference in the nature of the relationships, i.e. patron/freedman-client (Pliny) and master/slave (Paul). First, Pliny's letter (*Epist.* 9.21) offers a full description of the freedman's repentance and remorse. This seems a necessary element in any attempt to restore harmonious relationship between unequals where the blame was perceived to lie with the weaker party. It is also consistent with the definition of who is a fugitive and who is not, for if a person is defined as a fugitive by his intention, then the letter, one expects, will demonstrate that his actions and thoughts are consistent with an intention not to escape. Second, Pliny's letter is full of pleas for indulgence and mercy. As action and response, the repentance and remorse of the freedman should meet with his patron's indulgence and mercy. But neither element is present in Paul's letter to Philemon. There is no statement of Onesimus's repentance and remorse nor a plea that Philemon show mercy. Instead, Paul asks Philemon to receive Onesimus as the apostle himself (v.17) and writes an IOU to cover any wrong done to or debt owed to the master (vv.18-19), fully conscious, no doubt, that Philemon, sensitive to the social conventions of honour and shame, would not call in the debt.

To explain the difference between the letters of Paul and Pliny one can appeal, as Nordling[105] does, to variations in epistolary style and to the 'unique circumstances underlying the respective letters'. But then the unique circumstances are matters about which we are not informed and are therefore the product of conjecture. For example, Nordling alleges that Paul sought to refer to Onesimus's past wrongs 'in an oblique and euphemistic manner' because he wanted 'to present Onesimus in the best possible light'. This is but one way to construe Paul's rather vague use of language. And it must be remembered that however unclear his language might seem to us, it was not so to Philemon, who being fully aware of the wrong might have expected an expression of remorse from his slave. Also it is difficult to see how the two areas of difference can properly be omitted, if Paul's letter to Philemon is to be construed as a mediation between a slave and his wronged master. It seems almost essential to the genre to include some overt expression of or allusion to remorse.

A second difficulty concerns the assumption that Roman legal opinion would have applied in a matter between Philemon, a peregrine, and his slave. The relationship between multiple legal systems and how it worked in practice is a troubled issue. Roman law only directly applied to Roman citizens in territory subject to the jurisdiction of the *praetor urbanus*, e.g. in Italy and Roman colonies possessing *ius Italicum*. In a province the governor exercised an independent judicial authority which was defined by the *lex provinciae*, if one existed for his province, and by his own edict on taking up the *provincia*. The latter tended to approximate Roman law. Coexistent with the jurisdiction exercised by the Roman governor was the jurisdiction of local courts and judges. Here ancestral and Hellenistic law was applied. The division of jurisdiction between the Roman governor and the local courts is problematic. The governors tried cases of death or exile, appointed judges in cases between citizens of different cities, and heard cases involving Roman citizens or wealthy provincials. But they also interferred in the domestic affairs of the cities, especially where these affected the administration of the province, e.g. to restrain the excessive expenditure of cities and their granting of immunities from public service. Roman governors might also overturn ancestral laws and customs which they deemed to be harsh or barbaric, e.g. the right of a father to annul the marriage of his daughter (*P. Oxy.* II 237 (AD 186), esp. col. 7 *ll*.34-35), the right of a creditor to personal execution against a private debtor (the edict of T. Iulius Alexander, *OGIS* 669 = *MChr* 102; cf. esp. the appeal was to the βούλησις of Augustus). Returning to Paul's letter to Philemon, the issue is whether Roman law and legal opinion would have applied in a matter between a peregrine master and his slave. It might, if the matter was heard before a Roman governor or one of his deputies. But it is difficult to contemplate that a matter between a peregrine master and his slave would have been considered significant enough to be accepted within that jurisdiction.

Third, although intention determined whether a slave was a fugitive, the intention itself was determined in turn by the slave's ostensible acts. They had to have sought the intervention of friends of their masters, of their mothers or of the priests in the temple. If the slaves fled elsewhere first or did not approach a mediator immediately, then they were deemed fugitives by their actions. It did not count, if after fleeing a fugitive had a change of heart and sought the

---

[105] Nordling, *JSNT* 41 (1991) 100. Nordling actually argues that Onesimus was a fugitive. He must explain the differences between the letters of Pliny and Paul because he believes the freedman in Pliny's letter also to be a fugitive.

intervention of a mediator. In light of these considerations how might Onesimus's actions have been construed? The letter gives no indication that he made an immediate approach to Paul and it might even be inferred that there was some lapse of time between the flight and Paul's intervention. There are two indicators, albeit tentative, here. First, it is noted by Paul that Onesimus had been converted by him in prison (v.10). The assertion raises many questions. Did Paul know Onesimus and his situation before this? Did Onesimus only appraise Paul of it after his conversion? Indeed, was it his conversion that prompted him to seek mediation? Or are we to suppose that Onesimus's conversion followed immediately on his approach to Paul? Also relevant to the question of time is the fact that Paul not only observes that Onesimus is now useful but tacitly requests Philemon's consent to his continued presence with the apostle (vv.13-14). Are we not to suppose that Onesimus has had time to prove his worth to Paul? Second, Paul notes that Onesimus was perhaps separated from Philemon for a while (πρὸς ὥραν) that he might have him back forever (v.15). The temporal expression πρὸς ὥραν is vague as a comparison of NT usage will show (cf. John 5.35, 2 Cor. 7.8 and Gal. 2.5). The duration intended by it is determined not by some fixed external point of reference but by the perception of the speaker; cf. also πρὸς ὀλιγόν, 1 Tim 4.8 and James 4.14. This being so, Paul's comment clearly gives the impression that some considerable time-lapse has occurred, for this is the most reasonable way to construed the collocation of πρὸς ὥραν and αἰώνιον. Also it is difficult to see why the apostle would mention time, if his intervention was immediate. The verse seems to anticipate Philemon's response to a prolonged absence. This in turn influences the perception of the slave's intention.

Finally, the only support that Lampe can find in Paul's letter for his hypothesis that Onesimus was not a fugitive is the observation that if the slave had sought to disappear, there would have been more appropriate refuges than the apostle's Roman prison cell. The observation, of course, begs the question as to why Onesimus was there in the first place and if he was there by his own decision, what circumstances might have driven him to it. That Onesimus sought Paul to act as a mediator between himself and his master is but one possible explanation. Another is that Onesimus in fear of destitution and capture had a change of mind. Hearing of Paul's imprisonment he sought him out to mediate for him. But under Roman law he would still have been considered a fugitive (Caelius cited by Ulpian, *Dig.* 21.1.17.1; cf. also *Dig.* 21.1.17.12). Other scenarios might also be suggested. More importantly still, Lampe's hypothesis rests on the assumptions that Paul was actually imprisoned in a Roman prison cell and that the authorities would have been on the lookout for runaways. Both are questionable. Paul's imprisonment in Rome is described in Acts (28.16) as a form of house-arrest and there is no reason to believe that the type of confinement in which the apostle found himself when writing to Philemon was any different. Indeed, in view of the degree of access afforded his friends and fellow-workers (greetings are from Timothy, Mark, Aristarchus, Demas and Luke as well as Epaphras, who as a fellow prisoner should not perhaps be counted), one must suppose a rather loose form of imprisonment. One must not take a too literal interpretation of the expression ἐν τοῖς δεσμοῖς (vv. 10 and 13), for the same term is used in Philippians, which in all probability was written from Rome, to describe the apostle's imprisonment there. Regarding the assumption that the Roman authorities would have been on the lookout for fugitives it must be noted with Bellen that the engagement of the offices of government in the search was gradually introduced in the first two centuries of the principate and that an active pursuit was only instituted much later than the time of Paul's writing. In consequence, it may not have been altogether improbable that Onesimus, as a fugitive who found himself in dire straits, might seek out and find the apostle in his imprisonment.

Paul's letter to Philemon has also posed a difficulty to modern exegetes because of what appears to be its author's active support of the status quo with regard to slavery, as interpreted from the apostle's return of the fugitive. Numerous attempts have been made to explain his action. For example, Barclay, *NTS* 37 (1991), focuses on the vagueness of Paul's request to Philemon and concludes that Paul was himself struggling with the tension between the realities of slavery and the demands of Christian brotherhood. Paul did not know what to recommend and left the decision to Philemon. Bellen, *Studien zur Sklavenflucht* (1971), interprets Paul's decision to return Onesimus as an attempt to protect Christianity from the charge of kidnapping which would have adversely affected his missionary activity. Paul sought to stop slaves from using Christianity and its call to 'forsake everything' as a way of avoiding slavery. The lack of distinction in Christ between slave and free had for Paul and other New Testament writers, it is argued, no direct implication for social structures. So also in the view of Gnilka, *Philemonbrief* (1982) the equality affirmed at 1 Cor. 12.13 and Gal. 3.27-28 refers only to 'membership in the body of Christ', i.e. the church; it does not extend to social structures generally. As a practical outworking of this stance, Onesimus was returned to his master. Nothing at the political or legal level is said, but only that Philemon should receive Onesimus as a brother in Christ. Like Bellen, Derrett, *ZNTW* 79 (1988), argues that the epistle was a public manifesto to absolve the churches of the suspicion that they acted as an asylum for slaves. For Paul the churches' mission took precedence over the question of a slave's 'civil right'.

Still other authors offer mitigating arguments either in the form of a more positive description of the slave's lot or by placing the social considerations of the New Testament under the imperative of eschatology. For example, Gülzow, *Christentum und Sklaverei* (1969), argues that the oppressive nature of slavery was not apparent to first-century churches because most believing slaves belonged to believing masters. In the second century, however, persecution and the rise in the number of believing slaves in non-believing households brought the issue of slavery to a head. Yet another line is taken by those who would deny that Onesimus was a runaway. If Onesimus, as Lampe argues, had sought Paul's help as an intermediary, then the issue of Paul's active support of the institution is not really an issue, for the apostle was merely acting on the slave's wishes. Others believe that Onesimus was not even a slave. For example, Callahan[106] argues that he was Philemon's estranged brother (ἐν σαρκί, v.16), whom Paul sought to reconcile with his brother and sent home as the apostle's own emissary.

The above analysis of the documentary evidence suggests another possible way of explaining Paul's actions. If one assumes that in the areas of Philemon's residence and Paul's imprisonment the authorities were active in the pursuit and return of fugitives, then Paul's actions can be interpreted differently. Accordingly it might be argued that Paul was fully aware of Onesimus's status but that he kept it a secret from the prison authorities, wishing thereby to broker the reconciliation himself. As such Paul is seen not to be completely complicit in enforcing regulations governing the pursuit and return of fugitives. But the difficulty here is the lack of evidence concerning an official engagement in the pursuit at this time. The evidence from Egypt may not be typical for other provinces in the Roman East.

The above documentary evidence also allows one to test the hypothesis that Paul was imprisoned in Ephesus and that his letters to Philemon and Colossians were written from there.

---

[106] A.D. Callahan, 'Paul's Epistle to Philemon: Towards an Alternative Argumentum', *HTR* 86 (1993) 357-76.

There is no direct evidence for this imprisonment, for it is neither explicitly mentioned in Paul's letters nor does Acts record it. However, a number of considerations point to a composition of Philemon and Colossians in an area in close proximity to Colossae. For example, the command issued to Philemon, who lived in Colossae, to prepare quarters for Paul (Phm. 22) makes more sense if his imprisonment was nearby and release imminent. The presence of Epaphras (Col. 4.12 and Phm. 23), the evangelist of Colossae, is also easier to explain if Paul was imprisoned in Ephesus rather than in Caesarea or Rome. Again, still other considerations point to a composition in Ephesus.[107] Of particular interest to the present study is the argument that the presence of Onesimus is a strong indication for Paul's presence in the *metropolis* of Ephesus. The argument rests on the premise that it is improbable that a fugitive for whatever reason would need or be inclined to travel either to Caesarea or Rome to escape his master.

The documentary evidence suggests that runaway slaves either fled to their 'homes' (i.e. a place of former residence or where they knew people) or to a place where they could find work and not be conspicuous, e.g. in a large city. For example, the writer of *P. Heid.* 212 strongly believes the runaway to have been offered some form of protection by those who were acquainted with him. Two of the slaves in *P. Lond.* 2052 formerly belonged to Apollonios whose agent Zenon was. By addressing the memorandum to Zenon the writer may assume that they would return to their former home, no doubt bringing with them the foreign runaways. In *P. Cair. Zen.* 59015 (verso) the runaways, whilst being transported from Palestine to Egypt, fled and returned to their former owners and one might presume also their families. Movement between nomes is attested (e.g. *BGU* 1993 and *P. Harr.* 62) but it is generally assumed that slaves did not flee the country, e.g. *UPZ* 121. Scholl[108] holds that flight in Ptolemaic Egypt when declared or intimated is always internal. Bieżuńska-Małowist[109] notes that persons looking for fugitives frequently knew their place of hiding (e.g. *P. Cair. Zen.* 59015, 59837, *PSI* 329 and *BGU* 1993) or the names of those concealing them (e.g. *P. Cair. Zen.* 59822 and *P. Turner* 41). She thinks that such information was gained from informants rewarded for their effort. As a corollary it follows that the slaves could not have travelled too far afield. However, there might be some bias in data as the evidence is confined to Egypt and would thus tend to confirm internal flight only.

Literary evidence offers a helpful supplement. Suetonius records (*De gramm.* 15) that Lenaeus, the freedman of Pompey the Great, as a child escaped his master and returned to his birthplace, Athens. Cicero recounts (*Epist. ad Att.* 5.15.3 and 6.1.13) that a slave belonging to Atticus had joined a band of renegades in the Taurus mountains of Cilicia. Unfortunately the place from where he escaped is not known. Cicero's slave and reader, Dionysius, had fled to Illyricum (Cicero, *Epist. ad fam.* 5.9.2 and 13.77.3). The reason for his flight is unknown. Did he originally come from there? Cicero also records (*Epist. ad Q. frat.* 1.2.14) that Licinius, a slave of the actor Aesopus, had run away, presumably from Rome, to Athens where he posed as a free man and subsequently journeyed to Ephesus. A friend of his master,

---

[107] S.R. Llewelyn, *Tyndale Bulletin* 46.2 (1995) 351-2.

[108] Scholl, *Corpus* 300-1, and idem, *Sklaverei* 222-3.

[109] Bieżuńska-Małowist, *L'esclavage* I 131, II 142, and 'Les esclaves fugitifs' 85-6. A change in places of hiding is also noted between the earlier (the *chora*) and later periods (cities and large towns). The *chora* was a possible hiding place in the earlier period as the control and regulation of the population as a whole was in the process of establishment. A geographical/demographical reason is suggested for the later change. For example, Bieżuńska-Małowist, *L'esclavage* II 142, observes: 'In Roman Egypt there were no regions sparsely populated or covered with forests, and only the large towns were able to offer a refuge, ever so little safe, to fugitives.'

who was present in Athens at the time of the slave's arrival there but who only discovered later the fugitive's deceit, sent for him to be arrested in Ephesus and put into custody. Cicero is uncertain whether this was a public custody (*publica custodia*, i.e. prison) or labour in a mill (*pistrinum*). The purpose of Cicero's present letter was to request his brother to find the slave and, if possible, to send him to Rome. There is some disagreement whether *pistrinum* indicates a public or private mill. Watson[110] believes the mill to be private. Shackleton Bailey[111] considers it a publicly owned mill. If the custody was public, it can be explained variously. For example, it may relate to the slave's *scelus* and *audacia* which had so grieved his master. Again, it may be due to the political influence of which friendship to a person in a position of power could avail itself. More interestingly, it may indicate a greater involvement of the state in the procedure of apprehension and return of fugitives in the province of Asia, a practice which finds many parallels in the documentary evidence of Egypt.

S.R.L.

---

[110] A. Watson, *Cicero. Select Letters* (Oxford 1891) 102. So also W.W. How and A.C. Clark, *Cicero. Select Letters* vol. 2 (Oxford repr. 1971) 127.

[111] D.R. Shackleton Bailey, *Cicero: Epistulae ad Quintum fratrem et M. Brutum* (Cambridge 1980) 164.

TAXATION

§4 Tax Collection and the τελῶναι of the New Testament

Small Oasis 9.3 x 8.5 cm 8 April AD 187

Ed. pr. — P.J. Sijpesteijn, 'A female tax collector', *ZPE* 61 (1985) 71-3.

The papyrus has been regularly cut along its edges so that the free margins measure 2.7 to 2.5 (top) and 1.4 to 0.5 cm (left). The bottom is broken. The writing follows the fibres. The back is blank.

Ἔτους κζ Αὐρηλίου Κομμόδ(ου)	Year 27 of Aurelius Commodus
Ἀντωνίνου Καί[σαρος] τοῦ κυρίου	Antoninus Caesar, the lord,
Φαρμοῦθι ιγ. διεγράφη Σαραπιά-	Pharmouthi 13. There has been paid to Sarapias
δι Σαραπίωνος ἀσχοληθείσῃ τοὺς	daughter of Sarapion formerly engaged for the
5 καταλοχισμοὺς τοῦ Ὀξυρυγχίτου	registry (of catoecic land) for the Oxyrhynchite
καὶ ἄλλων νομῶν διὰ Ἀμμωνίου	and other nomes through Ammonius,
πραγματευτοῦ ὑπὸ Τετοέως	supervisor, her agent, by Tetoeus
ἀπελευθέρα[ς] Πανεχώτου ἀπὸ τοῦ	freedwoman of Panechotes from
Ἀφροδισίου τῆς Μικρᾶς	Aphrodision in the Small
Ὀάσεως 〚...〛	Oasis 〚...〛
10 ἀρούρης μ[ίας]	for one aroura [...]
τέλος σὺν σ[πονδῇ]	tax with [fee (?)]
ἔτι τὰ [ὀ]φει[λόμενα]	still that being owed [...]

------

7. ἐπιτ added in margin

The papyrus represents a receipt (σύμβολον) for the τέλος καταλοχισμῶν, i.e. the tax on registry of catoecic land[1] subsequent to its cession to a new owner. The right to collect this tax was presumably sold by auction to Sarapias, the former contracting tax-farmer.[2] It has been argued that the titles ὁ ἀσχολούμενος τοὺς καταλοχισμούς and ὁ δημοσιώνης (τέλους) καταλοχισμῶν refer to the same function, that of the tax-farmer for dues on the registry of catoecic land.[3] But the two titles appear in formally distinct types of documents: ὁ (δι)ασχολούμενος τοὺς καταλοχισμούς in notifications of cession addressed either to the *agoranomoi* of the Oxyrhynchite nome or the *syntaktikoi* of the Arsinoite nome;[4] and ὁ

---

[1] Catoecic land was royal land which in the Ptolemaic period had been ceded to soldier-settlers. In time it was treated like private property with the attendant rights pertaining to such, e.g. it could be sold (cession), given as a gift, or offered as security.

[2] See U. Wilcken, *Griechische Ostraka aus Aegypten und Nubien* (Leipzig 1899) 346 and 577. The contractors of other taxes were also designated by the title ὁ ἀσχολούμενος, e.g. ὁ τὸ ἐνκύκλιον ἀσχολούμενος, e.g. *P. Oxy.* I 44 and 185, and *P. Turner* 19; cf. also *P. Ant.* I 32 and *P. Batav.* I 11. On these tax-farmers and the procedure used to collect the *enkyklion* (a tax on all types of transactions affecting the ownership of property, e.g. sale, *hypotheke, epilysis* etc.) see most recently *P. Köln* V 219 and its introduction. The papyrus orders persons wishing to register such transactions to present themselves to the relevant tax-farmer that their contracts might be duly completed.

[3] See *BGU* VII 1565, *P. Mich.* VI 364, H.C. Youtie, *ZPE* 38 (1980) 273 and *ZPE* 40 (1980) 78-80, and F. Oertel, *Die Liturgie* (Leipzig 1917, reprinted 1965) 167 and 242-3.

[4] See Youtie, *ZPE* 40 (1980) 78, and *P. Oxy.* L 3556.

δημοσιώνης (τέλους) καταλοχισμῶν in receipts.[5] The above papyrus offers direct evidence for the identification of the titles, for a woman designated as ἀσχοληθεῖσα τοὺς καταλοχισμούς issues through her agent a receipt for an unspecified tax (*l*.11), presumably the τέλος καταλοχισμῶν. In view of the use of the aorist passive participle (ἀσχοληθείση) it would appear that the payment is an arrear which was due during her term but which was not paid till later.

The letters ἐπιτ have been added in the left margin of the papyrus slightly above *l*.7. The editor notes: 'We may presume that Ammonius either was promoted by the new tax-collector to ἐπιτηρητής or assumed this title by himself farming the tax (if this is what ἐπιτηρητής denotes here). Alternatively we may differently resolve the abbreviation and understand διὰ 'Ἀμμωνίου πραγματευτοῦ ἐπιτ(ηρήσεως).' An apparent difficulty with the suggestion is that the office of ἐπιτηρητής (supervisor) was by the date of this papyrus already a liturgical post. The office is first attested in AD 88 (*P. Oxy.* I 174) and was definitely a liturgy by AD 136. If the payment in the above papyrus is an arrear, then this might be seen to strengthen the possibility that Ammonios was a liturgical supervisor (ἐπιτηρητής). Such officials were involved in the collection of taxes (both those which were farmed and those which were collected directly by the state, e.g. by *praktores*) and could issue receipts in the name of the tax-farmer. Furthermore, from *SB* XVI 12504 *ll*.13-14 (the full text is reproduced below) it can be inferred that the officials were also responsible for the collection and payment of arrears to the public banks. If then Ammonios held a liturgical post, it could not properly be said that he had been promoted to it by the tax-contractor or that he had assumed the title himself. However, it should be borne in mind that the term here may not have carried a liturgical sense. Its usage elsewhere is quite general. As El Mosallamy[6] notes, 'the title ἐπιτηρητής is so general that our perception of the liturgical service of ἐπιτήρησις could be distorted by our inability to distinguish the liturgical officials from other persons using the same title in every instance'. This coincides with Oertel's assumption concerning the ἐπιτηρηταί of the καταλοχισμοί.[7] In his view they were probably not liturgists but supervisors appointed by the general tax-farmer for all Egypt to oversee the collection undertaken by subcontractors (οἱ ἀσχολούμενοι) in each nome.

The editor draws attention to the interesting fact that the tax-collector in this instance was a woman. Such a role for women has not otherwise been entertained by modern scholars. The editor suggests that the Romans were willing to accept female tax-farmers in circumstances where they offered the state a greater protection against loss of revenue. No doubt, this would imply that the woman was the person offering the highest bid for the tax. In a later publication[8] the editor offers as further evidence for the existence of female tax-contractors the papyrus *P. Princ.* II 50 (a receipt for *annona militum* dated AD 255).

---

[5] See Youtie, *ZPE* 40 (1980) 79, for a list of receipts for the tax on the registry of catoecic land. The above receipt differs from other receipts which use the title δημοσιώνης and are in the form of a *cheirographon*. As subject of the passive verb (διεγράφη, *l*.3) one expects a monetary amount. The tax would normally be expressed as a prepositional phrase (ὑπέρ + name of tax). However, receipts which use the passive regularly show confusion over case; cf. *P. Hamb.* I 83, *P. Gen.* II 108 and *P. Oxy.* VI 916. For a receipt similar to the above papyrus see *CPR* VI 4 (Tanis, AD 182). The text is a receipt of payment to a former *nomarches* and his associates for the φόρος νομῶν (rent on grazing rights to state pastures) issued through an unidentified official.

[6] A.H.S. El Mosallamy, 'Public Notices concerning Epitērēsis of the Ōnē Zytēras', *Proceedings of the XVI Int. Congr. of Papyrology* (Chico 1981) 221 n.20.

[7] Oertel, *Liturgie* 242-3.

[8] P.J. Sijpesteijn, 'Another Female Tax Collector', *ZPE* 64 (1986) 121-2.

Sijpesteijn observes that the evidence provided by the new papyrus on the role of women in the public life of Egypt will be unwelcome news to those who have sought to explain away the occurrence of γυμνασιαρχίς in *P. Amh.* II 64 *l*.6 (AD 107). The existence of female gymnasiarchs is well attested in other Roman provinces,[9] but the evidence from within Egypt is ambiguous and has been the subject of debate.[10] Most recently Hagedorn has argued on the basis of a rereading of *PSI XXI Congr.* 13 that women could undertake important municipal magistracies in Egypt. In particular the latter papyrus shows that a woman named Pompeia Heliodora was a perpetual gymnasiach of Alexandria, a municipal post she held no doubt due to her financial endowment of it.

Taxation in Ptolemaic Egypt

In Ptolemaic Egypt the farming and collection of taxes were carefully controlled by laws applying to Egypt generally (*P. Rev.*, the revenue law[11] of Ptolemaios II Philadelphos, 259 BC) and laws applying within a particular nome (*P. Paris* 62 = *UPZ* I 112; regulations of Ptolemaios V Epiphanes, 204 BC for the Oxyrhynchite nome). The system was founded on royal laws (νόμοι τελωνικοί) which were widened and supplemented by διαγράμματα, προστάγματα, διορθώματα etc. The two extant documents (i.e. the *P. Rev.* and *P. Par.* 62) together with the numerous receipts issued to taxpayers and tax-farmers are our major sources of information for the operation of the Ptolemaic system of taxation.

The tax-farmer (τελώνης) purchased by sale (τέλους ὠνή) at auction one or more taxes in a specific region. The object of the sale was a state tax which was figuratively given into the possession of the purchaser for a set period.[12] The sale was usually limited to a right to collect a tax or group of taxes for a village (the smallest administrative district), but sometimes the right extended to the whole nome (*UPZ* 112) or in the case of the Arsinoite nome to a *meris*. According to Wilcken, there was never a single bidder for a tax or group of taxes covering the whole country or its foreign territories.[13] The right was purchased annually at the beginning of

---

[9] For a list of evidence for women holding the magistracy of gymnasiarch outside Egypt see L. Casarico, 'Donne ginnasiarco', *ZPE* 48 (1982) 118-122. On the role of women in public life see also R.A. Kearsley, *New Docs* 6 (1992) 24-7. Kearsley notes that women more frequently appear to have held priestly magistracies than magistracies of a more secular nature, e.g. gymnasiarch, agonothete or secretary, and that their holding office was a function of wealth and family connections.

[10] E.g. *SB* XVI 12235 and *PSI XX Congr*.12. See discussion by D. Hagedorn, 'Noch einmal: Weibliche Gymnasiarchen in Ägypten?', *ZPE* 110 (1996) 157-8.

[11] B.P. Grenfell, *Revenue Laws of Ptolemy Philadelphus* (Oxford 1896); re-edited by J. Bingen, *Papyrus Revenue Laws* (Beihefte zum Sammelbuch griechischer Urkunden aus Ägypten 1, Göttingen 1952). J. Bingen, *Le Papyrus Revenue Laws — Tradition grecque et adaptation hellénistique* (Opladen 1978), argues that the Revenue Laws are a collection of originally independent documents, i.e. a law concerning the farming of money taxes (cols 1-22); a law concerning the ἀπόμοιρα on wine and the produce of orchards (cols 23-36); the declaration of auction and a list of obligations imposed on the buyer of the ἐλαϊκή or the monopoly of oils (cols 38-72); and the declaration of auction for the farming of banks and royal receipts in cash (cols 73-78). The documents do not represent a code. Rather they regulate contracts of lease between the king and the farmers of various revenues or institutions.

[12] M. Rostovtzeff, *Geschichte der Staatspacht in der römischen Kaiserzeit*, in *Philologus*, Supplementband 9 (1904) 338.

[13] Wilcken, *Griechische Ostraka* 520-1, argues that the account of Josephus, *AJ* 12.160 ff. is legendary when it relates that Joseph purchased the taxes for Coelesyria, Phoenecia, Judaea and Samaria together. Rostovtzeff, *Geschichte der Staatspacht* 360-1 and 366, agrees that in regions such as Asia Minor, Syria and Sicily, which were administered on the basis of the *polis*-system, the taxes of each *polis* were sold separately; however, he also believes that the account of Josephus to be possible. Such general sales of taxes, he suggests,

the New Year (Thoth). And even if the same tax-farmer was to purchase the sale for the following year, he had to enter into a new contract.

The auction was conducted in each nome by the *oikonomos* assisted by the *basilikogrammateus*.[14] In the administration and control of the system of taxation as a whole the *oikonomos* was assisted by an *antigrapheus*. The *oikonomos* himself was responsible to the central government through the *dioiketes*. The sale was by auction with the highest bidder winning the right to collect the tax. Wilcken[15] reconstructs the procedure of auction as follows: As a first step written offers were requested by the nome officials for the several taxes to be contracted. The offers were assessed by these officials (i.e. *oikonomos* and *basilikogrammateus*) and if accepted a minimal bid was posted together with the conditions of sale. During this time prospective bidders might consider the viability of the purchase by an inspection of the official records. The second step was the auction proper. The sale of taxes with the minimal bids and the conditions of sale was proclaimed by herald. After a set period the auction occurred. For a period of 10 days after the auction the highest bid (τὸ εὑρίσκον) was posted daily and higher bids accepted. The highest bid was reported to the *dioiketes* who was kept informed of proceedings. Thereafter the sale was knocked down to the highest bidder.[16] Harper[17] argues that the system of competitive bidding fostered a reasonable sale price which was neither artificially high (for this would restrict profits) nor low (for this would encourage competitors to offer a higher bid). Within 30 days after the knocking-down the written declarations of all guarantors (*symbola*)[18] endorsed occasionally by royal oath had to be lodged with the relevant official, either the *oikonomos* and/or the *basilikogrammateus* (*UPZ* 112 col. 1 *l*.13 to col. 2 *l*.2). Failing this the right of collection was put up to auction again. On receipt of the *symbola* the officials (the *oikonomos* and/or the *basilikogrammateus*) assessed the guarantees and, if in order, accepted them, confirming their assessment and depositing them at the royal bank (*UPZ* 112 col.2 *ll*.2-11).[19] If several guarantors combined to secure a

---

may have influenced the Roman introduction of such instruments in Asia under the Gracchi. According to Rostovtzeff, Joseph like the Roman *publicani* would have entered into separate contracts with each city for the collection of the taxes. In turn, the cities through their magistrates would have sold the taxes to smaller tax-farmers supervised by local officials (*dekaprotoi*).

[14] G.M. Harper, 'Tax Contractors and their Relation to Tax Collection in Ptolemaic Egypt', *Aegyptus* 14 (1934) 51.

[15] Wilcken, *Griechische Ostraka* 527-8 and 548 ff., and C. Préaux, *L'économie royale des Lagides* (Brussels 1939) 451-2.

[16] Even after the knocking-down a new offer might be accepted by the state if it exceeded the highest bid by at least 10%. See Wilcken, *UPZ* I, p.515, and Préaux, *L'économie royale des Lagides* 452.

[17] Harper, *Aegyptus* 14 (1934) 63.

[18] *P. Hib.* I 94, 95 and *P. Petr.* III 57 a, b, 58 c, d are identified as probable *symbola*.

[19] See Wilcken, *Griechische Ostraka* 548-555; idem, *UPZ* I, pp.511-7; Préaux, *L'économie royale des Lagides* 452-3; and G.M. Harper, 'The Relation of Ἀρχώνης, Μέτοχοι and Ἔγγυοι to each other, to the Government and to the Tax Contract in Ptolemaic Egypt', *Aegyptus* 14 (1934) 274-80. The guarantees covered the purchase price plus 5% (and 10% after 137 BC; see W. Schäfer, *P. Köln* V [Oplaten 1985] 142), the addition representing the sales tax (ἐγκύκλιον) on the purchase. The guarantors offered their property (usually real property such as houses, land, vineyards and gardens) under *hypotheke* as security for a defined sum. Rostovtzeff argues that the need for such types of guarantees was an important factor in the extension of private ownership of property in Egypt. Be that as it may, declarations (σύμβολα) obliging the guarantors to the state for a fixed sum of money (proportional to the liability which they underwrote) were given to the nome officials who deposited them with the royal bank. The guarantees, if not declared under royal oath, may also have been secured by βεβαιωταί (so Wilcken). Their property was subject to distraint by the government for any shortfall in revenue collection. Whether the government proceeded first against the tax-farmer and his associates is

contract, then each was liable with all or part of his property to a defined sum of money, i.e. the proportion of the contract which each underwrote. As a third and final step the government and tax-farmer entered into a contract (termed ὠνή or πρᾶσις) which stipulated the rights and obligations of the parties. The state gave the tax-farmer title to any tax yield over the contracted sale price (ἐπιγένημα) and guaranteed the payment of a reward (ὀψώνιον) on the satisfactory completion of the contract. For his part the tax-farmer contracted to pay the sale price[20] and offered security to cover it.

A recently published papyrus concerns the administrative procedures associated with the taking of guarantees. The papyrus is a report issued by the tax-farmer to the *oikonomos* of the nome. The first line which is written in a different hand records the report's date of receipt in the office of the *oikonomos*. Guarantees had to be lodged within 30 days of the sale. But the 30 day period was divided into 6 five-day periods. At the end of each five-day period a specified proportion of the guarantee had to have been obtained. If not, the contract was ended and the tax auctioned a second time with the contractor making good any loss in the subsequent sale price. The advantage to the government in this is clear, for it did not have to wait till the end of the thirty-day period before rescinding a contract which was unlikely to be able to offer sufficient security. If the auction in *SB* XVI 12506 occurred with the beginning of the New Year (1st of Thoth), then the guarantee was lodged within a fortnight (14th Thoth) or in the third five-day period.

The tax-farmer first declares his name and the taxes which he had bought (*SB* 12506 *ll*.3-8). Then he names his guarantor, describes the real property pledged as surety and declares the value of the guarantee (*ll*.8-14). He asks that the appropriate official be written to to record (?) the surety (*ll*.15-17). *SB* XVI 12507 (P. Hels. Inv. no. 22) may well represent one such official recording of sureties based on the submitted *symbola* of guarantors. Kaimio identifies the ἐγγύη of *l*.17 with the *symbolon* or the written declaration of the guarantor referred to in *UPZ* 112 col. 2 *l*.2. It would thus appear that the tax-farmer independently informed the *oikonomos* of his guarantees and that the guarantors themselves lodged their declarations with the relevant official for processing. As was customary, the guarantor by declaration was liable for a defined sum of money (here 20 talents).

---

unclear. Guarantors also appear to have entered into private agreements with the tax-farmer. This could occur either before their declarations were accepted by the *oikonomos*, or after it. At the end of the financial year each guarantor received the διαλογισμοί from the *oikonomos* certifying that all obligations of the contract had been met. Guarantors did not share in the profit (ἐπιγένημα) of the collection. Rather, in return for the risk they presumably had a claim on the ὀψώνιον which was paid from the rebated sales tax. These monies were paid by the bank to the tax-farmer after it had been satisified that all conditions of the farming contract had been met. Harper, *Aegyptus* 14 (1934) 285, surmises that the tax-farmer may have paid the total sum of the ὀψώνιον to his guarantors. More probably it was paid to the various parties (tax-farmer, associates and guarantors) in proportions stipulated by private contract and reflecting the value of the risk (liability) underwritten by each. Thus Rostovtzeff argues that the tax-farmer was also paid from the ὀψώνιον, and that in view of the increase of the ὀψώνιον from 5 to 10%, the profit of the ἐπιγένημα could not have been great (p.346). Préaux, *L'économie royale des Lagides* 455, ascribes the rise to difficult political times and believes that in other periods the collections were lucrative. In support she notes the ability of tax-farmers to find guarantors and *P. Tebt.* III 812.

[20] The sales tax (ἐγκύκλιον) does not appear to have been paid when the contract of sale was entered into. If the contract was not fulfilled, the sales tax had presumably to be paid by the parties. If, on the other hand, it was satisfactorily completed, the sales tax was rebated to the tax-farmer as a reward (ὀψώνιον). The implication must be that before the reward was paid, the tax collected must exceed the sale price plus the sales tax. In other words, the rebate was paid from the collection by the government waiving its claim to the sales tax.

Herakleopolis　　　　　　　　　　21 x 11.5 cm　　　　　　　　15 October 159 BC

Ed. pr. — M. Kaimio, 'On the sureties of tax contractors in Ptolemaic Egypt', in *Proceedings of the XVI Int. Congr. of Papyrology* (Chico 1981) 281-7 (= P.Hels.Inv.no.21 = *SB* XVI 12506).

The text is described as virtually complete except for the loss of the final greeting.

(m.1) ἐλ(ήφθη) (ἔτους) κγ Θωὺθ ιδ.	Received year 23 Thoth 14.
(m.2) Ἀλεξάνδρωι οἰκονόμωι	To Alexandros *oikonomos*
παρ' Ἡρακλείδου τοῦ Ἡρα-	from Herakleides son of Herakleides,
κλείδου τοῦ ἐξειληφότος	who has contracted
5　μετὰ μετόχων τὸ εἰσαγώγιον	with associates for the importation tax
τοῦ οἴνου καὶ τὴν (ἕκτην) τῶν	on wine, for the one-sixth tax on
παραδείσων καὶ τὴν (τρίτην) τῶν	gardens, and for the one-third tax on
βα[λ]ανείων· ἐπεὶ ὑποτί-	baths. Since Tnepheros son of Marres
θεται ἐν διενγυήματι	pledges in guarantee
10　ὑπὲρ ἐμοῦ εἰς τὰς δηλου-	on my behalf for the
μένας ὠνὰς Τνεφερῶς	said sales
Μαρρέους ἐπὶ ὑποθή(κη) οἰκίαι	by way of mortgage a house
καὶ αὐλῆι ἐν ἧι σιτοβολὼν	and a courtyard in which there is a granary
ἐν Ἡρακλέους πόλει πρὸς	in Herakleopolis for the amount of
(τάλαντα) λ,	20 talents,
15　ἀξιῶ γράψαι ὧι καθήκει	I ask you to write to whom it is appropriate
ἐνενεγκεῖν σοι τὴν	to record (?) for you the
ἐγγύην.	surety.

....

12-13. οἰκίαν καὶ αὐλήν

If a tax-farmer collected more (ἐπιγένημα) than the sum contracted to the state, it belonged to him. In other words, the tax-farmer received the surplus, if any, above the contracted sum and associated costs. This constituted his profit. If less (ἔγδεια) than the contracted sum was collected, the loss was his.[21] The tax-farmer was under an obligation to pay the contracted sum and a failure to pay meant that he and his guarantors were personally liable to make up the loss. The risk inherent in the system could be further shared by the tax-farmer (ἀρχώνης) taking fellow tax-farmers[22] and associates (μέτοχοι).[23] In Wilcken's view the use of

---

[21] A tax-farmer might contract to collect more than one tax. In this case, if a loss occurred in one and a profit in another, then the profit could be credited by the bank against the loss. So Wilcken, *UPZ* I, p.516.

[22] Wilcken, *Griechische Ostraka* 544-7. The tax-farmer could also sublet his contract with the assistance and approval of the *oikonomos* and *basilikogrammateus*.

[23] The function of associates is discussed by Wilcken, *Griechische Ostraka* 535-44, and Harper, *Aegyptus* 14 (1934) 270-2 and 282ff. The government only contracted with the tax-farmer and his associates were sharply differentiated from him. The associates only entered into the procedure in a secondary fashion by widening the property base of the tax-farmer (their property was also subject to distraint by the government in case of a loss) and in recompense for this risk by sharing in his profits (ἐπιγένημα). However, their names together with the

associates allowed persons of smaller means to bid and win the right to collect taxes.[24] The security of the government was undiminished and the pool of potential bidders widened thus fascilitating greater competition in the bidding process.

Royal officials, as well as slaves, were prohibited from various aspects of Ptolemaic system of tax-farming. They could neither be tax-farmers, associates of a tax-farmer nor the guarantors of one. A severe penalty consisting of a fine (5 talents), arrest and review of the case by the king awaited officials who illegally contracted for taxes (*P. Rev.* col. 13 *l*.7 - col. 14 *l*.1). Otherwise, whoever could offer the required security was permitted to bid and participate in the system. The significance of the prohibition on royal officials is usually interpreted as an indication of the government's concern to control the collection of taxes and to protect its taxpayers.[25] An independent administration was thought better able and inclined to control and supervise the collection of taxes.

The control exercised by the government is further seen in the regulation of personnel. The number of staff was determined by agreement jointly between the tax-farmer and the relevant nome officials, i.e. the *oikonomos* and his *antigrapheus*. It would seem to follow that a staff member could not be unilaterally removed by the tax-farmer.[26] The rates of pay (μισθός) were also fixed by the government. Supervision of collection was by an *ephodos* with a stipend of 100 dr. per month. The actual taxes were collected by *logeutai* and *hyperetai* whose stipends were fixed at 30 and 20 dr. per month respectively. *Symbolaphylakes*, who were probably the custodians of assessments agreed between the tax-farmer[27] and taxpayer as well as receipts, received 15 dr. Other staff included βοηθοί (second century BC) and the *antigrapheus*[28] of the

---

name of the tax-farmer were registered with the *oikonomos*, who conducted the auction, and allowed this official to consider their eligibility to contract for the tax. The names of the tax-contractor, his associates, guarantors and collectors were also listed in the γραφή which was lodged with the *oikonomos* and kept at the λογευτήριον, or tax bureau. The official list allowed the government to control the membership of tax companies and a heavy fine (20 talents) attended those who failed to disclose membership (by generalization from *UPZ* 112 col. 6 *ll*.10-14). The business relationship between the tax-farmer and his associates was regulated by an act of association (μετοχή) between the parties which stipulated their rights and obligations, and in particular the proportion of profit or loss carried by each party. Wilcken, *Griechische Ostraka* 548, surmises that perhaps guarantees were also lodged in these private contracts between the tax-farmer and his associates. The act of association was probably communicated to the government, perhaps being lodged with the royal bank together with the guarantees. In turn the *oikonomos* sent each associate a copy of the completed accounts (διαλογισμοί) so that they could satisfy themselves concerning the propriety of the tax-farmer. In the Roman period, Wilcken (pp.590-1) also argues that the same fundamental relationship of the tax-farmer with his associates pertained; the associate was only liable for a proportion of the capital and not for the collection itself. If the expression ὁ δεῖνα καὶ οἱ μέτοχοι τελῶναι is found in the Roman period, it only reflects popular usage which confused the associates with the tax-collector. Rostovtzeff, *Geschichte der Staatspacht* 348, holds a different view. He argues that the guarantors of the tax-farmer were mostly business partners (μέτοχοι) and that this explains why μέτοχοι did not place guarantees themselves. In fact the state recognized the company as a unity for the purpose of any deficit in collection: πρᾶξις ἔσται ἐξ ἑνὸς καὶ ἐκ πάντων (*P. Par.* 62 col. 6 *l*.14).

[24] Wilcken, *Griechische Ostraka* 523-4, notes the increasing participation of persons with Egyptian names in the period from the third to the second centuries. He also notes the high proportion of tax-farmers who had Jewish names.

[25] Wilcken, *Griechische Ostraka* 522, and Harper, *Aegyptus* 14 (1934) 52.

[26] So Rostovtzeff, *Geschichte der Staatspacht* 341.

[27] The tax-farmer appears to have acted as the assessor of taxes. But a disputed assessment might be adjudicated by the *oikonomos*. See Harper, *Aegyptus* 14 (1934) 55 and 58-9.

[28] The tax farmer was assisted by his own *antigrapheus* to whom collectors reported all payments. In turn, the *antigrapheus* reported payments to the government. Failure to report in either instance was subject to a hefty penalty. Monies collected were deposited with the royal bank to the credit of the tax-farmer. Payments in kind

tax-farmer. The staff were paid by the state from the proceeds of the tax and as a result presumably had no interest in any profit generated by the collection. The names and ethnic of all staff were included in a γραφή lodged with the nome officials; a person found acting in the interests of the tax-farmer but whose name was not on the list was fined and/or despatched to the king for punishment.[29] Rostovtzeff[30] observes that the list implies that nothing could be done by a tax-farmer without the knowledge or consent of the state. Given all the above considerations it is generally concluded that the staff were employees or subordinates of the state rather than agents of the tax-farmer.[31]

The tax-farmer was subject to state control in other ways as well. For example, though the tax-farmer acquired the right of distraint against tax-debtors, he could not unilaterally seize their property. Due process had to be followed and this involved the enlisting of the institutions of government.[32] If the taxpayer did not pay, then a penalty was awarded. If execution was necessary, it was accomplished by officials either through distraint or imprisonment. The role of the tax-farmer was confined to lodging a charge against the taxpayer; the tax-farmer could only proceed against the taxpayer by informing against him, a practice which fostered the abuse of συκοφαντεία, e.g. *P. Par.* 61 and 62, *P. Rev.* col. 5 *ll.*1-3, and from the Roman period *P. Oxy.* I 36). See also Luke 19.8. Government officials also intervened in the collection of taxes when the regular procedure could no longer be relied upon. For example, if the tax-farmer did not properly carry out his function or when arrears or penalties were owed from previous years, the collection of these amounts were the responsibility of the *oikonomos*[33] and exacted by his agents (πράκτορες). Otherwise the collection of taxes by officials was restricted by royal law. The tax-farmer could also be assisted in the collection of taxes through military escorts. The effect of this was to coerce payment.

Rostovtzeff[34] compares the control over tax collection exercised in Ptolemaic Egypt with that exercised in Athens, the model on which the Hellenistic tax systems were based. Lacking appropriate magistrates and officials, the Athenian state only asked the tax-farmer to pay the purchase price and limited its control to issuing regulations (i.e. a νόμος τελωνικός fixing the demands and obligations of the sale) to assure itself of payment. For example, a tax-farmer who failed to pay the purchase price was penalised by ἀτιμία, or loss of citizen status and its attendant benefits and protection. But the state did not interest itself in the business arrangements of the tax-farmer (e.g. whether he had associates) nor in the organization of the collection. This changed in the Hellenistic kingdom of the Ptolemies. Here there is clear evidence for the exercise of control over such areas as the tax-farmer's business arrangements, the agents of collection and the accounting procedures. The control of the state became all

---

were deposited with the local government treasury/granary. On the accounting procedure see Wilcken, *Griechische Ostraka* 569-70.

[29] Wilcken, *Griechische Ostraka* 543.

[30] Rostovtzeff, *Geschichte der Staatspacht* 341.

[31] Rostovtzeff, *Geschichte der Staatspacht* 341; idem, *The Social and Economic History of the Hellenistic World* (Oxford 1941) 328; Harper, *Aegyptus* 14 (1934) 53-4; and Préaux, *L'économie royale des Lagides* 456. Harper assumes that the salaries were physically paid by the state.

[32] On distraint see *New Docs* 7 (1994) 202-212.

[33] The property of the *oikonomos* was liable to distraint for uncollected arrears.

[34] Rostovtzeff, *Geschichte der Staatspacht* 332-49. On the use of tax-farming in Athens and classical Greece as the model for the Ptolemaic system see also Wilcken, *Griechische Ostraka* 513 and 515, and Bingen, *Le Papyrus Revenue Laws* 13-14.

pervasive.³⁵ The state through its officials and subordinates now calculated and collected taxes. Also the state no longer interested itself in the mere payment of the purchase price but was involved in the accounting process itself. Collectors notified the relevant nome official (i.e. the *antigrapheus*) of all payments immediately. He was also advised by banks of any taxes paid directly to them. The *antigrapheus* recorded all payments and thus exercised control over the accounting process through his custody of the books. All collected sums were transferred to the royal bank (or in the case of payment in kind to the royal storehouse) and were not at the disposal of the tax-farmer. As such the banks were also instruments of official control.³⁶ At the end of the year, the income from collection was calculated by the *oikonomos* at the annual γενικὸς διαλογισμός. If there was a profit (ἐπιγένημα), it was released to the tax-farmer and his associates according to the share of each. If there was a short-fall, payment was first sought from the tax-farmer, his associates and guarantors and, if this failed, satisfaction was achieved by distraint against their property.³⁷

The state also now interested itself in the internal relation of the tax-farmer with his associates and guarantors.³⁸ In Athens the city only dealt with the tax-farmer (ἀρχώνης); the relationship of the tax-farmer to his guarantors and associates was a private matter. In Ptolemaic Egypt, on the other hand, the names of all interested parties were entered in the γραφή lodged with the nome officials and the persons were recognized legally and for accounting purposes. For Rostovtzeff³⁹ the reason for the extension of state control in all these areas was the constitutional change from *polis* to kingdom and the presence now of permanent officials (rather than annually elected magistrates) who could oversee the administration of the tax system.

In sum, it is argued that the system of contracting the collection taxes had numerous checks and balances to protect the taxpayer:

(a) Royal officials could not bid at auctions, be associates in tax-corporations, or guarantors of successful bidders.
(b) The actual collection was by persons agreed on by both the tax-farmer and the nome officials. These persons, whose salaries were paid at a legally determined rate by the authorities from proceeds of the collection, could not be removed unilaterally by the tax-farmer.
(c) The office of the tax-farmer was supervised by a paid government official, the ἔφορος.
(d) The tax-farmer could not proceed directly against a recalcitrant taxpayer. He required the cooperation of nome officials.
(e) Though the tax-farmer played an important role in the assessment of properties to be taxed, the taxpayer had a right of recourse and of redress to the government. The three-party system of taxation (government, tax-farmer and taxpayer) offered a flexible arrangement of checks and balances.⁴⁰ Even so, abuse of the system was not eliminated.
(f) Revenues collected and accounting procedures were controlled by the royal bank (or storehouses) and nome officials.
(g) By the use of the γραφή the state now interested itself in the internal arrangements between the tax-farmer, his business associates and guarantors.

---

³⁵ Laws also regulated the obligations of taxpayers to register their taxable property and not to avoid payment, e.g. *P. Hib.* I 29 (265 BC) concerning a tax upon slaves. The ostensible reason for this law appears to have been to protect the tax-farmer from financial loss (*l.*3).

³⁶ Préaux, *L'économie royale des Lagides* 453. On the role of banks in the procedure of revenue collection see also Bingen, *Le Papyrus Revenue Laws* 30-31.

³⁷ See Harper, *Aegyptus* 14 (1934) 282-5. There was also monthly accounting with reports being sent to officials of the central government, i.e. the *dioiketes* and *eklogistes*.

³⁸ Préaux, *L'économie royale des Lagides* 457.

³⁹ Rostovtzeff, *Geschichte der Staatspacht* 337.

⁴⁰ Harper, *Aegyptus* 14 (1934) 63.

In view of the extensive involvement of the state in the procedure of revenue collection through its instruments of control, it must be asked why the system of tax-farming continued and why it was not replaced by a direct collection by the state itself. Préaux[41] answers that the function of tax-farming was not an instrument of collection but one of guarantee. It was adopted from the system of collection known from classical Greece to insure the state against fiscal risks. As Préaux observes:

> La recherche d'une garantie est, en effet, urgente lorsque les impôts sont dus en monnaie, dans un pays où l'usage de la monnaie vient d'être introduit, et où la fortune privée du contribuable, souvent très réduite, n'offre guère de prise à l'exécution réelle.

But the instrument was closely controlled and regulated by the Ptolemaic state. Legislation was produced to carefully define the rights and obligations of all interested and involved parties with the result that 'comme les banques grecques, comme la monnaie grecque, la ferme grecque introduite dans une royauté centralisée et forte perd sa signification: elle sert des fins d'Etat'.

According to Harper[42] the sale of taxes assured the government of a fixed and guaranteed revenue which allowed annual and central fiscal planning. Bingen[43] adopts a different position. It is argued that the continued use of tax-farming could not have been to guarantee the treasury against the risk of fiscal losses, as it is unlikely that individuals or groups of individuals could be found to take on such risks voluntarily. Rather the system was an adaptation (*ad hoc* rather than deliberate) resulting from the imposition of Greek fiscal conceptions on recently acquired terrritory used to the direct collection of taxes and tributes. For Bingen the farming of taxes and the leasing of royal banks highlight the existence of a independent economic force and the transfer to Egypt of the Greek monetary economy.[44] The tax-farmers did not collect the taxes but they did estimate the amounts payable by each taxpayer, oversee its collection by the instruments of government, and guarantee payment to the treasury. In this at least they continued the practices of Greek tax-farming. The removal of the collection of taxes from the tax-farmers was caused by the socio-political situation of the Ptolemaic kingdom, namely the shortage of Greeks (especially outside the nome capitals) and the presence of royal officials and functionaries administering each nome. In other words, the classical model of tax-farming could not function properly in Egypt as it lacked the necessary manpower to effect the collection of revenue. In order to overcome this problem the government used its own personnel. It was not the result of some deliberate and purposeful design to reinvent the institution, but necessitated by circumstances. As Bingen notes (p.16; see also p.32):

> j'ai le sentiment que on n'a pas imaginé un nouveau type de ferme qui fût destinée à s'intégrer dans un schéma voulu, mais que c'est l'inadéquation de la ferme au monde égyptien hellénistique qui a usé les mécanismes sans qu'on ait eu l'imagination nécessaire pour les refondre délibérément.

Other developments were forced on Greek fiscal administration by the change from the microeconomic nature of agriculture as practised in Greece (i.e. small-scale risky cultivation of mainly olives, vines and other dry-field crops) to the larger-scale and more homogenous cultivation of irrigated crops in Egypt. But though the developments were all embraced from a desire to maximise revenue collection, in essence the economy remained Greek in its conception, e.g. terminology, accountancy in terms of money, tax-farming, the clerouchy etc.

---

[41] Préaux, *L'économie royale des Lagides* 450-1 and 457-8.
[42] Harper, *Aegyptus* 14 (1934) 62.
[43] J. Bingen, *Le Papyrus Revenue Laws*.
[44] See also Préaux, *L'économie royale des Lagides* 451 n. 1.

Je ne crois pas, quoi qu'on ait dit sur le mercantilisme des Ptolémées, qu'il y ait de leur part un comportement économique qui, en dehors de la gestion du nouvel espace rural, dépasse vraiment les axes de l'empirisme de la cité grecque. (p.33)

The Ptolemaic administration thought in terms of the economic institutions and practices of the fourth-century Greek city. There was no fundamental revision, it is argued, to a centralized and planned economy as some have suggested.

Roman Tax-Farming

Early republican Rome was constrained by a similar set of circumstances as Athens, i.e. an annually elected magistracy without financial liability to the city. The state lacked the necessary machinery to carry out the estimation and collection of taxes. As a result it also turned to the use of tax-farmers to collect state revenue. Each tax was sold (*venditio*, ὠνή) by the *censor*[45] to a *manceps* (ἀρχώνης) who was liable with his property to the state and who offered guarantors (*praedes*) with property (*praedia*) mortgaged to the *aerarium* as security. If he possessed sufficient property himself and was willing, the *manceps* could secure the contract without guarantors. The mortgaged property was subject to seizure and distraint if the purchase price was not realised. Lintott[46] argues that on purchase no deposit was paid by the *manceps* and that the purchase price was only paid on completion of the contract's duration. The *manceps* could also take associates or partners (*socii*) to form a *societas*. The associates might in turn, though not necessarily, guarantee the contract. Directors (*magistri*) and local representatives (*promagistri*) might also be appointed by a *societas*. The conditions of the sale were regulated by a *lex censoria* (νόμος τελωνικός), but other than that the city interested itself little in the relationship between the *manceps* and his associates and guarantors. Also compliance with the *lex* proved difficult to supervise and enforce when the *societates* extended their activities to the provinces. With the gradual extension of Roman power beyond Latium the wealth and influence of the Roman tax-farmers (*publicani*) increased. At first direct taxes were collected by the cities and local communities so that the *publicani* were only afforded opportunities in the areas of money transfers and exchange. The decisive step was taken with the law of C. Gracchus (123 BC) which gave the *publicani* access to the *decumae* (tithes on crops) and *scriptura* (pasture dues) of Asia. The auctions occurred in Rome giving the successful bidder the taxes for a period of five years (*lustrum*). In turn the *publicani* subcontracted the collection of taxes to the cities which were often forced under the duress of complicit governors to enter into agreements (*pactiones*) of an arbitrary valuation.[47] The system was oppressive. According to Rostovtzeff this step broke with the model of tax-farming found in the Hellenistic kingdoms and led to the following developments:

(a) A new and closed class of tax-farmers was created, the *ordo publicanorum*. The equestrian order from which most *publicani* were drawn had a vested interest in the expansion of the system of taxation.
(b) The capital requirements to underwrite the taxes and to provide the resources and staff both in Rome and in the provinces required the formation now of large companies with the necessary capital to guarantee the sale price and inventory. Their influence increased as the state increasingly relied on their financial expertise.

---

[45] If there were no censor in office at the time of the sale, then other magistrates (usually the consuls) acted in his place. See A. Lintott, *Imperium Romanum* (London 1993) 88. The sale occurred probably at the beginning of a new financial period, the Ides of March.
[46] Lintott, *Imperium Romanum* 89.
[47] A.H.M. Jones, *The Greek City from Alexander to Justinian* (Oxford 1940, repr. 1966) 124-5.

(c) The partnership or *societas* was recognized at law as a legal entity or corporation. This was unusual under Roman law and was probably occasioned by the need to assure the continuity of the partnership, which otherwise would be dissolved by the death of a partner, over the duration of the contract. Furthermore, Rostovtzeff argues that though the contract was still let to the *manceps*, he lost his significance to the new representatives of the corporation, i.e. to the *magistri* and *promagistri*. These representatives now conducted the business of the *societas*. The *publicani* were legally recognized as the owners of the capital and inventory of the company which was presided over by a *magister* in association with the *socii* and represented in the provinces by *promagistri* appointed by them.

However, it should be noted with Lintott[48] that the system of taxation imposed on Asia was probably unique in the empire. For example, he cites the case of Cilicia where under the governorship of Cicero direct taxes continued to be collected by the communities. It is very difficult to make any generalization about the Roman systems of taxation as they varied considerably throughout the empire.

The power and influence of the *publicani* declined severely with the demise of the Republican order and the change to imperial rule and its consitutional implications. Already Caesar had changed the Gracchan system in Asia by reducing direct taxation and entrusting it to the cities and local communities to collect.[49] This was a relatively easy and natural step to take in that direct taxes had not actually been collected by the agents of the *publicani* but by the cities themselves. Here the services of the *publicani* were least necessary as the burden of collection had rested with the cities which continued to use the same system of tax-farming as employed under the Hellenistic monarchies.[50] With the abolition of the role of *publicani*, however, the city through its council and 'the first ten'/'first twenty' (a *munus* or liturgy with a necessary wealth/property qualification) became liable for the payment of direct taxes.[51] Within each city the tax was sold to a tax-farmer who was also liable for the taxes contracted by him. Revenue was thus assured by an extensive system of guarantees. It is also assumed with good reason that a system of taxation administered by the cities and local communities would have been more humane than that of the *publicani*. The change in the method of collection was, however, not immediate for the last we hear of *societates* active in the collection of direct taxes belongs to the reign of Tiberius (Tacitus, *Ann.* 4.6).[52] In the case of indirect taxes where the personnel of the *publicani* were more active in the collection the change was more gradual still.[53] Indirect taxes such as customs, market dues, licence fees, sales taxes etc. continued to be sold to *publicani*.[54] For example, the *portoria* for Asia was still sold at Rome and, although the payment of instalments and the provision of security were further regulated in the imperial

---

[48] Lintott, *Imperium Romanum* 76-7.

[49] Later Augustus instituted the *tributum soli* and *tributum capitis* assessed by regular census.

[50] Lintott, *Imperium Romanum* 77.

[51] In time the keeping of records and the assessment of taxes devolved on the cities. In other areas also the cities were imposed upon to assume an administrative role, e.g. the building of roads, the maintenance of the imperial post, the provision of recruits for the army etc. As Jones, *Greek City* 274 and 301-2, observes, the cities, fostered by the Roman policy of urbanization, gradually came to perform much of the routine administration of the empire.

[52] Wilcken, *Griechische Ostraka* 573, and Rostovtzeff, *Geschichte der Staatspacht* 379.

[53] Lintott, *Imperium Romanum* 85.

[54] It should be noted that cities and their leagues (*koina*) might also have administered the collection of indirect taxes. For example, it appears that the city of Myra through a concession from the Lycian *koinon* regulated and benefited from the collection of customs duty (*quadragesima* ?). See H. Engelmann, *ZPE* 59 (1985) 113-9, and J. Reynolds, *JRS* 66 (1976) 194. Also it should be borne in mind that a free city might collect its own taxes, e.g. customs duties.

period, the *societates publicanorum* continued to play an important role.⁵⁵ But even here the power, influence and income of the tax-farmers were much diminished by the introduction of imperial officials (financial procurators first attested in the time of Claudius) to control the collection of taxes and accounting procedures and by the dislocation of political relationships caused by the emergence of the imperial system. In particular any understanding between *publicani* and provincial governors for their mutual benefit became more precarious. In the imperial provinces governors and financial procurators owed their commission to the emperor and were answerable to him. In senatorial provinces this was not so; however, even here the presence of imperial procurators attending to the personal business affairs of the emperors,⁵⁶ as well as the other vehicles of information available to them (e.g. personnel attached to the imperial post), curbed and controlled the former excesses of the *publicani*. Rostovtzeff⁵⁷ notes that because of the status of the emperors, in a *de facto* way imperial procurators even in senatorial provinces stood between the provincials and the Roman magistrates hindering any understanding between them and the *publicani*. In effect the procurators (imperial freedmen and later *equites*) supplied the control which had been absent from the system of taxation operating in the provinces in the period of the Roman republic.

In time the engagement of *societates* for the collection of indirect taxes such as the *portoria* also ceased; they were replaced here by semi-official *conductores* under the control and supervision of imperial procurators.⁵⁸ But it is dangerous to assume that the change was orchestrated centrally and its introduction into the various provinces thereby coordinated. Rather the picture which Rostovtzeff offers is of independent but similar developments occurring in the provinces at different times and occasioned by the tendency towards imperial control and supervision.⁵⁹

The changes which occurred in the imperial period can be ascribed to various causes and motives. In the first place one might suggest a desire to undermine the power of the senate which had traditionally relied on the income raised by the sale of taxes. This is best seen in the instance of new taxes introduced by the emperors, e.g. the *vicesima hereditatum*. Here the

---

⁵⁵ Lintott, *Imperium Romanum* 123.

⁵⁶ In the initial imperial period the private property of the emperor and that of the state were separate. Receipts were paid to different accounts. The property of the emperor constantly increased through inheritance and confiscation. It is unclear when imperial procurators started to dominate public finances in senatorial provinces. In imperial provinces they were in charge of both public finances and the financial interests of the emperor from the beginning.

⁵⁷ Rostovtzeff, *Geschichte der Staatspacht* 382.

⁵⁸ The change was prompted by a reduction in profitability resulting from the increased control exercised by the government over the taxation system and by the creation of an experienced personnel effectively independent of the *societates* but involved in the collection of the indirect tax (*vectigal*). As a result the government now contracted with the *conductor* alone much as it had formerly done with the ἀρχώνης/*manceps*. This step also marked the transfer of the administration of the tax to the emperor and his representatives with all revenues now remaining in the provincial *fisci* to defray the costs of administration. See further Rostovtzeff, *Geschichte der Staatspacht* 504-6. Formerly the revenues of senatorial provinces were transferred to the *aerarium Saturni* in Rome; revenues of imperial provinces probably remained in the provincial *fisci*.

⁵⁹ Rostovtzeff, *Geschichte der Staatspacht* 405-6, cites a relevant example to illustrate differences between provinces. In the case of Palmyra in Syria the collection of *portoria* was purely municipal; the city sold customs revenue to tax-farmers who collected it under the supervision of an imperial procurator. Part of the collection, it is assumed, will have ended up in the imperial *fiscus*. In the case of border-customs Rostovtzeff assumes that these were probably sold by Rome to tax-farmers who were then supervised by imperial agents. Such tax-farmers were not, however, *conductores* but similar to those met in the Hellenistic kingdoms.

revenue was neither given to *publicani* to collect nor paid to the account of the state.[60] Rather the tax was collected by a system of tax-farming which was modelled on the system in use in Egypt, i.e. regulation to protect the taxpayers, imperial agents to control collection, collection by personnel independent of the tax-farmer, and possibly a system of accounting by imperial agents.[61] Rostovtzeff[62] argues that there was a change in the way the provinces were perceived. No longer were they seen as the foreign possessions of a city-state which as the *praedia populi Romani* could be milked for profit, but rather as part of a world-state possessing equal rights. Provincials had to be protected from the speculative profiteering of the tax-collectors.

The question is whether this concern for provincials was prompted by a general interest in their welfare or whether it was motivated by a desire to protect imperial revenue. For example, Macro[63] agrees that in the Republican period abuse by the *publicani* and provincial governors was prevalent due to the lack of central administrative control. A change occurred with Augustus. Whereas the Roman governor had previously seen the province as a service for a few years in which he could recoup the costs of his advancement, the emperor increasingly saw the empire as his own domain. The emperors were thus interested in maintaining its prosperity. In Asia, Caesar had replaced the farming of taxes to *publicani* with direct assessment and collection, and Augustus shifted the responsibility of their collection to the local, civic authorities (*decuriones*). But Roman governors kept a careful eye on civic expenditure, the reason being that as city vied with city to outdo each other extravagance and waste would ruin the tax base of the empire.[64] The imperial offices of *corrector* and *curator* (*rei publicae* or *civitatis*) were created to oversee civic expenditure, and the political power and authority of the provincial élite who occupied the magistracies was accordingly diminished.[65]

The Romans, like the Ptolemies, appear to have been sensitive to the need to safeguard the collection of revenue against corruption. For example, Trajan in the municipal constitution imposed on Irni (Spain) provided under one rubric that neither municipal magistrates nor persons related or associated with them could purchase the collection of public revenue or benefit in any way from the purchase.[66] Again, Hadrian enacted a law for Athens that councillors and their agents should not acquire tax-farming contracts (Dio 69.16.2). In the Republican period we also know that the senate controlled the sale of public contracts but its members were forbidden from bidding. These laws, however, regulated the participation of members of 'governing' councils only. Other evidence suggests that imperial officials were not necessarily excluded but could concurrently be tax-farmers (customs) and hold an administrative post, e.g. *praefectus vehiculorum* (*CIL* III 13283), *procurator Augusti* (*ILS* 8858), and λογιστὴς πόλεων Νεικομηδείας, Νεικέας, Προύσης (*curator civitatium*

---

[60] The tax was not called *publicum* nor was it paid into the *aerarium Saturni*. The *aerarium* was the state treasury receiving taxes from both imperial and senatorial provinces. It was increasingly under the control of the emperors. The *fiscus* and provincial *fisci* were the imperial treasuries.

[61] Rostovtzeff, *Geschichte der Staatspacht* 408, 498-9.

[62] Rostovtzeff, *Geschichte der Staatspacht* 407.

[63] A.D. Macro, 'The Cities of Asia Minor under the Roman Imperium', *ANRW* II, 7.2, 667-668.

[64] Macro, *ANRW* II, 7.2, 682ff. On the role of Pliny the younger in Bythinia see pp.668-9.

[65] Macro, *ANRW* II, 7.2, 690-695. The *curator rei publicae* is first attested in the Flavian period, but Lintott, *Imperium Romanum* 123, assumes that the post was probably created earlier.

[66] *Lex Irnitana* ch. J. For this law see J. González, *JRS* 76 (1986) 147-243, in particular 161.

Nicomediae Nicaeae Prusae, AE [1928] 97).[67] No doubt slaves and freedman attended to their tax-farming interest held in particular regions.

Taxation in Roman Egypt

In Wilcken's[68] view imperial laws formed the legal basis of the tax system. He surmises that Augustus probably added new tax laws to the Ptolemaic system but how extensive they were is disputed, as unfortunately we have no legislation in the Roman period comparable to that provided by *P. Par.* 62 and *P. Rev.* for the Ptolemaic period. However, on the basis of *P. Oxy.* I 36 it would appear that imperial regulations were just as detailed as the Ptolemaic. The surviving columns of the papyrus contain extracts of customs regulations concerning the rights and liabilities of tax-farmers to search ships and the procedure of issuing receipts to avoid false accusations of non-payment. The legal basis was further developed and adapted to changing circumstances by imperial rescripts as well as by the edicts of prefects, e.g. the edict of T. Julius Alexander (*OGIS* 669, AD 68) and the prefectorial *prostagmata* regulating methods of collection referred to by the plaintiff in *BGU* I 340 *ll*.20-25.

The administration of the taxation system was overseen by a hierarchy of officials. At its head was the Roman prefect; to him the *strategoi* of the nomes were directly responsible and accountable (see *P. Oxy.* I 44 for a case in point). They were the highest officials responsible for the taxes in their nomes and exercised general control over revenue collection. Rostovtzeff[69] notes the loss of the special financial personnel which was found in the Ptolemaic period, and the assumption of their functions by regular administrative officials, i.e. the prefect replaces the central *dioiketes*, and *strategos* replaces nome *oikonomos* and *dioiketes*. He surmises that, since Egypt was now a province and not an independent state, it no longer needed so extensive an administrative system.

The Romans never introduced *publicani* into Egypt, preferring instead to allow the Ptolemaic system essentially to continue. Sale by auction remained annual with the period of sale running from the beginning of the year to its end. Bids were made by written ὑπόμνημα now to the *epistrategos* (*procurator*). However, the sale itself was conducted by the *strategos* with the assistance of his *basilikogrammateus* (*P. Oxy.* I 44). An apparently new condition imposed on tax-farmers was the requirement that every four months their records (χρηματισμοί) had to be bound and given to an official for registration (*P. Grenf.* II 41, AD 46). Also the Roman model of handing the collection of direct taxes over to the cities was not at first adopted in Egypt as the cities there lacked the necessary municipal structure.[70] It was arguably for this reason that the role of *praktor* was revised, perhaps as early as the reign of Tiberius.[71] But other reasons can be suggested for the revision.

---

[67] H.-G. Pflaum, *Essai sur le cursus publicus dans le Haut-Empire Romain, Mém. de l'Acad. des Inscr. et Belles Lettres* XIV. 1 (1940) 264-273.

[68] Wilcken, *Griechische Ostraka* 570-1.

[69] Rostovtzeff, *Geschichte der Staatspacht* 461.

[70] The situation changed in AD 202 when the *metropoleis* of Egypt were granted *boulai*. From this period the municipalities and their office holders became responsible for the collection of revenues. See S.L. Wallace, *Taxation in Egypt from Augustus to Diocletian* (1938, reprinted New York 1969) 168. The system of taxation and its method of assessment was also further reformed under Diocletian. See *P. Cair. Isidor.* 1 and 8 and associated discussions (pp.23-9 and 71-5).

[71] See the discussion in *New Docs* 7 (1994) 93-4, for details and references.

Wilcken[72] argues that tax-farming had become less profitable in the Roman period due to the introduction of unfavourable contractual conditions and to the exercise of stricter control. Rostovtzeff is uncertain as to whether there was any tightening of control under Roman administration; the Ptolemaic offices of *oikonomos* and *antigrapheus* had disappeared and the new liturgy of ἐπιτηρητής (supervisor) introduced. The office is first attested in AD 88 (*P. Oxy.* I 174) and as definitely a liturgy by AD 136, but Rostovtzeff argues that their function was not so much that of control as that of assuring the government of full payment. As such they were involved in the collection of taxes (both those which were farmed and those which were collected directly by the state, e.g. by *praktores*) and could issue receipts in the name of the tax-farmer.[73] A recently published papyrus, *SB* XVI 12504, throws an important light onto the duties of the ἐπιτηρηταί.

Arsinoe   29.3 x 24.4 cm   AD 135/6

Ed. pr. — A.H.S. El Mosallamy, 'Public Notices concerning Epitērēsis of the Ōnē Zytēras', *Proceedings of the XVI Int. Congr. of Papyrology* (Chico 1981) 215-229 (= *SB* XVI 12504).

The papyrus is described as 'preserved on all sides' but 'difficult to read at many points because of holes, abrasions on the surface, and faded ink'. The two προγράμματα are written in separate columns and probably copied from a *tomos synkollesimos*. The hand is described as professional, skilful and neat.

Col. I

[ἀντίγρα(φον)] πρ[ο]γράμματος ἐξειλη[μ(μένον) ἐκ βιβλι]οθή-[κ(ης) δη]μοσίω(ν) λόγων.	Copy of *programma* extracted from the archive of public accounts.
Ο[ὐέ]γ[ετ]ο̣ς̣ ὁ καὶ Σαραπίων στρατηγὸ̣[ς 'Αρσι]νοίτου Θεμίστου μ[ερ]ί̣δ̣ο̣ς̣	I, Vegetus also called Sarapion, *strategos* of the Arsinoite nome, division of Themistos,
τοῖς ὑπογεγραμ[μέ]νοις ἀναδο[θ]εῖσί μοι ὑπὸ τῶν τῆς	order the underwritten, who were nominated to me by the
5 μ[ε]ρ[ίδος πραγ]ματικῶν ὡς εὔποροι καὶ ἐπιτήδειοι	officials of the division as of sufficient means and fit
ε[ἰς τὴν ἐπιτήρ]ησιν τῶν ὑπογεγραμμένων ἐν τῇ	for the superintendency of the underwritten
μ[ε]ρίδι τε[λ]ωνικῶν ὠνῶν καὶ ἄλλω(ν) τοῦ κ̅ (ἔτους)	tax-farming and other concessions in the division for year 20
Αὐτοκράτορος Καίσαρος Τραιανοῦ 'Αδρια[νοῦ] Σεβαστοῦ	of Imperator Caesar Trajan Hadrian Augustus,
παραγγέλλων ἀντιλαμβάνεσθαι τῆς ἐπιτηρήσεως	to take over the superintendency
10 μετὰ πάσης πίστεως καὶ ἐπιμελείας καὶ τοὺς	with all good-faith and care, and the

---

[72] Wilcken, *Griechische Ostraka* 594-5, 601.
[73] Wilcken, *Griechische Ostraka* 599-600.

§4 Tax Collection and the τελῶναι of the New Testament

λόγους τῶν προσπειπτόντων διὰ πενθημέρου	accounts of revenue in each five-day period
καταχωρίζειν, ὡς ἐκελεύσθη, ἐμοί τε καὶ	to record, as has been commanded, both for me and
οἷς δέον ἐστίν, τά τε ἐλλειλεμμέν[α] διαγράφειν	for whom it is necessary, the arrears (?) to pay
ἐπὶ τὴν δημοσίαν τράπεζαν μετ[ὰ τ]ῶν πρακτόρων	into the public bank with the *praktores*,
15 κινδύνου πρὸς τούτους ὄντος, ἐάν τ[ι] τῷ φίσκῳ	the risk being theirs, if any (harm) befall the *fiscus*
ἐμπέσῃ ἢ παρὰ τὸ δέον γένηται ἢ οὕτινος συκαμε	or if (anything) occurs contrary to what is proper or ...
. [. .]ου . [.]ς. (Ἔτους) ιθ̄ Αὐτοκράτορος Καίσαρος Τραιανοῦ	[...]. Year 19 of Imperator Caesar Trajan
Ἁ[δρ]ιανοῦ Σεβαστοῦ Μεσορὴ ἐπαγομ(ένων) γ̄.	Hadrian Augustus, Mesore, on 3rd of the intercalary (days).
ζυτηρᾶς ἔστι δέ·	For beer-tax it is:
20 Γάιος Ἀντώνιος Γαλλικὸς ἀπολύσιμος ἀπὸ	Gaius Antonius Gallicus veteran from
στρα[τ]ε̣ί[ας ἀπὸ Θε]α̣δ̣ελφίας	the cohort [at Th]eadelphia,
Πτολεμαῖος Σωπάτρου τοῦ Διδύμου ἀπὸ μητρο(πόλεως)	Ptolemaios son of Sopatros grandson of Didymos from the *metropolis*,
Ἁρποκρατίων Θέωνος ἀπὸ Μακεδόνων	Harpokration son of Theon from (the quarter of) Macedonians,
Ζωίλο(ς) τοῦ Χάρητος ἀπὸ [Ἱ]ερακίο[υ]	Zoilos son of Chares from (the quarter of) Hierakeios.

Col. 2

25 [ἀντί]γρα(φον) προγράμματος κ[ολλή]μ(ατος) [number] τόμου [number].	Copy of a *programma* from sheet (?) volume (?).
[Ἡ]ρακλείδης στρατη[γὸ]ς Ἀρσινοίτου Θεμίστ[ου μ]ερίδος.	Herakleides *strategos* of the Arsinoite nome, division of Themistos.
[Γ]ελλίου Βάσσου τοῦ κρατίστου ἐπι[σ]τρατήγου	Gellius Bassus, the most excellent *epistrategos*,
γράψαντός μοι ἀντὶ Γαίου Ἀντωνίου Γαλλικοῦ	having written to me to appoint in place of Gaius Antonius Gallicus,
διά γήρα[ς] ἀσθενοῦς τῷ σώματι καταστῆσαι	being weak in body through old age,
30 ἕτερον εἰς τὴν ἐπιτήρησιν ἐν ᾗ ἐδήλωσεν	another to the superintendency in which Gallicus declares

ὁ Γαλλικὸς εἶναι, ἀνεδόθη ὑπὸ τῶν τῆς μερίδος κωμογραμματέων ὧν δὲ κωμῶν μή εἰσιν κωμογραμματε[ῖ]ς πρεσβυτέρων διαδεχομένων τὰ κατὰ τὰς κωμογραμματείας	himself to be, there was nominated by the *komogrammateis* of the division and, for villages in which there are no *komogrammateis*, by the *presbyteroi* acting for the *komogrammateis*,
35 Ἀπίων Ἀμμωνίου τοῦ Μύσθου ἀπὸ Χηνοβοσκ(ῶν) εἰς τὴν ἐ[πι]τήρησιν ὠνῆς ζυτηρᾶς κώμης Θεαδελφία[ς]. Παραγγέλλ[ο]μεν αὐτῷ πιστῶς καὶ ἐπι[μελῶς] τ[ὴ]ν ἐπιτήρη[σ]ιν ποιεῖσθαι καὶ [τ]οὺς λόγο[υς] καταχωρί[ζειν] ἐμοί τε καὶ οἷς δέον ἐστὶν	Apion son of Ammonios grandson of Mysthes from the Chenoboskia quarter to the superintendency of the sale of beer-tax for the village of Theadelphia. We order him faithfully and carefully to perform the superintendency and to record the accounts for me and for whomever it is proper
40 τῶν περιουσῶν ἡμερῶν τοῦ ἐνεστῶτος ἔτους κ[αὶ] [το]ῦ ἰσιόντος κᾱ (ἔτους) Ἀδριανοῦ Καίσαρος τοῦ κυρίο[υ . . .]υ με . . . δηλον [ἀν]τὶ τοῦ Γαλλικοῦ διαπράττε[σθαι τ]ὴν χρείαν. Σεσημ(είωμαι).	for the remaining days of the present year and for the coming year 21 of Hadrian Caesar the lord [...] in place of Gallicus to finish the function. I have signed.
(Ἔτους) κ̄ Αὐτοκράτορος Καίσαρος Τραιανοῦ Ἀδριανοῦ Σε[β]αστοῦ Μεσορή.	Year 20 of Imperator Caesar Trajan Hadrian Augustus, Mesore.
45 Σαρα[πίων] . . . . . κλ . . ων ὑπηρέτης προθεὶς κατε(χώρησα).	I, Sarapion [...], assistant, having posted (the *programma*) have recorded (it).
(Ἔτους) κ̄ Αὐτοκράτορος Καίσαρος Τραιανοῦ Ἀδριανοῦ [Σεβαστοῦ] Μεσορὴ ἐπαγο(μένων) β̄.	Year 20 of Imperator Caesar Trajan Hadrian [Augustus], Mesore on the 2nd of the intercalary (days).

SB 12504 consists of two προγράμματα or public notices issued by successive *strategoi* approximately one year apart and extracted from the records of the 'archive of public accounts'.[74] Both concern the individual, Gaius Antonius Gallicus. The first public notice recorded his appointment with three other associates (μέτοχοι) to the liturgical supervision (ἐπιτήρησις) of the beer-tax (a capitation tax). The appointment was for one year, namely the

---

[74] All documents concerned with revenues and their collection were filed in the βιβλιοθήκη δημοσίων λόγων.

20th year of Hadrian or AD 135/6 (*l.*7).⁷⁵ The notice apparently concerned the appointment of ἐπιτηρηταί for farmed taxes generally (*l.*7) but in making the extract only the names of those appointed to the supervision of the beer-tax were copied.

The second notice concerns the release of the same individual from that liturgy and appoints another person in his place. Antonius Gallicus had apparently appealed to the *epistrategos* against his appointment and obtained release on the grounds of his age. The *strategos* was written to and a new appointment made presumably from the list of nominees for the next year. The new appointee would serve for the remainder of the present year and for the whole of the next year (*ll.*40-41). The slowness of the appeal procedure is attested by our extracts, for the notice of release was issued just 6 days before the expiry of the liturgical term. Whilst the appeal was being decided Antonius Gallicus would have had to serve in the liturgy himself or employ someone to act for him. The notice of release, however, did set a precedent for Antonius Gallicus to use, if he should be appointed in future to another similar liturgy. No doubt, it was for this reason that the present set of extracts was made.

Of interest for the present discussion is the list of obligations placed on those appointed to the liturgy of ἐπιτήρησις. Reports of the collected tax-payments were to be made every five days to the *strategos* and other concerned officials, possibly including the *nomarches* and *basilikogrammateus*⁷⁶ (*ll.*11-13). For examples of such five-day reports see *PIFAO* I 3 and other papyri cited there (p.5). Also arrears (?) were to be collected by the liturgists and deposited in the bank by them acting with the assistance of the *praktores* (*ll.*13-14). It would appear that if πρακτόρων is the correct restoration here, these officials might still be used in the Roman times to collect irregular payments (arrears and penalties) in the case of farmed taxes. See further the comments on *P. Ryl.* II 194 in *New Docs* 8 (1997) §5. The liturgists were personally liable for any loss accruing from their term of office (*ll.*15-17).⁷⁷

In Roman Egypt the characteristic trend of the taxation system was the movement from tax-farming to liturgy, i.e. the replacement of the τελώνης by the πράκτωρ. However, the trend towards the direct collection of taxes by state-appointed officials or liturgists was gradual and varied between nome and the type of tax to be collected. Rostovtzeff[78] surmises that as the farming of certain taxes in different regions became less profitable, it was harder for the government to find persons to farm them. As it was unsatisfactory for the government to rely on officials to force the tax-farmers contracted for the previous year to undertake the contract again,[79] it instead seized on the institution of the Ptolemaic *praktor* (an official formerly responsible for the collection of arrears and penalties)[80] and in the course of the first century made it into a liturgy or compulsory public service for the collection of regular taxes (mainly in

---

[75] Appointments for 1 year, 3 years and by iteration are attested. See N. Lewis, *The Compulsory Public Services of Roman Egypt* (Florence 1982) 29-31.

[76] See El Mosallamy, *Proceedings of the XVI Int. Congr. of Papyrology* 219 and 226.

[77] El Mosallamy, *Proceedings of the XVI Int. Congr. of Papyrology* 219, surmises that they may have also been in charge of leasing the right to brew beer.

[78] Rostovtzeff, *Geschichte der Staatspacht* 465.

[79] *P. Oxy.* I 44 (end of I AD) attests the difficulty of finding someone to bid for the ἀγορανομεῖον and ἐγκύκλιον. It implies that it was difficult to make a profit. Cf. the introduction of the μερισμὸς ὠνίων ἐνλείμματος τελωνικῶν in the second century AD (Wallace, *Taxation* 164-166). In *P. Oxy.* 44 the prefect is reported to have instructed the *strategos* to ease the burden of tax-farmers who failed to bid for the taxes. They had previously been financially harmed by the undertaking and threatened to flee should they be made to assume it again.

[80] Wilcken, *Griechische Ostraka* 601.

cash rather than kind) paid to the financial departments of the διοίκησις and ἴδιος λόγος.[81] The *praktores* are attested from the time of Tiberius (apparently not yet a liturgy) and the office, it has been suggested, may have been created as circumstances required to assist tax-farmers, who lacked the necessary coercive power. As such they assisted in the collection of irregular payments, i.e. arrears and penalties. Even so, their function appears to have quickly evolved and they soon became the collectors of numerous regular taxes.

The earliest pieces of evidence that the office of *praktor* had become a liturgy are *PSI* I 56 (AD 106) and *P. Giss.* 58 (AD 113). But it cannot be assumed that all *praktores* by this date had become liturgists. Also the farming of certain taxes still continued, e.g. the tax raised on catoecic land (*SB* XVI 12678 *l*.22, AD 179) and the various taxes on donkeys (see discussion in *New Docs* 8 [1997] §5). As Oertel[82] observes, the change from the farming of taxes to a system of state administration by liturgy was only gradual and not yet completely carried through at the end of the second century. Indeed, the two systems coexisted. With the demise of tax-farming the *praktores* replaced the farmers to become the regular collectors of taxes paid in cash. The duration of service was probably in most cases three years; property qualifications differed (600 dr. to 3 tal. 3,000 dr.), no doubt in line with the estimated value of the tax, and an allowance was given to cover expenses (approx. 2 dr. per day).[83]

The liturgy was based on the wealth qualification of the nominee and this was vouched for and guaranteed by the nominator. The *praktores* became the most important personnel involved in direct collection.[84] Like the tax-farmer, the *praktor* together with his associates (μέτοχοι) was personally liable with his property[85] and guarantors were sought for the sum to be collected.[86] Rostovtzeff[87] argues that the *praktoria* was modelled on the system of tax-farming (in particular the placing of guarantors, the assumption of personal liability with property, the presence of associates or μέτοχοι, and the ability to resell the tax or offer substitutes for its collection) which it was designed to replace. They had personnel who assisted in the collecting, receipting and recording of taxes (ὑπηρέται, βοηθοί, γραμματεῖς, χειρισταί). Collection was made on the basis of ἀπαιτήσιμα which were prepared officially and which listed what tax sum was to be paid by each taxpayer. The *praktor* was under the supervision of his nome *strategos*. Wilcken[88] surmises that there was also monthly reporting and accounting of collected payments with this official.

---

[81] A similar movement towards the use of liturgists to collect payments in kind is also attested. See Rostovtzeff, *Geschichte der Staatspacht* 474, and *New Docs* 7 (1994) 112-129.

[82] Oertel, *Liturgie* 196.

[83] See further Oertel, *Liturgie* 195-204, and Lewis, *The Compulsory Public Services* 44. Wilcken, *Griechische Ostraka* 606, believes that the *praktores* received in part a salary drawn from the tax designated πρακτορικόν. Rostovtzeff disagrees and sees this sum as a charge for late payment. Wallace, *Taxation* 324, believes both interpretations are possible on the basis of the evidence. Both Wilcken, *Griechische Ostraka* 605-6, and Rostovtzeff, *Geschichte der Staatspacht* 471, believe that the *praktores* like their predecessors, probably received the ἐπιγένημα of the collection.

[84] Other liturgists (e.g. ἀπαιτηταί, village elders etc.) were also involved in the collection of taxes. The ἀπαιτηταί were the agents for the collection of arrears, as tax-farmers and *praktores* could only collect taxes during the year of their contract or whilst contracted to collect taxes (Wilcken, *Griechische Ostraka* 609-10, 618).

[85] Wilcken, *Griechische Ostraka* 606. The government appointed two or more *praktores* (μέτοχοι) for one and the same tax.

[86] The *praktores* were nominated by village or *metropolis* communities who guaranteed the liturgists through their representatives, e.g. the village elders. See Wilcken, *Griechische Ostraka* 602.

[87] Rostovtzeff, *Geschichte der Staatspacht* 471.

[88] Wilcken, *Griechische Ostraka* 622-3.

Collectors could in theory seize a taxpayer who refused to pay and throw him in the debtor-prison (πρακτόρειον). However, in practice they might require the assistance of a military escort to exercise their coercive powers. Indeed, as early as AD 45 (*SB* IV 7461) we find that the *praktor* of the poll-tax in the village of Philadelphia required the assistance of the *strategos* to enforce payment. See also *BGU* I 8 col. 2 *l*.9.

Praktores came also to be used for the collection of newly introduced taxes such as the poll-tax, e.g. *SB* IV 7462 (AD 55-60). The Romans preferred and developed capitation taxes (e.g. poll-tax, bath-tax, trade taxes[89] etc.) as they offered an easy method of collecting a fairly steady revenue. As such they constituted a considerable tax burden on the lower strata of society.[90] Westermann and Keyes[91] offer the following reconstruction of the procedures used in the collection of the poll-tax by *praktores* in the second century:

(a) The taxpayer came into the office of the collector or the bank to make his payment, frequently by instalment.
(b) A receipt was issued to the taxpayer.
(c) The payments were entered into the day-book of the collector in the order in which they were received, i.e. date order.
(d) A copy was made of the day-book on a regular basis, e.g. *P. Col.* 1 recto 1a-b.
(e) Payments were transferred to the bank ledger and a check mark made in the copy of the day-book, e.g. *P. Col.* 1 recto 1a-b. The column number of the bank ledger where the taxpayer's name was found was also inserted against the record of payment in the copy of the day-book.
(f) Payments were entered into the bank ledger: the ledger had been prepared beforehand for the current year and contained the full list of taxpayers in the district arranged in alphabetical order (first two letters only), e.g. *P. Col.* 1 recto 2 and *P. Fay.* 153.[92] In preparing the bank ledger a space (1/2 inch) was left below each name to receive the record of payment. About 11 to 12 names were contained in each column of this ledger and the column was headed with a number.
(g) When all the tax was paid a check mark was placed against the taxpayer's name in the bank ledger.
(h) A summary of the bank ledger was made after the seventh month of the current tax year, e.g. *P. Col.* 1 recto 3. The names of those who had paid their poll-tax in full had a check mark against them, and no further follow-up was required. It was used by the *praktores* and banks to determine outstanding taxes which needed to be collected in the following months

---

[89] Trade taxes were collected through the guilds whose members were liable for the tax on their profession. See, for example, *P. Rainer Cent.* 122 (AD 429), *SB* XVI 12260 (AD 421) and discussion in *ZPE* 59 (1985) 67-70. Here the guild of Oxyrhynchite goldsmiths enters into agreements with one of its members for the collection (management) of the *chrysargyron*. The guild underwrites the expenses of the nominee.

[90] The poll-tax was a μερισμός as it was a tax 'assessed in equal amounts over the entire tax-paying populace of a given district' (Wallace, *Taxation* 135). The rates for various individuals was fixed; the numbers of variously rated individuals in a district was determined by the fourteen-year census; the total poll-tax was calculated for the district from the tax-rolls and remained the same for the fourteen-year cycle. A decrease in the population of a district meant that less tax was gathered and any loss had to made good by the collector and his guarantors. In the latter part of the reign of Trajan the μερισμός ἀνακ(εχωρηκότων) and the μερισμός ἀπόρων (perhaps identical) were instituted. This placed the loss back on the population of the district by distributing any shortfall on those who remained. It sought to stop connivance between villagers and absconding persons, and between officials and those seeking to declare themselves destitute. As one would expect, the value of the μερισμός, which probably also included other capitation taxes such as the χωματικόν, was small soon after the census but gradually increased up until the next census year, when the capitation taxes for the district were recalculated.

[91] W.L. Westermann and C.W. Keyes, *P. Col.* II (1932).

[92] The bank ledger of the previous year may have been used as the basis for the new ledger. Names of persons who had died or exceeded the taxable age were deleted, whilst other names were added from the register of minors. See *P. Col.* II (1932) pp.56-57. On the partial diminution of taxes after the death of the taxpayer see *P. Col.* II, pp.82-83. On *P. Fay.* 153 see F. Preisigke, *APF* 4 (1908) 95-114.

The move away from the sale of taxes can also be seen as early as the Augustan period in the interim measure introduced in the case of another capitation tax, the bath-tax. It was at first not sold but collected by the βαλανεύς before being given to a *praktor* by the later part of Tiberius's reign.[93] But in other areas (i.e. indirect taxes) the Ptolemaic system of tax-farming continued with its characteristics of the financial liability of tax-farmers, the requirement of guarantees, the making of an annual contract, the government's accounting and supervision of sums collected etc.

Abuse and Corruption

How effective the control exercised by imperial agents was is a mute point, for abuse in the collection of taxes was endemic in the Roman period. The problem appears to have been systemic in nature. Ramsay MacMullen[94] argues that the financial outlays and expenditures of the central imperial budget (the largest cost being the standing army) could easily have been met by a tax of a few per cent across the empire. With the exceptions of times of war or of the stationing of large numbers of soldiers in an area, increases in taxes and in the requisitioning of goods and services does not appear to have been in response to the needs of the central government. On the other hand, numerous complaints were lodged in response to individual instances of extortion and abuse by officials, soldiers and agents of the government. As he observes: 'So much depended on individual conduct in particular places by particular agents very, very loosely controlled from the centre'.[95] And the problem grew as a result of an increase in the number of officials from the late third century with imperial officials now usurping to a large measure the central power of the emperor(s) to control and shape tax policy by doubling or even trebling the authorized rates and pocketing the extorted sums.

In Egypt Lewis[96] notes the increased efficiency of collections in the change to Roman rule, but concerning the endemic nature of abuse he comments:

> the system of farming out the collection of taxes to the highest bidder — a system developed earlier, which the emperors retained practically unchanged for the first hundred years of Roman rule — was an open invitation to corruption. Once his bid had been accepted and he had contracted to pay the government the proffered lump sum, the first aim and overriding purpose of every tax-farmer was to show a profit in his enterprise. But more than one was not satisfied with that modest goal. More than one was eager to obtain the contract because he saw it as a get-rich-quick scheme; and once the contract was safely in his pocket he did not hesitate to employ any and all means, illegal as well as legal, to maximize his profit by wresting excessive and extortionate payments from his hapless and helpless victims. Such overbearing and violent behaviour was facilitated by the fact that collectors were frequently accompanied, ostensibly for their protection, by soldiers or armed guards, whom they could and did use to intimidate and maltreat the taxpayers.

Numerous instances of extortion and abuse can be cited; see Dio Cassius 57.10.5, Philo, *De spec. leg.* 3.159-162, and *P. Oxy.* II 284-5 (*ca* AD 50), 298 verso (first century), III 393 (= *SB* XIV 11902, AD 49-50) and 394, *SB* XVI 12678 (AD 179). The same types of abuse are

---

[93] Wilcken, *Griechische Ostraka* 585-6.

[94] R. MacMullen, 'Tax-Pressure in the Roman Empire', *Latomus* 46 (1987) 737-54.

[95] MacMullen, *Latomus* 46 (1987) 743. MacMullen (p.745) notes the erosion of collections in other areas of the system by: (a) imperial generosity in remitting tax debts and arrears in response to embassies, potential threats of rebellion or flight, or in seasons of bad harvest; and (b) the payment of customary gratuities to the emperor's servants. The flexibility of the system in these two areas is a function of the 'popular expectations of Greatness'. Under such expectations remission and reward were at the whim of the emperor rather than in response to any real need.

[96] N. Lewis, *Life in Egypt under Roman Rule* (Oxford 1983) 160-1.

recorded in the gospels, e.g. Luke 3.12-14, 18.9-14, 19.1-10 (esp. v.8), and the collocation of τελώνης and ἁμαρτωλός (Matt. 9.10-11 par. Mark 2.15-16 and Luke 5.30; Matt. 11.19 par. Luke 7.34; Luke 15.1), ἐθνικός (Matt. 18.17), πόρνη (Matt. 21.31).

SB XIV 11902 is a petition of complaint lodged with the *strategos* of the Oxyrhynchite nome against a tax-collector (*praktor*). In it the plaintiff alleges that the official had extorted certain sums of money, presumably for the trade-tax on weavers, i.e. the χειρωνάξιον γερδίων mentioned in the parallel petition of complaint, P. Oxy. 285. Wallace[97] proposes that the trade-tax in the Oxyrhychite nome was 36 dr. annually. In the present papyrus the extorted sums are 16 dr. in year 8 of the emperor Claudius and 24 dr. in the following year. In P. Oxy. 284 (also year 8 of Claudius) the amount is 16 dr., the same as for year 8 in SB 11902. It is tempting to interpret this coincidence as evidence for an attempt by the *praktores* (acting as associates) to distribute the shortfall in their revenue collection among the remaining members of the guild of weavers. This would make sense also of the expression κατὰ μέρος (P. Oxy. 284 l.10 and SB 11902 l.17), i.e. 'in part' or better 'among other people'. The action of the collectors may have in fact been legal as each guild through its membership was jointly responsible for the payment of the trade-tax. But the taxpayers may not have seen the matter in the same light. Unfortunately, the same coincidence of amounts is not found in the evidence for year 9 (24 dr. in SB 11902 and 12 dr. in P. Oxy. 285). The end of the present petition is lost; however, on the basis of similar petitions it can reasonably be assumed that it ended with a request that the *strategos* proceed against the tax-collector: διὸ ἀξιῶ διαλαβεῖν κατ' αὐτοῦ ὡς ἐάν σοι δοκῇ. εὐτύχει (cf. P. Oxy. 284 and 285). Interestingly, in the three similar complaints each plaintiff waited until the service of the *praktor* was completed before lodging his complaint.

Oxyrhynchus   6 x 14 cm   AD 49/50

Ed. pr. — G.M. Parássoglou, 'Greek Papyri from Roman Egypt', *Hellenika* 27 (1974) 233-5 (= P. Oxy. II 393 descr. = SB XIV 11902).

	Τιβερίωι Κλαυδίωι	To Tiberius Claudius
	Πασείωνει στρατηγῶι	Pasion *strategos*
	παρὰ 'Αριστᾶτος τοῦ	from Aristas son of
	Πλούτου, τῶν ἀπ' Ὀξυρύγ-	Ploutos, of those from
5	χων πόλεως γερδίων	Oxyrhynchus, weaver,
	λαύρας Ἱππέων Παρεμ-	of the quarter of the cavalry barracks.
	βολῆς. Διεσίσθην	I have suffered extortion
	ὑπὸ Δάμιτος	by Damis,
	γενομένου πράκτορος	former *praktor*,
10	τῷ μὲν η (ἔτει) Τιβερίου	in year 8 of Tiberius
	Κλαυδίου Καίσαρος	Claudius Caesar
	Σεβαστοῦ Γερμανικοῦ	Augustus Germanicus
	Αὐτοκράτορος	Imperator
	ἀργυρίου δραχμὰς δέκα	(to the amount of) sixteen silver
15	ἕξ, καὶ τῷ διελ(λ)ηλυθό-	drachmae, and in the past

---

[97] Wallace, *Taxation* 197.

τει θ̄ (ἔτει) ἄλλας ε̣ἴκ̣[οσι]	year 9 another twenty
τέσσαρος κατὰ μ[έρος]	four among in part
[ ]̣[ ]	[...]

....

2. Πασίωνι   7. διεσείσθην   15-16 διεληλυθότι   17. τέσσαρας

Lewis[98] argues that the change from the farming to the appointment of individuals to liturgies for the collection of money taxes started in the reign of Trajan and that this curtailed, though did not completely eliminate, extortion and abuse. For examples see *BGU* III 908 (reign of Trajan),[99] *SB* XIV 12087 (AD 162), 11904 (*ca* AD 184),[100] *BGU* II 515 (AD 193) and U. Wilcken, *Griechische Ostraka* (Leipzig 1899) 606. See also *SB* 9207, an account which in part lists payments for extortion. Extortion and abuse, no doubt, allowed the liturgist to show some profit for the risk to which he had become personally liable.

One abuse requiring the issuance of a number of imperial edicts over a short period (*P. Flor.* III 382 *ll.*17-23 of AD 199, *P. Mich.* X 529 *ll.*39-53 of AD 200 = *SB* XIV 11863) was that of demanding payment from persons other than the defaulter himself (ὑπέραλλα) as though by mutual guarantee. In particular the edicts note the demanding of payments from the father for the son and vice versa. *SB* XIV 12087 is a petition from a father who was suffering such an abuse from the *praktores* of the poll-tax.

Theadelphia   31.7 x 16 cm and 27.5 x 6.5 cm   Feb./Mar. AD 162

Ed. pr. — H. C. Youtie, 'P. Mich. inv. 160 + P. Oslo II 18: μηδένα ὑπέραλλα ἀπαιτεῖσθαι', *ZPE* 23 (1976) 131-8 (= *SB* XIV 12087).

The two pieces of the same petition are published by Youtie. The Michigan piece breaks off removing much of *ll.*21-22. The petition resumes with *P. Oslo* II 18. Margins are preserved on the top, bottom and left of the text. The text runs to the right edge of the papyrus. Written parallel to the fibres in the same hand throughout. The back is blank.

P. Mich. inv. 160

Ἁρποκρατί[ω]ν̣ι̣ στρατηγῷ	To Harpokrates *strategos* of the Arsinoite
Ἀρσι(νοείτου) Θεμίστου καὶ	nome, of the Themistos and
Πολέμωνος μερίδων	Polemon divisions
παρὰ Πτολεμαίο̣υ̣ Διοδώρου τοῦ κὲ	from Ptolemaios son of Diodoros, also
Διοσκόρου ἀπὸ κώμης	called Dioskoros from the village of
Θεαδελφείας. Οὗ ἀνέτεινα	Theadelphia. A copy of the petition
βιβλιδίου τῷ κρατίστῳ	which I presented to the most excellent

---

[98] Lewis, *Life in Egypt under Roman Rule* 178-9.
[99] Lewis, *The Compulsory Public Services* 47, cites AD 100 (*SB* VI 9050i) as the earliest evidence for the office of *sitologos* being a liturgy.
[100] Lewis, *Compulsory Public Services* 45, cites AD 118 (*P. Brem.* 38) as the earliest evidence for the office of *presbyteros* being a liturgy, but also observes that its introduction could have been earlier still.

§4 Tax Collection and the τελῶναι of the New Testament

ἐπιστρατήγῳ Ο[ὐηδ]ίῳ Φαύστῳ καὶ
ἧ[ς ἔ]σχον ἐπὶ σὲ ἱερᾶς
ὑπογραφῆς καὶ ἧς ἔσχον
ἡγεμονικῆς κρίσεως περὶ ὁμοίου πράγματος ἀντίγραφον ὑπέταξα πρὸς τὸ
ἀπαρενόχλητόν με γενέσθαι. Ἔστι
δέ· Οὐηδίῳ Φαύστῳ τῷ κρατίστῳ
ἐπιστρ(ατήγῳ)
5 παρὰ Πτολεμαίου [Δ]ιοδώρου τοῦ καὶ
Διοσκόρου τῶν ἀπὸ τοῦ
Ἀρσινοείτου νομοῦ. Κατελθὼν εἰς
Ἀλεξάνδρειαν ὡς μέλ-
λοντός μου ἀν[α]τ[εί]νειν σοι τῷ
κυρίῳ [βι]βλίδιον ἐν ᾧ ἡ [ἀ]ξίωσίς
μου δηλοῦται καὶ κατὰ τὸ παρὸν
μὴ εὑρών σε ἀνέτεινα τῷ
[κ]ρατίστῳ δικαιοδότῃ ['Ερενν]ίῳ
Φ[ιλώτᾳ καὶ] ἀνέπεμψέ με ἐπὶ σὲ
καὶ δέομαι ὑποτάξας τὸ βιβλίδιον
τυχεῖν τῆς ἀπὸ σοῦ βοηθείας
[ἵ]ν᾽ ὦ βεβοηθημένο[ς]. Διευτύχει.
Ἔστι δέ· Ἑρεννίῳ Φιλώτᾳ τῷ
κρατίστῳ δικαιοδότῃ παρὰ
Πτολεμαίου Διοδώρου
τοῦ καὶ Διοσκόρου τ[ῶν] ἀπὸ τοῦ
Ἀ[ρσιν]ο[εί]του νομοῦ. Πάσης
βίας ἐκκοπείσης ἐπὶ τῆς τοῦ
λαμπροτάτου ἡγεμόνος ἐπαρ-
10 χείας καὶ τῆς σῆς [δικ]αιοδοσίας ...
τος ἐντυγχάνω ἀδικούμενος καὶ
βιαζόμενος. Τὸ δὲ πρᾶγμα
τοιοῦτον· υἱὸν ἔχω, κύ-
ριε, τέλειον. Οὗτος ἀπὸ ιθ (ἔτους)
Αἰλίου Ἀντωνείνου ἀπ᾽ ἐμοῦ
ἐχωρίσθη καὶ οὔτε κοινόβιός μοι
ἐγένετο οὔτε ἐν τῇ κώ-
μῃ συννομιτεύεται. Οἱ δὲ τῆς
ἀργυρικῶ[ν] πράκτορες παρὰ τὰ
ἀπειρημένα ἀπαιτοῦσί με τὰ ὑπὲρ
αὐτοῦ ἐπικεφάλεια πάντων

epistrategos, Vedius Faustus,
of his sacred subscription which I
received for you, and of the prefectorial
judgement about a similar matter which I received
I append that I may be free from
harassment. It is:
To Vedius Faustus, the most excellent
epistrategos,
from Ptolemaios son of Diodoros also
called Dioskoros, of those from the
Arsinoite nome. Travelling down to
Alexandria to
present to you, my lord,
a petition in which my request
is made known and at the time
not finding you I presented (it) to
the most excellent *iuridicus* Herennius
Philotas and he referred me to you.
Appending the petition I ask
to receive your benefaction
that I might be helped. Farewell.
It is: To Herennius Philotas, the
most excellent *iuridicus*, from
Ptolemaios son of Diodoros
also called Dioskoros, of those from the
Arsinoite nome. All force being
eradicated under the governorship
of the most illustrious prefect
and your jurisdiction [...]
I petition as I am suffering wrongs and
violence. The matter is such:
I have, my lord, a grown son.
He left me from the 19th year of
Aelius Antoninus and
neither has he lived with me
nor does he live together with anyone
in the village. The *praktores
argyrikon* contrary to what is forbidden
demand from me the poll-taxes for him
though all

τῶν ἐπάρχων διατα[ξ]άντων μηδένα
ὑπέραλλα ἀπαιτεῖσθαι. Οὗτοι δὲ
περιφρονοῦντες τὰ ὡρισμένα
βιάζονται
εἰς τὸ διασεί‹ει›ν με ἐ[πὶ]
τοσοῦτον ὥ[στ]ε ὑπ' αὐτῶν
ἐκδιωχθῆναι ἐν καιρῷ κατασπορᾶς
καὶ χιμῶνος, ὅθεν ἐπὶ
15 σὲ κατέφυγον ὅπως [τ]ύχω τῶν
δικαί[ω]ν κἄν σου τῇ τύχῃ δόξῃ
κελεῦσαι γραφῆν[αι] τῷ τῆς
μερί[δ]ος στρ(ατηγῷ)
Ἁρποκρατίωνί
[με ἀ]παρενόχλητον φυλάξα[ι].
Λέγουσι γάρ με τὰ ἴδ[ι]ά μου
δημόσια ἐκτίλειν ἀμέμπτως.
Διευτύχει. Πτολεμαῖος
[ἐπιδέδ]ωκα. (Ἔτους) β̄
Ἁ[δρ]ιαν[οῦ] γ. Τῷ
κρατίστῳ ἐπιστρ(ατήγῳ)
ἔντυχε. Ἀπόδος.
Πτολεμαῖος ἐπιδέδωκα.
(Ἔτους) β̄ Τῦβι ῑϛ.
Ὁ [στρατηγ]ὸς [ὅ] τι πρὸ[ς] α[ὐτ]όν
ἐστ[ι]ν ποιήσει. Ἀπόδος.
Ἀντίγραφον ὑπομνηματισμοῦ·
(ἔτους) ῑε Ἀν[τ]ωνίνου Καίσαρος
τοῦ κυρίου Φαμενὼθ ¯ κληθέντος
Πετεχῶντος Πετεπειθῆς
Νεφθερῶντος [..] ὑποτυχὼν
εἶπεν· ου
20 τ[..]ει[.]...ο[.] συνι... τεθ..αι ἵνα
τὸν υἱὸν αὐτοῦ παραστήσῃ
ὀμνύοντα ἐν Ἀλεξανδρείᾳ
ἄντικρυς περὶ χει-
ριστείας ἧς ἔχει ἐν Σενδ[υ]πὲ εἰ
ἀνήρπασέν τινα...[   ]
θέ[σ]θαι φ....[   ]

the prefects have ordered that *hyperalla* be
demanded from no-one. These
persons defying their orders
use violence
to extort (money from) me to
such an extent as to be pursued by them
at harvest-time
and in winter, whence to
you I flee that I may receive
justice, and if it seems good to your
genius, order that the *strategos*
of the division, Harpokrates,
be written to
to keep me from harassment.
For they say that I pay all my
public dues faultlessly.
Farewell. I, Ptolemaios,
have delivered (the petition). Year 2 of
Hadrianus, day [.]3. Petition the
most excellent *epistrategos*.
Return (to the petitioner). I,
Ptolemaios, have delivered (the
petition). Year 2, Tybi 16.
The *strategos* will do what is in his
competence. Return (to the
petitioner). Copy of minutes:
Year 15 of Antoninus Caesar
the lord, Phamenoth [date lost]. Petechon
having been summoned, Petepeithes
son of Nephtheron [...] having
interrupted said
[...] that
he might produce his son
swearing in Alexandria
openly concerning
the agency which he holds in Sendypai if
he stole anything [...]
[...]

P. Oslo II 18

[ ]ον.........ισσο[.] αὐτόν,	[...] him,
περὶ ὧν Κάνωπος Δωρίων⟨ος⟩	concerning which Kanopos son of
ῥήτωρ παρεστὼς	Dorion, advocate defending
[Πετε]πειθῆ εἶπεν· [φη]μὶ δὴ	Petepeithes said: Indeed I declare
μηδεμίαν συνθήκην γεγονέναι	that there was no such
τοιαύτην. Ἁπλᾶ ἐστιν τὰ	agreement. Our point is
λεγό⟨με⟩να· χειρισ-	simple.
[τῆς] ὁ υἱός σου ἦν [τ]οῦ	Your son was an agent of my
συνηγορουμένου. Ἀνήρπασέν τινα.	client. He stole something.
Παράστησον αὐτόν. Μουνάτιος	Produce him. Munatius
εἶπεν· οὐκ ⟨ο⟩ἶδα	said: I do not understand
[οὐδ]ὲν περὶ ὧν λέγε[ις].	anything concerning what you are
Καὶ γὰρ εἰ ἀνδροφόνος ἐκεῖνος	speaking. For even if that man were to
λημφ⟨θ⟩είη, οὐ δεῖ τὸν πατέρα	have been apprehended as a murderer,
αὐτοῦ ὑπεύθυνον	his father should not be responsible.
5 [εἶνα]ι. Κάνωπος Δωρίωνος ῥήτωρ	Kanopos son of Dorion, advocate,
εἶπεν· ὀμοσάτω ὅτι μὴ συνέθετο	said: Let him swear that he did not
παραστῆσαι τὸν υἱόν. Μου-	agree to produce his son.
[νάτι]ος εἶπεν· τί ε[ἰ]σάγεις	Munatius said: Why do you prosecute this
ἔ[χ]ων τοῦτον ἀδίκως καὶ	man, when you hold him illegally, and
[ὅρ]κον αἰτεῖς; Πτολεμαῖος	demand an oath? I, Ptolemaios son of
Διοδώρου	Diodoros,
[ἐπή]νεγκα. (Ἔτους) β̄ Αἰλίων	have brought (this petition). Year 2 of the
Ἀντωνίνου καὶ Οὐήρου Καισ[άρ]ων	Aelii Antoninus and Verus, Caesars our
τῶν κυρίων Φαμενώθ.	lords, Phamenoth.

....

Col. 1: 2. καί   12. τῶν instead of τῆς   16. ἐκτίνειν   19. ἐπιτυχών (?)

As the decision of the *strategos* is lacking at the end of the text, it may be assumed that the petition is a copy made before its submission to that official. This is consistent with the fact that the entire petition is written in the same hand. The copy was presumably retained by the plaintiff for his own records. The original petition was made to the *iuridicus*, Herennius Philotas (*ll*.8-17). It was answered with his subscription to petition the *epistrategos* (*l*.17). The *epistrategos* was duly petitioned (*ll*.4-8) and a copy of the original petition appended. His reply was to refer the matter to the *strategos* (*l*.18). In the present document the petitioner refers the matter to the *strategos* (*ll*.1-4) including copies of the petition to the *epistrategos* and his subscription (*ll*.8-18). To this was added a copy of the minutes of a judicial hearing (AD 152) before the prefect, Lucius Munatius Felix.

The petitioner is known from the census declaration *P. Wisc.* I 36 to have been 25 years old in AD 147. At that time he had only one child, Dioskoros also called Heron, aged 3. If this is the child who had disappeared in AD 155/6 (*SB* 12087 *l*.11) — as Dioskoros would have been the oldest child, the assumption is reasonable — then he would have been only 12 years old when this occurred. Youtie comments: 'Ptolemaios offers no explanation, but as we have good reason to know, there is nothing far-fetched in this situation.' In AD 161/2 the *praktores* were seeking to exact arrears from the father for his long-since disappeared son. Such an abuse was strictly prohibited by later imperial decree (AD 199-200). From the present text the petitioner refers to prohibition by decrees of the prefects (*ll*.12-13). In view of the similarity of language between the petition and later imperial edicts Youtie assumes that their language was 'borrowed from an earlier edict aimed at the same abuse' and that 'the phraseology had become traditional in edicts of this class'. The assumption of a borrowing is consistent with the statement in *ll*.12-13. But a query can be raised concerning the general acceptance of these edicts at the time of our petition. For surely the point of the appended minutes (i.e. the judicial hearing before the prefect Munatius) is to argue by analogy that a father is not responsible for his adult son, an argument which would have been superfluous if earlier prefectorial edicts on ὑπέραλλα were generally recognized.

Taxation in Judaea

The financial administration of Judaea in the Roman period is understood by Rostovtzeff[101] by analogy with that in operation in Egypt. After a brief period in which *publicani* were used to collect the *stipendium* (56-44 BC),[102] the former Hellenistic system of taxation was restored by Caesar. Small tax-farmers (mostly indigenous provincials as in Egypt) purchased the various taxes in cash and *ad valorem* duties and could only demand within the limits of a fixed amount (Luke 3.12-13). As well, since they denounced taxpayers to officials (Luke 19.8), it would appear that the tax-farmer in Palestine could not unilaterally proceed against a recalcitrant taxpayer but had to proceed through the official institutions.[103] Arrears, as in Egypt, were collected by officials.

In asserting the similarity between the tax systems of Egypt and Judaea/Palestine Rostovtzeff is followed by most other scholars. For example, Youtie argues that in the Roman period from the time of Augustus only indirect taxes (custom duties, tolls, market-taxes, trade-taxes etc.) were sold to the tax-farmers of Egypt and Palestine. Direct taxes were collected by government agent, e.g. the *praktores* in Egypt. He seeks to distance somewhat the tax-farmers of Palestine from the corruption and abuse known to have been practised by the τελῶναι of the Greek city-states and the Roman *publicani* operating in western provinces before the principate.[104] Instead he argues for a closer parallel between them and the tax-farmers of Graeco-Roman Egypt. Points of similarity include:

(a) Both groups were predominantly small local businessmen; the larger corporation was absent.
(b) The government regulated both groups with respect to the collection of taxes.

---

[101] Rostovtzeff, *Geschichte der Staatspacht* 475. Cf. also *P. Dura* 13 (first century AD), an application of a tax-farmer. The editor argues that the tax system of the Arsacid Parthians continued that of their Seleucid predecessors and was very like that known to operate in Ptolemaic Egypt and its external territories. The document attests then the similarity of administrative concepts held in the Hellenistic world.

[102] Rostovtzeff argues that Judaea was organized into five parts each with a central city and an aristocratic *synhedrion*. The *publicani* concluded contracts (*pactiones*) with these cities who were then responsible for the collection of taxes through the *synhedrion*.

[103] H.C. Youtie, 'Publicans and Sinners', *ZPE* 1 (1967) 574, also argues from the use of ἐσυκοφάντησα ('I have brought false charges') in the Zacchaeus story (Luke 19.8) that the tax-farmer could not unilaterally proceed against a recalcitrant taxpayer.

[104] Youtie, *ZPE* 1 (1967) 562-566.

Youtie notes the ambivalence of Jesus's attitude to the tax-farmers. Jesus seemed to recognize, it is argued, the right of Rome to raise taxes ('Render to Caesar') and thus the right of tax-collectors, and he associated with tax-farmers, yet in the collocations such as 'sinners and tax-farmers' an antipathy is manifested. It might be objected against Youtie's argument that the meaning of Jesus's teaching, 'Render to Caesar' is quite ambiguous. For example, Daube[105] has noted that 'this in the mouth of Jesus is by no means a counsel of subservience to the state, rather one of minimum performance'. It might also be addeed that the saying's intention is deliberately ambiguous with the interpretation of its meaning very much dependent on the perspective of the hearer. If one was inclined to view Rome as a hostile and blasphemous power as the Zealots did, then the saying would be construed quite differently.

To return to MacMullen's point that complaints regarding matters of taxation were in response to individual instances of extortion and abuse, it can reasonably be asked whether the documentary and legal evidence for this assertion is somewhat biased. An official complaint would more probably concern a matter of abuse or an illegal action. To question the system through official channels potentially entailed a criticism of the government itself and would tend only to be entertained by individuals, associations or cities who could rely on the emperor's favourable hearing. This is not to say that such complaints and criticisms were not made, but these are largely unofficial in nature, e.g. the Jewish and Christian use of 'prophetic' literature to express criticism of Rome.[106] MacMullen and Fuchs[107] cite the criticism of Rabbi Gamaliel II (first/second century AD) concerned with 'cultural smothering' and the 'economic exploitation' of the system of taxation: 'This empire gnaws at our substance through four things: its tolls, its bath buildings, its theatres, and its taxes in kind.'

Youtie tries to delineate between opinion and reality, nationalistic bias and religious disposition in the matter of tax-farmers. He uses the documentary evidence from Egypt to argue his case. He contrasts the difference between the common impression that tax-farmers were given to extortion and oppression, and the infrequency of actual evidence (e.g. petitions and edicts) against them. Youtie also suggests that when considering the reputation of tax-farmers one needs also to reckon with the inclination of the taxpayer to avoid or understate his liabilities. The actions of the tax-farmer should be viewed in the light of his own personal liabilities for any short-fall in collections and the unwillingness of taxpayers to pay their dues. He also notes the difference between the general perception that tax-farmers were wealthy and other evidence which suggests that profits were not excessive, perhaps a little higher than an annual return of 12% on their investment (witness government inducements to take up contracts). Youtie suggests that the latter perception is explained by the fact that within their communities tax-farmers as the local bourgeois were comparatively better off than the small landholders and tenants who made up the bulk of taxpayers. Nationalistic bias may also have sharpened the perception. On the question as to whether Jesus's stance was motivated by a nationalistic bias, Youtie suggests that the religious stance of Jesus and his attitude to the poor (opposition to the rich) may have influenced his view but that Jesus was always ready to accept tax-farmers. He concludes that the negative collocation 'sinners and tax-collectors' was a

---

[105] D. Daube, 'Responsibilities of Masters and Disciples in the Gospels', *NTS* 19 (1972/3) 15.

[106] See R. MacMullen, *Enemies of the Roman Order. Treason, Unrest, and Alienation in the Empire* (Cambridge, Mass. 1966) 128-162, and A.Y. Collins, *Crisis and Catharsis. The Power of the Apocalypse* (Philadelphia 1984) 90-4.

[107] MacMullen, *Enemies of the Roman Order* 148-9, and H. Fuchs, *Der geistige Widerstand gegen Rom in der antiken Welt* (1938, repr. Berlin 1964) 70. Fuchs (p.71) cites further examples of rabbinic criticism against the perceived greed of Rome and its system of taxation.

pedagogical device which like many of his parables involves a less than morally commendable action.

Herrenbrück[108] also argues against the view that the τελῶναι of the gospels were *publicani* (Roman *equites* whose *societas publicanorum* had contracted the collection of tributes and taxes in a province) or *portitores* (collectors of custom duties). He follows Rostovtzeff and Youtie in identifying them rather as Hellenistic small tax-farmers whose function and role can be clarified by the evidence from Graeco-Roman Egypt. Appeal to evidence from Egypt is justified by a common heritage; the Ptolemaic system of taxation was introduced into Palestine by Ptolemy I Soter and Ptolemy II Philadelphos and was continued and maintained under Seleucid, Hasmonean and Roman rule (with a brief interlude of *publicani* between 63 and 47/44 BC). Tax-farming in Palestine was finally replaced by liturgies in the third and fourth centuries AD. But Herrenbrück disagrees with certain assumptions of Rostovtzeff and Youtie: (a) that Augustus changed the system of taxation by limiting the farming of taxes to indirect taxes; (b) that the tax-farmers were in the service of Rome; and (c) that the τελῶναι of Egypt had nothing to do with the collection of taxes. He argues that the tax-farmers of Palestine were wealthy individuals who belonged to the upper-middle or upper classes of society.

S.R.L.

---

[108] F. Herrenbrück, 'Wer waren die >Zöllner<?', *ZNTW* 72 (1981) 178-194, and idem, *Jesus und die Zöllner* (Tübingen 1990).

§5 Taxes on Donkeys: An Illustration of Indirect Taxation at Work in Roman Egypt

Hermopolite or Oxyrhynchite nome   11 x 12.5 cm   3 Sept. AD 65

Ed. pr. — C. Wehrli, 'Reçu délivré par un τελώνης ἑξαδραχμίας', ZPE 40 (1980) 181-183 (= *P. Gen.* II 95).

The text of the papyrus is written parallel to the fibres with margins of 2.5 cm (top), 1 cm (bottom), 1.5 cm (left), and 3.5 cm (right). The back is blank.

Ἑρμαῖο(ς) Διογᾶ(τος) τελ(ώνης)	Hermaios son of Diogas farmer of the
(ἑξαδραχμίας) ὄνω(ν)	six-drachma tax on donkeys
ια (ἔτους) Νέρωνος τοῦ κυρίου	for (year) 11 of Nero, the lord,
Μητόκωι Στράτωνος	to Metokos son of Straton
χ(αίρειν). ἀπέχω παρὰ σοῦ ἃς	greeting. I receive from you
ὀφείλ(εις)	the
5 κατὰ χειρόγρα(φον) ἀργ(υρίου)	sixteen silver dr. which you owe
(δραχμὰς) δεκαέξ,	by note-of-hand,
(γίνονται) (δραχμαὶ) ις, (ἔτους) ιβ	(total) 16 dr., (year) 12
Νέρωνος	of Nero
Κλαυδίου Καίσαρος Σεβαστοῦ	Claudius Caesar Augustus
Γερμανικοῦ Αὐτοκράτορος	Germanicus Imperator
μη(νὸς) Σεβαστοῦ ς.	in the month of Augustus, 6.

The provenance of the papyrus is suggested by the name of the tax (see below). As *P. Gen.* 95 does not possess the usual form of a fiscal receipt but makes specific mention of the lender's position as τελώνης ἑξαδραχμίας, Wehrli conjectures that the debt was not a simple loan but associated with the collection of the six-drachma tax. The reconstruction is as follows: Hermaios, as the tax-farmer of the six-drachma tax on donkeys, had not exacted from Metokos an immediate payment of the tax. Instead he had taken upon himself the responsibility of paying the tax owed by Metokos. The taxpayer's debt had been transformed into a loan and secured by a *cheirographon* or note-of-hand made out by Metokos in favour of Hermaios. As the farmer of the tax for year 11 and thus liable for any shortfall in the sum tendered for the collection of that year, Hermaios appears to have preferred to convert a public arrear into a private debt. According to this explanation *P. Gen.* 95 represents Hermaios's receipt of repayment in the subsequent year 12.

To account for the amount paid Wehrli suggests that there were three donkeys charged at 5 dr. 1 ob. each (the amount charged in *P. Oxy.* XII 1438) together with an interest payment of 3 ob. The small interest payment can be explained by the short term of the loan with repayment occurring a few days after the end of the financial year.

Oxyrhynchite nome?   11.5 x 7.3 cm   second/third century AD

Ed. pr. — P.J. Sijpesteijn, 'Three Papyri from the Michigan Collection', *ZPE* 33 (1979) 244-248 (= *P. Mich.* XV 709).

The text of the papyrus runs parallel to the fibres with margins of c. 3.5 cm (bottom), c. 1.5 cm (top), and 1 cm (left). There are four vertical folds. The back is blank. The papyrus has been dated on palaeographical grounds to the end of the second or the beginning of the third century AD. The date of ιη (ἔτος) in *l*.8 suggests two possibilities, AD 176/7 or 208/9.

['Η]ρακλείδης καὶ 'Αρτεμᾶς	We, Herakleides, Artemas
[κ]αὶ οἱ μ[έ]τοχ(οι) ἀπ⟨αιτ⟩ητ(αὶ)	and associates, collectors of the
(ἑξαδραχμίας) ὄνων	six-drachma (tax) on donkeys
[π]όλεως ὅρμου νομοῦ	of the city, harbour (and) nome
[ἐ]νχωροῦμεν Ἑρεννίωι	permit Herennius
5 ἀπὸ Φιλαδελφίας τοῦ 'Αρσινοΐ-	from Philadelphia of the Arsinoite
[το]υ νομοῦ ἐμπορεύσασθαι	nome to trade
[ἐν τῶι] νομῶι η...[..]..π..	[in the] nome [...]
σ.[....]. πρὸς τὸ ἐνεστὸ(ς)	[...] for the present
ιη (ἔτος)	(year) 18
δραχμὰς ἓξ ὀβολ(οὺς) β̄,	six drachmae 2 obols.
10 (γίνονται) (δραχμαὶ) ϛ̄ (δυόβολος).	(Total) 6 dr. two ob.

The papyrus does not state the nome in which the collectors of the ἑξαδραχμία operated. However, as a tax of this name is only attested in the Hermopolite and Oxyrhynchite nomes, the editor suggests that the receipt could have been issued in either. The Oxyrhynchite nome is favoured because of the scarcity of papyri from the Hermopolite nome in the Michigan collection. If so, it would appear that the six-drachma tax was paid by Herennius (from Philadelphia in the Arsinoite nome) in order that he might trade in another nome. On the preference for capitation taxes placed on trades by the Roman government see Wallace, *Taxation*, pp.191-193. As Wallace observes (p.213): 'Capitation taxes on trades were one of the most important sources of revenue exploited by the Roman administration in Egypt'.

Unlike *P. Gen.* 95 which was issued by a tax-farmer (τελώνης), *P. Mich.* 709 is made out by two ἀπαιτηταί and their associates. The persons were probably liturgists. Persons who held the office collected payments in cash exclusively, at least until the end of the second century. By contrast registrations of donkeys in the Oxyrhynchite and Hermopolite nomes are addressed to οἱ ἐξειληφότες τὴν ἑξαδραχμίαν τῶν ὄνων. The latter were tax-farmers.[1] See Table 6 below. The registrations are dated to between 4 BC and AD 119. Between the last registration and *P. Mich.* 709 (second/third century AD) the collection of the tax had probably become a liturgical office.[2] Lewis[3] cites *P. Rein.* 135 (AD 129) as the earliest attestation of ἀπαιτηταί. However, the earliest evidence that the office had become liturgical does not occur until the late third century, but by implication Lewis believes that the change occurred earlier.

---

[1] According to U. Wilcken, *Griechische Ostraka* (Leipzig 1899) 575, the titles ἀπαιτηταί and ἐξειληφότες represented liturgists and tax-farmers respectively.

[2] Cf. also the receipt *O. Tait* II 1078 (Thebaid, AD 129). Here the receipt is also issued by a tax farmer for a six-drachma tax on donkeys.

[3] N. Lewis, *The Compulsory Public Services of Roman Egypt* (Florence 1982) 14.

§5 Taxes on Donkeys: An Illustration of Indirect Taxation at Work in Roman Egypt

Euhemeria (in the Arsinoite nome)   14.6 x 8.3 cm   AD 204-206

Ed. pr. — C.A. Nelson, *BGU* XV 2520 (Berlin 1983) 125-129.

The papyrus is broken at the bottom and on the left with over half of each line missing. A blank space of 2 cm is left at the top. The script is described as 'average size, slanted, and moderately experienced. Several letters have been made with a dull pen and are larger than the others ... The third hand is more careless and inexperienced than the first two.' The editor detects at least three different hands with each apparently recording payments for a single year. The back is blank.

[ἔτους ιγ(?) Λουκίου Σεπτιμίου	[Year 13(?) of Lucius Septimius
Σεουήρου Ε]ὐσεβοῦ[ς] Περτίνακος	Severus] Pius Pertinax
καὶ Μάρκου	and Marcus
[Αὐρηλίου Ἀντωνείνου Εὐσεβοῦς	[Aurelius Antoninus Pius,
Σεβαστῶν 〚καὶ Που〛βλίου	Augusti, 〚and of Pu〛blius
Σεπτιμίου Γέτα Καίσαρος	Septimius Geta Caesar
〚Σεβαστοῦ〛, (month and day).	Augustus〛, (month and day).
διέγρ(αψεν) (name)	Marcus [... has paid to (name) and his
καὶ μετόχ(οις) πράκτορ]σι σιτικ(ῶν)	associates, *praktores*] of grain (taxes)
Εὐημερείας Μάρκου	at Euhemeria,
[± 30 letters ὑπ(ὲρ) διπ(λώματος)]	[... for the licence] of
ιγ (ἔτους) δραχ(μὰς) τέσσαρες	(year) 13 four drachmae
τετρώβολ(ον),	four obols,
5 [(γίνονται) (δραχμαὶ) δ τετρώβολ(ον)	[(total) 4 (drachmae) four obols and
καὶ (month and day) ὑπ(ὲρ)	(month and day) for the
διπ(λώματος) ιγ(?) (ἔτους) δραχ(μὰς)]	licence of (year) 13(?)] twelve
δώδεκα ὀβολ(οὺς) δώδεκα,	[drachmae] twelve obols,
(γίν.) (δρ.) ιβ (ὀβ.) ιβ	(total) 12 dr. 12 ob.
[καὶ (month and day) ὑπ(ὲρ) διπ(λώματος)	[and (month and day) for the licence of
ιγ(?) (ἔτους) δραχ(μὰς) ὀκτὼ(?)	(year) 13(?) 8(?) drachmae
ὀβολ(οὺς) ὀκτώ(?), (γίν.) (δρ.) η(?) (ὀβ.)	8(?) obols, (total) 8(?) dr. 8(?) ob.]
η(?)] καὶ Μεχεὶρ κη ὑπ(ὲρ)	and Mecheir 28 for the
διπ(λώματος) ιγ (ἔτους)	licence of (year) 13
[δραχ(μὰς) ὀκτὼ(?) ὀβολ(οὺς) ὀκτώ(?),	[8(?) drachmae 8(?) obols,
(γίν.) (δρ.) η(?) (ὀβ.) η(?) (m.2) (month	(total) 8(?) dr. 8(?) ob. (m.2) (month
and day)] διὰ Νεμεσιανοῦ	and day)] through Nemesianos,
τοῦ καὶ	also called
[(name) ὑπ(ὲρ) διπ(λώματος) ιδ(?) (ἔτους)	[(name), for the licence of (year) 14(?),
δραχ(μὰς) ὀκτὼ ὀβολ(οὺς) ὀκτώ,]	8 drachmae 8 obols],
(γίν.) (δρ.) η (ὀβ.) η καὶ Ἀθὺρ	(total) 8 dr. 8 ob. and Hathyr
λ δι(ὰ) Ποσιδω[νίου]	30 through Posidonios

[ὑπ(ὲρ) διπ(λώματος) ιδ(?) (ἔτους) δραχ(μὰς) ὀκτώ(?) ὀβολ(οὺς) ὀκτώ(?), (γίν.) (δρ.) η̄(?) (ὀβ.) η̄(?) καὶ (month)] λ̄ διὰ Νεμεσιανὸς τοῦ καὶ	[for the licence of (year) 14(?) 8(?) drachmae 8(?) obols, (total) 8(?) dr. 8(?) ob. and (month)] 30 through Nemesianos, also called
10 [(name) ὑπ(ὲρ) διπ(λώματος) ιδ(?) (ἔτους) δραχ(μὰς) ὀκτὼ ὀβολ(οὺς) ὀκτ]ώ, (γίν.) (δρ.) η̄ (ὀβ.) η̄ καὶ Φαρμοῦθι λ̄	[(name), for the licence of (year) 14(?), 8 drachmae 8 obols], (total) 8 dr. 8 ob. and Pharmouthi 30
[ὑπ(ὲρ) διπ(λώματος) ιδ(?) (ἔτους) δραχ(μὰς) ὀκτώ(?) ὀβολ(οὺς) ὀκτώ(?), (γίν.) (δρ.) η̄(?) (ὀβ.) η̄(?) (m.3) καὶ Θ]ωθ(?) λ̄ ὑπ(ὲρ) διπ(λώματος) ιε̄ (ἔτους) δραχ(μὰς) ὀκτὼ (ὀβολοὺς) η̄,	[for the licence of (year) 14(?), 8(?) drachmae) 8(?) obols, (total) 8(?) dr. 8(?) ob. (m.3) and] Thoth(?) 30 for the licence of (year) 15, 8 drachmae 8 (obols),
[(γίν.) (δρ.) η̄ (ὀβ.) η̄ καὶ (month and day) ὑπ(ὲρ) διπ(λώματος) ιε̄ (ἔτους) δραχ(μὰς) τέσσαρες τετρώβολ(ον), (γίν.)] (δρ.) δ̄ (τετρώβ.) [. . .]εχ ὑπ(ὲρ) τέλ(ους) ιε̄ (ἔτους) [δρα]χ(μὰς)	[(total) 8 dr. 8 ob. and (month and year) for the licence of (year) 15, 4 drachmae 4 obols, (total)] 4 dr. (4 ob.) [...] for the tax of (year) 15,
[τέσσαρες τετρώβολ(ον), (γίν.) (δρ.) δ̄ (τετρώβ.) καὶ (month and day) ὑπ(ὲρ) διπ(λώματος) ιε̄(?) (ἔτους) δραχ(μὰς) ὀκτὼ (ὀβολοὺς) ὀκτώ, (γίν.) (δρ.)] η̄ (ὀβ.) η̄ [καὶ Χο]ίακ ῑ ὑπ(ὲρ) [διπ(λώματος)] ιε̄ (ἔτους) δραχ(μὰς)	[4 drachmae 4 obols, (total) 4 dr. (4 ob.) and (month and day) for the licence of (year) 15 eight drachmae eight (obols), (total)] 8 dr. 8 ob. [and] Choiak 10 for the licence of (year) 15,
[ὀκτώ(?) (ὀβολοὺς) ὀκτώ(?), (γίν.) (δρ.) η̄(?) (ὀβ.) η̄(?) ±15 letters] (traces of letters)	[8(?)] drachmae [8(?) (obols), (total) 8(?) dr. 8(?) ob. ...]

....

4. τέσσαρας   9. Νεμεσιανοῦ

The editor describes the papyrus as a record of payment for the *diploma* (see abbreviated designation in *ll*.6, 11) or the licence-tax[4] over a three-year period. Payments usually of 8 dr. 8 ob. appear to have been made four times each year. Interestingly in *ll*.4-5 a 4 dr. 4 ob. payment is followed by another for 12 dr. 12 ob. From this it would appear that a reduced fractional payment for the *diploma* might be made up by a larger subsequent payment. It is assumed that this also was the case with the reduced payment recorded in *l*.12. Though the amount is not preserved, in *l*.12 a payment ὑπ(ὲρ) τέλ(ους) is recorded. In view of the fact

---

[4] That the *diploma* should be considered to be a licence-tax is articulated by several scholars, e.g. Grenfell-Hunt, *P. Tebt.* II 360 (p.197); P.M. Meyer, *P. Hamb.* I 9 (p.32); and A.C. Johnson, *Roman Egypt* (New Jersey 1959) 557. The use of *diplomata* for other purposes is also attested. For example, they were issued to some individuals allowing them to use the official post/transport system. They were also issued to troops to allow them to requisition means of transport. See *New Docs* 7 (1994) 13-25 and 62-87.

that all other payments appear to have been for the *diploma* the editor suggests that the term τέλος is to be understood as an alternate designation for the *diploma*.

Payments of the *diploma* appear to have been made by one Marcus to the πράκτορες σιτικῶν (*l*.3) of Euhemeria. The names of two assistants of the tax officials are given as Nemesianos and Poseidonios respectively (*ll*.7, 9). Though the tax officials' title gives no indication as to the reason for the payment, the editor surmises both from the designation of the payment (δίπλωμα), its amount (8 dr. 8 ob.) and the use of a running record of payment[5] that it was a tax on donkeys. It is unclear why the payment was made to the *praktores* of the grain tax, especially as here the payments are in cash rather than kind; cf. *P. Ryl.* II 194 where the payment for what appears to be the δίπλωμα ὄνων was made to the πράκτωρ ἀργυρικῶν. But the impost appears to have been given in the Arsinoite nome to a range of different officials to collect. See Table 2 below. Until at least AD 146 the *diploma* was farmed, though the contractors were variously named μισθωτής (*BGU* I 213), ἐγλήμπτωρ (*P. Hamb.* I 9) and πραγματευτής (*P. Tebt.* II 360). In the case of *BGU* XV 2520 (AD 204-206) I assume that the collection was made by liturgists. The anomaly is *P. Ryl.* 194 (AD 134-136) in which the collection is again made by a person who may be assumed to hold a liturgy, i.e. a πράκτωρ ἀργυρικῶν. But importantly the papyrus is dated earlier than both *P. Hamb.* 9 (AD 143-146) and *P. Tebt.* 360 (AD 146) which attest the continued collection of the impost by tax-farmers. The amount of the payment of 4 obols in *P. Ryl.* 194 is also anomalous. In view of both difficulties it seems preferable to consider the payment of 4 obols not as an instalment of a regular payment but rather as an irregular payment. Such irregular payments (e.g. arrears or penalties) were collected by *praktores* in the Ptolemaic period and may well have continued to be collected by them under Roman rule.

Returning to *BGU* 2520, a partial explanation for the collection of the *diploma* by the *praktores* of the grain tax might be that the latter liturgists had extensive dealings with the owners of donkeys and other animals of burden. See *New Docs* 7 (1994) 112-127. The step may also have only been an interim one. But caution is necessary as the exact purpose of the *diploma* is only inferred from and not stated in *BGU* 2520.

Registration and Licence-Taxes

In Roman Egypt various livestock in private ownership (e.g. sheep, goats, camels, horses and donkeys) were subject to annual registration or ἀπογραφή.[6] Tax-lists were prepared from these and owners paid a fixed licence-tax (τὸ καθῆκον τέλος, i.e. it was not a fluctuating *ad valorem* tax on property) on each mature animal.[7] The amount of the licence-tax varied according to the type of animal; sheep were taxed at one rate, donkeys (and perhaps horses) at another and camels at a different rate again. For the same type of animal the licence-tax also varied between nomes. The evidence for the licence-tax on donkeys is quite diverse as the

---

[5] Cf. *P. Hamb.* 9. Meyer observes that 'with each new payment the sheet was submitted to him (i.e. to the assistant of Maximus, the ἐγλήμπτωρ διπλώματος ὄνων νομοῦ καὶ ἄλλων ὠνῶν) for receipting'. An annual amount of 8 dr. 8 ob. was paid for each beast.

[6] From the reign of Claudius there were two registrations of sheep annually. By the end of the first century it had reverted to one again. See *P. Köln* VII 188 (pp.188-189).

[7] Those who leased animals from the crown paid a φόρος; those who owned animals paid a fixed τέλος. The topic is treated by S. Wallace, *Taxation in Egypt from Augustus to Diocletian* (1938: reprinted New York 1969) 77-95. Wallace (pp.143-145) holds that because of recording difficulties the ὑϊκή (a tax on pigs) in some nomes was a μερισμός rather than licence-tax, i.e. an amount that was assessed and distributed over the entire tax-paying populace of a district.

following tables indicate. In AD 112-113 (see *BGU* 213) the licence-tax on donkeys (δίπλωμα ὄνων) in the Arsinoite nome was 8 drachmae. Some thirty years later in the same nome (see *P. Hamb.* 9, AD 143-146) the licence-tax on horses was 8 dr. 8 ob. However; as the payments were made to the ἐγλήμπτωρ διπλώματος ὄνων νομοῦ καὶ ἄλλων ὠνῶν, Wallace[8] holds that the same amount was paid on donkeys as on horses, the 8 ob. difference from the payments recorded in *BGU* 213 being due to an increase in the tax over the thirty-year period. Documents from other nomes again show a lower annual rate. For example, from the Oxyrhynchite nome in 4-3 BC a rate of 5 dr. 1 ob. is recorded for a payment called ἑξαδραχμία τῶν ὄνων (see *P. Oxy.* XII 1438 and 1457). The tax rolls from Karanis (AD 171-174) record a 6 dr. payment for donkeys in a tax called πενταδραχμία (*P. Mich.* IV 223 *ll*.3028 and 3034; 224 *ll*.1902, 2520, 3474, 3749, 4563 and 5087; and 225 *l*.983).[9] Of interest is the lack of correspondence between the name of the payment and its amount.

Meyer[10] argues that the 8 dr. 8 ob. payment was made for animals employed in a trade, e.g. *P. Amh.* II 92 in the retail of oil, *P. Tebt.* II 360 in the retail of vegetables[11] and *P. Hamb.* 9, a running receipt of payments by the superintendant of the guild of machine-operators. Kortenbeutel[12] identifies the πενταδραχμία with the ἑξαδραχμία and the δίπλωμα ὄνων, which he believes were a trade-tax paid by ὀνηλάται on their donkeys. Wallace, despite the variation in the names (δίπλωμα, ἑξαδραχμία and πενταδραχμία) and in the amounts of the payment, surmises that all the payments represent a tax on privately owned donkeys (and horses)[13] and that one and the same tax applied throughout Egypt. He also notes two points of careful differentiation in the registrations of donkeys: (a) between the business and private use of donkeys: μὴ ἐργαζομένο(υς) μισθοῦ ἀλλ' εἰς ἰδίαν χρεί(α)ν (*P. Sarap.* 3 *ll*.5-6); ἐργαζομένας μου τὰ ἴδια ἔργα (*P. Oxy.* XII 1457); μὴ ἐργατικ(ὴν) μισθ(οῦ) ἀλλ' εἰς τὴ(ν) ἰδίαν χρείαν (*PSI* VII 785); and (b) between the numbers of male and female donkeys. He suggests that either one of these criteria (i.e. nature of use or sex) may have accounted for differences in recorded payments, i.e. 5 and 8 dr. payments. Youtie[14] observes the discrepancies between the names of two taxes (i.e. ἑξαδραχμία and πενταδραχμία) and the amounts paid. In the Hermopolite and Oxyrhynchite nomes where the six-drachma tax applied payments of 5 dr. and 5 dr. 1 ob. were made. In the Arsinoite nome where the five-drachma tax applied, the actual payment was 6 dr. (= 4 dr. 14 ob.). After a consideration of the procedures used to calculate payments Youtie suggests that 'the same tax was called πενταδραχμία ὄνων in the Fayum and ἑξαδραχμία ὄνων in the Hermopolite and Oxyrhynchite nomes'. 5 dr. was the basic charge and 6 dr. its effective rate (basic charge + additional charges) in both nomes. In the Arsinoite nome the impost was named after the basic charge and in the Oxyrhynchite after the effective amount. Sijpesteijn[15], who disagrees with Youtie, makes two objections. First, the actual or

---

[8] Wallace, *Taxation* 91.

[9] The payment of 4 ob. in *P. Ryl.* II 194 is considered an instalment by Wallace, *Taxation* 91.

[10] Meyer, *P. Hamb.* 9 (1913) 32.

[11] So also Wallace, *Taxation* 207. The donkey is frequently mentioned in relation to the transport of vegetables or vegetable-seeds, e.g. *BGU* XI 2110; *P. Aberd.* 40h, 41d and e; *P. Alex. Giss.* 13; *P. Customs* 306, 333, 422 (see also p.64); *P. Mil. Vogl.* II 57; *P. Wisc.* II 80 r 4; *SB* VI 9234; and *O. Deiss.* 81.

[12] H. Kortenbeutel, *BGU* IX 1894 (1937) 100.

[13] Wallace appears to have been followed by Johnson, *Roman Egypt* 405 and 557. He suggests that the *diploma* was 'a licence for private ownership of horses, donkeys, or camels or for their use in private transport'.

[14] H.C. Youtie, *Scriptiunculae* II (Amersterdam 1973) 33-34.

[15] P.J. Sijpesteijn, *P. Mich.* XV 709 (1982) 48, and idem, *ZPE* 33 (1979) 246.

effective payments for the ἑξαδραχμία in the Oxyrhynchite nome were 5 dr. and 5 dr. 1 ob. Second, the name of the tax would have expressed the basic charge and not the total amount paid.[16] He argues that the basic charges were thus 5 dr. in the Arsinoite nome and 6 dr. in the Hermopolite and Oxyrhynchite nomes. To both of these amounts extra charges might be added. Thus in *P. Mich.* XV 709 where 6 dr. 2 ob. is paid, the basic charge is 6 dr. to which an extra charge of 2 ob. for the προσδιαγραφόμενα has been added. A problem resides in the existence of 5 dr. and 5 dr. 1 ob. payments for the ἑξαδραχμία in the Oxyrhynchite nome. Sijpesteijn explains them as partial payments. He proposes that 'all the known payments for the ἑξαδραχμία/ πενταδραχμία ὄνων were connected with employment of the animals in nomes different from the ones in which their owners lived or with animals hired out by their owners', and uses the latter case to explain the statement in all three registrations that the donkeys were for private use.

The *Diploma* on Donkeys in the Arsinoite Nome

It will be noted that all applications for lease (see Table 1 below) which require the lessee to pay a *diploma* are from the Arsinoite nome. The amount to be paid is not specified.[17] Wallace, who considers the three documents *Stud. Pal.* XXII 177, *P. Amh.* II 92 and *PSI* VII 787, suggests that the *diploma* in these instances was a certificate 'connected with the concession of a monopoly of retail sales' (*Stud. Pal.* XXII 177 and *P. Amh.* 92) or a certificate 'apparently required for the privilege of making a different type of flour or bread' (*PSI* 787).[18] The publication of *P. Mil. Vogl.* II 53 castes considerable doubt over Wallace's interpretation of the *diploma* in connection with the application for lease, for in this document it becomes clear that the *diploma* was to be paid on animals used in the milling of grain. The conclusion affects the interpretation of the remaining evidence. First, one is inclined to accept that the *diploma* referred to in *PSI* VII 787 will also have been paid on animals used in the milling procedure. Second, the suggested restoration διπλώματος ἵππω[ν] δύο for *P. Amh.* 92 *ll.*21-22 seems more probable.[19] In other words, the *diploma* was to be paid in these three leases on animals used in the trade. In *Stud. Pal.* XXII 177, however, the purpose of the payment remains obscure. It should be noted, however, that in *BGU* IX 1894 *l.*77 (Theadelphia in the Arsinoite nome) payment of the δίπλωμα Τείτου θρεμμάτων is booked to the account of the ἱερατικά (*l.*59) by the civil administration. Presumably Titus was a large transport contractor

---

[16] Sijpesteijn's argument rests on the premise that the name of the tax had not become fossilized. By fossilization one means that the rate of tax had changed whilst its name had remained the same. The premise seems reasonable as it is unlikely that the rate of taxation would have declined. Indeed, commonsense and the evidence suggest the opposite; cf. the upward movement in the rate of the *diploma* between *BGU* I 213 on the one hand and *P. Hamb.* 9, *P. Tebt.* 360 and *BGU* 2520 on the other. On the possible fossilization of the names of customs duties see P.J. Sijpesteijn, *Customs Duties in Graeco-Roman Egypt* (Zutphen 1987) 79-82. As a further possible example of fossilization consider the discussion of the ἕκτον by Wallace, *Taxation* 28 and 54.

[17] The editor of *BGU* 2520 entertains the possibility that the text relates to a licence for a concession similar to the four documents of Table 1. However, because of similarities with *P. Hamb.* 9 he dismisses this possibility.

[18] Wallace, *Taxation* 186-187. Wallace suggests that the same word probably followed δίπλωμα in both *Stud. Pal.* XXII 177 and *P. Amh.* II 92.

[19] Meyer, *P. Hamb.* 9 (1913) 32.

who paid for a *diploma* on his animals (donkeys or horses).[20] Was the licence-tax in this instance paid to the temples and if so, why?

Table 1: Applications for Lease

	Date	Nome	Business	To be paid
Stud. Pal. XXII 177	AD 137	Arsinoite (Sok.Nes.)	oil-press	τέλεσμα [δ]ι̣πλώματος ἱερῶν to be paid by lessee
P. Mil. Vogl. II 53	AD 152-153	Arsinoite (Tebtynis)	mill and equipment	δίπλωμα κτηνῶν to be paid by lessee
P. Amh. II 92	AD 162-163	Arsinoite	right to retail oil	δίπλωμα ιπ . [.] to be paid by lessee
PSI VII 787	II AD	Arsinoite?	mill and equipment	δ]ι̣πλωμα̣ [?] to be paid by lessee

As noted above, Meyer[21] had already argued that the *diploma* was paid for animals employed in a trade. Following Rostovtzeff, he further suggests that on payment each animal was provided with a *diploma*, the term indicating both the tax and its associated documentation. In support of his argument he further draws attention to *P. Tebt.* 360, a receipt for the *diploma* possibly issued to a retailer of vegetables, and to *P. Hamb.* 9, a running receipt for the *diploma* paid on horses by the superintendent of the guild of machine-operators. It seems plausible to suggest that both documents refer to payments made on animals used in trade. Cf. *BGU* 213, 1894 *l.*77, *P. Ryl.* 194 and *P. Hamb.* 9. By way of analogy one might also note the stated purpose of the ἑξαδραχμία in *P. Mich.* XV 709, i.e. to trade (ἐμπορεύσασθαι), and the apparent identification between it and the τέλος ὀνηλ(ασίας) in *O. Tait* II 1078. Table 2 lists other references to the *diploma* which are not made in applications for lease.

Table 2: *Diplomata* apart from References in Applications for Lease

	Date	Nome	Paid to or through	Amount
BGU I 213	AD 112-113	Arsinoite (Karanis)	μισθωτὴς διπλώματος ὄνων	8 dr.
P. Ryl. II 194	AD 134-136	Arsinoite?	πρά[κ(τωρ) ἀργ(υρικῶν) for the 4 ob. [δί]πλ(ωμα) ὄνων	
P. Hamb. I 9	AD 143-146	Arsinoite (Theadelphia)	ἐγλήμπτωρ διπλώματος ὄνων νομοῦ καὶ ἄλλων νομῶν	8 dr. 8 ob.
P. Tebt. II 360	AD 146	Arsinoite (Tebtynis)	πραγματευταί for διπ(λώματα ?) λαχα(νοπώλου ?)	8 dr. 8 ob.
BGU IX 1894 *l.*77	AD 157	Arsinoite (Theadelphia)	δίπλωμα Τε̣ί̣τ̣(ου) θρεμμάτ(ων)	not given
BGU XV 2520	AD 204-206	Arsinoite (Euhemeria)	πράκτωρ] σιτικ(ῶν) for δίπλωμα and τέλος	8 dr. 8 ob.

As in the case of applications for lease it will be noted from Table 2 that all extant payments of the *diploma* are from the Arsinoite nome.[22] The amounts vary as do also the titles of the

---

[20] From the Thinite nome there is a possible mention of a payment called the (ἑξάδραχμος) ἱερῶν in *PIFAO* I 3 (AD 143).

[21] Meyer, *P. Hamb.* 9 (1913) 32.

[22] *P. Edfou* 272 (AD 109) from Apollonopolis Magna in the Thebaid also records a payment for a τέλ(ος) δι(πλώματος) ὄνων. However, it is not included in the list because (a) it is not in the form of a bank *diagraphe*

persons to whom they were made. Every payment uses the verb διαγράφω with the one exception of *BGU* 1894 (an extracted list of entries for all taxes paid in money). Also with the exception of *P. Ryl.* 194 (a list of payments for various taxes) all payments, where declared, are approximately 8 dr. What was the purpose of the payment? It has already been noted above that in *P. Tebt.* 360 and *P. Hamb.* 9 the *diploma* was paid on animals used in a trade. In the case of *BGU* 1894 the editor suggests that Titus was the holder of the *diploma* and was probably a large transport contractor.[23] Unfortunately, the other receipts for the *diploma* fail to give an indication of the occupation of the payee. Wilcken, whose only evidence when writing was *BGU* 213, tentatively suggested that the licence on donkeys was obtained from the imperial government to permit their use on public roads.[24] Another understanding of the tax's purpose is suggested by consideration of the five-drachma tax (Table 3) and the *penthemeros* payments on donkeys (Table 4). From this evidence it might be argued that the payment was made in lieu of providing the animals for public service.

Table 3: Five-Drachma Tax[25]

	Date	Nome	Paid	Amount
Tax Lists				
P. Col. V 1 verso 1a	AD 160	Arsinoite (Theadelphia)	(πεντάδραχμος)[26]	34 dr. $\frac{1}{2}$ ob.
BGU IX 1894 *l.*28	AD 157	Arsinoite (Theadelphia)	(πενταδραχμία) ὄνων	not given
P. Mich. IV 360	AD 171-174	Arsinoite (Karanis)	(πενταδραχμία) ὄνων	basic rate 5 dr. paid 6 dr.

As well as the eight-drachma amount collected in the Arsinoite nome for the *diploma*, there is evidence for a five-drachma tax (see Table 3). The only indication as to the nature of this lower tax is given in the wording of *P. Mich.* IV 360:

(δρ.) $\overline{\delta}$ (ὀβ.) $\overline{\iota\delta}$ (πενταδραχμίας) ὄνων τ$\overline{\gamma}$ (ἔτους) ἀπεργ(ασίας) τ$\overline{α}$ (ἔτους) (δρ.) $\overline{\epsilon}$
               προσ(διαγραφομένων) (ὀβ. $\overline{β}$), (γίν.) (δρ.) $\overline{\epsilon}$ (ὀβ. $\overline{β}$).
4 dr. 14 ob.   For the five-drachma tax on donkeys for year 13 for (public) service for year 11, 5 dr. plus 2 ob., total 5 dr. 2 ob.

The amount actually paid is that recorded in the left column, 4 dr. 14 ob. (= 6 dr.). On the method of calculation see H.C. Youtie, *Scriptiunculae* II (Amsterdam 1973) 1023-1024. In view of the use of the term ἀπεργασία it appears that this tax may have been paid in lieu of giving the donkeys for the prescribed five-day service of the state. Wallace surmises that the licence-tax of 5 or 8 drachmae may have in fact 'exempted the donkey from service in the

---

and (b) it is for an amount of 4 dr. which agrees with the amounts paid in other receipts from the Thebaid, i.e. *P. Edfou* 397 (AD 4) for a τέλ(ος) ὄνων, *P. Edfou* 270 (AD 88-89) for a τέλ(ος) ὀνη(λασίας), *O. Tait* II 1079-1081 (AD 193, AD 233 and III AD) and *O. ROM* II 160 (II-III AD) also for a τέλ(ος) ὀνη(λασίας). See below for further details. The payment thus appears to belong with the other 4 dr. payments from the Thebaid.

[23] *BGU* IX (1937) 105.
[24] Wilcken, *Griechische Ostraka* 360-361.
[25] The name of the tax appears as an abbrevation, i.e. as the number 5 (ε) followed by the drachma sign.
[26] The listing of the tax among the garden and vineyard taxes suggests to the editor (p.61) the possibility that the tax may have been the rarer πεντάδραχμος levied on garden lands in the Mendesian nome and not the πεντάδραχμος ὄνων.

corvée' (e.g. work on the embankments or government transport).²⁷ Tentative support for the suggestion, it is alleged, is provided by the amount paid for the *penthemeros* on donkeys in *P. Ryl.* 195. See Table 4.

Table 4: *Penthemeros* for Donkeys

	Date	Nome	Paid	Amount
BGU III 969 (trial)	AD 142	Arsinoite	Grain delivered to treasury in lieu of πενθήμερος ὄνων	?
P. Petaus 44 (tax list)	before AD 185	Herakleopolite (Ptol. Hormou)	πενθήμ(ερος) ὄνων	31.5 art. of wheat
P. Ryl. II 195 (tax list)	II AD	Arsinoite?	πενθήμ(ερος) ὄνων	8 dr.

We need to look more closely at Wallace's suggestion that the taxes exempted owners from providing their animals in public service. To this end *BGU* 969 needs to be considered in greater detail. The papyrus is a copy from the day-book of the judge Harpochration (Harpocration?). The issue behind the case can be pieced together with the help of *BGU* 136 (AD 135), a copy from the day-book of the *archidikastes*, Claudius Philoxenus, concerning the same dispute, and *BGU* I 77 (AD 161-180), a receipt which appears to represent a settlement of the dispute. From this evidence it would appear that on the death of the Petheus (the grandfather of Tapontos), the estate was divided between the three sons with Petheus (senior) receiving a double share as the eldest son. Petheus (senior) had conveyed his property to his daughter, Tapontos, but as she was still a minor at the time of her father's death, both Panomieus and Petheus (junior) became her guardians. See Table 5 for the family tree.

Table 5: The Family Tree of Petheus

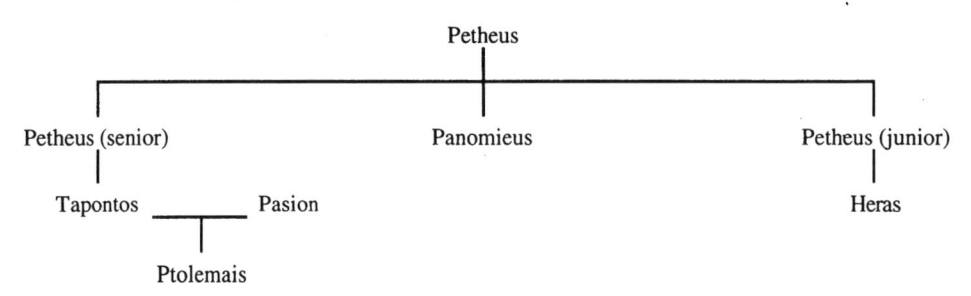

```
                          Petheus
         ┌───────────────────┼───────────────────┐
   Petheus (senior)      Panomieus          Petheus (junior)
         │                                        │
   Tapontos ──── Pasion                         Heras
         ┬
     Ptolemais
```

Tapontos alleges in *BGU* 136 that her uncles had failed to provide for her and to render an account of the estate. The uncles in reply state that her father (and their brother) had been a public donkey-driver and that they had run into expenses paying off his debts. If she wanted her inheritance, then she should indemnify them for the expenditure. Pasion, the husband of Tapontos, counter-claimed that Petheus (senior) had not been a donkey driver, and as a result Claudius Philoxenus referred the matter to the nome *strategos* for investigation. In *BGU* 969 we pick up the dispute some years later. In the meantime at least one other hearing before Harpochration had occurred (*l.*9). It now appears that the three brothers had been at one time

---

²⁷ Wallace, *Taxation* 92. On the possible interpretation of the παραζυγὴ ζυγῶν as an *adaeratio* in lieu of supplying animals for liturgical service see Wallace, *Taxation* 280-281.

κτηνοτρόφοι but that the younger brothers had been freed from κτηνοτροφία. The two uncles assert that they had met the cost of the *penthemeros* for their brother. No doubt this was one of the debts which they had earlier alleged they were owed from the estate. In *BGU* I 77 we find a receipt issued by Ptolemais to Heras for an amount owed by Heras's father (i.e. Petheus, junior) to her grandfather (i.e. Petheus, senior).

Arsinoite nome   20 cm x 19 cm   AD 142?

Ed. pr. — U. Wilcken, *BGU* III 969 (Berlin 1903) 289-291.

The papyrus is an extract from the day-book of a judge. Only col. 1 is reproduced below. Col. 2 is fragmentary due to the loss of the right edge of the papyrus sheet. From what survives it is clear that col. 2 concerns the same case and appears to have completed the extract. The hand is described as 'a clear cursive which approaches an uncial'.

     Ἀντίγραφον. Ἐξ ὑπομνηματισμοῦ
     Ἁρποχρατίωνος τοῦ καὶ Θλεσίωνος
     γεγυμνασιαρχ(ηκότος) κριτοῦ (ἔτους)
     ε̄ Ἀντωνίνου
     Καίσαρος τοῦ κυρίου Φαμενὼθ δ̄.
     Ἐπὶ
5   τῶν κατὰ Πανομιέα καὶ Πεθέα ἀμφοτέ-
     ρους Πεθέως πρὸς Πασίωνα Χαιρήμονος
     πρόδικον γυναικὸς ἑαυτοῦ. Ἀθηνόδωρος
     ῥήτ(ωρ) ὑπὲρ Πασίωνος εἶπ(εν)·
     Ἐκέλευσας διὰ τοῦ
     προτέρου ὑπομνηματισμοῦ τὸν
10 κωμογραμματέα προσφωνῆσαι, πό-
     τερός ἐστιν ὁ κτηνοτρόφος.
     Ἀπηλλάγη-
     σαν μὲν οὖν οἱ ἀντίδικοι τῆς κτηνοτρο-
     φία[ς] ἧς ἐκοινώνουν τῷ τετελευτηκότι
     καὶ εἰς τὸν συνηγορούμενον κατήντηκεν
15 ἡ κτηνοτ[ρ]οφία. Δίδυμος ῥήτ(ωρ)
     ὑ[π]ὲρ Πανο-
     μιέως καὶ Πεθέως ἀπεκρείνατ[ο]· Οἱ συνη-

Copy. From the day-book of Harpochration, also called Thlesion, former gymnasiarch, judge, year 5 of Antoninus Caesar, the lord, Phamenoth 4. Concerning the action of Panomieus and Petheus both sons of Petheus against Pasion, son of Chairemon, representative of his wife. Athenodoros, advocate for Pasion said: 'You ordered in the former day-book that the village-scribe make a report (concerning) which of the two is the animal-keeper. Therefore, the defendants were freed from the animal-keeping which they shared with the deceased and it fell to the plaintiff.'

Didymos, advocate for Panomieus and Petheus answered: 'The

γορ[ο]ύμενοι . [. .]. λε . αν ὡς κτηνοτρόφος.	accused [...] as animal-keeper.
. [. . .]. [. . . . . .]ου πατὴ[ρ] καὶ περὶ αὐτοῦ	[...] father and concerning it
οὐδεμία λοιπὸν ἀμφισ[βή]τησ[ί]ς ἐστιν	there is no dispute remaining
20 κα[ὶ] γὰρ ἐμετρήσαμεν πλῖστα ὑπὲρ τῆς	for we paid much for the
πενθ[η]μέρου. Ἐπὶ γὰρ [ο]ὐκ εἶχεν ὄνους	penthemeros. For since he had no donkeys,
ἐκεῖνος, ἡμεῖς ἐδώκαμεν τὰ μετρήματα. Ἔθος δ' ἐστὶν τὸν ἔχοντα ἰδίους ὄ-	we delivered the payments ourselves. It is a custom for the owner of private
νους τούτοις ἀπεργάσεσθαι, εἰ δὲ μὴ ἔχοι,	donkeys to serve[28] with these and if he owns none,
25 πενθήμερον μετρῖν εἰς τὸ δημόσιον.	to measure out the *penthemeros* (in grain) to the treasury.

The wording of col. 1 has proved somewhat confusing. At first sight it appears to say that owners of donkeys had to give them in service to the state for the corvée (i.e. 5 days' work) and those who owned none had to pay the equivalent value of the service in grain. If so, the impost would have amounted to a capitation tax placed on all persons. Considering the payment to have been made by persons who did not possess a donkey, Preisigke[29] uses it to interpret the rather obscure tax of the Ptolemaic period called ἀνιππίας, i.e. he suggests that the latter impost was paid by cleruchs who could not or did not wish to provide horses for the postal system.[30] The example, unfortunately, is not contemporary. Wilcken[31] states in

---

[28] For the use of ἀπεργασία with reference to liturgical work see F. Preisigke, *Wörterbuch*, s.v. ἀπεργασία, *P. Oxy.* XII 1409 *l*.10, *BGU* XIII 2327 *l*.5 and the several examples in *P. Mich.* IV 360 (cited above).

[29] F. Preisigke, 'Die ptolemäische Staatspost', *Klio* 7 (1907) 270-271. So also U. Wilcken, *Grundzüge und Chrestomathie der Papyruskunde* I, 1 (Hildesheim 1963) 373.

[30] On the basis of *P. Petrie* II 39, III 110, *PSI* IV 388, *P. Tebt.* I 99, and III 1036 (cf. also *P. Petrie* III 54b and *P. Tebt.* III 1061) it may be concluded that the ἀνιππίας was an impost placed on cleruchs which was paid annually in grain. Opinions have varied as to the purpose of the ἀνιππίας. J.P. Mahaffy, *P. Petrie* II (1893) 130, very tentatively suggested that it was a tax 'for having no horse'. Wilcken, *Griechische Ostraca* 344-345, rejected this suggestion, arguing that as the same cleruch, Pythagoras, also paid a tax called φόρος ἵππων, he presumably possessed a horse. Furthermore, in view of the fact that ἄνιππος does not appear to mean 'unmounted, without a horse', Wilcken suggests that the term may qualify land rather than persons and finds support for his hypothesis in Herodotus, *Hist.* 2.108. Accordingly, he postulated that the impost was used to defray the cost of improving difficult terrain (πεδιὰς ἄνιππος) for use by horses. But Wilcken also expresses doubt over the name, for one would properly expect that it would reflect the positive outcome of the expenditure rather than the negative property of the terrain. However, J.G. Smyly, *P. Petrie* III (1905) 277-278, observes that the marginal note in *P. Petrie* 39 alongside the entry for the φόρος ἵππων weakens the force of Wilcken's argument. The marginal note 'apparently directs the transference of this item to the next account'. Against Wilcken's argument that ἄνιππος does not appear to be used of persons, Smyly points to two occurrences of the term (Plutarch, *Mor.* 100a and Poll., 1.210) with the meaning 'unskilled in horsemanship'. Accordingly he suggests that the impost was 'a kind of fine imposed on such military cleruchs as were unable to ride'. In this

reference to the papyrus: 'Owners of donkeys had to place a donkey at the disposal of the state for land transport, while those who had no donkey had to pay a compensation to the state instead'. Rostovtzeff[32] holds the same view: 'Everyone is obliged to supply beasts of burden; those who possess several animals are the professional donkey-drivers and they supply three animals for state caravans (camel-owners perhaps one animal ...), the others paid money instead.' He considers the amounts in *WO* 392, 395, 684, 1054, 1057 and 1261 to be payments by persons who could not supply animals for the corvée. Cf. also *P. Ryl.* 195 *l.*5 (second century AD) where the πενθήμερος ὄνων is paid in cash — πενθημ(έρου) ὄνων (δραχμὰς) η̄ (8 drachmae) — and *P. Charite* 20 *ll.*10-16 (*ca* AD 320-350) where it appears that Charite had to pay 7/96th of the cost of one or more donkeys for the mines. As far as I can see, Rostovtzeff makes no attempt to explain the larger amounts paid in the first two ostraca. Nor is there any explanation for the payment in wheat in *P. Petaus* 44. On the other hand, Wallace assumes that the tax only applied to owners of donkeys; they could either 'give the use of them for five days or else measure into the government's granary a supply of grain of value equivalent to five days' work'.[33] In other words the tax only applied to owners of donkeys who then had a choice of how to pay. Further support for this position can be found in the observation of Grenfell and Hunt that the πενθήμερος ὄνων 'being rarely mentioned does not seem to have been a far-reaching impost'.[34]

In support of the last interpretation one might consider the example of a somewhat similar tax, the payment of which exempted certain individuals from the corvée. For example, in the Ptolemaic period Greeks were exempted from compulsory service by the payment of the tax called χωματικόν, from the second century BC called ναύβιον. However, there is a problem with this example. In the Roman period the basis of revenue collection and of compulsory service was widened; payment of the ναύβιον does not appear to have exempted the cultivator from compulsory service nor did the performance of compulsory service exempt him from payment of the ναύβιον. A capitation tax, χωματικόν (not to be confused with the earlier tax exempting Greeks from compulsory service), was also raised on the population for the maintenance of the irrigation system.[35] In other words, the ναύβιον cannot serve as an

---

interpretation he is followed by A. Bouché-Leclercq, *Histoire des Lagides*, III (Paris 1906, reprinted 1978) 236. The editors of *P. Petrie* 39 and the recently published *P. Med. Bar.* 5 (*Aegyptus* 66 [1986] 24-30) associate the payment (though not exclusively, cf. *P. Tebt.* I 99) with cleruchs who are designated as orphans. *P. Med. Bar.* 5 further shows that the impost was paid on an estate of 100 arouras which is administered for the orphaned cleruch, Menoitas, by his guardian, Ptolemaios (also a cleruch). As Menoitas was a minor, the conclusion seems to follow that the ἀνιππίας was an impost raised on those either who were unable to ride (i.e. *P. Petrie* 39 and 110) or who did not support a mount (*P. Petrie* III 54b, *P. Tebt.* I 99 and III 1036). C. Préaux, *L' économie royale des Lagides* (Brussels 1939) 214-217, points to both the military importance of the horse and its relatively high cost. No doubt it was in the government's interest to place an impost on those who benefited from their privileged position but could not fully meet their obligations. There is no reason, however, to associate the payment with the postal service. We turn briefly now to the βύρσης. It appears to have been an impost paid by cleruchs in cash annually. There is no indication of an association between it and the ἀνιππίας. The purpose of the βύρσης (= 'hide' or 'tanned skin') is obscure. Cf. Mahaffy, *P. Petrie* II (1893) 130, and Wilcken, *Griechische Ostraka* 352. The term appears to be too general to support Preisigke's more specific interpretation of it. Indeed, the use of hides was so extensive even in military circles that it seems to stretch credibility to suggest a particular purpose for this impost.

[31] Wilcken, *Griechische Ostraka* 377.
[32] M. Rostovtzeff, 'Angariae', *Klio* 6 (1906) 254.
[33] Wallace, *Taxation* 92.
[34] Grenfell and Hunt, *P. Oxy.* XII (1916) 20.
[35] Wallace, *Taxation* 59-61.

analogous example because the point of comparison is no longer contemporary. Indeed, the tax and its historical development could actually be used to argue the opposite case with regard to the πενθήμερος ὄνων. What then of this tax? The interpretation of the papyrus depends on how one completes the ellipsis in *l.*24 (εἰ δὲ μὴ ἔχοι). It is quite evident that it is to be completed from the immediately preceding clause and the expression τὸν ἔχοντα ἰδίους ὄνους. In other words, owners of private donkeys supplied them for use in the corvée, whilst those who had no private donkeys paid an amount of grain of equivalent value to the work. This conforms with the actions of the accused who in *ll.*20-23 state that since their brother had no donkeys, they paid most of the grain. The problem, however, is to reconcile this interpretation with the fact that Petheus (senior) was, it would seem, subject to κτηνοτροφία.[36] Was he a κτηνοτρόφος who had in his charge only public animals? This would at least explain why he was liable to pay the πενθήμερος ὄνων in grain. Be that as it may, Wallace's interpretation of the payment is not supported by the document and this in turn throws doubt on his suggestion that the *diploma* exempted donkeys from service in the corvée. It would seem that the latter impost, like many of the other taxes on donkeys, was a tax on trade and thus should be distinguished from the πενθήμερος ὄνων and its grain payment, which was a tax in lieu of work.

There are a few other difficulties in Wallace's suggestion. First, it relies heavily on a coincidence in the amounts payable for the *diploma* and *penthemeros*. This is risky as there is only one piece of evidence for the monetary value of the *penthemeros*, i.e. *P. Ryl.* 195. In addition, there is no reason other than this coincidence to associate the two payments unless one also associates the *diploma* and five-drachma taxes. In that case the qualification of the latter as ἀπεργ(ασίας) may then be used to interpret the former. However, it is here that one strikes a second difficulty, for there is no apparent reason why these two taxes should be identified. For the suggested identification to be viable one must also explain the differences in the amounts paid. Wallace suggests the considerations of sex and use (private use or hire). But these reasons are derived from documents (i.e. registrations of donkeys – see Table 6) which are not from the Arsinoite nome. As Wallace[37] himself notes, the paucity of evidence prevents a clear picture as to the nature and purpose of these taxes from emerging. Third, Wallace's suggestion rests on what now appears to be a misunderstanding of the *diploma* in applications for lease (see *P. Mil. Vogl.* II 53 and the discussion above). If the *diploma* was paid on animals used in a trade, then it would appear to be a quite different payment from the five-drachma tax.

The Six-Drachma Tax on Donkeys in the Oxyrhynchite and Hermopolite Nomes

The scarcity of ἀπογραφαὶ ὄνων (see Table 6) given the supposed number of donkeys in use in Egypt has long been recognized. Wallace[38] suggests two possible reasons for this: (i) that not all animals were subject to taxation; or (ii) that a different method was used to record donkeys for taxation purposes. Of further interest is the fact that all three extant returns come from either the Oxyrhynchite or Hermopolite nomes and were sent to the farmers of the six-

---

[36] It is well to note the apparent contradiction between the assertion of Pasion that Petheus (senior) was not an ὀνηλάτης (δημόσιος), i.e. *BGU* 136 *l.*21 (cf. also 136 *l.*15), and his advocate's later acceptance of the fact that he was a κτηνοτρόφος, *BGU* 969 *ll.*14-15.

[37] Wallace, *Taxation* 93.

[38] Wallace, *Taxation* 90.

drachma tax on donkeys. In this respect the registration of donkeys was quite different from the registration of other animals (e.g. sheep, goats, cattle and camels) which were sent to officials of the nome's financial administration, i.e. to the *strategos* or the *basilikogrammateus*. Meyer[39] has suggested that the nome officials compiled lists from annual registrations and that these in turn formed the basis for the calculation and exaction of the various taxes on donkeys. His argument can no longer be accepted as it is based on the assumptions that registrations were sent to the nome officials and that *P. Hamb*. I 33 (verso) was a list of publicly and privately owned donkeys compiled for taxation purposes. The three extant registrations show the first assumption to be unfounded. The second assumption is also problematic for the document could equally have been prepared as a record of ὀνηλάται and the number of their donkeys used to transport grain, cf. *P. Col*. II 1 recto 5.[40]

Table 6: Registrations of Donkeys

	Date	Nome	Lodged with
P. Oxy. XII 1457	4-3 BC	Oxyrhynchite	οἱ ἐξειληφότες τὴν ἐξαδραχμίαν τῶν ὄνων
PSI VII 785	AD 93	Hermopolite	οἱ [ἐξειληφότες τὴν (ἐξαδραχμίαν) τῶν] ὄνω(ν)[41]
P. Sarap. 3 (= *SB* I 4516)	AD 119	Hermopolite (Herm.Mag.)	οἱ ἐξειληφότες τῆς (ἐξαδραχμίας) τῶν ὄνων[42]

What then was the purpose of these registrations? Sijpesteijn[43] suggests that the registration may have served to exempt persons using donkeys in farming or in their trade from paying custom duties on those animals each time they brought them in or out of their villages or cities. However, as the registrations were addressed to the farmers of the six-drachma tax (and not the customs collectors) and all emphasize the fact that the animals were for private use, it seems more plausible to think that the persons were seeking either an exemption from or reduction in the six-drachma tax itself. If a reduction was granted for personal use, then this may well account for the discrepancy between the name of the tax and the amounts paid, i.e. 5 dr. in *P.Oxy*. XXIV 2414 and 5 dr. 1 ob. in *P.Oxy*. XII 1438, but 6 dr. 2 ob. in *P. Mich*. XV 709 for trade.[44] See Table 7 for the relevant evidence from receipts, tax lists etc. But a question is raised by the assumption that registration was not universal. How did the financial administration maintain its record of the number of donkeys for the purpose of taxation? One suggestion is that the registers of customs houses were used to estimate numbers. As Sijpesteijn[45] observes, most receipts mention the number of animals (mostly donkeys and

---

[39] Meyer, *P. Hamb*. 33 (1913) 143.

[40] Wallace, *Taxation* 226, has suggested that the 4 dr. paid for each donkey in *P. Hamb*. 33 may have been a 2% tax on purchase. However, the suggestion is improbable as an *ad valorem* tax would not result in equal payments for all donkeys.

[41] For corrections to text see H.C. Youtie, *Scriptiunculae* II 1021-1024.

[42] Ibid.

[43] Sijpesteijn, *Customs Duties in Graeco-Roman Egypt* 59 n.5.

[44] One might seek to explain the discrepancies in the amounts paid by analogy to the ἀπογραφαί of unflooded land (ἄβροχος γῆ) whereby a reduction or exemption from relevant taxes was sought. But even so the addressees of the three declarations of private donkeys pose a problem. The ἀπογραφαί of unflooded land like the ἀπογραφαί of sheep and goats were addressed to the *strategos* and *basilikogrammateus* (also to the *komogrammateus*) but not to the farmers of the tax.

[45] Sijpesteijn, *Customs Duties in Graeco-Roman Egypt* 52.

camels) involved. Still if this suggestion is accepted, the consequent discrepancy between the methods of record-keeping for the numbers of camels (which were registered) and donkeys will need explanation.

Table 7: Six-Drachma Tax[46]

	Date	Nome	Paid to	Amount	For
Receipts					
P. Gen. II 95	AD 65	Hermopolite/ Oxyrhynchite	τελ(ώνης) (ἑξαδραχμίας) ὄνω(ν)	16 dr.	3 donkeys + interest?
O. Tait II 1078	AD 129	Thebaid	μισθωταὶ ἑξαδραχμίας, τέλ(ους) ὀνηλασίας) and τέλους ὄνου	not given	2 donkeys
P. Mich. XV 709	II/III	Oxyrhynchite ?	ἀπαιτηταὶ (ἑξαδραχμίας) ὄνων	6 dr. 2 ob.	trade
Tax Lists					
P.Oxy. 1438[47]	late II	Oxyrhynchite	(ἑξαδραχμία) ὄνω(ν) in list of capitation taxes owed	5 dr. 1 ob.	1 donkey?
P. Iand. VII 143	c. 200	Great Oasis (Kysis)?	(ἑξαδραχμία)[48]	5 dr. $1\frac{1}{2}$ ob.?	?
P.Oxy. 2414	II-III	Oxyrhynchite	(ἑξαδραχμία) ὄνων	5 dr.	donkeys
Other					
PIFAO I 3 d (declaration)	AD 143	Thinite	ἐπιτηρηταὶ ὠνῆς for (ἑξάδραχμος) ἱερῶν	not given	?
SB VIII 9842 (letter ?)	early II	Hermopolite	ἑξαδραχμία[49]	not given	?

---

[46] In *P. Oxy.* XII 1517 (Oxyrhynchite nome, AD 272 or 278), possibly a list of capitation taxes on trades (or χειρωνάξια), Chosion, an ὀνηλάτης, is recorded as having paid 60 dr. The nature of this payment is unclear — Χωσίων ὀνηλάτης (δρ.) ξ̄ (*l.*8). Wallace, *Taxation* 206, suggests that it was 'perhaps the monthly tax paid by an ὀνηλάτης'. I have not listed the payment in Table 7 as the nature of the tax is uncertain.

[47] In *P.Oxy.* XII 1438 the donkey-tax (ἑξαδραχμία ὄνων) is listed under the rubric of capitation taxes for fugitives, ἀπὸ ἐπικεφαλίων τινῶν [ἀναχωρησάντων] εἰς ἀγνοουμένους τόπους, and together with other taxes collected on a per capita basis, e.g. the poll-tax (ἐπικεφάλαιον) and the embankment-tax (χωματικόν). On such lists for fugitives in the Arsinoite nome see *New Docs* 8 (1997) §6. The listing is problematic as the tax would seem only to have been levied on those owning or licensing donkeys. Several factors point in this direction. If the impost was exacted on a per capita basis, (a) the addition of ὄνων to the name of the tax would in time have seemed meaningless and (b) one might reasonably have expected more extant evidence of the impost. Furthermore, it is noted by way of analogy that (i) other imposts on animals were generally levied on the number of animals owned; (ii) receipts for the *diploma* and six-drachma tax (*P. Gen.* II 95) indicate that payments were made for each donkey owned; and (iii) the application for lease indicates that the impost (*diploma* only) was on the animals used in a trade and not on the person. Moreover, it is difficult to see what sense there would have been in making ἀπογραφαί emphasizing the private use of donkeys, if the tax was raised as a μερισμός and thus distributed in equal amounts to all taxpayers.

[48] See the discussion of the editor of *P. Iand.* VII 143 (p.334). H.C. Youtie, *Classical Philology* 30 (1935) 283, questions whether (ἑξαδραχμία) is the right resolution of the symbol. The fact that the additional charges differ between cols 2 and 3 indicates that the taxes are different and therefore that the symbol 'must be something other than the name of a tax'.

[49] K.H. Gerschmann, *Aegyptus* 42 (1962) 238-239, notes the use of the article with ἑξαδραχμία but observes that the tax may not have been the same as that known from *P. Oxy.* XII 1457. The reason appears to be that the only sure reference to the six-drachma tax (*P. Oxy.* 1457 4-3 BC) is early and that by the second

Taxes on Donkeys in Thebaid

Wilcken[50] argues that in the Thebaid the τέλ(ος) ὀνηλ(ασίας) was a trade-tax paid by professional donkey-drivers and as such was distinct from the τέλος ὄνων (a tax on the ownership of donkeys) and the τέλος ἁμάξης (a tax on the ownership of a wagon) with which it is frequently associated;[51] cf. *WO* 392 and 395 in which the same persons pay both ὑπ(ὲρ) ὀνηλ(ασίας) καὶ ἁμαξ(ῶν). Rostovtzeff agrees that ὀνηλάται paid taxes both on their profession and on their animals[52] but considers the amounts in *WO* 392, 395, 684, 1054,

---

century (the date of *SB* VIII 9842) it had increased to 8 dr./8 dr. 8 ob. His argument appears to confuse the six-drachma tax with the *diploma* on donkeys. It also fails to consider the possible identification between the term ἑξαδραχμία and the symbol used to indicate 6 dr. in various other documents. It at least seems reasonable to assume that *SB* 9842 refers to the six-drachma tax known from these. Gerschmann gives either Eschmunên (Hermopolis Magna) or the Fayûm as possible origins of the letter. In view of the mention of the six-drachma tax the former provenance is to be preferred. Cf. the two registrations of donkeys from that nome which are delivered to οἱ ἐξειληφότες τῆς (ἑξαδραχμίας) τῶν ὄνων.

[50] Wilcken, *Griechische Ostraka* 145-146.

[51] Related to the tax on donkey-drivers is the tax on wagons. See Table 8. The relation is indicated by the frequency with which the collectors of both taxes are the same. In the Table below an asterisk marks that the payment was made to the τελ(ῶναι) or μισθω(ταὶ) ὀνη(λασίας) καὶ ἁμαξῶν. It will be noted that the taxes were still farmed at least until the end of the second century. This coincides with the other evidence on the collection of imposts on donkeys. Why the two taxes should be associated is unclear, for donkeys, like camels, carried their loads. See Wilcken, *Griechische Ostraka* 272 and Meyer, *P. Hamb.* I (1911) 31. The draught-animal was predominantly the ox. The tax was paid by the owner of the wagon; cf. the use of σοῦ in *WO* 1054, 1057, 1261 and *O. Tait* II 1076. Wilcken, *ibid.* 145, surmises that there was an annual registration of wagons with the tax being paid either annually or monthly according to the number and sorts of wagons owned.

Table 8: The Wagon Tax

	Date	Nome	Paid	Amount
O. Leiden 49	AD 31	Thebaid	τέλος ἁμάξ(ης)	? for payment until Mecheir
**WO* 392	AD 44-45	Thebaid	ὑπ(ὲρ) ὀνηλ(ασίας) καὶ ἁμαξ(ῶν)	75 dr. and later another 30 dr.
**WO* 395	AD 47	Thebaid	ὑπ(ὲρ) ὀνηλ(ασίας) καὶ ἁμαξ(ῶν)	150 dr.
**O. Tait* II 1074	AD 96	Thebaid	τέλ(ος) ἁμάξης	?
**O. Leiden* 390	AD 98-138	Thebaid	τέλ(ος) ἁμάξ(ης)	8 dr. for Ha[thyr?]
**O. Tait* II 1075	AD 102	Thebaid	τὰ ἀπὸ σ[υμ]φωνία(ς)	4 dr.
**WO* 1054	AD 104-105	Thebaid	τέλ(ος) τῆς ἁμάξης σο(ῦ)	? until Mesore
O. Leiden 90	AD 112	Thebaid	[τέλ(ος)] τῆς ἁμάξης	?
WO 1057	AD 116	Thebaid	τέλ(ος) ἁμάξης σοῦ	? until Mesore
**O. Tait* II 1076	AD 193	Thebaid	τέλ(ος) ἁμάξης σοῦ	8 dr.
**O. Leiden* 151	II-III	Thebaid	?	12 dr.
**WO* 1261	?	Thebaid	[τέλ(ος)] τῆς σου ἁμάξης	?

[52] M. Rostovtzeff, 'Kornerhebung und -transport im griechisch-römischen Ägypten', *APF* 3 (1906) 220. See also Wallace, *Taxation* 206. Wallace considers that *WO* 1054 was a tax on the wagon but *WO* 684 was a capitation tax placed on the trade.

1057 and 1261 to be payments by persons who could not supply animals for the corvée.[53] The editors of *O. Tait* 1078 by identifying the ἑξαδραχμία (*ll*.5-6, 9) with the tax paid to the μισθω(ταὶ) τέλ(ους) ὀνηλ(ασίας) allow the possibility that the τέλ(ος) ὀνηλ(ασίας), like the ἑξαδραχμία in Oxyrhychite nome, was a tax paid on the ownership of donkeys. Bagnall and Samuel[54] raise two objections to the identification: (a) *O. Tait* 1078 'is dated to 129, several decades before the type of receipt that we have here, and conclusions of this era may not be true later'; and (b) the amounts recorded for the τέλ(ος) ὀνηλ(ασίας) are not multiples of 6 dr., which would have been expected if it was the six-drachma tax. The first objection is simply invalid as the documents from Edfou show. The second objection fails to consider the variations in recorded payments of the six-drachma tax itself (see Table 7). Disregarding the question of the relationship of the ἑξαδραχμία to the other taxes in the Thebaid, there are two factors which suggest the identity of both the τέλ(ος) ὄνων and the τέλ(ος) ὀνη(λασίας). These are: (a) they are apparently charged at the same rate of 4 dr.; and (b) in *O. Tait* 1078 the τέλ(ος) ὄνων is paid to the farmers of the τέλ(ος) ὀνη(λασίας). It may thus be tentatively concluded that the two taxes are the same and that the τέλ(ος) ὀνη(λασίας) was paid on the animals owned by the ὀνηλάται. This possibility may also explain why the payment made in *P. Edfou* 272 by the same payee as in *P. Edfou* 270 (i.e. Philippos, son of Thedetos) is called a *diploma*, a licence-tax on animals used in a trade. The evidence is collected in Table 9. But all this does not explain why the tax in *O. Tait*. 1078 should be designated as ἑξαδραχμία. By way of explanation, however, one notes that the evidence may once again illustrate the discrepancy to be found between the name and the rate of taxes on donkeys; cf. above for the discrepancies with the ἑξαδραχμία and the πενταδραχμία ὄνων.

Table 9: The Four-Drachma Tax

	Date	Nome	Paid	Amount
P. Edfou 397	AD 4	Thebaid (Apoll. Mag)	τέλ(ος) ὄνων	4 dr.
P. Edfou 270	AD 88-89	Thebaid (Apoll. Mag)	τέλ(ος) ὀνη(λασίας)	4 dr.
P. Edfou 272	AD 109	Thebaid (Apoll. Mag)	τέλ(ος) δι(πλώματος) ὄνων	4 dr.
O. Tait II 1078	AD 129	Thebaid	ἑξαδραχμία, τέλ(ος) ὀνηλ(ασίας) and τέλος ὄνου	?
P. Edfou 446	AD 129-130	Thebaid (Apoll. Mag)	τέλ(ος) ὄνων	8 dr.
O. Tait II 1079	AD 193	Thebaid	τέλ(ος) ὀνη(λασίας)	8 dr.
WO 684	II-III AD	Thebaid	τέλ(ος) ὀνη(λασίας)	2 dr. 1 ob.
O. ROM II 160	II-III AD	Thebaid	τέλ(ος) ὀνη(λασίας)	4 dr.
O. Tait II 1080	AD 233	Thebaid	τέλ(ος) ὀνη(λασίας)	2 dr. 1 ob.
O. Tait II 1081	III AD	Thebaid	τέλ(ος) ὀνη(λασίας)	12 dr.

---

[53] Rostovtzeff, *Klio* 6 (1906) 254.
[54] R.S. Bagnall and A.E. Samuel, *O. ROM* II (p.43).

Conclusion

The above discussion of tax on donkeys illustrates the continued use of tax-farming at least until the end of the second century. This is in agreement with Oertel's[55] observation that the change from the farming of taxes to a system of state administration by liturgy was only gradual and not yet completely carried through at the end of the second century. This was at a time when the collection of other types of taxes were increasingly being imposed by way of liturgy on the propertied classes of Egypt. Thus the two systems coexisted. According to Johnson[56] fixed taxes (e.g. such capitation taxes as the poll-tax and dike-tax, as well as rentals of garden lands and other garden taxes) were collected by *praktores* (liturgists), whilst variable taxes (e.g. sales-tax, customs and revenues from monopolies) continued to be farmed. The reasons for the coexistence of the two systems of collections are unclear. The change has been explained variously. For example, it has been argued that the profitability of contracting the collection of fixed taxes decreased forcing the government to compel individuals to undertake the office. In the case of fixed taxes the government would be able to make a good estimate of the potential revenue of the tax and thus be more demanding as to the value of the bid accepted. This in turn would put pressure of the profits of the contractor. The tax on donkeys does not appear to fit Johnson's hypothesis, for despite the variation of its value (as well as name) between nomes and even within nomes the impost was apparently at a fixed rate. In this regard the tax differs little from the poll-tax, the value of which varied both between and within nomes. Johnson[57] observes:

> Although certain taxes were universally applied in all the nomes, the rate of taxation and the method of collection varied considerably. Each nome apparently had certain taxes which were characteristic of the locality and may not have been imposed elsewhere.

The above discussion illustrates the fragmented nature of Roman taxation. There was no universal system, either in terms of rates or methods of collection, for Egypt, let alone for the empire as a whole. But such a system is understandable given the dimensions and diversity of the empire, the inefficiencies and difficulties of communication and the absence of a truly professional administration. Under such circumstances the system was divided into small regional units under local officials. Taxes within these regions were either collected directly or sold to tax-farmers. Again, there was no uniformity here across the various regions. Rates and methods of collection varied. Tax-farmers, it would appear, continued to be employed in areas of taxation where assessment and collection were of a more irregular nature. They were the collectors of such regional taxes as the various imposts on donkeys besides many others. They operated under the supervision of regional officials and the collection was controlled through the accounting procedure. See further the discussion in the preceding entry.

The discussion has focused on Egypt for it is from there that we have the greatest amount of information. But the system, it is argued, applied also in Judaea and Syria. The tax-farmers encountered in the pages of the NT and the system under which they operated were very much like those attested in the papyri of Egypt. However, one must be guarded in how the evidence is used. For example, Cassidy has proposed that the didrachma in the pericope Matt. 17.24-27

---

[55] F. Oertel, *Die Liturgie*, 196.
[56] Johnson, *Roman Egypt* 493-4.
[57] Johnson, *Roman Egypt* 490. On the variations in rates of poll-tax see Wallace, *Taxation* 121-134. Besides variations between the rates operative in different nomes, the rate was also affected by the tax-status of the individual, e.g. Roman citizens were exempt whilst metropolites paid at a reduced rate.

is not the temple tax but one of the Roman civil capitation taxes. The terminology,[58] it is plausibly argued, better suits a civil than a religious tax. Furthermore, he holds that the tax systems of Roman Egypt and Judaea (Syria) were similar. Finding numerous capitation taxes in Egypt of similar value, Cassidy suggests that the tax was one of these and that a simple confusion has occurred due the coincidence in the value of the temple impost and the particular capitation tax. There are a number of difficulties[59] with the argument. The one that is of interest here is the assumption that the Romans imposed a somewhat uniform tax system across the provinces. This was not so. They often accepted the system which was in place and developed it. Capitation taxes were favoured by Romans and developed by them. But the rates and methods of collection differed between tax regions within the provinces and between the various provinces.

One consequence of the system of taxation was the financial burden it placed on the poorer strata of society. This was so in Egypt and may be assumed to have been the case in Palestine as well. One remedy was *anachoresis* or flight.

S.R.L.

---

[58] I.e. οἱ βασιλεῖς τῆς γῆς, τέλος and κῆνσος. See R.J. Cassidy, 'Matthew 17:24-27 — A Word on Civil Taxes', *CBQ* 41 (1979) 572-3.

[59] The other difficulties which might be argued are:

(a) Cassidy assumes that the terminology is the verba ipsissima of Jesus. One may have to reckon with the possibility that the reference has been changed in transmission of the account or its translation into Greek. Also the legendary character of the fish and the coin in its mouth casts doubt over the authenticity of the pericope as a whole.

(b) The pericope locates the incident in Capernaum which at that time was not part of a Roman province but of a client kingdom. Presumably, the system of taxation was that of the kingdom, presumably Hellenistic.

(c) If the terminology belongs to the civil register, the use of ἐλεύθερος (Matt. 17.26) instead of ἀτελής is unexpected. Perhaps this more general term was used because taxation was perceived as a mark of subjugation.

(d) It seems odd that the collectors just accept Peter's answer. This is not what one would have expected.

§6 Flight from Personal Obligations to the State

Ibion (Tebtynis) 15.6 x 16.6 cm AD 57/8

Ed. pr. — M.H. de Kat Eliassen, 'Three Papyri from the Oslo Collection', *Symbolae Osloenses* 51 (1976) 145-8 (*SB* XIV 12015), and idem, *Symbolae Osloenses* 52 (1977) 97-102 (*SB* XIV 12018).

No description of the papyrus is offered in the ed. pr. But importantly Sijpesteijn notes a free margin of approx. 3 cm. at the top. This and several other grammatical features of the text are strange. Corrections noted by Sijpesteijn are added to the text.

Bibliography: P.J. Sijpesteijn, *ZPE* 55 (1984) 157-8.

SB XIV 12015

Π[το]λεμαίου πράκτορος λαογραφίας
  Ἰβιῶνος
κατὰ [δ]έησιν ο[ἱ] ὀφιλοῦντες εἰς
  μῆνα Σεβαστὸν
τοῦ ἐνεστῶτος δ̄ (ἔτους) [Ν]έρωνος
  Κλαυδί[ο]υ
Καίσαρος Σεβαστοῦ Γερμανικοῦ
  Αὐτοκράτορος
5 ὑπὲρ λαογραφίας γ̄ (ἔτους) καὶ
  χωμάτων β̄ (ἔτους)
ἀπόρων ἀνευρέτων, οἱ καὶ
  ὄντες
ἀνευρέτων καὶ ἐν ἀναχωρήσι εἰς
  ἀγνοου-
μένους τόπους λαογραφίας ἀργ(υρίου)
  (δραχμὰς) Ατιη (ὀβολὸν ἕνα ἥμισυ)
καὶ χωμάτων (δραχμὰς) σλβ (γίνονται)
  αἱ ἐπὶ τὸ (αὐτὸ) (δραχμαὶ) Αφν
  (ὀβολός εἷς ἥμισυ).
10 Ὑπὲρ δέησι<ν> ἐπικλασμὸν
  γενέσθαι
ὧν τὸ κατ' ἄνδρα·
Ἀμοννεὺς πρεσβ(ύτερος) Σαρᾶτος
  λαο(γραφίας) (δραχμὰς) μ̄ς̄
  (τριώβολον) χω(μάτων) (δραχμὰς) ς̄
  (τετρώβολον)
['Αμο]ννεὺς νεώ(τερος) Σαρᾶτος
  λαο(γραφίας) (δραχμὰς) [μ̄ς̄]
  (τριώβολον) χω(μάτων) (δραχμὰς) ς̄
  (τετρώβολον)

(From) Ptolemaios, *praktor* of the poll-tax for Ibion, as requested: Those owing to the month of Sebastos in the present year 4 of Nero Claudius Caesar Augustus Germanicus Imperator for the poll-tax of year 3 and dike-tax of year 2 of untraceable tax delinquents, these consisting of untraceable (persons) and (persons) in flight to unknown places: poll-tax 1318 silver dr. 1½ ob. and dike-tax 232 dr.; total altogether 1550 dr. 1½ ob. That beyond the request there is an extraordinary levy (on taxpayers) of whom the list is: Ammonius, the elder, son of Saras, for the poll-tax 46 dr. 3 ob., for the dike-tax 6 dr. 4 ob. Ammonius, the younger, son of Saras, for the poll-tax [46] dr. 3 ob., for the dike-tax 6 dr. 4 ob.

SB XIV 12018

Δίδυμ[ο]ς [ ]	Didymos [...]
Θσαφῖβις Ἁρπά[λου]	Thsaphibis son of Harpalos [...]
Ἁρμιῦσις Ἁρμι[ύσεως]	Harmiysis son of Harmiysis [...]
Ψοσνεῦς ὁς ... [ ]	Psosneus, also called [...]
5 Ψοσνεῦς Πετενου( ) λαο(γραφίας)	Psosneus son of Petenou( ) for the poll-tax
(δραχμὰς) μ̄ς̄ (τριώβολον)	46 dr. 3 ob.,
[χω(ματικοῦ) (δραχμὰς)] ς̄	[for the dike-tax] 6 [dr.]
(τετρώβολον)	4 ob.
Ἡρακλᾶς Κενταύρο(υ) λ(αογραφίας)	Heraklas son of Kentauros for the poll-tax
(δραχμὰς) μ̄ς̄ (τριώβολον)	46 dr. 3 ob.,
χω(ματικοῦ) (δραχμὰς) ς̄	for the dike-tax 6 dr.
(τετρώβολον)	4 ob.
ὁ αὐτὸς ὑπὲρ Ὀξυρύνχ(ων) πόλ(εως)	The same for Oxyrhynchus
λαο(γραφίας) (δραχμὰς) ῑς̄ (ὀβολόν	for the poll-tax 16 dr. $1\frac{1}{2}$ ob.,
ἕνα ἥμισυ) χω(ματικοῦ) (δραχμὰς)	
ῑγ̄ (διώβολον)	for the dike-tax 13 dr. 2 ob.
(Ἔτους) δ̄ Νέρωνος Κλαυδίου	Year 4 of Nero Claudius
Καίσαρος Σεβαστοῦ	Caesar Augustus
Γερμανικοῦ Αὐτοκράτορος μη(νὸς)	Germanicus Imperator, for the month of
Σεβαστοῦ κ̄ᾱ	Sebastos, (day) 21.

....
SB 12015 *l*.1. sc. Παρά (*P. Corn.* 24 and *P. Ryl.* IV 595) *l*.7. ἀναχωρήσει

The above papyri were published in subsequent editions of *Symbolae Osloenses*. In view of the facts that the two texts belong to the same year and month (year 4, Sebastos), were discovered at the same find-spot and show similar hand-writing, the editor entertained the possibility that the second text (*SB* 12018) represented a lower portion of *SB* 12015. However, it is dismissed as 'neither the colour of papyrus and ink, nor the folds seem to correspond exactly'. The possibility is reconsidered again by Sijpesteijn. He discounts the objection of de Kat Eliassen as not carrying 'much weight in view of the similarity in contents of the two fragments, the same month and year, the same find-spot and the rather similar hand-writing'. Sijpesteijn further notes the presence of a κόλλησις or join approx. 3 cm from the right border of *SB* 12015. The same is found on the left edge of *SB* 12018. Presumably the two sheets were at one time joined by this κόλλησις. Sijpesteijn further notes that the structure of the fibres (presumably the right and left edges of *SB* 12015 and 12018 respectively) 'also points in the direction of one and the same papyrus'.

The papyri attest the drawing up of lists of tax delinquents who had turned to flight. *SB* 12015 + 12018 is the copy of the list made by the *praktor* of the poll-tax. The list names two capitation taxes, the poll-tax and the dike-tax. Both were collected by the same official. De Kat Eliassen surmises that the original list was sent to the *strategos* or the *basilikogrammateus* as the principal tax officials of the nome. Of interest for us is the use of the term ἀναχώρησις (*l*.7). Braunert[1] has discussed the connection between ἀναχώρησις and the concept of ἰδία. He argues that in the reign of Nero (a time of particular difficulty for taxpayers)[2] the Romans attempted a new remedy to the old and endemic practice of flight. This involved the creation of a stronger bond between the individual and the community in a particular place by the introduction of the concept of ἰδία, i.e. a person's fiscal/legal domicile or the community in which he was registered. So defined, the ἰδία became the place where the individual fulfilled his obligations to the state. At the same time, the word ἀναχώρησις is first met as a *terminus technicus* to describe flight from one's fiscal/legal domicile.

The amount of the poll-tax in *SB* 12015 + 12018 is unusual and may be made up by the addition of other taxes as well.[3] In view of the stated total of the dike-tax and the fixity of its amount[4] de Kat Eliassen proposes that the list of those owing this tax may have contained 34-35 names. She estimates approximately 30 for the number owing the poll-tax. It might reasonably be proposed that the list was compiled from the bank ledger or other list of taxpayers against which payments were marked. But if this were the case, one would have expected an alphabetical listing of names.[5] Unfortunately this is not so for *SB* 12015 + 12018 and other similar lists for the Arsinoite nome (*P. Corn.* 24 and *P. Ryl.* IV 595). In view of this, some other procedure for the compilation of the list must be conjectured. The list was compiled and dated in the 4th year of Nero for the taxes owed in the 2nd (dike-tax) and 3rd years (poll-tax). Also unusual is the fact that an individual (Heraklas) owes taxes in both the Arsinoite and Oxyrhynchite nomes. It was customary for each adult male to be assessed only for the capitation taxes of his own fiscal domicile or ἰδία. If he resided elsewhere, the payment was made either through the local collectors or through a bank and transferred to the relevant account in his fiscal domicile.

De Kat Eliassen suggests that *SB* 12015 was compiled for the calculation of the μερισμὸς ἀπόρων.[6] The difficulty with the suggestion, as de Kat Eliassen realises and later qualifies,[7] is that the μερισμὸς ἀπόρων is not otherwise attested until the second century[8] and neither this papyrus nor the contemporary tax list of ἄποροι ἀνεύρετοι (*P. Corn.* 24 and *P. Ryl.* 595) give any indication as to their exact purpose. They could just as easily have been compiled in preparation for a hearing before a higher official. In view of the association between *SB* IV 7462, *P. Corn.* 24 and *P. Ryl.* 595, this has actually been suggested as the reason. In the case

---

[1] H. Braunert, 'ΙΔΙΑ: Studien zur Bevölkerungsgeschichte des ptolemäischen und römischen Ägyptens', *JJP* 9/10 (1955/6) 211-328, esp. 240ff. See also S.R. Llewelyn, *New Docs* 6 (1992) 112-119, and *New Docs* 7 (1994) 103-5.

[2] The difficulty of the times is not only attested by our papyrus but also by *SB* IV 7461 (Claudius), *P. Mich.* X 594 (Claudius), *P. Ryl.* 595, *P. Corn.* 24, and *SB* IV 7462. As Philo's description (*De spec. leg.* 3.159-162) and the numerous threats contained in petitions show, flight was one remedy which taxpayers took to avoid their liability to the state.

[3] I.e. the λαογραφία (poll-tax), ἁλική (salt-tax), πορθμεῖον (ferry-tax) and ὑική (pig-tax). See Sijpesteijn, *ZPE* 55 (1984) 158 n.13.

[4] See *P. Mich.* X 594, p.65.

[5] For the compilation and marking of alphabetical tax-lists see the discussion of Westermann and Keyes in *P. Col.* II (1932). The discussion is summarized above in *New Docs* 8 (1997) §4.

[6] The μερισμός or tax assessment was made for each ἰδία and any shortfall arising from individuals who failed to pay – i.e. those who were without means (ἄποροι) or those who had fled (ἀνακεχωρηκότες) – was met by the other taxpayers of the ἰδία.

[7] De Kat Eliassen, *Symbolae Osloenses* 52 (1977) 98.

[8] S.L. Wallace, *Taxation in Egypt from Augustus to Diocletian* (1938, reprinted New York 1969) 137. Braunert also argues that the μερισμός belongs to the reign of Trajan.

of *SB* 7462 six *praktores* of the poll-tax, each from different villages in the Heraclid division of the Arsinoite nome, petition the prefect (Balbillus, AD 55-59) when faced with financial loss arising from the depopulation occasioned by flight and death. Threatening to abandon the *praktoreia* they request the prefect to write to the *strategos*, as the chief fiscal officer of the nome, not to trouble them but to await the prefect's decision to be issued during his assize. The document is of interest in that the *praktor* of one of the villages (Philadelphia) is named as Nemesion. This same individual is the author of a list of delinquent taxpayers (*P. Ryl.* 595), amongst whom are the names of 105 persons[9] who were missing, (ἄποροι) ἀνακεχωρηκότες (εἰς ἀγνοουμένους τόπους), *ll*.11-113, as well as the names of 4 who had died (*ll*.125-130). The document is dated October AD 57. Also in the same hand as *P. Ryl.* 595 and from the same collector is *P. Corn.* 24. The document is again a list of tax delinquents (44 ἄποροι ἀνεύρετοι). The names of 34 missing taxpayers are shared between the lists of *P. Ryl.* 595 and *P. Corn.* 24. The editor of *P. Ryl.* 595 proposes that the two lists may have formed part of the dossier collected in preparation for the assize of the prefect referred to in *SB* 7462. In this case the intended addressee of the lists was not the *strategos* or *basilikogrammateus*, as suggested by de Kat Eliassen, but the prefect himself.

The Notification of *Anachoresis*

Notifications of flight were submitted to the Roman authorities asking that the person be registered ἐν τῇ τῶν ἀνακεχωρηκότων τάξει. Braunert[10] assumes the declaration to be compulsory. Lewis[11] merely suggests that it was in the interests of the declarant to lodge a notification. By so doing he would avoid the harassment of tax-collectors seeking to learn of the fugitive's whereabouts. Also by declaring that the person was ἄπορος he hoped to avoid any obligation to the state which might attend the possession of a fugitive's property. A village official was asked to verify the truth of the notification and upon his certification the person's name was entered on the list of fugitives. It might be argued that the lists were used to calculate the μερισμὸς ἀνακεχωρηκότων, i.e. an additional capitation tax placed on the remaining taxpayers of an ἰδία[12] to make up the short-fall in revenue arising from the flight of individuals who no longer met their obligations to the state.[13] This removed the loss from the tax-collectors and placed it instead on the population of the district. It sought to stop connivance between villagers and absconding persons, and between officials and those seeking to declare themselves destitute. However, the μερισμός is not attested until the second century, whereas all declarations are from the reign of Nero or earlier.

An interesting addition (*SB* XIV 11974) to the few already extant notifications (*P. Oxy.* II 251, AD 44; 252, AD 19-20; 253, AD 19; XXXIII 2669, AD 41/53; and *P. Mich.* X 580, AD 19/20) has recently been published. All come from Oxyrhynchus and fall in the reigns of Tiberius, Claudius, and Nero. This makes any generalization about other nomes and later

---

[9] The editor of *P. Ryl.* 595 (p.69) estimates that the number of missing persons (105) would represent 10% or over of the male population of Philadelphia.

[10] Braunert, *JJP* 9/10 (1955/6) 265 fn. 124.

[11] N. Lewis, Μερισμὸς ἀνακεχωρηκότων, *JEA* 23 (1937) 68.

[12] The ἰδία was the taxpayer's fiscal domicile. *Anachoresis* is flight from one's ἰδία, i.e. ἀναχώρησις εἰς τὴν ξένην where ξένη is to be opposed to ἰδία. See H. Braunert, *Die Binnenwanderung* (Bonn 1964) 26.

[13] Wallace held that the μερισμὸς ἀνακεχωρηκότων and the μερισμὸς ἀπόρων (perhaps identical) were instituted in the latter part of the reign of Trajan.

periods difficult. The declarant is usually a relative, though not necessarily.[14] To judge from those texts whose address has survived, declarations were submitted to persons holding the joint office of *topogrammateus* and *komogrammateus*. Their formal characteristics are:

    Address: τῷ δεῖνι παρὰ τοῦ δεῖνος

    Notification
- Name of disappeared person
- Place of his registration
- Statement of flight: ἀνεχώρησεν εἰς τὴν ξένην
- Statement that the person lacks property (πόρος)
- Oath that the matters of notification are true
- Request that the person be registered in the list of ἀνακεχωρηκότες, i.e. ἀναγράφεσθαι ἐν τοῖς ἀνακεχωρηκόσι
- Farewell: εὐτυχεῖτε

    Subscription of the declarant

    Date of declaration

The change from notification to subscription, as might be expected, is characterized by a change in handwriting. The oath can be located either in the notification proper (e.g. *SB* XIV 11974) or in its subscription (*P. Oxy.* 253). Oaths are absent in *P. Oxy.* 252 and *P. Mich.* 580, but as in both papyri the ends are lost or very fragmentary, the oath may have been lost.

Oxyrhynchus   25 x 6.5 cm   AD 63/64

Ed. pr. — C. Wehrli, 'Déclaration d' anachôrèsis', *Museum Helveticum* 35 (1978) 245-249 (= *SB* XIV 11974).

Written parallel to fibres with margins of 1.5 cm top and left. Right and bottom margins are preserved. The right side of the text has been effaced but the lost text can be restored from other similar types of documents.

Ἀν[τίγ]ρ[αφον].	Copy.
Ἀπολλοφ[ά]νει καὶ Δι[ο]-	To Apollophanes and Diogenes
γένει τοπογρ(αμματεῦσι) καὶ	*topogrammateis* and
[κωμογρ(αμματεῦσι)]	[*komogrammateis*]
Ὀξυρύγχ(ων) πόλ(εως)	of Oxyrhynchus
5 παρὰ Ἐπιμάχου τοῦ	from Epimachos son of
Ἐπιμάχο[υ ἀπ᾽ Ὀξυρ]ύγχ(ων)	Epimachos from Oxyrhynchus.
πόλεως. Ὁ υἱός μου	My son
Ἰσχυρίων [ἀνα-]	Ischyrion being re-
γραφόμενο[ς] ἐπ᾽ ἀμ-	gistered in the district
10 φόδου Ἱππέων [Παρ]εμ-	of the cavalry's barracks
βολῆς ἀνεχώρησεν	has run off
εἰς τὴν ξένη[ν] τῷ	to foreign parts in
ἐνεστῶτι δεκάτῳ (ἔτει)	the present tenth (year)

---

[14] Braunert, *JJP* 9/10 (1955/6) 265. *P. Oxy.* II 251 (mother declares son), 252 (brother declares brother), 253 (relationship not clear), XXXIII 2669 (landlords declare their tenant), *P. Mich.* X 580 (mother declares son), and *SB* XIV 11974 (father declares son).

	Νέρωνος Κλαυδίου	of Nero Claudius
15	Καίσαρος Σεβαστοῦ	Caesar Augustus
	[Γερ]μανικοῦ Αὐ[τοκ]ράτορος	Germanicus Imperator
	[καὶ] ὀμνύω Νέρωνα	[and] I swear by Nero
	Κλαύδιον Καίσαρα	Claudius Caesar
	Σεβαστ[ὸν Γερμανικὸν]	Augustus [Germanicus]
20	Αὐτοκράτορα ἀλη-	Imperator that
	θῆ εἶναι τὰ προγε-	the aforewritten is true
	γραμμένα καὶ μη-	and that
	δένα πόρον ὑπάρχειν	Ischyrion is without means
	τῷ ['Ι]σχυρίωνι μηδὲ μὴν	nor indeed that
25	[ἐστ]ρατεῦσθαι, ἐὰν δὲ	he has joined the army, but if
	[. . . . .]. καὶ στρατεύση-	[ ] and he will join the army
	ται ἢ κα[ὶ]αι	or even [ ]
	προσανεν[εγκεῖν ὑ]μῖν·	(that I will) report (it) to you.
	διὸ [ἀξιῶ] ἀναγρα-	Therefore [I ask] that
30	φῆναι αὐτὸν [ἐν τοῖς]	he be registered [among those]
	ἀνακεχωρη[κόσιν]	who [have] run off
	ἀπὸ τ[οῦ ἐνεστῶτος (δεκάτου ἔτους)]	from [the present tenth year]
	ὡς καθήκει.	as is appropriate.
	[. . . . . .]ος ἀντι-	[...]
35	[ ]νη σεσημ(είωμαι).	[...] I have signed.

SB 11974 is interestingly the only declaration of disappearance which is a copy. This fact may well explain the loss of three elements: a closing farewell (εὐτυχεῖτε); the subscription of the declarant; and the date. As well it would account for the apparent use of the same hand throughout. The text is also unique in ruling a line after *l*.33 and in using the signature σεσημείωμαι (*l*.35). These do not appear to form part of the declarant's subscription. A solution is suggested by the analogy offered in *PSI* VIII 871 (Oxyrhychus, AD 66). The latter text is also a notification but in this case it requests that the declarant's son be registered in the list of coppersmiths. It is addressed in part to the same officials as *SB* 11974. Also like *SB* 11974 the text is a copy (*PSI* 871 *l*.1). When changing to the subscription of the addressed officials (cf. *P. Mich.* III 170 and 171) the text uses the formula: ὑπογραφῆς ἀντίγραφον (name of official) σεσημείωμαι (date). The expression ὑπογραφῆς ἀντίγραφον indicates that the formally distinct subscription, like the declaration itself, is only a copy. If the analogy is correct, then the last two lines of *SB* 11974 should be amended to read: ὑπογραφῆς ἀντίγραφον ... σεσημ(είωμαι). Unfortunately, the parallel is not complete because (a) the letters νη, if correctly read, are not consistent with the name of either official; and (b) there is apparently no date after the official's signature. However, both might be explained as some form of abbreviation made when making the copy of the document. Cf. the loss of parts of the notification itself.

If the analogy is allowed to hold and the suggested reconstruction accepted, it may be surmised that the declarant received back a copy of his notification which had been duly subscribed by an official. Cf. *PSI* 871 *ll*.28-29 The subscription verified the facts of the notification. This may then have been used by the declarant to avoid any future harassment (e.g. by tax-collectors for the arrears of the fugitive) or as proof that notification had been given. For one reason or another an abbreviated copy of this document was later made.

Conclusion

The evidence of hardship arising in part from the onerous nature of the tax burden and its unfair distribution especially on the poorer classes of Egypt raises serious questions over the benevolence of imperial motives. In Roman Egypt *anachoresis* or the flight of individuals from their obligations towards the state was a problem which grew as the obligations became heavier and harder to meet. It was seized upon as a means to escape the burdens of both taxation and compulsory public service. As already observed, it was a step taken especially by the poorer classes of society.[15]

Préaux[16] notes the attitude of Rome which considered the Egyptian economy as an economy of tribute to be exploited by her, and which was founded on a deep prejudice against the native inhabitants. Johnson[17] observes that 'a study of the various taxes collected by the Romans shows that their ingenuity was pretty well exhausted in exploring all possible sources of revenue'. On expenditures against this collection he further comments:[18] 'In most cases no estimate can be made for expenditures, but in general it may be said that Rome gave little in return for the annual tribute except a certain measure of the pax Romana.' Wallace[19] finds a principal cause of flight to be the burden of capitation taxes placed on the populace:

> The poll-tax was but one of the taxes which had caused a large part of the populace to flee from their homes and abandon the cultivation of the soil; but the steady drain of wealth from Egypt caused by the collection of the poll-tax, for which there is no evidence that the Romans gave anything in return, must have played an important part in the economic decline which became so severe in the third century.

The above list of persons in arrears for capitation taxes who had turned to flight confirms Wallace's view.

There is little evidence for *anachoresis* in provinces of the Roman empire other than Egypt. However, it is reasonable to assume that it would have occurred elsewhere when two conditions were present: (a) the provincials were tied to a location or place of work in some way or other, much as the inhabitants of the *chora* were tied to an ἰδία; and (b) the obligations

---

[15] For example, there was an increase in *anachoresis* among tenant farmers of state land in the second century AD. See A.C. Johnson, *Roman Egypt* (New Jersey 1959) 435-436 and 482-483. The *anachoresis* of tenant farmers occurred even though the price of their crops was increasing. As taxes in money, generally speaking, remained constant in the first two centuries of Roman rule, Johnson surmises that the flight was caused either by a general increase in payments in kind (particularly rent) or a decline in general productivity caused by overcropping and failure to maintain the canal system.

[16] C. Préaux, 'L'attache à la terre: continuités de l'Égypte ptolémaïque à l'Égypte romaine', *Das römisch-byzantinische Ägypten*, edd. G. Grimm, H. Heinen and E. Winter (Mainz am Rhein 1983) 4-5. Préaux notes that the Roman attitude differed little from that of the Ptolemies. She argues that the ultimate effect of Roman policy and the flight of individuals to patrons was the centralization of economic power in the hands of a few large estate holders and the creation of a type of serfdom (the colonate) whereby a person was bonded to the land of his patron.

[17] Johnson, *Roman Egypt* 484.

[18] Johnson, *Roman Egypt* 490. Cf. A. Lintott, *Imperium Romanum* (London 1993) 74, regarding the effect of Roman taxation on Macedonia. Lintott observes that the funds which had previously been spent in Macedonia on the army and administration were now exported.

[19] Wallace, *Taxation* 134.

imposed on these provincials were oppressive, causing them to turn to flight. Such flight is threatened by the coloni of the saltus Burunitanus in Africa (see Dessau, *ILS* 6870) and the peasants of Aga Bey in Lydia.[20] Both situations are matters of petition to the emperor. Another indication of the prevalence of flight is that its was a typical question asked of oracles: εἰ φυγαδεύσομαι — *Will I be a fugitive?*; to which one answer was: οὐ λανθάνι σου ὁ δρασμός — *Your flight is not undetected*.[21] Evidence for flight is also to be found in the presence of outlawry in the various provinces. That ordinary people fled and turned to brigandage was a mark of significant economic, political and social dislocation. [22]

MacMullen[23] points to the connection between *anachoresis* and the ascetic life and argues that the growth of monasticism owed much to the flight of individuals from their economic perils.

> Each in his own way, rich and poor, became what we would call displaced persons. And from both types together monasticism drew the majority of its recruits. That ancient recourse of desperation, *anachoresis*, turned into asceticism.

It was for this reason that the monks were called at the time *anchorites*. The connection between *anachoresis* and monasticism was noted by Libanius (*Or.* 2.32):

> I have said that in the past the workers of the land used to have money chests, clothes, and cash, and marriages with dowry. Nowadays, though, you can go through miles of deserted farmland. The burden of taxation has emptied it, and there is another and worse trouble besides — that crew who pack themselves tight into caves, those models of sobriety, only as far as their dress is concerned.   (Tr. Norman, Loeb)

The allusion in the last sentence is to Christian monks. The text attests the burden which taxation had caused the poorer classes. They had turned to flight and to asceticism. Obligation to the state also fell heavily upon the wealthier classes of the cities, especially through the imposition of liturgies. Thus *Cod. Theod.* 12.1.63 seeks to correct the flight of persons of the decurion class to monasticism.

> Certain devotees of idleness have deserted the compulsory services of the municipalities, have betaken themselves to solitude and secret places, and under the pretext of religion have joined with bands of hermit monks. We command, therefore, by Our well considered precept, that such persons and others of this kind who have been apprehended within Egypt shall be routed out from their hiding places by the Count of the Orient and shall be recalled to the performance of the compulsory public services of their municipalities, or in accordance with the tenor of our sanction, they shall forfeit the allurements of the family property, which We decree shall be vindicated by those persons who are going to undertake the performance of their compulsory public services.   (Trans. by C. Pharr, Greenwood Press, New York 1969)

Persons are to be searched out under threat of the loss of family property, the loss arising from the claim of persons serving the liturgy in their place. Libanius was also keen to point out the alleged lawlessness of the monks. See, for example, Libanius, *Or.* 30.8-31 and 45.26. The allegation need not be mere bias, for it is evident that the monks provided refuge and protection to outlaws. The matter was of such significance that it required imperial legislation (*Cod. Theod.* 9.40.16).

---

[20] The inscription is cited in M. Rostovtzeff, *The Social and Economic History of the Roman Empire* (Oxford, repr. 1966) 409.

[21] See G.H.R. Horsley, *New Docs* 2 (1982) 42-3.

[22] R. MacMullen, *Enemies of the Roman Order. Treason, Unrest, and Alienation in the Empire* (Cambridge Mass., 1966) 192-200 and 255-68, discusses the issue of brigandage.

[23] MacMullen, *Enemies of the Roman Order* 210, 235, 355 n.18, 357 n.21.

The practice of *anachoresis* also touches on the nature of the early Jesus movement. Theissen[24] has argued that the sociological origin of the movement was one of 'wandering radicals/itinerant charismatics'; these were persons who had renounced their permanent abodes, family ties, wealth and property and who as a result were homeless. This essentially rural movement was responsible for the transmission of a number of *logia* in the Jesus tradition which chiefly advocated ethical radicalism. However, it will be noted that the adherents gave to their *anachoresis*, no doubt much as the later monks did, a religious significance. In so acting they were following the life and words of Jesus. The underlying political and social causes which made such a retreat attractive can be read between the lines of the gospel narrative and its stories, e.g. the burden of the system of taxation (Luke 3.13 and 19.8), absent foreign landlords (Mark 12.1-12), insecure employment and the exploitation of labour (Matt. 20.1-16), and compulsory public services (Matt. 5.41 and 27.32).

S.R.L.

---

[24] G. Theissen, 'Wanderradikalismus. Literatursoziologische Aspekte der Überlieferung von Worten Jesu im Urchristentum', in *Studien zur Soziologie des Urchristentums* (Tübingen 1983) 79-105 — ET: 'The Wandering Radicals', in *Social Reality and the Early Christians* (Minneapolis 1992) 33-59.

PUBLIC COURTESIES AND CONVENTIONS

§7 Benefaction Ideology and Christian Responsibility for Widows

Gazoros   Early third century BC

Ed. — C. Veligianni, 'Ein hellenistisches Ehrendekret aus Gazoros (Ostmakedonien)', *ZPE* 51 (1983) 105-114.

Inscribed on a stone found in 1964 three kilometres east of modern Gazoros at the western base of a hill. On the basis of the script the editor assigns the decree to the early third century BC. The stone is broken at the top right and left-hand side and also at the bottom edge. The middle portion of the preserved text is badly damaged, with the reverse roughly pitted. Of grey marble: height, 0.73m.; width, 0.45m.; depth, 0.12m.; line spacing, 0.11m.; number of letters in the completely preserved lines, 27-36.

```
          - - - - - - - - δραχμῶν ἐ[πὶ πο]-     (As one was) for a long time
      λὺ [ο]ὐ [δ]υναμένων εὑρεῖν                 not able to obtain (a medimnus of grain at
      ἐντα[ῦθα],                                  such and such) drachmae here,
      ἐπηνγείλατο τοῖς πολίταις                  he promised to the citizens
      πωλήσ[ειν]                                  to sell
      ἕως τ νεῶν σῖτον, τῶν μὲν πυρῶν            grain up to 10 shiploads, wheat by
      τὸν μέ-                                     the
  5   διμνον δραχνῶν δύ' ὀβολῶν                  medianus at 2 drachmae
      τεσάρων,                                    4 obols,
      τῶν δὲ κριθῶν μιᾶς ὀβολῶν                  barley at 1 drachma 4 obols;
      τεσσάρων·
      ὃς καὶ ἐκεῖνό τε τὸ ἔτος                   he had also both in that year
      ἐπεποιήκει τοῦ-                            done this
      το καὶ ἐν τῶι ἕκτωι ἔτει [ὁ]μ[ο]ίως         and in the sixth year has equally not ceased
      οὐ διαλέλοι-                                selling
      πεν πωλῶν. Ἐπεὶ οὖν ἀξίως τοῦ τε           (grain). Therefore since he, in a manner
      βα-                                         worthy of both the
 10   σιλέως καὶ τῶν πολιτῶν                     King and his fellow-citizens,
      πρ[ο]ενοήσατο τῆ-                           provided for
      ς χώρας τοῦ διασωθῆ[να]ι καὶ               the land that those who remain
      [δ]ύνασθαι τοὺς
      μένοντας ἐν οἴκωι τὰς λῃτ[ο]υργίας          at home might be preserved and be able to
      συντ-                                       perform the liturgies,
      ελεῖν καὶ τὰς συ[νκυρο]ύσας κώμας          and (since) he sought to keep safe the
      ἐζ-                                         neighbouring villages
      ἤτησεν διασ[ῶ]ι[σ]αι κοινῆι καὶ καθ'        in common and separately,
      ἰδίαν,                                      it was decided
 15   ἔδοξεν Γαζ[ωρίοις] κ[α]ὶ ταῖς              by (the citizens) of Gazoros and the
      συ[νκ]υρούσαις κώ-                          neighbouring villages
      μαις τό τε ψήφ[ισ]μα πεμ[φ]θῆναι            that the decree be sent
      πρὸς τὸν βασι-                              to the King
```

λέα καὶ αἱ[ρεθῆναι πρέσβεις] τρεῖς	and that three [ambassadors] be chosen,
[ο]ἵτινες πορεύ-	who will travel
σονται πρ[ὸς τὸν βασιλέα	to [the King], in order to
δια]λεγησόμενοι ὑπὲ-	report concerning
ρ τοῦ ψηφίσμ[ατος· στήσουσιν δ]ὲ	the decree. And those
οἱ αἱρεθέντες	chosen [will set up]
20 στήλην λιθίν[ην ἐν . . c.7 . . .]ος	a stone stele in the temple of [. . .]
[ἱε]ρῶ[ι] ᾗ ἂν αἱρῆται Πλῆστ-	wherever Pleistis chooses
ις καὶ ἀναγρά[ψου]σιν τὸ ψήφισμα·	and they will inscribe the decree;
στεφα-	and they will crown
νώσουσιν δὲ στεφάνωι θαλλίνωι, ἵνα	(him) with a crown of young shoots, in
καὶ οἱ λ-	order that the rest also
οιποὶ ὁρῶντες τὴν γεγενημένην	seeing the favour accorded
εὐεργε-	(him)
σίαν ὑπο τῶν πολιτῶν πρόνοιαν	by the citizens may show care that
ἔχωσίν τοῦ	they might
25 διασώιζειν τοὺς ἰδίους πολίτας.	preserve their own citizens.
Εἱρέθησαν	There were chosen (as ambassadors)
[κα]ὶ ἐπεψηφίσθη· Κοζισιοτος	and it was put to the vote: Kozisiotos, son
Βαστικιλα, Διονύ-	of Bastikillas,
[σ]ιος Ἀπολοδόρου, Μαντ[ας]	Dionysios, son of Apollodoros, Mantas,
Κερζουλα	son of Kerzoulas.

20. Possibly λιθίν[ην ἐν Ἀρτέμιδ]ος, *ZPE* 51 (1983) 108   25. ᾑρέθησαν

The above inscription honours a person for his benefaction to the city of Gazoros and the villages of its surrounding territory. Unfortunately the name of the benefactor is lost at the top of the stone. However, the editor (p.109) assumes that besides being a citizen of Gazoros he was also a royal functionary. This, it is argued, explains a number of features in the inscription.[1] The city itself appears to have been organised after the model of the Greek city. The citizens form a group distinct from the villagers and the latter, unable to initiate their own decree, joined their vote of gratitude for the particular benefits received by them to that of the city. Three honours were voted: (a) the sending of an embassy to the king; (b) the erection of a stele with the text of the decree; and (c) the awarding of a crown. The benefaction of the person honoured consisted in the supply of grain at a fixed price at a time of need. The act is significantly referred to in terms of πρόνοια (προενοήσατο *l*.10). The situation which occasioned the benefaction is not specified. However, the editor (p.109) notes that elsewhere expressions parallel to *ll*.10-11 refer to situations caused by war. She associates the crisis with the Celtic incursion and its aftermath in the early third century. More particularly she dates the inscription to the time when Ptolemy II (Philadelphus) was in control in the regions of eastern

---

[1] The editor argues that an embassy to the king reporting a vote of honours to an individual is more easily explained if that person was a royal official rather than a private individual. As well, it is noted that the choice of the concept of πρόνοια (*l*.10) to describe the benefaction points to a person holding either a public or royal office. The fact that the act is conceived as a service over against the king and the citizens indicates the nexus between king and city; the act is thus more easily conceived as that of a royal functionary since as such the individual mediated between king and city. J. and L. Robert, *BE* (1984) no.259, argue against this, and note that Pleistis (*l*.20) must be the benefactor.

Macedonia (pp.111-2). The sixth year of Ptolemy II (*l*.8) was 277/6 BC. The hypothesis hangs on the observation that the mediated relationship between the king and Gazoros, which is implied by the inscription, fails to suit the Antigonid period for during this time the city was integrated into the state of Macedonia. The nature of the benefaction (i.e. the supply of grain) also appears to be consistent with what is known of other benefactions of Ptolemy II in this period (p.112 n.21). J. and L. Robert, however, are not persuaded.

The honorific inscriptions regularly called upon aspiring καλοὶ κἀγαθοί to fill the breach left in civic beneficence by their much-vaunted predecessors. The ethical dimensions of this civic modelling are well rendered in a Boeotian decree which honours its benefactor Epaminondas

> in order that (ἵνα), when these (foregoing honours) are contributed in this manner, our city may appear (to be) grateful towards the benefactors, and many may become zealous imitators (ζηλ[ωταί]) of the virtuous (acts [τῶν ἀγαθῶν]) of the foremost (τῶν πρώτων), which are attested (μαρτυρουμένων) to the city.[2]

From the above decree we see that all future imitation of meritorious actions (τὰ ἀγαθά) is rigidly confined to aristocratic models (οἱ πρῶτοι) whose reputation for civic honour has been made known (μαρτυρεῖν) to the citizens.

It is rare for the inscriptions to highlight a particular moral virtue that aspiring benefactors should imitate. The merit of the καλοὶ κἀγαθοί was simply assumed. Precisely because the benefactions themselves amply testified to the moral rectitude of benefactors, there was no need to underscore a *specific* moral characteristic when encouraging prospective benefactors to be generous. Furthermore, when the inscriptions paid tribute to a benefactor, they usually employed a *range* of moral terms to establish his credentials as an ethical model.[3] Occasionally, an inscription does more sharply focus the mind of its audience by providing its own portrait of a civic luminary who worthily imitated the moral qualities of another benefactor:

> Epigone, indeed, a woman of saintly dignity and devoted to her husband, imitated his example herself by taking up the priesthood ordained for every goddess, worshipping the gods reverently at sacrificial expense, in providing all men alike with a festive banquet.[4]

At one level, the Gazoros decree is entirely typical of the honorific descriptions. But the use of πρόνοια and προνοεῖν in this decree may have struck its original readers as unusual. The surprising feature involves the nexus forged between the ethical example of the benefactor and the munificent role of his successors. Here our decree is highly explicit in its parallelism: the care that the benefactor of Gazoros had lavished upon the city should be duplicated in his aspirants (πρ[ο]ενοήσατο τοῦ διασωθῆ[να]ι [*ll*.10-12]; πρόνοιαν τοῦ διασώιζειν [*ll*.24-25]). The ethical concentration of the Gazoros decree upon πρόνοια invites comparison with its clearest New Testament counterpart: the use of προνοεῖν for the care that the Christian

---

[2] *IG* VII (2) 2712 (AD 37). In a second-century BC decree, the Ephesian people agree that a statue in honour of the gymnasiarch Diodoros be set up in the gymnasium, thereby 'guiding everyone to become emulators (ζηλωτάς) of excellent deeds' (*I. Ephesos* 6). For further examples employing ζηλωτής, see *Michel* 1011; *SEG* XVI 94, XXI 452; *ID* IV 1520, 1521; *IG* XII(9) 239, 899.

[3] See E.A. Judge, 'Moral terms in the eulogistic tradition', *New Docs* 2 (1982) 105-106.

[4] A.R. Hands, *Charities and Social Aid in Greece and Rome* (London and Southampton 1968) D13. In *SEG* XVIII 27 honours are accorded a priest of Asklepios so that the other priests might be zealous imitators (ζηλωταί) of their peers.

community should exercise towards its widows (1Tim. 5.8).⁵ What would the auditors of 1 Timothy have understood its writer to be saying against the backdrop of inscriptions similar to the Gazoros decree? The question gains force when one remembers that the writer of 1Tim. 5.1-8 also employs stock reciprocity terminology seen in the inscriptions to facilitate his moral argument.⁶

At the outset, we will survey the use of πρόνοια in the documentary and literary evidence.⁷ From there we will be better placed to understand 1Tim. 5.1-8 from a Graeco-Roman benefaction perspective. It will be argued that the writer of 1 Timothy, whilst operating within traditional Jewish-Christian theological perspectives, endorses the Graeco-Roman reciprocity ethos and instances πρόνοια as its crowning expression in kinship relationships.

1. πρόνοια and Ancient Benefaction Ideology: Survey of the Documentary Evidence

In the honorific inscriptions πρόνοια is regularly used of the detailed attention that benefactors devoted to their communities. It is pre-eminently a public virtue, civic in its focus and largely restricted to the καλοὶ κἀγαθοί. Those credited with πρόνοια in our survey below have usually exhibited military or judicial expertise, liberality in a wide range of civic affairs, or a flair for political diplomacy.⁸ The far-ranging administrative and strategic abilities required of such luminaries explain why πρόνοια was the obvious lexical choice as an honorific.

Three inscriptions illustrate the πρόνοια of rulers and officials in military and judicial affairs. In 119 BC the Macedonian city Lete honoured the Roman *quaestor*, M. Annius, 'for exhibiting the greatest forethought (πλείστην πρόνοιαν ποιούμενος) for things of importance'.⁹ The specific occasion of Annius's honour was his routing of the Gallic forces which had seriously threatened Macedonian Argos. Eumenes II of Pergamum boasts that he 'had undertaken many great struggles against the barbarians, exercising all zeal and forethought (σπουδὴν καὶ πρόνοιαν ποιούμ[εν]ος) that the inhabitants of the Greek cities might always

---

⁵ For discussions of πρόνοια (and cognates) in the New Testament, see J. Behm, *TDNT* Vol.4, 1009-1016; P. Jacobs and H. Krienke, *DNTT* Vol.1, 693-95; F.W. Danker, *Benefactor: Epigraphic Study of a Graeco-Roman and New Testament Semantic Field* (St Louis 1982) 359-360. On θεία πρόνοια (absent from the New Testament), see *New Docs* 3 (1983) 143-144; J.T. Squires, *The Plan of God in Luke-Acts* (Cambridge 1993) passim.

⁶ For reciprocity motifs in 1Tim. 5.1-8, see section 3 below. On hellenistic reciprocity more generally, see S.C. Mott, 'The Power of Giving and Receiving: Reciprocity in Hellenistic Benevolence', in G.F. Hawthorne (ed.), *Current Issues in Biblical and Patristic Interpretation: Studies in Honor of Merrill C. Tenney* (Grand Rapids 1975) 60-72. The unpublished dissertation of G.W. Peterman, *Giving and Receiving in Paul's Epistles: Greco-Roman Social Conventions in Philippians 4 and Selected Pauline Texts* (University of London 1992) 31-104 surveys a range of reciprocity texts from the Jewish and Graeco-Roman world.

⁷ In this article several terms will be used to render πρόνοια in the documentary and literary evidence. These reflect the semantic range of the noun (πρόνοια: 'foresight'; 'forethought'; 'care'; 'thought') and the verb (προνοεῖν: 'foresee'; 'think of'; 'plan beforehand'; 'provide/provide for'; 'take thought for'; 'take care for/to/that'; 'superintend'; 'attend to') when applied to human beings and their affairs. See LSJ *Suppl.*

⁸ Occasionally, the inscriptions merely acknowledge the πρόνοια of καλοὶ κἀγαθοί without elaboration. For example, *IG* II² 3449 dedicates a monument to Iulia Berenike 'because of her foresight (διὰ τῆς προνοίας)'. Elsewhere, a husband recognises the care of his deceased wife (*CIJ* I 123: εὐχαριστῶ τῇ προνοίᾳ).

⁹ *SIG*³ 700.

dwell in peace and the utmost prosperity'.[10] Last, the Thessalians praise the resident Mylasan judges for settling trials fairly and exhibiting the greatest care in their piety towards the god.[11]

Munificence in civic administration was a hallmark of those who were credited with πρόνοια. Tiberius Julius Alexander, the prefect of Egypt, outlined in his AD 68 edict several revisions of oppressive fiscal policies. The prefect assured his Alexandrian audience of his concern (πρόνοια) that the city retain its imperial privileges. As a demonstration of good faith, the prefect promised to write to the emperor about the Alexandrian grievances over taxation. The emperor would eradicate such injustices because (as Tiberius Alexander dutifully asserts) his 'constant kindness and concern ([εὐ]εργεσία‹ι› καὶ πρόνοια) is for the security (σωτηρίας) of us all'.[12]

Other examples from the inscriptions illustrate the civic-mindedness characteristic of the benefactors praised for their πρόνοια. In 160 BC Attalus of Pergamum evinces his concern for the city of Amlada, reducing their tribute by 12000 drachmae in toto.[13] In a Jewish inscription several benefactors are honoured for their care in restoring a synagogue.[14] Skythes is praised for his zeal (σπουδή) and foresight (πρόνοια) in regard to the sacrifices and public affairs at Ephesos.[15] Xenokleas had exercised the greatest care on behalf of his citizens by distributing corn in pressing times.[16] Last, Aristokles as secretary of the Council had manifested foresight in meeting the needs of the city from his own expenses. Accordingly, he was to be honoured with a statue and a painted image because (as the inscription elaborates):

> it is fitting to praise and honour with appropriate honours (those) virtuous (individuals) amongst men who exercise with all fairness love of country and care (φιλοπάτριδας καὶ πρόνοιαν ποιουμένους) concerning public affairs.[17]

The honorific inscriptions often apply πρόνοια to the judicious political diplomacy of rulers or their emissaries. In 197-196 BC the city of Lampsakos honoured Hegesias for his successful role as an ambassador to the Romans. He had met with the Roman commissioners and consul and zealously urged them to take thought of Lampsakos by preserving its autonomy and democracy.[18] Of particular interest is the famous AD 67 inscription of Nero in which he proclaims the (short-lived) freedom of Hellas. According to Nero, his magnanimous act of liberation reciprocates the Greek deities for the πρόνοια they had frequently displayed towards himself:

> And now it is goodwill (δι' εὔνοιαν), not pity (οὐ δι' ἔλεον), that prompts me to be your benefactor; and I take the opportunity to requite (ἀμείβομαι) your gods, of whose concern

---

[10] C.B. Welles, *Royal Correspondence in the Hellenistic Period: A Study in Epigraphy* (London 1934), No. 52 (1A, *ll*.8-13: 167-166 BC).

[11] *IG* IX(2) 507 (*ll*.21-23: τὴν πλείστην πρόνοιαν ποιούμενοι). For another case of judicial πρόνοια, *I. Erythrai* 122. For further examples of πρόνοια towards the god(s), *SIG*³ 399, 734; *I. Magnesia* 86; *JHS* 14 (1894) 377-380; *IG* II² 1132.

[12] *OGIS* 669 (*ll*.1-2, 66).

[13] Ibid, 751 (*l*.11: τῇ ἑαυ[τῶν] προνοίᾳ).

[14] *CIJ* I 682 (πρόνοια).

[15] *I. Ephesos* 1390.

[16] *IG* VII(2) 4132 (τὴν καλλίστην πρόνοιαν ποι[ού]μενος).

[17] *IG* V(1) 1432 (*ll*.40-41).

[18] *SIG*³ 591 (*ll*.73-75: ἵνα πρόνοιαν ποιῶνται). Similarly, *I. Iasos* 150. In *SIG*³ 618 (190 BC) L. Cornelius Scipio and his brother affirm their care (πρόνοιαν ποιεῖσθαι) for Herakleia through their bestowal of (restricted) freedom upon the city.

(προνοουμένων) for me on land and sea I have made trial, and they have granted me the opportunity to practise benefactions (εὐεργετεῖν) on unparalleled scale.[19]

However, πρόνοια was not the preserve of the καλοὶ κἀγαθοί alone. When the Greek *poleis* asserted their watchfulness over constitutional affairs, πρόνοια was the preferred word. For example, a first-century BC Athenian reform reminds its people to exercise proper care over the written legislation.[20] The Greek *poleis* also resorted to πρόνοια when they wanted to express scrupulousness in the return of honour to their benefactors, whether human or divine. The city of the Eretrians, for instance, honoured Eunomos Karustios in order that their forethought (πρόνοια) on behalf of valuable φίλοι would be universally recognised.[21] Owing to the ancestral status and beneficence of the oracle of Apollo Koropaios, the city of Magnesia vowed that it would exercise 'more careful forethought (πρόνοιαν ἐπιμελεστέραν)' as to the orderly behaviour of its cult.[22] The full text of the decision of an Egyptian βουλή was given to the priest on a white notice-board:

> so that he may have it on view daily in front of the temple, in order that when these (affairs) are completed the Council may manifestly exercise the greatest forethought for piety towards the goddess (πλίστην πρόνοιαν ποιουμέν[η] τῆς πρὸς τὴν θεὸν εὐσεβείας).[23]

The papyri replicate the same patterns of lexical use for πρόνοια as those outlined above. πρόνοια, as we have seen, is the preserve of officials: petitioners flatter a prefect with a view to investigating the loss of several archival documents;[24] a *strategos* is to oversee the collection of grain for the fiscus;[25] a legionary acknowledges the just care of a centurion;[26] and a prefect demonstrates his sympathy and concern over oppressive liturgies.[27] Last, in AD 41 the newly invested emperor Claudius affirms his own solicitude for the interests of Alexandria (πρόνοια τῆς πόλεως).[28]

2. πρόνοια and Ancient Benefaction Ideology: Survey of the Literary Evidence

Greek authors, in their stereotyped presentation of the ideal ruler, understood πρόνοια to be one of the fundamental qualities that differentiates the ruler from his subjects. In the view of Lucian, it is appropriate that the emperor be recompensed with honours from his subjects. The very quality of the imperial care demands no less:

> ... the king's most important reward (μισθὸς μέγιστος) is praise, universal fame, reverence for his benefactions, statues and temples and shrines bestowed on him by his subjects — all these are payment

---

[19] *SIG*³ 814 (*ll*.20-25 [cf. *ll*.35-37: πρόνοια]). In sharp contrast to Nero, the Gospel writers and Paul portray benefaction as an expression of mercy (Matt. 9.27, 15.22, 17.15; Mark 10.47-48 *et par*; Luke 10.37, 17.13; Rom. 12.8). See also the interesting graffito (dedicated either to Apollo or a mortal named Eulalius) in *I. Ephesos* 555: 'you offer your friendship with good care (προνοίας) to all men'. For discussion, see M. Marcovich, 'A New *Graffito* from Ephesus', *GRBS* 14 (1973) 61-63.

[20] *SEG* XXX 80 ([ποιεῖσθαι τῶν ἐν τοῖς νόμοις γε]γρ‹α›μμένων π[ρ]όνοιαν). Similarly, *IG* XII(9) 905 ([μετὰ πάσης περὶ τῶν] νόμων προνοίας).

[21] *IG* XII(9) 211. Additional examples: *SIG*³ 740; *SEG* XXIII 77; *I. Priene* 19; *IG* II² 1040, 1041.

[22] *IG* IX(2) 1109.

[23] *SEG* XXII 114.

[24] *P. Fam. Tebt.* 15 (AD 114-115): 'may it please your gracious caution (πρόνοια) and benevolence'.

[25] *P. Petaus* 53 (AD 184-185: ποιεῖσθαι πρόνοιαν).

[26] *BGU* XI 2012 (διὰ τῆς προ[ν]οίας τῶν δικαίων: second century AD).

[27] *P. Oslo* III 79 (AD 134-135: πρόνοια[ν ποιούμενος]).

[28] *P. Lond.* VI 1912 (*ll*.103, 105).

(μισθοί) for the thought and care (προνοίας) which such men evidence in their continual watch over the common weal and its improvement.[29]

In Stoic fashion, Dio Chrysostom argues that 'it is natural (κατὰ φύσιν) for the stronger to govern and care (τὴν ἀρχὴν καὶ πρόνοιαν) for the weaker'.[30] The ruler is aware that his own oversight (πρόνοια) will bring advantage to others, as the rule of the gods will bring advantage to himself.[31] Accordingly, the πρόνοια of the ruler — in contrast to the ephemeral labours of the leisured class at the gymnasia — accomplishes wide-ranging benefits for all his subjects.[32] Plutarch, too, requires that the speech of statesmen exhibit foresight (πρόνοια) and thoughtful concern for others.[33]

At a less ideological level, Josephus restricts the expression of πρόνοια to the patriarchs and kings of Israel,[34] and to non-Jewish royalty and officials.[35] Josephus underscores his own attention (πρόνοια) to the welfare of Galilee whilst commissioner of the Sanhedrin in AD 66-67.[36] Philo also highlights the πρόνοια of Joseph as the viceroy of Egypt in storing up food against a time of famine.[37] In each case, the mark of royalty or officialdom is far-reaching foresight for the needs of their subjects: but in making the expression of πρόνοια the preserve of the socially powerful the Greeks — in contrast to the New Testament — promoted an elitist ethic.[38]

Finally, in the Roman West *providentia* — the Latin equivalent of πρόνοια — features as a prized attribute of the ideal ruler. From the late-first century BC, as the Julian house eclipsed its rivals, *providentia* was monopolised by the Caesars as an honorific. To be sure, various Latin authors praise the foresight (*providentia*) of earlier Roman generals and dictators in efficiently managing state crises.[39] Valerius Maximus, relates how Hiero of Syracuse had sent benefactions of grain and gold to the Romans after their military disaster at Lake Trasimene (217 BC). The diplomatic astuteness of Hiero's munificence is graphically rendered by Valerius:

> And not being ignorant of the modesty of the Romans in receiving such gifts, he made as if he had presented them a congratulation of Victory, that he might compel them, moved by religion, to accept

---

[29] Lucian, *Apology* 13. Philo contrasts the λειτουργίαι of private citizens, rendered under compulsion, with the unconditioned munificence of rulers who provide for the future well-being of their subjects (πρόνοια: id., *Leg.* 51).

[30] Dio Chrysostom, *Or.* 3.50. Elsewhere, Dio compares the king to a shepherd who cares for his flock (πρόνοια: ibid., 4.44). In a metaphor reminiscent of Paul, Dio likens his pity for the commons to the care that one lavishes upon an ailing limb of the body (πλείονα ποιούμεθα πρόνοιαν: ibid, 50.3; cf. 1 Cor. 12.14-26).

[31] Ibid, 3.52.

[32] Ibid, 3.127.

[33] Plutarch, *Mor.* 802F; cf. *Mor.* 789D.

[34] Patriarchs: Joseph (Josephus, *AJ* 2.40); Moses (3.13; 3.69). Royalty: David (7.259); Solomon (8.124). Others: Joseph, the son of Tobias (12.160).

[35] Royalty: Ptolemy Philadelphus (Josephus, *AJ* 12.37); Queen Alexandra (12.409); Herod (14.181, 482; id., *BJ* 1.308); Artabanes and Izates (id., *AJ* 20.57). Officials: Nebuzaradan (id., *AJ*, 10.157); Albinus (20.204).

[36] Josephus, *Vit.* 62, 68, 77, 121, 389.

[37] Philo, *Jos.* 161. Also, id., *Leg.* 253. Other authors: Plutarch, *Eum.* 8.3; Diog. Laert., 7.30; 2Macc. 4.5; *LetAris* 290.

[38] Caution is warranted here, given the bias of our evidence. The inscriptions were erected in honour of the civic elite and our literary evidence reflects aristocratic concerns. It is therefore possible that πρόνοια had a wider social currency in the eastern Mediterranean basin than I am suggesting. Unfortunately, our available evidence — apart from 1Tim 5.8 — does not allow us to confirm this hypothesis.

[39] Livy, *AUC* 4.46; Vell. Pat. 2.115; Tacitus, *Hist.* 2.19.

his munificence. Liberal first in his ready will to send, and prudent in taking care (*providentia*) that it should not be sent back.[40]

However, in 43 BC Augustus asserts that the Senate had ordered him as *propraetor* and the consuls 'to see (*pro*[*videre*]) that the republic suffered no harm'.[41] In the early empire Seneca argues that if a philosopher was to repay his benefactions worthily, he must first acknowledge his debt to the ruler who, through careful management and foresight (*providentia*), had provided the favourable conditions of state for uninterrupted philosophical reflection.[42] Last, the legends of the imperial coins highlight the *providentia* of the emperors in referring to the beneficent nature of their rule.[43]

Thus the Romans found *providentia* to be a useful word for the foresight of rulers who, either by their munificence or administrative and military abilities, ameliorated the living conditions of their subjects. Like their Greek precursors, the ethic thus promoted is elitist.

3. προνοεῖν and Christian Benefaction Ethics: 1Tim. 5.8

Debate continues regarding the unity of 1Tim. 5.3-16 and the arguments are well covered elsewhere.[44] Irrespective of any particular position taken on the question of unity, the crucial role of reciprocity terminology in Paul's argumentation appears to have been overlooked. In 1 Timothy Paul employs conventional benefaction terminology (εὐσεβεῖν, προνοεῖν) and reciprocity motifs (τιμᾶν, ἀμοιβὰς ἀποδιδόναι) to undergird church and kinship responsibilities towards widows.[45] This oversight has blunted appreciation of the double-edged ethic that Paul wields. He endorses stock Graeco-Roman norms of good behaviour towards parental benefactors, whilst subsuming its ethical motivation under traditional Jewish-Christian motifs.[46]

Paul's sympathy for Graeco-Roman norms of behaviour is evident when he calls upon Timothy — and the church he represents — 'to honour' the real widows (1Tim. 5.3: τίμα). Traditionally, exegetes have understood the imperative to involve either financial payment (should v.3 allude to an official order of enrolled widows) or unspecified material assistance

---

[40] Val. Max., *Factorum ac dictorum memorabilium libri IX*, 4.8 (ext.) 1.

[41] Augustus, *Res Gestae* 1.3.

[42] Seneca, *Ep.* 73.10. Note, too, Josephus's acknowledgment of the πρόνοια of Vespasian (*Vit.* 423). The Lukan reference to the πρόνοια of the Roman official Felix (Acts 24.2) is consonant with these uses.

[43] See M.P. Charlesworth, 'Providentia and Aeternitas', *HTR* 29 (1936) 107-132.

[44] Commentators are divided over the unity of 1Tim. 5.3-16. It is either a single unit solely devoted to the relief of destitute widows (eg: M. Dibelius/H. Conzelmann; D. Guthrie; G.W. Knight; P.H. Towner), or a two-pronged discussion of the material support for 'true' widows and the membership qualifications for an official order of widows (eg: J.N.D. Kelly; C. Spicq; A.T. Hanson). For more recent discussion, see D.C. Verner, *The Household of God: The Social World of the Pastoral Epistles* (Chico 1983) 161-166; J.M. Bassler, 'The Widow's Tale: a Fresh Look at 1 Tim 5:3-16', *JBL* 103/1 (1984) 23-41; B.W. Winter, 'Providentia for the Widows of 1 Timothy 5:3-16', *TynBul* 39 (1988) 83-99; P.H. Towner, *The Goal of Our Instruction: The Structure of Theology and Ethics in the Pastoral Epistles* (Sheffield 1989) 180-190; B.B. Thurston, *The Widows: A Woman's Ministry in the Early Church* (Minneapolis 1989) 36-55; M.D. Moore, 'The "Widows" in 1 Tim 5:3-16', in C.D. Osburn (ed.), *Essays on Women in Earliest Christianity* Vol.1 (Joplin 1993) 322-366; F. Young, *The Theology of the Pastoral Letters* (Cambridge 1994) 114-120.

[45] In referring to Paul as the writer of the Pastoral epistles, I am not precluding the possibility that 1Tim. was written by Paul's secretary or a pseudonymous author.

[46] According to G.W. Peterman, *Giving and Receiving* 212, 1Tim. 5.4 demonstrates that traditional social expectations concerning reciprocity had been incorporated into the teaching of the early church.

and social recognition (if, alternatively, destitute widows are in view).[47] Such conclusions underestimate the honour-driven nature of Graeco-Roman society.[48] The real issue for Paul — both ethically and theologically — is the maintenance of culturally appropriate norms of reciprocity.

We see this in 1Tim. 5.8b where Paul implies that even unbelievers set store by the reciprocal obligations of their society.[49] The honorific inscriptions insisted upon the return of honour being commensurate with the original benefactions. This is apparent in *SEG* XI 948 (first century AD) where the people of Cardamylae act reciprocally in honouring their benefactor, Poseidippos:

> It was resolved by the people and the city and the ephors to praise Poseidippos (the son) of Attalos on account of the aforesaid kindnesses and also to bring never-ending gratitude (ἀτελῆ χάριν) in recompense of ([ἀμοι]βῆς) (his bestowal) of benefits; and also to give to him both the front seats at the theatre and the first place in procession and (the privilege of) eating in the public festivals which are celebrated amongst us and to offer willingly (χαρ[ιζομέ]νους) all (the) honour (τειμήν) given to a good and fine man in return for (ἀντί) the many (kindnesses) which he provided, while giving a share of the lesser favour (ἐλάττονος χάριτος), (nevertheless) offering thankfulness (εὐχαριστίας) to the benefactors of ourselves as an incentive to the others, so that choosing the same favour (χάριν) some of them may win (the same) honours (τειμῶν). And (it was resolved) to set up this decree on a stone stele in the most conspicuous place in the gymnasium, while the ephors make the solemn procession to the building without hindrance, in order that those who confer benefits may receive favour (χάριν) in return for (ἀντί) love of honour (φιλοτειμίας), and that those who have been benefited, returning honours (ἀποδιδόντες τειμάς), may have a reputation for thankfulness (εὐχαριστίας) before all people, never coming too late for the sake of recompense (ἀμοιβήν) of those who wish to do kindly (acts).

Here we see the incentives for the benefactor and the beneficiary carefully tabulated through the use of reciprocity terminology (ἀντί, ἀποδιδόντες, ἀμοιβή). Poseidippos receives favour from Cardamylae in exchange for his love of honour, whilst Cardamylae receives the coveted reputation for gratitude in its return of honour to Poseidippos. The reciprocation of honour, as formulated in the Cardamylae decree, is striking for its calculation of the benefits to both parties.

This ideology of reciprocity embraced household relations as much as the civic arena. The popular philosophers urged the reciprocation of parental benefaction by their progeny.[50] Even the honorific inscriptions occasionally highlighted cases of parental munificence that were worthy of honour. Queen Apollonis Eusebes, to cite one example, dealt with her children with such concord that she earned their conspicuous thanks and eternal commendation.[51]

Thus Paul reinforces the reciprocity motif implicit in τιμή when he exhorts all children, as a mark of family piety (εὐσεβεῖν), to make a return to their parents (1Tim. 5.4: ἀμοιβὰς ἀποδιδόναι τοῖς προγόνοις). This was a traditional motif in Graeco-Roman benefaction ideology. Of all the philosophers, Hierocles gives this doctrine of the pious reciprocation of parental favour its fullest and finest exposition:

---

[47] See especially P.H. Towner, *Our Instruction* 181-182.
[48] In section 1 above, several examples are cited of *poleis* choosing πρόνοια to express their scrupulousness in the return of honour.
[49] J.N.D. Kelly, *A Commentary on the Pastoral Epistles* (London 1963) 115.
[50] See Dio Chrysostom, *Or.* 12.42-43; Aristotle, *Mag. Mor.* 2.12.1; id., *Pol.* 7.14.2; Plutarch, *Mor.* 479F; id., *Cor.* 4.4, 36.3; Seneca, *Ben.* 2.11.5; 5.5.2-4; 6.24.1-2.
[51] *Michel* 541 (second half second century BC).

> But we must begin with the assumption that the only measure of our gratitude (εὐχαριστίας) to them is perpetual and unyielding eagerness to repay their beneficence (προθυμία πρὸς τὸ ἀμείβεσθαι τὰς εὐεργεσίας αὐτῶν), since, even if we were to do a great deal for them, that would be far too inadequate . . . So, in order to choose our duties to them easily, we should have this summary statement at hand, namely, that our parents are the images of the gods (θεῶν εἰκόνες), and, by Zeus, domestic gods, benefactors (εὐεργέται), kinsmen, creditors, lords, and the warmest of friends . . . They are lenders of the most valuable things, and take back only things which will benefit us (ἡμῶν εὐεργεσία) when we repay (ἡ ἀπόδοσις) them. For what gain is so great to a child as piety (εὐσεβής) and gratitude (εὐχάριστον) to his parents?[52]

As with Hierocles, Paul also brings to the fore the religious motivation for πρόνοια to widows in 1Tim. 5.4 and 5.8. The reciprocation of parental favour is pleasing in God's sight (v.4), whereas a failure to render appropriate honour and assistance to relatives (vv.3, 16b) marks the offender as one who has disowned the faith (v.8). The theological contours of Paul's thought here, as we have noted, are not without counterpart in the wider Graeco-Roman landscape. Pythagoras, as rendered by Iamblichus, reminds the young men at the gymnasium of Kroton that they owed their parents gratitude as benefactors:

> Our parents alone are the first in benefactions (εὐεργεσίαις), even before our birth, and ancestors are responsible for all the achievements of their descendants. We cannot go wrong if we show the gods that we do good to our parents (ἑαυτοὺς εὐεργετεῖν) before all others. The gods, we may suppose, will pardon those who honour (τιμῶσι) their parents above all, for our parents taught us to honour (τιμᾶν) the gods.[53]

We have seen how Paul positively endorses Graeco-Roman reciprocity ethics within the household. What, then, is the force of Paul's use of προνοεῖν in 1Tim. 5.8a? On the one hand, Paul is simply reinforcing prevalent community norms. When Christian children and the wider body of believers exercise πρόνοια towards widows, they should reflect the same far-ranging care that the καλοὶ κἀγαθοί and emperors display towards their own communities. On the other hand, in contrast to the Graeco-Roman context, πρόνοια is no longer the preserve of a powerful elite: it is transported by Paul without fanfare into the realm of everyday kinship relationships.[54] Moreover, πρόνοια has become for Paul the crowning expression of genuine faith in action within the Christian household (1Tim. 5.8b: πίστις, ἄπιστος), whether that is directed towards one's immediate family or more distant relatives.

Notwithstanding Paul's endorsement of Graeco-Roman reciprocity ethics in this instance, his thought retains its Jewish-Christian moorings. Given that the LXX employs τίμα in rendering the fifth commandment (Ex. 20.12; Dt. 5.16: cf. 1Tim. 5.3a), Paul adeptly engages the attention of his Graeco-Roman audience by adopting familiar reciprocity terminology in his exposition of the Mosaic Law concerning parents (vv.3-4: τιμᾶν; ἀμοιβὰς ἀποδιδόναι).[55] While Paul affirms what is honourable in Graeco-Roman culture (eg; 1Tim. 5.8b; cf. Phil. 4.8), he rejects the idea that the human return of favour somehow reciprocates divine πρόνοια

---

[52] Hierocles, Περὶ καθηκόντων, 'How to Conduct Oneself Toward One's Parents' (Stob. 3.52.).

[53] Iamblichus, *Vit. Pyth.* 38.

[54] πρόνοια is seldom used of kinship relationships in the inscriptions. For a counter example, see n.8.

[55] In similar vein, Philo (*Decal.* 111-115) discusses the fifth commandment of the Decalogue from a reciprocity perspective. In his view, all impiety (ἀσέβεια) towards parents is reprehensible precisely because their beneficence exceeds any possibility of repayment (ἀμοιβάς). Furthermore, although children are unable to make a complete return (ἀντιχαρίζεσθαι) to their parents, they would do well to ponder the faithfulness of animals in returning the kindnesses (ἐν χαρίτων ἀμοιβαῖς) of their human benefactors. Similarly, Sir. 7.28 and Josephus, *Ap.* 2.206. However, the LXX — notwithstanding narrative texts such as 1Sam. 25 — does not explicitly teach a reciprocation of favour or gratitude. See G.W. Peterman, *Giving and Receiving* 62.

or impels divine forgiveness. This was the position of, respectively, Nero and Pythagoras, as outlined previously. Rather, reciprocity in kinship relationships upholds the true value of the Christian household in the sight of God and is an important litmus test of the believer's adherence to the apostolic faith (1Tim. 5.4b, 8b).[56] Finally, in the case of the 'real' widow, recompense ultimately resides in her hope in God (1Tim. 5.5: ἡ ὄντως χήρα ἤλπικεν ἐπὶ θεόν), because He has repeatedly promised to answer the cries of the widow and orphan (Ex. 22.22-24; Dt. 10.18; 24.17-21; Pss. 68.5; 146.9 [LXX, χήρα], cf. v.5 [ἡ ἐλπὶς αὐτοῦ ἐπὶ Κύριον τὸν Θεὸν αὐτοῦ]; Pr. 15.25).[57]

J.R. Harrison

---

[56] While Paul's perspective on kinship relations is grounded in the Decalogue (Exod. 20.12; Lev. 19.3; Deut. 5.16; 1Tim. 5.4b) and the apostolic faith (1Tim. 5.8b; cf. Eph. 6.1-2), it is interesting to note that the third/second-century BC Pythagorean philosopher Pempelos reproduces similar sentiments: 'For he who honours his parents by gifts will be recompensed by God, for without this the divinities will not pay any attention to the prayers of such parents for their children . . . The profane person who is deaf to these considerations will by all intelligent persons be considered as odious to both gods and men.' (Περὶ γονέων, Stob. 4.25.52)

[57] F. Young, *Pastoral Letters* 116, suggests that the fervent prayers of the 'real' widow for others in 1Tim.5.5 is a case of reciprocation of church patronage. This tantalising speculation fails to convince because of a telling absence of any reciprocity terminology in vv.5-6. Rather, the widow's tireless prayer points to her total reliance upon God as benefactor. Paul's restraint in describing the prayers of the widow can be gauged from a comparison with Pempelos. According to Pempelos (Περὶ γονέων, Stob. 4.25.52), the prayers of parents reciprocate both the piety and impiety of their progeny: 'For our parents, who are divine images that are animated, when they are continually adorned and worthily honoured by us, pray for us, and implore the gods to bestow on us the most excellent gifts, and do the contrary when we despise them . . . Every intelligent person, therefore, should honour and venerate his parents, and should dread their execrations and unfavourable prayers, knowing that many of them take effect.'

§8 The Epitaph of a Student Who Died Away from Home

Necropolis of Claudiopolis First century AD

Ed. pr. — R. Merkelbach, *EA* 3 (1984) 137-141.

Bibliography: *I. Klaudiupolis* 70; *SEG* XXXIV 1259; *BE* (1984) §478.

The inscription is one of two surviving but separate, consolation decrees for a deceased student. The inscriptions on two limestone blocks are relatively well preserved. Every second line is coloured red to facilitate ease of reading. Only the first of the inscriptions is reproduced below. The surface is corroded in many places, no doubt as a result of its use as a lid on the Byzantine tomb where its inscribed side faced outwards. There is also a peg in the middle of its left edge which was used to secure it. At the bottom 1-2 lines have splintered off and perhaps also part of the stone. Height: 1.99m; breadth: 0.68m; depth 0.03-0.04m. The second inscription, which was later used to form a side of the Byzantine tomb, is damaged along its left side and a number of letters are missing from this margin. The meaning of its text is difficult to discern and for this reason it is not reproduced here.

[Στρα]τηγῶν προθέν-	The *strategoi* having given leave,
[τω]ν· Μητρόδωρος Φι-	Metrodoros son of
[λί]ππου εἶπεν· ἐπεὶ Θεό-	Philippos proposed: Since
δωρος ᾽Αττάλου ᾽Αγριπ-	Theodoros son of Attalos from
5 εὺς ἕνεκεν σχολῆς ἀφ-	Agrippeia having come
ιγμένος εἰς τὴν πόλιν	to this city to sudy
δείλαιος οὐδὲ τῆς ἐλπ-	but not, poor wretch,
ίδος ἀπολαύσας ἐπὶ	enjoying his hope further,
πλέον ἔφθη μὲν τὰς εὐ-	forestalled his wishes
10 χὰς δυσμοίρῳ τύχῃ καὶ	by ill-fated chance, and
τῆς ἀποδημίας καὶ τῆ-	away from home and in the
ς ἡλικίας ἀνόνητον σ-	prime of life having hastened an
πουδὴν ταχύνας ἐφ᾽ ἃ	unprofitable zeal perished
μὲν ἐξῆλθεν πάντων π-	before (attaining) everything
15 ροαπολόμενος, τοῖς δ᾽	on which he had set forth, and (since)
οἴκοθεν ἀγαθοῖς μηδ᾽	not even enjoying the good things
εἰς τάφου καὶ νεκροῦ κό-	from home for the
σμον χρησάμενος ξέν-	adorning of grave and corpse
ῃ γε οὖν ἐνθάπτεται γῇ κα-	he is then buried in a foreign land
20 ὶ πρὸς ἀλλοτρίοις ἀπέπ-	and expired in alien
νευσε κόλποις ὁ μητρὶ χ-	bosoms stretching out his hands
εῖρας ὀρέξας οὐδὲ πα-	to his mother nor even
τρὸς ὕστατα προσστερ-	clasping the last
νισάμενος ἀσπάσμ-	embraces of his father,
25 ατα πικρᾶς μνημόσυνα	memorials of bitter
τ‹ύ›χης· ἐρανίσζεται δὲ ἡ	chance; his circle has
περίστασις ἐπ᾽ αὐτῷ τ-	contributed for him

ὃν τοῦ τέλους οἶκον· κ-	this house of death. Even
ἂν πάντες τοῦ πάθους	all of us kinsmen
30 συνγενεῖς ὁμολογοῦμε-	of suffering concede
ν ἐν αὐτῷ, τοῦ δαίμονος	one thing to him; (that) the daemon[1]
χαρισαμένου ἐντὸς	granting him
τῇ πόλει τελευτᾶν ἧς [ἐ-]	to die in the city which
ράσθη μὲν δείλαιος [εἰς ἡ-]	he loved, he, poor wretch, coming
35 χητὸν λόγων τῶν πε[ρὶ ἐπ-]	as a student of rhetoric — that
αίνου ἢ καὶ ἠθῶν κα[ὶ κλαυθ-]	of praise, or even of characterisations and
μῶν μαθητὴς τ[ῶν περὶ]	of laments for
ἑτέρων ἀφικόμ[ενος μὴ ἀ-]	others — did not have
[π]ολαύει δοὺς . . [ ]	the enjoyment (of it) having given [...]
40 [.]νοσ[ ]	[...]

The inscription was found in the region of the necropolis of Claudiopolis together with another inscription which also originally belonged to the same grave of a deceased student, Theodoros, son of Attalos. The grave was of the Roman period. Both stones had, however, been moved and reused in the building of a tomb of the Byzantine period. The date of the decrees recorded on both stones is determined by the mention of Agrippeia (*ll*.4-5). The only other evidence for a city of the name Agrippeia in Bithynia is found in the enumeration of cities of that region to be found in Pliny the Elder, *Nat. Hist.* 5.149. Merkelbach believes Agrippeia to be the earlier name for Cretia-Flaviopolis. It had acquired its name when Agrippa in company with king Herod (Josephus, *AJ* 16.23, and Nikolaos of Damascus, 90 F 134) passed through the province of Pontus-Bithynia in 14 BC. The inscriptions are thus to be dated between 14 BC and the renaming of the city as Flaviopolis under the Flavian emperors (AD 69-96).

The above inscription mentions *strategoi* (*l*.1). These were no doubt officials in the city administration of Claudiopolis. Their exact function within the administration is unknown. In the above inscription they are responsible for the vote of consolation. *Strategoi* are known elsewhere in Bithynia only for the city of Kios (*I. Kios* 16). In this latter inscription five are named in the dating formula of an ephebic list.

In Merkelbach's opinion the texts represent two separate decrees of consolation for the deceased student, Theodoros. J. and L. Robert, *BE* (1984) §478, concede that the text starts in the form of a decree (*ll*.1-3) but note that what follows is not in the form of a decree of consolation. Rather it is described as 'a long rhetorical lament over the misfortune of a young man who died so young in a town where he had come to study'.

Theodoros had come to Claudiopolis as a student of rhetoric. This is made explicit by *ll*.34-37. The text was very probably composed by a teacher or fellow student, for it appears to have rhetorical pretensions. Merkelbach notes the presence of numerous antitheses and participial constructions; the editors of *I. Klaudiupolis* 70 note the use of μέν (*l*.9) and δέ (*l*.26), as well as the two *topoi* of (a) death at a young age (*ll*.9-15) and (b) death in a foreign land (*ll*.16-26). However, the style of the epitaph does not appear to match its pretensions. Merkelbach describes the text as in no way a masterpiece; its sentences pass over into one another in tape-

---

[1] On δαίμων meaning 'death', 'Hades' see R. Lattimore, *Themes in Greek and Latin Epitaphs* (Urbana 1942, repr. 1962) 148. He considers this 'a more cautious way of accusing Hades without naming him, thus averting further disaster'.

worm fashion; classical Greek was a foreign speech to the composer. Merkelbach concludes: 'One has the impression that Greek language and culture had not had a foothold for long in this region and that a rhetor, who could elaborate complicated sentences, was seen as an embodiment of all higher culture.'

The purpose of a funerary inscription was 'to put its reader in the mood, to evoke memory of the deceased and to incite reflection about life and death'.[2] This was mostly achieved through the use of common *topoi*. As noted above the inscription uses the two *topoi* of death at a young age and death in a foreign land. Lattimore[3] discusses both. Death as a young person (ἄωρος) was a chief cause of lament for three reasons: (a) the deceased had no time to enjoy life; (b) the parent or older person outlived the child; and (c) premature death threatened the continuity of the family.

Death abroad was often lamented because it precluded proper ceremonies. Lattimore discusses funerals conducted by or monuments and epitaphs set up by public ordinance. These were at first reserved for soldiers commemorating their ultimate sacrifice for the state but in time the practice degenerated with private individuals honoured 'for virtue'. Examples of *proxenoi* representing their own states abroad and voted public burial by their cities of residence are noted.[4] Lattimore considers these as 'compensations for the lack of a funeral at home'. The above epitaph of the students seeks to fulfil the same function.

A second example of the *topos* of death abroad is provided by the funerary inscription (second or third century AD) of an athelete from Termessos who died and was buried far from home and whose friends erected a stele for him in Termessos.[5] Interestingly this inscription complements that of the student, for whereas the former was erected at home by friends, the latter was set up away from home at the place of study. The inscription notes the pain of the surviving father as well as the youthfulness and athletic success of the deceased and offers the consolation that all die and fail to find their way home. In view of the fate of the deceased the advice is given to rejoice, eat and drink and to enjoy the gifts of Aphrodite.

The 'carpe diem' motif, φάγωμεν καὶ πίωμεν, is another important *topos* of funerary inscriptions. The *topos* is found twice in the New Testament at 1 Cor. 15.32 and Luke 12.19. Ameling[6] discusses these verses in relation to the relevant documentary evidence. He notes that though Paul's use is a citation of Isaiah 22.13, the Lukan use is neither dependent on Paul nor on Isaiah. Even so, both were probably influenced by the prevalence of the *topos*. The premise behind the funerary *topos* was either that there is no life after death or that such life as there was was only a poor imitation of one's present existence. Therefore each individual was to make the most of his life now. In the case of the parable told in Luke the rich man built his larger barns but before he could enjoy the ease which his wealth created, he died. The advice was of no use to him. It should further be noted that the conclusion of the parable counters the attitude of the rich man, for a person should not lay up treasures for himself but with God. The assumption here is of a future judgement and life beyond the grave. In the case of 1 Cor. 15.32 the incongruity of the premise behind the *topos* and of the theme of the chapter (i.e. the resurrection of the dead) is apparent. Paul in addressing his discussion to the Corinthians,

---

[2] J. Nollé, 'Grabepigramme und Reliefdarstellungen aus Kleinasien', *ZPE* 60 (1985) 117.

[3] Lattimore, *Themes* 178, 184-191 and 201.

[4] Lattimore, *Themes* 224-6.

[5] Nollé, *ZPE* 60 (1985) 121-6. On the funerary *topos* of life as a race in the stadium (cf. also 1 Cor. 9.24-27) see pp.133-5.

[6] W. Ameling, φάγωμεν καὶ πίωμεν, *ZPE* 60 (1985) 35-43.

who would no doubt have encountered the *topos* in numerous cemeteries, could not allow this godless point of view to go unopposed.

The text illustrates the importance of rhetorical training for individuals who aspired to positions of status or rank in their cities. The educational system was narrowly based on rhetorical exercises. Rhetoric played an integral role in civic life. And even as the cities began to lose their independence and the significance of oratory in the political process of decision-making diminished (especially from the second century in the Greek east), it continued to play an important part on the various public occasions which called for displays of epideictic oratory, e.g. the celebrations of victory and holidays, the birthdays or deaths of rulers etc. In Cameron's view, its purpose was to affirm the social order.[7] Kennedy[8] holds that oratory performed on such occasions important cultural, social and political functions. These included the display of civic and national unity, the transmission of cultural values, the expression of loyalty to the state, and within limits the offering of advice to or criticism of the addressee.

In our inscription Theodoros had left home and journeyed elsewhere in an effort to gain an education in rhetoric. Travel for educational purposes was not an uncommon phenomenon amongst the elite classes. The ethos and value systems of the city and its institutions fostered and promoted Greek language and culture. *P. Yale* II 105 (Theban nome, first century AD) further confirms the point. The text appears to be the inner two columns of a papyrus roll and contains what is interpreted as a rhetorical exercise copied (first century AD) for personal use. The surviving text is the surviving part of a deliberative exercise (*pragmatikai*) modelled on the events and aftermath of the naval battle of Arginusae; in particular, it attacks a general for his having abandoned his men, both living and dead, after the battle had been won.[9] The dialect is Attic. However, the style is thought by the editor to be 'too polished to have been the product of a local Theban talent'.[10] She suggests a composition in 'Alexandria if not outside Egypt' in the first century BC. The point of interest is the find of a rhetorical exercise at the fringe of the Graeco-Roman world and the importance which a person living there apparently placed on Greek rhetorical training.

The phenomenon is significant for the growth of early Christianity. From Jesus to Paul Christianity changed from a rural to an urban movement. Once this bridge had been crossed, the new belief was able to spread throughout the eastern provinces of the Roman Empire, hopping from one city to another. The change also entailed the embracing of the new linguistic medium of Greek and in time an acceptance of its stylistic values. We know that from the time of the first Christian apologists a certain discomfort was felt about the style in which the Scriptures were written.[11] The more educated and elite classes in pagan society could not help

---

[7] A. Cameron, *Christianity and the Rhetoric of Empire* (Berkeley 1991) 82-3.

[8] G.A. Kennedy, *Greek Rhetoric under Christian Emperors* (Princeton 1983) 23-25.

[9] Deliberative exercises treated mythological or historical themes. In the latter case they did not necessarily make an attempt to preserve historicity. See Kennedy, *Greek Rhetoric under Christian Emperors* 81.

[10] S.A. Stephens, *P. Yale* II, p.56.

[11] For example, see Justin Martyr, *Cohort. ad Graec.* 8 and 35, *Orat. ad Graec.* 5, Clement of Alex., *Protrepticus* 8, Origen, *Contra Celsum* 1.62, 7.58-9, Eusebius, *H.E.* 3.24, John Chrysostom, *Hom. in Ioan.* 2.2, Basil, *Epist. ad Libanium* 339, and Jerome, *Epist.* 22.30. On the pseudepigraphical letters between Paul and Seneca, P. de Labriolle, *History and Literature of Christianity from Tertullian to Boethius* (London 1924, repr. 1968) 23 n.3, comments: 'The apocryphal collection of letters exchanged between Seneca and St Paul had been forged in order to combat by indirect means in the minds of the lettered pagans their repugnance to the form of the *Epistles*; the forger represents the admiration of Seneca for the basic matter of these *Epistles*, in order to entice the scrupulous to pierce beneath the outer covering which displeased them.'

comparing the Christian corpus of alleged apostolic authorship[12] with its own literature and noting the stylistic failings of the former. In addressing the issue appeal was often made to 1 Cor. 2.4-5 and the importance of content over form. Leaving aside apologetics and turning to the question of Christian education the churches showed a certain ambivalence towards classical literature. For example, injunctions could be made against the reading of profane literature (*Const. apost.* 1.6); here it was argued that the OT and NT covered all the types of literature one could wish to read (history, wisdom, poetry, song, law etc.). John Chrysostom was fearful of the effects of pagan literature on students, an echo of Plato's criticism of Homer and other artists in his Republic. But Christians did not abandon the traditional classical curriculum. And when Julian excluded Christians teachers from teaching the classics,[13] his actions caused great consternation and in order to fill the void a literature was created from biblical sources modelled on the classics (Sozomen, *H.E.* 5.18). Such an action discloses the importance which the church attached to form and style despite what it might have said in other contexts. Also, as Kennedy[14] observes, the rescript awakened some Christians (e.g. Gregory of Nazianzus) to defend their right to Hellenistic culture. But this is not to say that the churches followed unquestioningly the canons of classical literature. An important exception here was their preference for the more socially inclusive genre of 'lives', which in the view of Cameron[15] functioned as a sign on how to live and to interpret the past and present. She argues that the preference broke the mould of the traditionally elitist culture and that the genre's emphasis on the inner person brought the private/inward sphere of the individual to the fore. In doing so new classes of persons were treated, e.g. women and the poor.

Kennedy[16] argues for another important change, namely that the divine authority of Scripture replaced the ethos of the speaker and his dramatic brilliance. The changed focus provided new topics and a distinctive style modelled to a large degree on the language of the psalms and prophets. Homily became the dominant genre of Christian rhetoric and integral to it was the exegesis of Scripture. The implication and outworking of this shift is significant and can be illustrated from the works of Eusebius. The writing of history, it is argued, is a classical concept; however, Eusebius reflects the values of Christian rhetoric rather than the conventions of classical tradition in that he did not compose speeches for his historical characters but preferred to quote the original writings and documents. He attempted to establish the authority of his work rather than to display dramatic brilliance.

S.R.L.

---

[12] E.A. Judge (per lit.) notes: 'It remained a matter of disagreement which works were in the corpus anyway, the point at issue being precisely who their authors were, and of course the 'poor' literacy of the apostles (by atticising standards) was the heart of the problem.'

[13] Julian, *Epist.* 36. The rescript is ostensibly motivated by a desire to stop teachers believing one thing and teaching another (422a-b, 423c). Julian strives for integrity among teachers. Christian teachers should teach their texts (Matthew and Luke are cited) in the churches and leave the teaching of classical literature to those who believe in Hermes and the Muses who inspired it. Christian youth, however, were not excluded from a classical eduction (424a).

[14] Kennedy, *Greek Rhetoric under Christian Emperors* 32.

[15] Cameron, *Christianity and the Rhetoric of Empire* 146.

[16] Kennedy, *Greek Rhetoric under Christian Emperors* 180 ff.

§9 Prescripts and Addresses in Ancient Letters

Oxyrhynchus   13 x 7 cm   Third century AD

Ed. pr. — J.R. Rea, *P. Oxy.* LI 3645 (London 1984) 126-9.

The papyrus appears complete. All four margins survive and there is evidence of neither preceding nor following columns. The folding and ink offsets on the back of the papyrus show the letter to have been rolled up. The back is otherwise blank. The hand is described as a 'good sloping cursive, showing some influence from the severe or mixed style of book hand'. This is especially so for the last line and a half (from καὶ σὺν αὐτῷ κτλ) which may have been written later but by the same hand.

εἰ, ὡς ἀκούω, κατὰ τὰς εὐχὰς ἡμῶν ὁ κύ- ριος ἡμῶν φίλος εἰσαῦθις ἄρχει, δύναν- ται ἐκ ταύτης τῆς προφάσεως ἀμφοτέ- ρους ἡμᾶς καὶ αὐτὸς καὶ ὁ ἀδελφὸς ῥύσα- 5 σθαι παρὰ τῷ φίλῳ αὐτῶν, τῷ εἰς Ὄασιν ἀναβάντι ὁπότε καὶ ἐπεδήμει ὁ βρα- χύτερος αὐτῶν καὶ σὺν αὐτῷ ἐκεῖ ἐγέ- νετο. ἐπιδ[ὰ]ν παρ' ὑμῖν γένηται, γνωρίσθητι αὐτῷ.	If, as I hear, in accord with our prayers our lord friend again holds a magistracy, on this pretext can he himself and his brother deliver us both by their friend, the one who went up to the Oasis when also the shorter (younger?) of them was at home and went with him there. Whenever he arrives, make acquaintance with him.

....

8. ἐπειδάν

The editor suggests that the letter may have been prompted by the imposition on the writer of some compulsory public service or liturgy. The context is suggested by the use of ῥύσασθαι in *ll.*4-5; cf. *P. Oxy.* XII 1424 *ll.*9-10: σπούδασον τοίνυν, ἄδελφε, τοῦτον ῥύσασθαι τοῦ λειτουργήματος — 'Hasten therefore, brother, to deliver him from the liturgy'. The magistrate and his brother together with a friend may in some way or other be able to offer help. At any rate when the friend arrives, the recipient is told to make himself known to him. A surprising feature of the letter is the absence of any names. Five different persons are referred to in the text but not one of them is named. Why? The editor connects the phenomenon with the absence of a prescript and farewell in the letter proper and of an inscription or address on its back. He notes:

> Probably ... the absence of prescript, farewell formula, and address, is deliberate and was part of the same marvellous discretion which forbade the mention of names and makes it so difficult now to understand what the writer's predicament was.

A reason for the silence may be that the letter concerns an illicit act. If, as the editor suggests, the letter deals with the avoidance of a liturgy by the intervention of friends and acquaintances, then the silence is understandable. The nature of the illicit act can only be guessed. However, two possibilities suggest themselves:

(a) σκέπη, i.e. 'protection' where an official deliberately fails to nominate a person who is eligible and due to serve; or

(b) ἀναχώρησις, i.e. 'flight' from one's fiscal domicile.

In the case of (b), one must assume some official complicity in the flight.

A second interpretation, which neither relies on construing the reference of ῥύσασθαι to deliverance from a liturgy nor assumes any illegal activity, can also be suggested. It rests on the observation that from time to time, and for reasons which are not always apparent, writers omitted to add an epistolary prescript. As an example of a similar omission of personal details see *P. Oxy.* XLIII 3150 (sixth century AD). Obviously the important element of the letter for the transmission of such details is the prescript, for it is unusual for the writer and recipient to be named in the letter's farewell (i.e. the simple imperative ἔρρωσο or ἐρρῶσθαί σε εὔχομαι) and not all letters carried an address (55.7% carried an address according to Ziemann's statistics). The relevance of the second interpretation depends on whether evidence for the omission of the prescript is extant in the same period. A number of letters are important here:

— *P. Lips.* III 105 (first or second century) carries neither a prescript nor a farewell. There are traces of writing (now effaced) on the verso. This may have been an address, but any decision is risky.

— *P. Oxy.* III 525 (early second century) carries neither a prescript nor an address. Accordingly, the names of the writer and recipient are unknown.

— *P. Stras.* IV 170 (second century) employs instead of the usual prescript a greeting in the optative, χαίροις κυρία. Neither the writer nor the recipient is named here. The letter carries no address. The back of the papyrus is blank.

— *P. Tebt.* II 417 (third century) appears to employ a greeting in the optative, [χαίρ]οις πολλά. Neither the writer nor the recipient is named here. The letter is written on the verso of an earlier document of which the ends and beginnings of lines from two columns survive. The letter carries no address.

Ziemann[1] has argued that the mutual accommodation of the form of the prescript and that of the address led to the gradual omission of the former from the beginning of letters. The address was retained, however, as it carried the same information but in a more accessible and useful location. Ziemann seems to date the beginning of omissions from the fifth century AD, though anomalies are noted at an earlier date, e.g. *P. Lips.* 105 (I/II AD) and *P. Oxy.* III 525 (II AD).

Koskenniemi[2] like Ziemann notes the overlap of information contained in the prescript and in the address, i.e. the naming of the writer and recipient; however, he argues that the prescript remained distinct just so long as it retained χαίρειν. The essential function of the prescript was perceived to be that of greeting. It is only as this word began to disappear from the prescript (IV AD) that the significance of the prescript itself waned and it began to disappear. Koskenniemi thus pins the disappearance of the prescript to that of χαίρειν; however, his position is ambiguous. On the one hand, it is observed that the infinitive, at least in part, was gradually perceived as a meaningless characteristic of the prescript.[3] This would, no doubt, offer a reasonable explanation for the term's disappearance and with it in time the disappearance of the prescript. On the other hand, Koskenniemi[4] cites a number of phenomena which indicate that the significance of the word in the prescript was not lost, i.e. its omission

---

[1] F. Ziemann, *De epistularum graecarum formulis solemnibus quaestiones selectae* (diss. Halle 1910) 284. See also *New Docs* 7 (1994) 35.

[2] H. Koskenniemi, *Studien zur Idee und Phraseologie des griechischen Briefes bis 400 n. Chr.* (Helsinki 1956) 155-8.

[3] Koskenniemi, *Studien zur Idee* 161.

[4] Koskenniemi, *Studien zur Idee* 161-7.

from letters of condolence, modification by Christian phrases (ἐν κυρίῳ etc.), variation by philosophical writers (εὖ πράττειν etc.), and the replacement of its infinitive form by either an imperative (χαῖρε) or an optative (χαίροις) form. Each phenomenon points to the continued significance of the term's usage in the prescript.

It is also unclear whether Koskenniemi is correct in believing that the essential function of the prescript was perceived to be that of greeting. With the advent of the new forms of prescript in the imperative and optative, if the naming of the writer and recipient were now perceived to be unessential, why did writers still seek to identify themselves and their addressees at the beginnings of letters? Note especially here the addition of ὁ δεῖνα σε προσαγορεύω (ἀσπάζομαι) or παρὰ τοῦ δεῖνος after the greeting in approximately 70% of cases (based on the data of Koskenniemi). It would be of interest to know whether there is any correlation between the addition of details concerning the writer and recipient at the beginning of the letter and the absence of an address on its verso. However, as far as I can see, no such information is provided.

Table 1:[5] The Mention of Writer and Recipient

In the letter	In the address	χαῖρε	χαίροις
W&R	W&R	12	8
W&R	R	5	4
W&R	—	8	5
W&R	?	3	2
R	W&R	0	0
R	R	0	4
R	—	2	3
R	?	4	1
—	W&R	0	0
—	R	1	0
—	—	0	2
—	?	0	2
?	W&R	1	0
?	?	0	1

---

[5] In compiling the table a number decisions were made. They are:
(a) Papyrus letters were omitted where it was judged that they were not despatched but kept as copies or as part of a writing exercise. There were two such texts, *P. Oxy.* 1185 and *P. Phil.* 34.
(b) In *P. Oxy.* 1587 χαῖρε was read.
(c) It is assumed that where the writer's name stood in a fragmentary address, the recipient's name also stood in the lost part. For ease of classification, cases where the name of the recipient survives in a fragmentary address have been assigned to R, i.e. it is assumed that the name of the writer was absent. Likewise cases where only ἀπόδος survives in an address have been assigned to R.
(d) There was only one example of an illegible address (R and ?). But there are 12 other cases in which the address is absent but the fragmentary nature of the papyrus does not permit one to be certain. In these cases it is a pity that photographs of the letters could not be consulted as they might have permitted a more definite decision concerning whether the address was absent or not. It is likely, I believe, that in many cases the address was absent; however, to be on the safe side I have assigned these instances to an uncertain category.

Table 1 was created by using the list of prescripts in the imperative and optative provided by Exler and supplemented by further examples found by a search of the Duke data-base.[6] It is to be read as follows: 'W' indicates that the writer's name occurs; 'R' indicates that the recipient's name occurs; '—' indicates the absence of a prescript or address, and therefore any occurrence of names; '?' indicates either that the prescript or address is illegible, or that the prescript or address is absent but the fragmentary nature of the papyrus does not permit one to be certain whether it was once there.

In a number of examples the absence of the address might be explained by factors other than mere fortune. Letters of introduction do not appear to carry an address (4 examples found in W&R and —). This is easily explained by the fact that such letters were carried by the person to be introduced. One suspects that such persons knew the relevant details or again had no particular recipient in mind. In either case an address was irrelevant. Also of interest is the fact that a number of letters without an address were actually written on the back of an older document ('W&R' = 4 examples, 'R' = 1 example, and '—' = 1 example). This will have precluded in many cases the possibility of writing an address on the back of the letter. However, it did not preclude absolutely the writing of an address as *P. Coll. Youtie* 54 (R and R) shows. In this case the address was written in the margin of the letter and the letter folded so that the address was exposed. It should also be borne in mind that if the address was important, then in most cases a blank sheet could have been used.

To return to the question at issue, the above statistics show that the presence of an address did not influence the addition or omission of details of writer and recipient in the letter proper. In the vast majority of cases ($\chi\alpha\hat{\imath}\rho\epsilon$ = 34, $\chi\alpha\hat{\imath}\rho o\iota\varsigma$ = 27) either the writer or recipient or both were mentioned in the letter regardless of the presence or absence of an address. There is no example where both details were given in the address and omitted in the letter proper and only one example (*P. Fay.* 129, third century AD) where the recipient was mentioned in the address and details of writer and recipient omitted in the letter.

More generally, if it is assumed that the overlap of information between the prescript and address led to the demise of the former, then one might reasonably assume that this would be preceded by an increased use of addresses on the backs of letters. In the period from the third century BC to the fourth/fifth century AD, Ziemann[7] gives the statistic that in 368 private letters

---

[6] F.J. Exler, *A Study in Greek Epistolography* (Washington 1923) 35-36. The examples are:

$\chi\alpha\hat{\imath}\rho o\iota\varsigma$: *P. Bas.* 16, *PBM* II 144, *P. Brem.* 19, *P. Coll. Youtie* I 54, *P. Flor.* II 140, *P. Haun* II 33, *P. Iand* II 12, VI 94, *P. Köln* III 163, *P. Mil.* II 75, 77, *P. Oxy.* I 112, III 526, VI 933, VII 1063, XX 2274, XLI 2986, XLIX 3469, *P. Princ.* II 71, 74, III 165, *P. Ross. Georg.* III 4, *PSI* 206, *PSI* IX 1049, *P. Stras.* I 37, *P. Tebt.* II 417, IV 170, *SB* V 8004, XIV 12082, 12107, 12176, XVI 12590 (=32).

$\chi\alpha\hat{\imath}\rho\epsilon$: *BGU* II 435, III 821, *P. Alex.* 27 and 29, *PBM* III 899, *P. Brem.* 56, *P. Fay.* 129, *P. Flor.* II 345, *P. Gron.* 17 and 18, *P. Herm.* 45, *P. Lond.* VI 1917, *P. Mich. Michael* 27, *P. Oxy.* I 122, VIII 1156, (IX 1185), XII 1492, 1587, XIV 1664, 1667, 1675, 1677, XVIII 2193, XXXVI 2785, XLI 2985, XLIII 3094, XLIX 3507, (*P. Phil.* 34), *P. Rein.* 48, *P. Ryl*, IV 691, *PSI* III 208, IX 1041, XIV 1420 (= *SB* VI 9452), *PSI. Congr.* XI 11, *SB* VI 9524, XII 11009, XIV 11588, 12177 (= 36).

[7] Ziemann, *De epistularum graecarum formulis solemnibus quaestiones selectae* 277. It is disappointing that data was not also given for the period after IV/V AD as this would permit a statistical analysis for the use of the address between periods when the use of the prescript was almost ubiquitous and when it was in sharp decline. One would expect that if an overlap of information played any part in the demise of the prescript, then this would be reflected in an increased use of the address. In the absence of this data, it is assumed above that the increased use of the address might have been evident in the period immediately preceding the loss of the prescript and that this would have contributed to the development.

205 or approx. 55.7% carry an address. Clearly the number of unaddressed letters in which there was no overlap of information may have been sufficiently large to cause the continued retention of the prescript. What is surprising, however, is the data for the period from the first AD to fourth/fifth century AD. Dividing the data into two periods, (i) first to third/fourth centuries AD and (ii) fourth to fourth/fifth centuries AD, one finds no significant difference between the proportion of private letters with an address and those without it.[8] There is no evidence to suggest that the proportion of addressed letters increased in time giving rise to the disappearance of the prescript. Another explanation must be sought.

The use of expressions found at the beginning of letters and containing the verb προσαγορεύω or ἀσπάζομαι is worthy of further study. A quick survey[9] of uses with προσαγορεύω indicates that in 9 cases no new information is added by the use of the expression. In other words it extends a further greeting to the recipient. In 5 cases it occurs after the initial greeting in χαῖρε or χαίροις and allows the writer to name himself. In 4 cases it is used to widen the greeting to persons other than the immediate addressee. There is also one use in an ἀφορμή-formula. The chronological distribution of the data indicates that its use after χαῖρε or χαίροις in order to allow the writer to name himself is earlier (III to III/IV AD). It can therefore be suggested that this use was earlier and it was only later extended (III/IV to IV AD) to include the other functions. The conclusion is further confirmed by a closer inspection of the papyri in the *P. Oxy.* series.[10] Again the earliest examples of expressions at the beginning of letters containing the verb προσαγορεύω are associated with a greeting in χαῖρε or χαίροις. The name of the writer could then be declared at the top of the letter. It would then appear that such expressions became conventional and their function extended even to the point of adding a superfluous additional greeting with no new information. The practice shows the continued importance of the naming of individuals at the beginning of the letter, regardless of the presence or absence of an address.

There are also formal grounds on which to distinguish the address and prescript beyond their positions and the information contained in them, for whereas the address was spoken to the letter's courier, the prescript was spoken to the letter's recipient.

---

[8] The contingency table is given below. The numbers in brackets indicate the expected values and the numbers above them the observed values. It will be observed that there is no significant variation between observed and expected values. The p-value of Table 2 is 0.379.

Table 2: The Proportions of Addressed Letters

	Number of letters with an address	Number of letters without an address
Earlier period (I to III/IV AD)	146 (143.3)	97 (99.7)
Later period (IV to IV/V AD)	25 (27.7)	22 (19.3)

[9] The papyri surveyed for the use of προσαγορεύω at the beginnings of letters are: *P. Alex.* 29 (III/IV AD), *P. Ant.* II 93 (IV AD), *P. Bas.* 16 (AD 200-250), *P. Erl.* 118 (III-IV AD), *P. Freib.* IV 57 (I/II AD), *P. Herm.* 4 (IV AD), *P. Meyer* 21 (III/IV AD), *P. Mich.* VIII 519 (IV AD), *P. Michael* 29 (IV AD), *P. Nag. Ham.* 66 (IV AD), *P. Neph.* 12 (AD IV), *P. Ryl.* IV 691 (III AD), *PSI* VII 826 (IV/V AD), *PSI* IX 1041 (III/IV AD), *SB* III 7243 (IV AD), *SB* XII 10773 (V AD), *SB* XIV 11881 (IV AD) and *SB* XIV 12177 (III AD). *P. Neph.* 12 serves two of the classified functions and has been counted twice in the statistics.

[10] The *P. Oxy.* numbers are: 123, 526, 1300, 1350, 1492, 1587, 1664, 1667, 1774, 2150, 2275, 2785, 3150, 3507, 3819, 3863.

Prescripts in New Testament Letters

The formulation and transmission of the prescript was important in the writing and textual history of NT letters respectively. The importance of the prescript in giving the orientation of the letter is apparent from a consideration of its usage in the NT.

(1) The tendency apparent in the text history of Pauline letters to widen the audience beyond the original circle of recipients. The tendency appears to give expression to the view that the Pauline letter was not merely occasional in nature, i.e. addressed to a particular church in a particular situation. Its application extended beyond the confines of just one congregation.

(2) A generalisation of the audience is also attested in the catholic epistles, cf. James 1.1, 1 Pet. 1.1-2, 2 Pet. 1.1 and Jude 1. In these cases, however, the generalisation is not so much part of the textual histories of the letters as of the pseudepigraphical character of the composition itself. It is not as Harnack[11] held because these letters emanated from apostles, prophets and teachers who felt that their mission was to the church as a whole. More probably it belongs to the genre which, as Schnider and Stenger[12] argue, follows features of the Jewish diaspora letter, i.e. a broad or universal address, a fictive authorship by a past figure of authority, an author who is often the recipient of revelation and a *Sitz im Leben* of a threatened loss of identity.

(3) Though the Pauline letters use an oriental form of the prescript (e.g. ὁ δεῖνα τῷ δεῖνι. χάρις ὑμῖν καὶ εἰρήνη πληθυνθείη),[13] Paul shows great flexibility expanding on the intitulations of the sender and the recipient, as well as the salutation itself, to flag major themes in the letter.[14]

(4) Hebrews, which is a text more akin to a homily than to a letter, lacks a prescript. However, it does possess an epistolary conclusion (chapter 13), and as such was generally recognized as a letter by the early church and collected together with the letters in the various codices and canons of the church. Naturally, it has been debated whether chapter 13 was original to the composition of the text or whether it was a later interpolation to give the document the appearance of a letter. In view of the evidence adduced above one must be careful in using the absence of a prescript to argue for or against either position.

(5) The Greek form of the prescript (e.g. ὁ δεῖνα τῷ δεῖνι χαίρειν) is only attested at James 1.1 and in the letters of Acts (15.23 and 23.26). The Greek form of the letters recorded in Acts can be easily explained. Luke was a Hellenistic writer who used the epistolary convention of his day. Its use at James 1.1, however, is noteworthy. James is properly a collection of paraenetic material which has been given the ostensible form of a letter by the same addition of the prescript. That the Greek form of the prescript was used may indicate the provenance of that innovation as the Hellenised church. Harnack[15] has argued that the compilation of materials in James was made earlier (probably in

---

[11] A Harnack, *The Mission and Expansion of Christianity in the First Three Centuries* (tr. 1908, repr. Gloucester Mass. 1972) 341-3.

[12] F. Schnider and W. Stenger, *Studien zum neutestamentlichen Briefformular* (Leiden 1987) 34-40.

[13] On the difference between the Greek and oriental forms of the prescript see P. Vielhauer, *Geschichte der urchristlichen Literatur* (Berlin 1978) 65.

[14] Schnider and Stenger, *Studien zum neutestamentlichen Briefformular* 1-33.

[15] A. Harnack, *Geschichte der altchristlichen Literatur bis Eusebius*, II, *Die Chronologie*, vol.1 (Leipzig 1897) 488-90.

Palestine before the middle of the second century) with the document remaining in obscurity until the name of James was added in its prescript at the end of second century. Dibelius[16] differs from Harnack arguing that though the document is clearly pseudonymous and ascribed to James as its literary patron, James 1.1 is not a later interpolation. Against the hypothesis of a later addition of the prescript Dibelius notes:[17] (a) the presence of a play on the words $\chi\alpha\acute{\iota}\rho\epsilon\iota\nu$ (v.1) and $\chi\alpha\rho\acute{\alpha}\nu$ (v.2), a rhetorical device used elsewhere; and (b) the absence of any heroizing of James in the prescript, e.g as 'brother of the Lord'. Neither of Dibelius's points is convincing.[18]

It is worth bearing in mind that the prescript which marks James as pseudepigraphical need not have been added with any intention to deceive. Should the compilation have first circulated without a prescript but with a traditional attribution to James, it can plausibly be argued that the later addition of the prescript was made by a person or persons who merely wished to make explicit its supposed authorship. The text is not otherwise overtly pseudepigraphic. The change in form (i.e. from paraenesis to letter) entailed in the addition of the prescript may also not have been intentional. As already noted, one of the tendencies of epistolary practice was the loss of the prescript. The addition of the prescript may have been prompted by a desire to restore the traditional attribution of authorship to the letter itself.

S.R.L.

---

[16] M. Dibelius, *Der Brief des Jakobus*, revised by H. Greeven (Göttingen repr. 1964) — ET, *James* (Philadelphia 1981) 23-4.

[17] Dibelius, *James*, 18 and 53.

[18] I argue elsewhere against the two points made by Dibelius. See my forthcoming article in *Novum Testamentum* entitled, 'The Prescript of James'.

§10 A Rescript to the Victors of Sacred Games

Oxyrhynchus ca AD 253-7?
Ed. pr. — J.R. Rea, *P. Oxy.* LI 3611 (London 1984) 26-30.

The bottom edge of the papyrus is lost, though the text itself appears complete (so ed. pr. note to *l*.21). The rescript is dated by reference to the named emperors and prefect. See ed pr. note to *ll*.1-4 and 15. As the endorsement (m.2) shows the text to be a copy, it might have been made afterwards and used as a precedent in a later case. The hand is described as 'a practised official cursive, much influenced by the "Chancery" style', the hand of the endorsement as 'less formal'.

Αὐτοκράτωρ Καῖσαρ Πούπλιος Λικίννιος	Imperator Caesar Publius Licinius
Οὐαλεριανὸς Εὐσεβὴς Εὐτυχὴς Σεβαστὸς καὶ	Valerianus Pius Felix Augustus and
Αὐτοκράτωρ Καῖσαρ Πούπλιος Λικίννιος	Imperator Caesar Publius Licinius
Οὐ[α]λεριανὸς Γαλλιηνὸς Εὐ[σ]εβ(ὴς) Ε[ὐτ]υχ(ὴς) Σ[εβασ]τ(ὸς)	Valerianus Gallienus Pius Felix Augustus
5 ἱερονείκαις τοῖς ἐν Ἀντ[ινόου π]όλει δ[ι]ὰ	to the victors of sacred games in Antinoopolis through
Σεπτιμίου Καλλικλέους. (v.) [ ] (vac.)	Septimius Kallikles.
ἐπεὶ κατὰ τὸν ἔν[α μ]ὲν χρόνον δυοῖν	Since for a period of two
ἀφαιρέσεων τῶν καλουμένων παρὰ	'retractions' as they are called among
Ἀλεξανδρεῦσι, τὸ[ν] τῶν πεντεκαίδεκά τε	the Alexandrians, amounting to fifteen
10 μηνῶν καὶ ἡμερῶν ἑπτὰ γενόμενον,	months and seven days,
τοὺς μὲν Ἀλε[ξ]ανδρέας ἱερονείκας εἰληφέ-	the Alexandrian victors of sacred games have
ναι τὰς ἐπὶ τοῖς ἀγῶσι συντάξεις παρὰ τοῦ	received the game allowances from the
ταμείου φατέ, τὸ δ[ὲ] κατ[ὰ] τοὺς Ἀντινοέας	treasury, you say, but the one pertaining to you Antinoites
ὑμᾶς ἐπεσχῆ[σθαι, πρόσ]ιτε τῷ φίλῳ ἡμῶν	has been stopped, apply to our friend
15 καὶ ἐπάρχῳ τ[ῆς Αἰγύπ]του Μαγνίῳ Φήλικι	and prefect of Egypt, Magnius Felix,
παρεχόμενοι ταῦτα, [ὅς,] ἐὰν μηδενὶ λόγῳ	presenting these (matters), who, should he
τὸ καθ᾽ ὑμᾶς ἐπεσχημένον εὑρίσκῃ, προστάξει	find that the one pertaining to you was stopped for no reason, will command
τὰς τοῦ ῥηθέντος χρόνου συντάξεις ἀποδο-	the allowances for the said period to be

θῆναι καὶ ἰς τὸ λοιπὸν ὑμῖν δίδοσθαι ὅσα
20 καὶ διὰ παντὸς τοῦ πρόσθεν χρόνου τετυ-
χήκατε. (v.) [ ] (vac.)

paid and in future to be given to you as
much as you have obtained over all the
preceding period. [ ]

Back, downwards (m.2)
ἀ(ντίγραφον) ἀντιγραφῆς Καίσαρος

Copy of a rescript of Caesar

5, 11. ἱερονικ-   19. εἰς

Before commenting on the above papyrus, it is well to clarify first a few matters and the terminology associated with rescripts. Corporate bodies (including cities), officials or important individuals might deliver their requests and petitions to the emperor in the form of *epistulae* delivered by an embassy, the imperial post or a messenger respectively; the emperor's reply also in the form of an *epistula* was then carried back by the same means. An individual of humbler status, on the other hand, delivered his/her petition (*libellus*), generally speaking in person or through an agent who was closely related to himself/herself, to the emperor who replied by subscribing (*subscriptio*) his decision underneath the *libellus*. The currency of the term *subscriptio* is confined to the second and early third centuries.[1] Thereafter, imperial responses to *libelli* attained an independent status headed by a prescript consisting of the names of the emperor(s) and petitioner(s). See *P. Oxy.* 3611 *ll*.1-6. They were now termed rescripts (*rescriptiones*). The distinction between *epistulae* and *subscriptiones* derives from Wilcken's influential article titled 'Zu den Kaiserreskripten' (*Hermes* 55 [1920] 1-42). Table 1 below lists a number of the important differences which have been alleged to pertain between the two types of rescripts. Some are disputed and the debate will be described below.

The text of *P. Oxy.* 3611 represents a copy of an imperial rescript issued to the victors of sacred games in Antinoopolis (ἱερονείκαις τοῖς ἐν Ἀντ[ινόου π]ό̣λει). It may reasonably be assumed that the association of athletes had written to the emperor through their representative, Septimius Kallikles. The latter then awaited the emperor's decision, carrying it back to his fellow-athletes. It is unclear whether the approach to the emperors was made whilst they were in Rome or in the East. The point at issue is the non-payment of allowances for a period of fifteen months and seven days. The payment was one of the benefits which accrued to the victors of sacred games and apparently was made by the imperial treasury.[2] The petitioners are told to approach the prefect of Egypt, Magnius Felix, who would rectify the matter.

---

[1] Nörr, 'Apokrimata apokrimaton (P. Columbia 123)' in *Proceedings of XVI Int. Congr. of Papyrology* (Chico 1981) 591-2, observes that there is only one use of the Greek equivalent of *subscriptio*, i.e. ὑπογραφή, in our sources, i.e. *P. Harr.* 67 belonging to the reign of Antoninus Pius. He suggests that this limited usage might result from the fact that ὑπογραφή had a special currency with the corresponding activity of provincial governors. On the vagary of Roman legal terminology with respect to imperial constitutions see Nörr, 'Apokrimata' 581-96.

[2] Various privileges accrued to successful athletes from both imperial and civic authorities, e.g. a right to public maintenance usually from a civic fund (*CPH* 55 and 70; from *P. Lond.* 1164i we learn that the right could be sold); release from taxation and public liturgies (*BGU* 1073 and *WChr* 158). Diplomata listing imperial privileges and immunities might be issued to eligible members (*BGU* 1074).

The editor of *P. Oxy.* 3611 concludes that the text contained no formula of greeting (note to *l.*6) and probably no formula of farewell (note to *l.*21). The absence of these two formal features indicates that the text cannot have been an imperial *epistula*. The heading consisting of imperial titles further confirms that a private rescript is involved here. The form is somewhat surprising as it was usual for corporate bodies, such as one might suppose the victors of sacred games to have been, to write to an emperor by *epistula* and to receive his reply by *epistula*. But there was no hard and fast rule as *P. Lips.* 44 cols. 2 and 3 (= *MChr* 381) shows.[3]

Table 1: Differences between *Epistulae* and *Subscriptiones*

	Epistulae	*Subscriptiones*
(a)	Beginning: Name of emperor in nominative and of recipient in dative followed by greeting to recipient(s) (*salutem* or *salutem dicit*)	Name of emperor in nominative and of recipient in dative but no greeting
(b)	End: *Vale* — Farewell in emperor's hand	*Scripsi* or *rescripsi* in the emperor's hand;[4] *recognovi* in the hand of the *a libellis*
(c)	Length: Longer	Briefer and to the point[5]
(d)	Position: A separate text	Text of subscription added underneath the petition
(e)	Language: Latin or Greek	Latin but Greek translations might be made[6]
(f)	Occasion: Issued in response to an *epistula*	Issued in response to a *libellus*[7]
(g)	Mode: Sent as a letter to petitioner[8]	Added underneath the *libellus* and posted at the residence of the emperor at the time of issuance[9]

---

[3] *P. Lips.* 44 contains the Latin text of an imperial rescript to the synod of gymnasts and stage-performers, probably from Alexandria. It concerns the criteria of eligibility for immunity from civic liturgies. The facts that the text is in Latin and that it lacks the formulaic greetings are strong indications that it is not an *epistula*.

[4] The emperor by writing *scripsi* or *rescripsi* authenticated the rescript. His seal appears to have been applied below. Before this, however, the *a libellis* had drafted the rescript and checked the final copy prepared by a subordinate clerk adding *recognovi* in his own hand. See Wilcken, *Hermes* 55 (1920) 6-7. Nörr, *ZSS* (Roman Abt.) 98 (1981) 12 and 32, holds that *recognovi* was added after the emperor had added his mark of authentification.

[5] See also Honoré, *Emperors and Lawyers* 36.

[6] See also Williams, *JRS* 64 (1974) 101-3, and Honoré, *Emperors and Lawyers* 37-8 (but see p.42 where it is suggested that trivial rescripts were composed in Greek). See below for the view of Nörr.

[7] Wilcken, *Hermes* 55 (1920) 9-7.

[8] Wilcken, *Hermes* 55 (1920) 15 and 38.

[9] R. Katzoff, 'On the Intended Use of P. Col. 123', in *Proceedings of XVI Int. Congr. of Papyrology* (Chico 1981) 561, observes: 'imperial bureaucracy never took the trouble to post rescripts anywhere except at the residence of the emperor at the time.' Rescripts were not only issued by emperors. The procedure of the prefects of Egypt was different; copies of their decision were remitted to the nome metropolis and posted there for the petitioner to copy. Though whilst in Egypt the prefectorial bureaucracy, which was concerned to have its rescripts posted locally, may have handled paperwork and followed its own procedure. On prefectural rescripts

The language of the rescript is also noteworthy. It was the standard administrative practice of the office of *a libellis* to compose its rescripts in Latin. Cf. again *P. Lips.* 44. A number of rescripts in Greek are extant, of which *P. Oxy.* 3611 is one, but it is unclear whether these were actually composed in Greek or whether they are just Greek translations of Latin originals. In the matter of composition the office of *a libellis* differed from the offices in charge of responses to *epistulae*. The latter responses were assigned to either the office of *ab epistulis Latinis* or the office of *ab epistulis Graecis* for composition in the language of the city or corporate body.

Wilcken[10] reconstructs the following features of a subscribed *libellus*:

(1) Upper margin: page number in the roll of the imperial archive.
(2) Above the *libellus*: date of the presentation of the *libellus* to Caesar.
(3) The text of the *libellus*.
(4) The text of the *subscriptio* (prescript and context) in the hand of a chancellery clerk.
(5) *Recognovi* in the hand of the head of the chancellery.
(6) *Rescripsi* (*scripsi*) in the hand of Caesar followed by imperial seal and the seals of witnesses.
(7) In one text the number of *libelli* in the roll of the imperial archive is added after *rescripsi* and before the text was posted.
(8) Date and place of imperial undersigning.
(9) Date and place of *propositio* added by the imperial chancellery.

P. Oxy. 3611, as is the case with all other imperial rescripts, only bears the text of the response (4). All other formal elements are absent. In particular the *libellus* is not reproduced. Wilcken notes the usual absence of such features but concludes that they were omitted in making the copy. In this regard, it will be noted that *P. Oxy.* 3611 is itself a copy (m.2). However, it is questioned whether Wilcken's conclusion is correct.

Subscriptiones and *Epistulae*

Fergus Millar[11] recounts a commonplace told variously about Hellenistic rulers but told by Cassius Dio (59.6.3) about Hadrian:

> When the emperor was on a journey, so the story runs, a woman approached him and asked for his attention. Hadrian replied that he had no time, at which the woman shouted, 'Then do not be a king!' So he turned round and gave her leave to speak.

The story illustrates an important perception about the Graeco-Roman ruler. In particular, Romans and provincials expected that they could approach their emperor with requests and petitions. Many of the approaches concerned indulgences and privileges, but a great number also were of a legal nature, especially seeking an interpretation or clarification of the law. He was the ultimate legal authority in the empire and his opinion carried great weight.[12] Dutiful

---

from Egypt see Wilcken, *Hermes* 55 (1920) 27-37. Besides some formal differences (see pp.27-29) Wilcken considers the procedures of imperial and prefectural rescripts similar.

[10] Wilcken, *Hermes* 55 (1920) 38-41.

[11] Fergus Millar, *The Emperor in the Roman World* (London 1977) 3.

[12] The issuing of imperial rescripts on points of law is similar to the giving of *responsa* by private lawyers. See A.M. Honoré, '"Imperial" rescripts AD 193-305: Authorship and authenticity', *JRS* 69 (1979) 51-2, and idem, *Emperors and Lawyers* (London 1981) 6. Honoré describes the imperial practice as a 'free legal advice service'.

emperors were conscious of their subjects' expectations and spent considerable time giving decisions on the numerous requests brought before them.[13] On the basis of *P. Col.* 123 (a papyrus containing 13 rescripts issued by Severus on three consecutive days whilst visiting Egypt in AD 200) Williams[14] estimates that approximately 1,500 rescripts were issued annually. The emperor was assisted in this task by the office of the *a libellis*,[15] a professional lawyer whose responsibility it was to formulate a legal opinion and to draft the rescript[16] even before the emperor decided the matter.[17] In fact the emperor only wrote *rescripsi* (or *scripsi*) at the end of the rescript.[18] The addition appears to have been necessary to authenticate the rescript.[19] The rescript was then executed by an official in the chancellery writing *recognovi*.

As already noted above, approach to the emperor varied according to the status of the petitioner. If the petitioner was a city, corporate body or an influential individual or high official, *epistulae* were the usual vehicle of communication between the parties. An embassy or messenger carried the petitioner's *epistula* to the emperor. The embassy or messenger either awaited the emperor's *epistula* in reply (e.g. in the case of a city or incorporated body) or the *epistula* was sent by the *cursus publicus* (e.g. in the case of a Roman official). Such correspondence was handled by the offices either of the *ab epistulis Latinis* or of the *ab epistulis Graecis*. An individual of humbler status, on the other hand, delivered his/her *libellus*, generally speaking in person or through a closely related agent,[20] to the emperor who replied by subscribing his decision underneath the *libellus*. The procedures involved here have been a matter of some dispute.

Wilcken argues that *libelli* addressed to the emperor were delivered in person either to the emperor or to the governor of the petitioner's province. If delivered to the emperor, the original *libellus* was subscribed and handed back to the petitioner, with only a copy being retained by the imperial *scrinium*.[21] After the reforms of Hadrian the procedure changed. The

---

[13] For a survey of the handling of requests for legal advice and the issuing of rescripts by the emperors from Augustus to Gordian see Honoré, *Emperors and Lawyers* 1-23.

[14] W. Williams, 'The *Libellus* Procedure and the Severan Papyri', *JRS* 64 (1974) 92.

[15] The earliest evidence for the issuing of rescripts comes from the reign of Tiberius (*Dig.* 48.5.39.10), though the practice was possibly initiated by Augustus. It is not known when the office of *a libellis* was created. The earliest known equestrian to hold the office was L. Volusius Maecianus (*CIL* XIV 5347) during the reign of Hadrian. The average tenure of office was approximately three years (Honoré, *JRS* 69 [1979] 56, and idem, *Emperors and Lawyers* 55). Before the creation of the office of *a libellis* the emperors may have delegated the right of response to respected lawyers and in addition may have set up their own legal service to answer others (presumably the more important *libelli*) themselves (Honoré, *Emperors and Lawyers* 5).

[16] On stylistic variation between rescripts and the identification of their respective authors see Honoré, *JRS* 69 (1979) 51-64, and idem, *Emperors and Lawyers* 46ff. Honoré observes: 'The availability of the emperor determines the number of rescripts, the personality of the secretary their style.'

[17] The emperor does not appear to have normally been assisted by members of his *concilium* in deciding a legal issue subject to petition. See Williams, *ZPE* 17 (1975) 70-8, and Nörr, *ZSS* 98 (1981) 12.

[18] The use of *subscriptio* to refer to an emperor's subscription of a petitioner's *libellus* is only attested for the second century AD. It is for this reason that the general term rescript is used to refer to the subscribed response.

[19] Honoré, *Emperors and Lawyers* 42.

[20] Wilcken, *Hermes* 55 (1920) 11, Williams, *JRS* 64 (1974) 93-8, and Nörr, *ZSS* 98 (1981) 11. Nörr (pp. 35-6) does consider as possible one exception to the rule that *libelli* were delivered in person. That is when the emperor was absent from Rome. Then he conjectures somewhat tentatively that the petition could be delivered either to the emperor or to Rome. In the latter case the libellus was dispatched to the emperor (his chancellery travelling with him) and once authorized was sent back to Rome for posting there.

[21] Cf. Millar, *The Emperor in the Roman World* 538 and 544. He argues that in the first century petitions were addressed verbally to the emperor and it was only from the second century that written *libelli* come to any preponderance.

original *libellus* was subscribed and posted outside the residence of the emperor, either in Rome if the emperor was resident there at the time or outside his headquarters if the emperor was travelling. Petitioners could make a copy of the subscription and have it attested. Approximately 30 days after posting, the *libellus* with *subscriptio* was removed and retained by the imperial *scrinium*.[22] Because of what Wilcken perceived to be the function of *libelli* in the legal process he argues that the services of the provincial governors after Hadrian's innovation were used to deliver *libelli* to the emperor and to receive back the subscribed original *libelli* for posting.[23] Again the petitioner could make his copy and have it attested. However, in this case the originals were added to a roll containing correspondence between the emperor and his governor and preserved in the provincial archive. Only a copy was retained in Rome.

Wilcken's view is followed by Garnsey.[24] This is particularly so with regard to *libelli* appealing judicial sentences, where a petitioner's movements would naturally have been restricted. In such instances a *libellus* could be sent to the emperor through the governor and his response sent back. See *Dig*. 28.3.6.9 and 49.4.1.7 and 10. Cf. also *Dig*. 49.1.25. Garnsey distinguishes criminal (petition against a sentence or sanction) from civil appeals. The former type of appeal functioned to correct perceived injustices or the inexperience of judges. As Millar[25] observes, the imperial responses show 'the role of the emperor in redressing the rigour of the law, making allowances for ignorance of it and giving guidance on procedure'. They also reflect, for Garnsey, the growth of the criminal *cognitio* procedure. In such a procedure the judge or magistrate had a greater power to discriminate and to determine penalties than had previously been the case under the formulary procedure of the *ius civile* with its pecuniary penalties. In particular rescripts attest the desire to protect the social elite from the harsher penalties associated with *cognitio*.

Wilcken's proposal regarding the role played by provincial governors in the transfer of *libelli* is disputed. For example, Williams[26] admits contrary examples but argues that these are exceptional cases in which the government went out of its way to help the petitioner. As individuals had to present their petitions in person, Williams surmises that most petitions would be from persons living in close proximity to Rome. This, he suggests, explains why it was never considered necessary to create a Greek-speaking *a libellis* on analogy with the *ab epistulis Graecis*. Further, Williams argues that the requirement to deliver petitions in person was a 'necessary act of economy' to limit the flow of requests from the provinces. Only face-to-face business was heard.[27]

Dispute also surrounds the promulgation of rescripts. Wilcken[28] had originally argued that before the introduction of *propositio* or posting by Hadrian the subscribed original *libellus* was handed back to the petitioner or his agent. According to Wilcken only copies were retained in the imperial *scrinium*. After the introduction of *propositio* by Hadrian, Wilcken maintained against Mommsen that all rescripts in the form of *subscriptiones* were posted, not just those

---

[22] Wilcken, *Hermes* 55 (1920) 26.

[23] Wilcken, *Hermes* 55 (1920) 19-27. *Epistulae* were, in Wilcken's view, another matter and for the most part were generally not dispatched through the governor.

[24] P. Garnsey, *Social Status and Legal Privilege in the Roman Empire* (Oxford 1970) 67, 69, and 70-71.

[25] Millar, *The Emperor in the Roman World* 547.

[26] Williams, *ZPE* 17 (1975) 58-62. So also Nörr, *ZSS* 98 (1981) 11 and 37, who notes that governors seldom intervened in the process.

[27] See further Williams, 'The publication of imperial subscripts', *ZPE* 40 (1980) 284-7.

[28] Wilcken, *Hermes* 55 (1920) 11-12 and 20.

which represented a change of law.[29] On the other hand, no rescripts in the form of *epistulae* were posted. However, Wilcken[30] holds that the purpose of posting was not to bring to public knowledge matters of fundamental and general significance. The rescript, it is argued, was usually posted up outside his residence, e.g. in the portico of Trajan's baths in Rome.[31] As the subscribed petition was not returned to the petitioner, it was up to him/her to make copies of the posted rescript and have them attested. (After the period of posting, copies could only be made from the imperial archives. To obtain such a copy a special petition to the emperor was made.[32]) Clearly posting was a form of publication and copies of the decisions could be made by lawyers or other interested members of the public, though this was not its intended purpose. The original subscribed petition was glued to other petitions to form a roll, the *liber libellorum rescriptorum*, and filed in the imperial archive at Rome. If the emperor's decision was made in response to a petition presented to him during a provincial visit, the original was probably carried back to Rome; in addition if an official translation of the decision was made, it may have been filed in the archive of the provincial governor where it might later be consulted.[33]

Honoré[34] allows for greater variation in practice of posting. Rescripts were usually posted up outside the emperor's residence but if he was on the move or some delay had occurred in dealing with the request (delays appear to be usual, p.49), the subscribed *libellus* might be sent back to Rome or to the petitioner's provincial capital for posting. Also Honoré maintains the possibility that rescripts were handed back to the petitioner or his agent even after Hadrian.[35]

Nörr, who looks at the period between Hadrian and Diocletian, finds two particular problems with Wilcken's treatment of imperial subscripts, namely his use of the procedures associated with prefectorial subscripts in Egypt to fill the gaps in our knowledge and an undervaluation of the constitutions transmitted in the Roman legal tradition.[36] After considering the different promulgation marks (e.g. pp., acc., d, s) Nörr concludes that Wilcken's view that all subscripts were posted is too simple. The evidence provided by texts bearing the marks *d(ata)* and *acc(epta)* implies that the subscript, presumably only a copy with the original retained in the imperial archive, was handed back to the petitioner. Nörr also argues against the procedure proposed by Wilcken, namely that the subscript was placed below the original *libellus* together with the marks of imperial authorization and verification by the chancellery (i.e. the *(re)scripsi/recognovi*-clause) and was then posted. He concedes that this

---

[29] Wilcken, *Hermes* 55 (1920) 17.

[30] Wilcken, *Hermes* 55 (1920) 19.

[31] Williams, *JRS* 64 (1974) 98-101, and *ZPE* 40 (1980) 283-94. The earliest direct evidence for posting is Pius's subscript to Sextilius Acutianus of Smyrna (*CIL* III 411, AD 139). Williams (*pace* Mommsen and Wilcken) argues that the practice might have gone back to the reign of Augustus. (The keeping of rolls of petitions in the archive is also thought to go back to Augustus; see Williams, *ZPE* 17 [1975] 61.) The subscriptions were not necessarily posted on the day of decision but were allowed to accumulate until a suitable number could be put up together. But see also Nörr, *ZSS* 98 (1981) 13, who thinks that rescripts might have also been posted singly. Williams suggests that the subscription may then have been left on display for approx. one month (so also Wilcken, *Hermes* 55 (1920) 17) or, if outside Rome, for the duration of an emperor's visit.

[32] Wilcken, *Hermes* 55 (1920) 37, and Williams, *ZPE* 17 (1975) 59 n.51.

[33] Williams differs from Wilcken on these points. See above.

[34] Honoré, *Emperors and Lawyers* 27-9.

[35] Honoré, *Emperors and Lawyers* 32 and 35.

[36] Nörr, *ZSS* 98 (1981) 4-6, holds that there were numerous and significant differences between imperial and prefectorial subscripts. On the difficulties of using the Roman legal tradition as a source of evidence see Nörr, *ZSS* 98 (1981) 6-11. Of particular significance here is the difficulty in determining to which categories (e.g. *edicta, decreta, epistula, subscriptio* etc.) the constitutions belong.

may have been an earlier practice but notes that it had changed at least by the second half of the second century and perhaps as early as the time of Hadrian's reform of the procedure. Rather the original *libellus* with its subscript was added to a roll in the imperial archive where it could later be accessed and a copy taken with the emperor's consent. Only a copy of the subscript without the mark of imperial authorization and verification was subjected to the physical risks of posting. Further, it is argued that as the *libelli* were not promulgated but only the subscripts, the latter acquired an independent form. In particular, an address was added to the beginning of the subscript,[37] and the facts of the case were carefully repeated in the subscript. The nexus between *libellus* and rescript was loosened with the result that the *subscriptio* was no longer in a 'pure' form.[38] The changes also relativized to a degree the distinction between *epistulae* and *subscriptiones*.[39] The later term disappeared from the beginning of the third century and both types of constitution were now called *rescriptiones*.

The office of the *a libellis* and the issuance of rescripts ceased as a result of the codification of imperial rescripts. Acting on the assumption that the same problems would constantly recur and be the subject of repeated petitions, Diocletian ordered new codes of rescripts to be compiled. In future petitioners and their legal representatives would be able to consult these.[40]

The Legal Status of Rescripts

Rescripts were originally sought by petitioners for a particular case. Their usefulness did not, however, end there. Other petitioners or litigants in a law-suit also quoted relevant rescripts (without the preceding *libelli*) as precedents in support of their cases. Rescripts stated the rules of private or administrative law and as such possessed imperial authority. Their legal force and quality, however, is difficult to determine and therefore disputed. For example, Honoré[41] maintains that rescripts did not have 'the force of a judgement or any other executive force'; they were neither pieces of legislation nor judgements but rather were declarations of what the law was.[42] As such they were only 'authoritative opinions' which petitioners could use in any way they pleased. If favourable, a rescript could be used to exert pressure on the judge. Alternatively, if unfavourable, the petitioner might decide not to produce it. As Millar[43] observes, the acquisition and use of rescripts depended entirely on the petitioner. Even as an authoritative opinion a rescript might be ignored by a provincial governor or other judge if the actual facts of the case did not conform to those alleged in the petition. The judge found the facts of the case and if these were not consistent with those assumed in the rescript, he was not bound by its ruling. Moreover, rescripts did not interfere in the course of legal proceedings;

---

[37] See also Nörr, 'Apokrimata' 599.

[38] See also Nörr, 'Apokrimata' 576 and 598-9.

[39] Cf. also Nörr, 'Apokrimata' 577. Other points of distinction between epistulae and subscriptiones are also questioned. For example, Nörr, *ZSS* 98 (1981) 9-10, argues that length is not the sure criterion that it is often thought. A better criterion to distinguish *epistulae* from *subscriptiones*, in his view, is the status of the addressee, if known. It is also argued that though composition in Latin was the usual administrative practice, some composition in Greek may have occurred ('Apokrimata' 600). If a translation was made, it is unclear whether this was undertaken by the chancellery or the person having the copy made (p.601).

[40] See further Honoré, *Emperors and Lawyers* 135-8.

[41] Honoré, *JRS* 69 (1979) 52, and idem, *Emperors and Lawyers* 24-6 and 127. In issuing rescripts emperors appear to have respected the law. Only very seldom were rescripts issued in which indulgences were given.

[42] Honoré, *Emperors and Lawyers* viii, 6 and 24.

[43] Millar, *The Emperor in the Roman World* 546-7.

trials were not postponed to await rescripts and if a rescript arrived too late, the judgement was not affected.

On the other hand, Katzoff[44] holds that decisions on particular cases such as rescripts and *decreta* (i.e. judicial decisions of the emperor) had binding force in the cases for which they were given. The point of dispute for him is whether rescripts had a more general application beyond that one case.

Was the rescript *lex* (generally valid) or *exemplum* (precedent) only? Whilst Ulpian's opinion is quite clear, holding that rescripts were law (*legem esse constat*, *Dig.* 1.4.1.1), the earlier opinion of Gaius is more tentative (*id legis vicem optineat*, *Instit.* 1.5). Rescripts (only *epistulae* are named), as imperial constitutions, have the force of law as the emperor derived his *imperium* through law. Nörr[45] sees Gaius's position as both identifying and distancing. The actions of the emperor Macrinus (AD 217-218) are informative. He abolished the rescripts of earlier emperors believing that it was wrong that the inclinations and wishes of the likes of Commodus and Caracalla should appear to be law (*leges videri*, *SHA* 13.1). It is also observed that Trajan refused to answer private petitioners lest the favour done in a particular case might be applied in other cases as well. Clearly, the legal tendency was to give rescripts a more general application and thus the force of law. The same can be seen to apply to the *decreta* of emperors (Fronto, *Epist. ad M. Caes.* 1.6.2).

Nörr[46] argues that a full, harmonized and clear picture of the legal quality of rescripts is meaningless. However, the concepts of *lex* and *exemplum* need not be mutually contradictory. Some prescripts may have had binding force in the particular case for which they were issued, but only served as *exempla* for future cases. But the tendency was for the authority of the imperial *exempla* to increase and for them to become general rules. As Garnsey[47] observes the ad hoc decisions of emperors were treated as *ius* and as such they could not be ignored. But their validity as law was only de facto, for people held them to be law. Also it is important to distinguish between types of decisions. Some were personal and particular, whilst others more general. In the latter cases the *exempla* might have been issued with future cases in mind, thus approaching the concept of law. The form of promulgation is also important to the question of the legal quality of rescripts. If the rescript was delivered to the petitioner and not posted publicly, then any intention to give it general force is questionable.

As an example of a legal rescript and the procedure which surrounded it one can consider *BGU* I 267 and *P. Strassb.* 22, two copies of the same rescript concerned with the *longi temporis praescriptio*. The text of *BGU* 267 is reproduced below.

Fayum   21 x 13 cm   Third century (?)

Ed pr. — F. Krebs, *BGU* I 267 (Berlin 1895) 266.

[. . . . .]λογ [Αὐτοκ]ρ[άτωρ]	[...] Imperator
Καῖσαρ	Caesar
[Λούκιος Σεπτίμιος Σεουῆρ]ος	[Lucius Septimius Severus]
Πέρ[τ]ιναξ [Σε]βαστὸς	Pertinax Augustus

---

[44] Katzoff, 'On the Intended Use of P. Col. 123' 569.
[45] Nörr, *ZSS* 98 (1981) 40.
[46] Nörr, *ZSS* 98 (1981) 37-45.
[47] Garnsey, *Social Status and Legal Privilege* 174-5.

['Αραβικὸς 'Αδιαβη]νικὸς [Arabicus] Adiabenicus
[Παρθικὸς Μέγιστος] καὶ Αὐτοκρά[τωρ] [Parthicus Maximus] and Imperator
Καῖσαρ Caesar
5 [Μάρκος Αὐρή]λιος 'Αντωνεῖνος [Marcus] Aurelius Antoninus
Σεβαστὸς Augustus
'Ιουλιανῇ Σω[σθ]ενιανοῦ διὰ to Juliana, daughter of Sosthenianus
Σωσθένους through Sosthenes
ἀνδρός· [Μ]ακρᾶς νομῆς her husband. *Longae possessionis*
παραγραφῆς (sic) *praescriptio*
τοῖς δικαία[ν] αἰτ[ί]αν ἐσχηκόσι καὶ is guaranteed to those having *iusta*
ἄνευ *causa*
τινὸς ἀμφισβητήσεως ἐν τῇ νομῇ and having been in undisputed possession
10 γενομ[έν]οις πρὸς μὲν τοὺς ἐν ἀλλο- with respect to those
τρίᾳ πόλει διατρείβοντας ἐτῶν εἴκοσι living in another city for twenty years
ἀριθμῷ βεβαιοῦται, τοὺς δὲ ἐπὶ τῆς in number, those (living) in the
αὐτῆς ἐτῶν δέκα. Προετέθη ἐν 'Α- same for ten years. It was posted in
λεξανδρείᾳ. ῆ (ἔτει) Τῦβι γ̄ Alexandria, (year) 8 Tybi 3.

....

7. παραγραφή   11. διατρίβοντας

A method of acquiring property by possession or taking hold (i.e. *usucapio*) was known to Roman law already in the time of the *XII Tables* (451-449 BCE). Undisturbed possession of one year for movables and two years for immovables (lands and buildings) vested the right of ownership in the *possessor* (*XII Tables* 6.3). The intention of the legal institution was to remove uncertainty of title when this might arise, e.g. when property was delivered or transferred informally or when the vendor under Roman law lacked the appropriate legal right over the property. Even so certain criteria had to be met for *usucapio* to apply, i.e. possession for the required period, the *bona fides* of the *possessor* at the time of acquisition and the presence of a genuine *causa* or ground for possession. Also the property cannot have been stolen or taken by force. But there was a major shortcoming in *usucapio*, for it only applied to Roman citizens and to property susceptible to Quiritarian ownership, e.g. Italic land including *coloniae* located outside Italy which possessed *ius Italicum* and apparently also movable property of Romans in the provinces. Peregrines and provincial lands (Gaius, *Instit.*, 2.46, and Justinian, *Instit.*, 2.6) were not covered by it. To avoid the difficulties presented by these limitations an affected *possessor* was allowed to plead an objection which extinguished the opposing claim, i.e. the *longi temporis praescriptio*. The *praescriptio* applied to provincial land and allowed the person holding undisturbed possession (ἄνευ τινὸς ἀμφισβητήσεως, *ll*.8-9) for the determined period (10 years for persons living in the same *metropolis* with its surrounding district and 20 years persons living in different *metropoleis*) a defensive plea defeating any action for recovery.[48] Even so the *possessor* had to show *iusta causa* (δικαία αἰτία, *l*.8) for his possession of the property. The conditions thus reflect those of *usucapio*.

---

[48] Unlike *usucapio* in Roman law which formed part of the substantial law (*ius civile*) and conferred ownership on the possessor, *longi temporis praescriptio*, as a defensive plea, was a piece of procedural law which only permitted the possessor to extinguish the claim of another to the property. In this respect it very much reflects the legal remedies afforded plaintiffs under the *ius praetorium*.

There are a number of indications that the rescript is not an *epistula*. In particular, it will be noted that the prescript lacks any greeting and that the text was posted. The posting occurred in Alexandria on 3rd day of Tybi in the 8th year of Septimius Severus and Caracalla, i.e. 30 December AD 199. From December AD 199 till April AD 200 the emperors are known to have been in Alexandria, possibly with interruptions. The rescript was thus posted at the place of their residence at the time. Contrary to Wilcken's general view, the rescript was issued without any evidence of the *libellus* which initiated it. It will also be noted that the text is in Greek. Was the rescript issued in Greek or is the text translated from Latin? As the legal idiom is clearly based on Roman law and its conceptual constructs, an original composition in Latin seems the preferred alternative.

The text of *P. Strassb.* 22 is of further interest for our understanding of the *praescriptio*.

Hermopolis magna   32 x 24.5 cm   Third century AD

Ed. pr. — F. Preisigke, *P. Strassb.* 22 (Strassburg 1906) 78-87.

The extracts are written on the back of a papyrus sheet constituted by gluing together two or three pieces of scrap paper. The scrap pieces (*P. Strassb.* 23) contain summaries of shortages in the land tax dating from the middle of the first century to the beginning of the second. The script is described as that of the chancellery style of the third century. The extracts were apparently made after the death of the emperors (note the abbreviated prescript with θεοί — *divi* l.1) and after the end of the prefectship of Subatianus Aquila (ἡγεμονεύσαντος l.10).

Θεοὶ Σεουῆρος καὶ Ἀντωνῖνος Ἰου[λ]ιανῇ	*Divi* Severus and Antoninus to Juliana
Σωσθένους διὰ Σωσθένους ἀνδρός.	daughter of Sosthenes through Sosthenes her husband.
Μακρᾶς νομῆς παραγραφὴ τοῖς δικαί[αν]	*Longae possessionis praescriptio* assist(s) those
αἰτίαν ἐσχηκόσι καὶ ἄνευ τινὸς ἀμφισβ[η]-	having *iusta causa* and having been in undisputed
5 τήσεως ἐν τῇ νομῇ γενομένοις πρὸς μ[ὲ]ν	possession, with respect to
τοὺς ἐν ἄλλῃ πόλει διατρείψαντας ἐτῶν εἴκοσι	those living in another city for twenty years
ἀριθμῷ βοηθοῦνται, πρὸς δὲ τοὺς ἐπὶ τῆς αὐτῆς	in number, with respect to those in the same (city)
δέκα. Προετέθη ἐν Ἀλεξανδ[ρ]είᾳ ᾗ (ἔτει) Φαρμοῦθι κδ̄.	for ten years. It was posted in Alexandria, (year) 8, Pharmouthi 24.
10 Σουβατιανοῦ Ἀκύλα ἡγεμονεύσαντος.	When Subatianus Aquila was prefect.
(Ἔτους) ῑε Φαμενὼθ ῑζ κληθέν[τ]ων Σαβείνου	(Year) 15, Phamenoth 17. Sabinus
καὶ Μαξίμου Διονυσίου καὶ ὑπακο[υ]σάντων	and Maximus Dionysius having been summoned and obeying,
μεθ' ἕτερα· Ἀκύλας εἶπεν· Τί ἀποκρείνῃ	after other matters Aquila said: "What do you answer

πρὸς τὸν χρόνον [τ]ῆς νο[μ]ῆς, ὥς φησι[ν] με-	regarding the duration of *possessio* when he says
15 τὰ τὴν ὠνὴν τῆς Παυσοράπιος ἐτῶ[ν] σχε-	after the purchase by Pausorapis (there have passed) nearly
δὸν δέκα τεσσάρων, καὶ τὴν ἐν τούτῳ σιωπήν;	fourteen years, and during that time silence."
Ἀσκληπιάδης ῥήτωρ εἶπεν· Γέγονεν. Ἀκύ-	Asklepiades the advocate said: "It was so." Aquila
λας εἶπεν· Διατάξεις εἰσὶν τῶν κυρίων περὶ	said: "There are imperial constitutions concerning
τῶν ἐν τοῖς ἔθνεσιν οἰκούντων· ἂν ἄλλα-	those living in the provinces that if
20 χόσε νομῇ παρακολουθήσῃ ἔχοντός τινος	the transfer is accompanied with the one having
ἀφορμὴν κἂν βραχεῖαν δικαίαν κατοχῆς,	*bonum initium possessionis* even if insignificant (?),
σιωπήσαντος τοῦ νομίζοντος αὐτῷ διαφέρειν	the one who thinks (the property) to belong to himself being silent
καὶ ἀνασχομένου ὑπὲρ δεκαετίαν, ἔχειν τ[ὸ] βέ-	and waiting more than ten years, those
βαιον τοὺς κατασχόντας.	in possession have security."
25 Μεττίου Ῥούφου ἡγεμονεύσαντος. (Ἔτους) ι	When Mettius Rufus was prefect. Year 10,
Ἀθὺρ κδ κληθέντος Σαλουστίου Καπί-	Hathyr 24, Sallustius Kapiton being summoned
τωνος πρὸς Ἰουλίαν Πυθαροῦν καὶ εἰπόντο[ς]	against Julia Pytharous and having said

Col. 2

τὸ[ν] ὑ]π[ο]μνηματογρ[ά]φον Μαικιανὸν ἀκηκοέναι περὶ τοῦ	that Maecianus, the memorandum-taker, had heard about the
πρ[ά]γμ[α]τος, μεθ᾽ ἕτερα· Μέττιος Ῥοῦφος	matter, after other matters, Mettius Rufus
30 Καπίτωνι εἶπε[ν]· Οὐδεμίαν παρείσδυσιν ἔχεις,	said to Kapiton: "You have no means of entry,
ἡ γὰρ γ[υν]ὴ ἐν τῇ νομῇ γέγονεν πολλῷ χρόνῳ. Παρ᾽ ἡ-	for the woman has been in possession for a long time.
μεῖν δ[ὲ ἰ]δοὺ ἡ [δ]ι᾽ ἐνιαυτοῦ νομὴ αὐτάρκης	Observe, with us possession for a year
ἐστὶν [...] δ. [.] ... ιαν.	is sufficient [...]

§10 A Rescript to the Victors of Sacred Games   141

The above papyrus contains three different legal rulings or hearings concerned with the acquisition of property. They appear to have been ordered by their importance and not their dates. The chancellery style in which the extracts were made indicates that they were possibly made for use by some official. The protocols of cases before the prefects may have been taken from their day-books.

The first extract (*ll*.1-9) is a copy of the imperial rescript already known from *BGU* 267. But interestingly its text varies from that of the other copy. Preisigke (p.82) notes that in the copying of an important text the same care for precise accuracy is not shown as we expect today. Of particular interest is the difference in the recorded date of posting. Whereas *BGU* 267 is dated 30 December 199, the date of posting for *P. Strassb.* 22 is recorded as 19 April 200. Various reasons for the difference can be alleged, e.g. scribal carelessness (Preisigke), or that there were two postings in different locations in Alexandria and on different dates (Mitteis).

The second extract (*ll*.10-24) concerns a hearing before the prefect of Egypt, Subatianus Aquila, dated 13 March 207. Both the rescript and the prefectorial hearing refer to the *longi temporis praescriptio*. The δικαία ἀφορμή (*iustum initium*, *l*.21) of the prefect's decision corresponds to δικαία αἰτία (*iusta causa*, *ll*.3-4) in the rescript. The meaning of βραχεῖα (*l*.21) is unclear but in Mitteis's opinion refers to the *bona fides* of the *possessor*.[49] Of further interest in the protocol of the case before Aquila is the mention of διατάξεις (plural) and the expression ἐν τοῖς ἔθνεσιν οἰκοῦντες. Are we to suppose several constitutions on the same subject matter by various emperors? If so, only the one cited survives. The second expression is important in that it indicates that the *praescriptio* was issued specifically with provincials in mind. It was issued to meet a legal need in the provinces. In the *fundus Italicus*, *usucapio* continued to apply and so initially *longi temporis praescriptio* was not available there. Finally the clause σιωπήσαντος τοῦ νομίζοντος αὐτῷ διαφέρειν indicates that perhaps it was only the person claiming ownership of the property against its *possessor*, rather than any third party, who could disturb possession and thus annul one of the necessary conditions on which *longi temporis praescriptio* was based.

The third extract (*ll*.25-33) concerns a much earlier hearing before the prefect Mettius Rufus. It is dated 20 November 90, and concerns *usucapio*, an older institution of the *ius civile*. Mitteis quite correctly infers from the decision that the case concerned persons of Roman citizenship (παρ' ἡμῖν, *ll*.31-2, and the names of the parties) and the usucaption of movable property (ἐνιαυτός *l*.32).

From the rescript it would appear that the emperor does not create law but only restates it in response to the petitioner. This is consistent with Honoré's discussion of the legal status of rescripts, i.e. they were neither pieces of legislation nor judgements but rather were declarations of what the law was (see above). Of further interest is the use of the rescript by

---

[49] Mitteis, *P. Strassb.* p.86: 'in my opinion the prefect can only mean by βραχεῖα ἀφορμή that *mala fides superveniens* does not prejudice (the matter) ... For Subatianus Aquila δικαία ἀφορμή thus has two sides, one objective (*iustus titulus*) and the other subjective (*bona fides*) and βραχεῖα refers to the latter'. If Mitteis is correct, then clearly the prefect, when adjudicating a case, placed greater importance on the objective condition. This is sensible as it is the easiest condition to substantiate. One might compare the conditions which applied in the case of *usucapio*. Here the *bona fides* of the *possessor* at the time of acquisition and the presence of a genuine *causa* or ground for possession (i.e. *iusta causa* or *iustus titulus* such as transfer by sale, gift, legacy etc.) were necessary conditions (Gaius, *Instit.*, 2.43 and Justinian, *Instit.*, 2.6 and 2.6.11). In Zulueta's opinion *iusta causa/iustus titulus* is 'practically the more important of the two requisites', the reasons for this being that without it, '*bona fides* would be unreasonable'. See F. de Zulueta, *The Institutes of Gaius*, vol. 2 (Oxford 1953) 69-70.

the prefect of Egypt in his hearing of a case. The imperial constitutions are appealed to by him to decide a matter between persons apparently from the same nome, to judge from a reference to the ten-year period only. It is unclear whether the constitutions where tendered in the hearing by the person seeking the *praescriptio*, or invoked by the prefect or his *consilium*. Be that as it may, the constitutions declare the law which the Roman judge sought to apply after he had determined the facts of the case.

The rescript concerned with *longi temporis praescriptio* has been used as one example of the function which imperial constitutions played in the judicial procedures of the Roman empire. Its interest does not end there. A similar law to that of *usucapio* is found in Rabbinic law, namely acquisition by *hazaqah*. It appears that *hazaqah* was introduced late into Jewish law in the period of Graeco-Roman influence. Freyne[50] proposes that, like the law of confiscation, it first occurred in the period of Roman *dominium* when the Jewish law yielded to the imperial pressure to recognise use rather than absolute ownership. The suggestion is improbable as *usucapio* did not apply to peregrines nor to provincial lands. It is therefore unlikely that the rabbis would have often come in contact with it. On the other hand, the *longi temporis praescriptio*, which did concern peregrines and provincial land, is not attested before AD 199. The silence of Gaius' *Institutes* (*ca* AD 161) further supports the contention that its introduction was late. It is therefore highly improbable that the *praescriptio* could have influenced the formulation of *hazaqah*, which is first attested (*m. Ket.* 2.2) in a comment by R. Joshua, a second-generation teacher (AD 80-120). De Zulueta[51] suggests that before the introduction of the *praescriptio* the local law of each province will have applied. In the case of Jewish law this would have been *hazaqah*. Whence then was it introduced into Jewish law? If Roman law is an improbable source of influence, is its introduction to be credited to Hellenistic law? I have argued elsewhere that Ptolemaic law was the vehicle through which acquisition by possession found its way into Jewish law.[52]

Rescripts and the Early Church

Rescripts issued by emperors in response to *libelli* and *epistulae* provide us with the earliest evidence for imperial opinions and decisions concerned with Christianity. Pliny's *epistula* to Trajan (*Epist.* 10.96) and the emperor's rescript (*Epist.* 10.97) is the earliest example. Here we see a provincial governor consulting the emperor on the examination and punishment of Christians. Of particular concern is what to do with persons who had once been Christians but who now denied their allegiance. This was confirmed by their offering of prayers and sacrifices to the gods and to the image of the emperor also. The issue is important in Pliny's eyes due to the number of persons affected and the opportunity offered by leniency to rectify the situation and restore traditional religious affiliations and practices. In response Trajan commended Pliny's course of action: Christians were not to be actively sought out by the provincial administration but if they were brought to trial before the governor and the case against them proved, the same persons were to be given opportunity to repent and offer sacrifices to the gods. As Millar[53] observes, the rescript set the pattern for the general treatment of Christianity in the courts.

---

[50] S. Freyne, *Galilee from Alexander the Great to Hadrian 323 BCE to 135 CE* (Delaware 1980) 168-9.

[51] F. de Zulueta, *The Institutes of Gaius* II, 8 and 70-71.

[52] S.R. Llewelyn, 'The introduction of *hazaqah* into Jewish law', *Journal for the Study of Judaism* 27 (1996) 155-67.

[53] Millar, *The Emperor in the Roman World* 558.

Another important early example is Hadrian's response to a proconsul of Asia concerning criminal procedure. The governor's predecessor had addressed an *epistula* to the emperor; however, as the matter was of considerable importance and would continue to concern the administration of the province, the emperor felt impelled to respond to the new office-holder. The text is preserved by Justin Martyr (*Apol.* 1.69). Inhabitants of the province were accusing Christians of acting contrary to the laws. But the accusations appear to have been made as pure calumny and without proof. The accusers are required by the rescript either to bring the matter before a court of law or to desist. If not, they are to be subject to severe punishment.

Both the above rescripts are responses to official enquiries addressed to the emperor as *epistulae* by provincial governors. An early instance of a *libellus* (βιβλίδιον) addressed by a Christian woman to the emperor is recorded by Justin Martyr (*Apol.* II.2). After the woman had divorced her husband because of his debauchery, in counter-response he accused her of being a Christian. She delivered a *libellus* to the emperor asking that she might first be allowed to order her affairs before defending herself against the accusation. The request was granted.

Καὶ ἡ μὲν βιβλίδιόν σοι τῷ αὐτοκράτορι ἀναδέδωκε, πρότερον συγχωρηθῆναι αὐτῇ διοικήσασθαι τὰ ἑαυτῆς ἀξιοῦσα· ἔπειτα ἀπολογήσασθαι περὶ τοῦ κατηγορήματος μετὰ τὴν τῶν πραγμάτων αὐτῆς διοίκησιν. Καὶ συνεχώρησας τοῦτο.

The above instance is alleged to have occurred in the reign of Antoninus Pius. It is not until the time of Gallienus that we have a copy of the emperor's rescript in reply to a Christian petition. The text, a translation into Greek from the Latin, is given by Eusebius (*HE* 7.13). On becoming sole emperor (AD 260) Gallienus ended by general *edicta* the persecution of the Christians which had occurred under his joint rule with his father, Valerian. Confiscated property was to be restored to the churches. Millar[54] argues that it was such confiscations of property and its subsequent restoration which marked the beginning of correspondence and direct relations between the church and the emperors. An official named Aurelius Quirinius had apparently not complied with the imperial order and as a result a number of bishops had written a *libellus* to the emperor. His rescript ran:

Αὐτοκράτωρ Καῖσαρ Πούπλιος Λικίνιος Γαλλιῆνος Εὐσεβὴς Εὐτυχὴς Σεβαστὸς Διονυσίῳ καὶ Πίννᾳ καὶ Δημητρίῳ καὶ τοῖς λοιποῖς ἐπισκόποις. τὴν εὐεργεσίαν τῆς ἐμῆς δωρεᾶς διὰ παντὸς τοῦ κόσμου ἐκβιβασθῆναι προσέταξα, ὅπως ἀπὸ τῶν τόπων τῶν θρησκευσίμων ἀποχωρήσωσιν, καὶ διὰ τοῦτο καὶ ὑμεῖς τῆς ἀντιγραφῆς τῆς ἐμῆς τῷ τύπῳ χρῆσθαι δύνασθε, ὥστε μηδένα ὑμῖν ἐνοχλεῖν. καὶ τοῦτο, ὅπερ κατὰ τὸ ἐξὸν δύναται ὑφ' ὑμῶν ἀναπληροῦσθαι, ἤδη πρὸ πολλοῦ ὑπ' ἐμοῦ συγκεχώρηται, καὶ διὰ τοῦτο Αὐρήλιος Κυρίνιος, ὁ τοῦ μεγίστου πράγματος προστατεύων, τὸν τύπον τὸν ὑπ' ἐμοῦ δοθέντα διαφυλάξει.

Imperator Caesar Publius Licinius Gallienus Pius Felix Augustus to Dionysius and Pinnas and Demetrius and the other bishops. I have commanded the benefit of my bounty to be carried out throughout all the world that they should depart from the places of worship, and because of this you also can use the decision of my rescript, so that none may trouble you. And this thing, which can by permission be accomplished by you, has long since been consented by me; because of this Aurelius Quirinius, *magister summae rei*, will observe the decision given by me.

---

[54] Millar, *The Emperor in the Roman World* 571.

The text of *P. Oxy.* 3611 is of particular interest because it is a rescript for a non-territorial association. As observed above, numerous professional associations (e.g of athletes, actors, musicians, *grammatici*, rhetors and doctors) could petition the emperor by *epistulae*. They shared this capacity with other corporate entities such as cities and provincial leagues. What is significant, however, is the possibility that such non-territorial associations formed the model on which the relations between the church and the emperors were developed. A number of features are shared between the two relationships of professional association to emperor and church to emperor. These include the imperial granting of privileges and immunities to both,[55] their capacity to address *epistulae* to emperors, and the appeal to the emperor to decide matters involving internal dispute and schism. Millar[56] observes:

> These relations are also not without relevance to the history of the contacts of church and emperor. For those contacts themselves have to be considered in the light of the fact that for centuries the emperors had been granting rights, privileges and exemptions to the world-wide, 'oecumenical' associations of athletes and performers, which had their own officers and priests, and whose members took part in the religious festivals, great and small, of the Greek world; and more recently at least, had been laying down the rules as to who qualified for membership, and responding to individual petitions on this question.

The facilities offered the church and its leadership, however, appear after Constantine to have extended beyond that offered to the associations. In particular one notes the use of the provincial governors and the imperial post by the church for the delivery of *libelli* to the emperor (Augustine, *Epist.* 88.2) and the use of the same post for the conveyance of bishops to various synods.

S.R.L.

---

[55] Millar, *The Emperor in the Roman World* 493 and 502.
[56] Millar, *The Emperor in the Roman World* 462.

JUDAICA

§11 A Hebrew Congregational Prayer from Egypt

This text was published, with a description of the text and a brief discussion of its content, in *ZPE* 51 (1983) 80-84 (+ plate Va) by Felix Klein-Franke of the Institute of Asian and African Studies in the Department of Islamic Civilization at the Hebrew University, Jerusalem.

The text is a nine line prayer written on parchment in 'free-style', to borrow Joseph Heinemann's phrase for the style of non-statutory prose prayer.[1] Klein-Franke further identifies the prayer as a lamentation. It must be pointed out, however, that the prayer contains more praise than lament which is restricted to the urgent petition of *ll.*6-7. The text originates from Oxyrhynchus, a town in which there was a Jewish presence, albeit beleaguered, in the era following the Jewish revolt that occurred in Egypt at the end of the reign of Trajan and put down by Hadrian (see Hugh MacLennan, *Oxyrhynchus: An Economic and Social Study* [repr. Amsterdam 1968] 20-21).

Klein-Franke ascribes the date of the script 'to the period prior to the fifth century A.D.'. This seems a fair supposition. The formation of the letters of our text approximates to that encountered in plate 182, a fourth century CE text also from Oxyrhynchus, in S. A. Birnbaum's, *The Jewish Scripts: Text* (Leiden 1971) and *Plates* (London 1957). The tetragrammaton is rendered by four yods (יייי) in *ll.*1, 5, 6 and 9 and the word 'God', אֱלֹהִים, has been abbreviated to אים in *ll.*4 and 6.

The prayer alludes to biblical events in *ll.*1-6 and closes with an anachronistic allusion to the worship of God in the Jerusalem temple and a citation from Psa. 92.1 in *l.*9.

מודים אנחנו לך יייי אנו	We praise you LORD our God.
שמואל קדש את שמך בטלה חלב	Samuel sanctified your name with a sucking lamb
במצפה	at Mizpah,
ואליה קדש את שמך בהר הכרמל	and Elijah sanctified your name on Mt. Carmel.
כי אתה	For you are
אים ואין זולתך וכל העם	God and there is none besides you. All the people
ראו את קדושתך	saw your holiness
5 ונפלו על פניהם וככה אמרו	and fell on their faces and said as follows:
יייי הוא האים	'The LORD is God,
יייי הוא האים כן קדש את	The LORD is God'. So sanctify
שמך בפרק הזה	your name in this epoch,
בימי צרינו כי החרימו קרן	in the days of our oppressors, for they have put a horn to death.
ונודה לך בחצרות	And we praise you in the courts
קדשך וביריעות משכנותיך	of your sanctuary and among the curtains of your dwellings
ואהליך וכתוב מזמר שיר	and your tents. A psalm is written, a song
ליום השבח טוב להודות לייי	for the day of the Sabbath: 'It is good to praise the LORD and to
ולזמר	sing praise'.

---

[1] See his *Prayer in the Talmud: Forms and Patterns* (New York/Berlin 1977) 125.

Klein-Franke rightly points out that the prayer begins with an echo of the eighteenth benediction of the Amidah in its Babylonian recension ('we praise you . . . ').[2] The references to Samuel and Elijah, both of whom prayed for divine deliverance in the context of confrontation (see 1 Samuel 7 [the battle at Mizpah] and 1 Kings 18 [the defeat of the priests of Baal on Mt. Carmel]) and were heard, are designed to encourage the Jewish faithful in their present distress as they, in their turn, wait in hope for salvation.[3]

Line 7 of the text alludes to an outrage committed against Jews by their enemies. There is no way of accurately identifying the particular event the author has in mind. E. Mary Smallwood's discussion of the situation of Jews in Egypt immediately after the revolt of 115-117 is largely limited to Alexandria, though she does refer to *P. Oxy.* 705, one of the few documents to shed light on the situation of the Jews in Egypt after the revolt (see her *The Jews Under Roman Rule* [Leiden 1981] 402). This papyrus, written in 200-202 CE, alludes to an annual remembrance by Gentile Egyptians of the crushing of this revolt. *P. Oxy.* 1189 appears to allude to confiscations of Jewish property in the wake of the revolt. This papyrus, dated 117 CE, was written by the *strategos* of Heracleopolis to his opposite number in Oxyrhynchus. The writer refers to property, now confiscated, that had belonged to Jews (*ll*.9-10; περὶ γραφῆς τῶν τοῖς ['Ι]ουδαοῖς ὑπαρξάντων), and directs the addressee to keep one of the two enclosed copies of the schedule of confiscated land and to send the other to the *strategos* of Cynopolis to provide a model for confiscations of Jewish property both at Oxyrhynchus and Cynopolis. *P. Oxy.* 500 *ll*.11-12 (130 CE) testifies to the alienation of land that had belonged to Jews. This papyrus takes the form of an application to Hierax, *strategos* of the Athribite nome, on behalf of a group of people to lease land, some of which had been confiscated 'from Jews who have been killed (no doubt in the revolt of 115-117)' (ἀ[π' 'Ι]ουδαίων ἀνειρη[μ]ένων) and from 'Greeks who have died without heirs' (καὶ Ἑλλήνων ἀ[κλ]ηρονομήτων).[4]

For his part, Klein-Franke, although he is fully informed about the situation of the Jews implied in the Oxyrhynchus papyri and Jewish revolt of 115-117, surmises that the text was written in the wake of the 'sequestration of a ritual fund' (Klein-Franke, p. 82). This, I feel, is a rather forced translation of *l*.7, החרימו קרן, which I take to mean: 'they have put a horn to death'.

Klein-Franke translates the word פרק of the previous line as 'robbery', a meaning it has in Nah. 3.1. In Obad. 14 the word means 'cross roads'. However, this word denotes the

---

[2] For text of the Babylonian version of the Amidah, see E. Schürer, *The History of the Jewish People in the Age of Jesus Christ,* vol. 2, ed. G. Vermes et al. (Edinburgh 1979) 456-8. See also the formula נודה לך discussed in Heinemann, *Prayer* 42 and 189, and the frequent use of the formula אודך יהוה in the Dead Sea Scrolls (esp. 1QH).

[3] Klein-Franke draws parallels with mTa'an 2.4 which deals with the forms prescribed for the liturgy of Sukkot: 'He who answered Samuel at Mispeh will answer you and hear the sound of your cry this day. Blessed are you, O Lord, who hears a cry . . . He who answered Elijah at Mount Carmel will answer you and hear the sound of your cry this day. Blessed are you, O Lord, who hears prayer' (Neusner). See also Heinemann, *Prayer* 195 and 248.

[4] See the text and discussion by Fuks in *CPJ* 2.255-7 (#448), and brief comment in Smallwood, *Jews Under Roman Rule* 405. The editor of *P. Oxy.* V (p.314) had construed the Greek differently, however, reading εἰρ[η]μένων where Fuks was to read ἀνειρη[μ]ένων at *l*.11.

chapter divisions in the Mishnah and also frequently means 'era' in the rabbinic literature, as an examination of the entry in Marcus Jastrow's *Dictionary* (s.v. פֶּרֶק) will establish.[5]

Klein-Franke's translation of חרם (hi.), 'to take unlawful possession', is also open to debate. In biblical Hebrew the verb means 'to devote to sacred use', to 'place (something or someone) under the ban' without possibility of redemption (see Lev. 27.28; Mic. 4.13). Numerous examples exist in the Hebrew Bible of חרם taking on the subsidiary meaning of 'to put to death' or 'to destroy', as in the MT of Exod. 22.19 ('the one who sacrifices to gods shall be destroyed' [זֹבֵחַ לָאֱלֹהִים יָחֳרָם]), Lev. 27.29 ('every person who is devoted to destruction shall not be ransomed but be put to death' [אֲשֶׁר יָחֳרַם מִן־הָאָדָם לֹא יִפָּדֶה מוֹת יוּמָת כָּל־חֵרֶם]) and Isa. 34.2 ('he [the Lord] has devoted them [the nations] to destruction' [לְטֶבַח הֶחֱרִימָם נְתָנָם]). In Jer. 25.9 God will totally destroy (הַחֲרַמְתִּים) his own people together with all the surrounding nations by the hand of the 'tribes of the north' led by Nebuchadrezzar. Israel is the destroyer of cities, people or nations in Deut. 2.34; 3.6; 7.2; 20.17; Josh. 8.26; 10.28, 37 and Jer. 50.21. I know of no passage in which חרם means 'to confiscate' or 'to sequestrate'.

However, Klein-Franke may be on firmer ground when he translates קרן in *l.*7 by the term 'ritual fund'. The mishnaic tractate Peah 1.1 speaks of enjoying the 'fruits' (living on the interest) in this world and the 'horn' (i.e. the principal) in the world to come. However, קרן, a word denoting the concept of might and power, has a wide range of derived meanings in the Bible and in the Rabbinic corpus. It can denote a deliverer, as in Ezek. 29.21 ('I will raise up a horn for the house of Israel' [אַצְמִיחַ קֶרֶן לְבֵית יִשְׂרָאֵל]) and Psa. 132.17 ('I will make a horn to sprout for David' [אַצְמִיחַ קֶרֶן לְדָוִד]). In other passages the word denotes the strength of a people, as in Lam. 2.3 ('he has cut down in fierce anger the whole horn of Israel' [קֶרֶן יִשְׂרָאֵל כֹּל]) and Jer. 48.25 ('the horn of Moab is broken' [קֶרֶן מוֹאָב]). A further parallel can be found at 1QM 1.4 ('. . . that his fury may root out [הכרית] and eliminate [השמיד] the horn [קרן] [of Israel]').

While there is evidence for confiscations of Jewish land in *P.Oxy.* 1189, these can be dated to the year the revolt was quelled (i.e. 117 CE). *P. Oxy.* 500 speaks of the alienation of Jewish land in the period immediately after the revolt. However, I know of no evidence in the papyri to suggest that confiscations of Jewish land or property were an ongoing fact of life for Jews in Oxyrhynchus up to the time our text was written (i.e. some time in the fourth century CE). On the contrary, I suggest that the the petition recorded in *ll.*6-7 of the prayer is alluding to the putting to death of Jews, the 'horn' of God, in the uprising of 115-117 CE in Egypt, and seeking divine redress. *P.Oxy.* 705 demonstrates that even at the beginning of the third century there was still an annual (and no doubt rancorous) commemoration of this defeat of the Jews. It is also possible, though less likely in my opinion, that our text is alluding to the massacres of Jews in the revolts in the land of Israel in 66-70 and 132-135 CE.

Mark Harding

---

[5] See bPes. 117a ('the prophets among them [the people of Israel] ordained that Israel should recite it [the Hallel] at every important epoch [כל פרק] and at every misfortune'). Frank I. Andersen (per litt.) suggests 'juncture'.

§12 An Association of Samaritans in Delos

Ed. pr. — P. Bruneau, 'Les Israélites de Délos et la juiverie délienne', *BCH* 106 (1982) 465-504.

Bibliography: *SEG* XXXII (1982) §809-810, A.T. Kraabel, 'New Evidence of the Samaritan Diaspora has been Found on Delos', *Biblical Archaeologist* 47 (1984) 44-6.

(a) Delos   150-50 BC

Found 92.5 m north of the synagogue and like the latter edifice also beside the sea. White marble: height 48 cm; width 40.5 cm at base and 33 cm at top; thickness 11 cm at base and 7.5 cm at top; width of inscribed portion 34.2 cm; height of letters 15 cm ± and sometimes 10 cm. The top is broken but retains in relief part of a wreath of somewhat exceptional height; moulding below. Even lines of the inscription are painted red; odd lines black.

Οἱ ἐν Δήλῳ Ἰσραελεῖται οἱ ἀ- παρχόμενοι εἰς ἱερὸν Ἀργα- ριζεὶν στεφανοῦσιν χρυσῷ στεφάνῳ Σαραπίωνα Ἰάσο- 5 νος Κνώσιον εὐεργεσίας ἕνεκεν τῆς εἰς ἑαυτούς.	The Israelites of Delos who contribute to sacred Mount Gerizim crown with a golden crown Sarapion, son of Jason, from Knossos because of his benefaction towards them.

(b) Delos   250-175 BC

Found with previous stone. White marble: height 70 cm; width at base 54.2 (without moulding), 56 cm (with moulding restored); width at top 53 cm; thickness 9.5 (max.) and 6 cm (min.); width of inscribed portion 52 cm; height of letters 12 cm ± and 8 cm for omicron. Very mutilated at the bottom. As a result the second half of the text is almost all lost. The top also carries the relief of a wreath. The text is inscribed below *in rasura* (i.e. the stone has been reused). Lines 2, 4 and 6 of the inscription are painted red; lines 1 and 3 black. Line 5 appears not to be inscribed but only painted. Οἱ ἐν Δήλῳ must be restored. As there is no trace of these letters immediately above *l*.1, Bruneau supposes that it was placed above the wreath at the top of the stone (now broken off). To explain the unusual position he appeals to the fact that the stone appears to have been reused. As there was insufficient space below the wreath, the initial letters of the inscription were placed at the top of the stone.

[Οἱ ἐν Δήλῳ]
1 Ἰσραηλῖται οἱ ἀπαρχόμενοι εἰς ἱερὸν
      ἅγιον Ἀρ-
    γαριζεὶν ἐτίμησαν (vac.) Μένιππον
      Ἀρτεμιδώρου Ἡρά-
    κλειον αὐτὸν καὶ τοὺς ἐγγόνους
      αὐτοῦ κατασκευ-
    άσαντα καὶ ἀναθέντα ἐκ τῶν ἰδίων
      ἐπὶ προσευχῇ τοῦ
5 θε[οῦ] ΤΟΝ[- - - - - - - - - - - -]
    ΟΛΟΝΚΑΙΤΟ[- *ca* 6-8 letters - - καὶ
      ἐστεφάνωσαν] χρυσῷ στε[φά-]
    νῳ καὶ [- - - - - - - - - - -]
    ΚΑ- -
    Τ- -
	[The Israelites of Delos]
	who contribute to sacred
	and holy Mount Gerizim
	have honoured Menippos, son of
	Artemidoros
	from Herakleia, himself and his descendants
	for having
	constructed and dedicated at his own expense
	in fulfilment of a vow
	to God [the ...]
	[... and they have crowned] with a golden
	crown
	and [...]
	[...]
	[...]

§12 An Association of Samaritans in Delos

The presence of a Jewish colony in Delos is variously attested by 1 Macc 15.23, Josephus, *AJ* 14.10, 19.213-216,[1] *I. Delos* 2532, and the identification of certain ruins as a synagogue. The colony is thought to date from the second century BC. Kraabel (p.44) notes that the synagogue is the oldest yet discovered in the Mediterranean diaspora. An instance of an isolated Samaritan was also already known: *I. Delos* 2616 is a list of subscribers found at the Sarapion in Delos and names Πραῦλος Σαμαρεύς (col. 2 *l*.53). His religious affiliation is naturally disputed.[2] The above inscriptions now attest the presence of an association of schismatic Jews, i.e. Samaritans, in Delos. The identification is implicit in the mention of Mount Gerizim, the form Ἀργαριζείν being explained by the prefix of הר (*har* = mountain) to the name.[3] That they designate themselves as Ἰσραηλῖται rather than Ἰουδαῖοι also implies their identification as Samaritans. The choice of that name rather than Samaritans was prompted (so Bruneau, p.478) by a desire to proclaim a descent from Jacob-Israel (indicating in a gentile world a cultural and religious affiliation) and to differentiate themselves from the Ἰουδαῖοι by the adoption of a name recalling the earlier unity of the ancient kingdoms. Kraabel (p.45) sees in the use of the title an attempt by the Samaritans to lay claim to it in the face of Jewish usage, thus the qualifying addition of the prepositional phrase οἱ ἀπαρχόμενοι εἰς ἱερὸν ἅγιον Ἀργαριζείν, which supposedly functioned to differentiate this group of Israelites from the others using the title. From the two inscriptions it is apparent that the Samaritans of Delos paid contributions (ἀπάρχεσθαι) to the temple at Mount Gerizim. Thus both Samaritans and Ἰουδαῖοι appear to have made annual payments to their respective sanctuaries.

The two texts are honorary inscriptions set up by the Samaritans of Delos in recognition of two benefactors. As Bruneau (p.481) observes, the benefaction in the first inscription is not specified; the wording is general. The second benefactor paid for constructions the nature of which is unknown due to the mutilated condition of the text. Kraabel (p.45) notes how the forms and styles of both stelai and the honours voted in them are properly Greek. They are also taken as an indication of the settled nature of the colony, which had most probably been brought there by trade. The two benefactors are otherwise unknown; however, Bruneau (p.481) surmises that they were fellow-Samaritans. Kraabel questions this, adducing evidence of Jews honouring benevolent gentile rulers and suggesting that the individuals here could equally have been gentile benefactors.

Dating of the inscriptions is difficult; the tools of prosopography, orthography and palaeography are of little help in determining a date before or after 129 BC, the year in which the temple on Mount Gerizim was destroyed (Josephus, *AJ* 13.256). The fact that contributions to Mount Gerizim are mentioned in both texts does not of itself assist in dating the texts, for even after that date the cult may have continued with contributions still being made.[4] It is also noted (Bruneau, p.485) that the expression οἱ ἀπαρχόμενοι κτλ. may still

---

[1] On the identification of the Roman magistrate who authored the letter at *AJ* 19.213-216 see most recently M. Pucci ben Zeev, 'Who wrote a letter concerning Delian Jews?', *Revue biblique* 103 (1996) 237-243. She identifies the author as Octavian and dates the letter between 19 August and 27 November 43 BC.

[2] See Bruneau, *BCH* 106 (1982) 479, and J and L. Robert, *BE* (1969) 478.

[3] On the rivalry of the two temples see Bruneau, *BCH* 106 (1982) 475-7. Just as the adherents of the temple in Jerusalem considered it to be ἱερός and ἅγιος, so also the Samaritans used the same epithets to describe their own temple (cf. also Josephus, *AJ* 12.10, and *BJ* 3.307). Bruneau (p.478) considers the epithets to be usual, expressing a belief in the authenticity of their temple.

[4] Bruneau, *BCH* 106 (1982) 482. The woman at the well supposes the cult to have ended (John 4.20), though as Bruneau points out the mountain was still considered holy; cf. Josephus, *AJ* 18.85 and *BJ* 3.307 (for later examples see Bruneau, *BCH* 106 [1982] 482). Bruneau states that the Johannine dialogue is a redactional

have been used to distinguish the association even if contributions were no longer made to Mount Gerizim; it may have been one of those fossilised terms which did not change, though the circumstances to which it referred did. On palaeographical grounds Bruneau assigns the first inscription to the period 150-50 BC and the second to 250-175 BC.

The inscriptions attest an organised association of Samaritans in Delos at least some time in the first half of the second century (inscription b) and lasting for between 25 and 125 years at least (inscription a). The text of the second inscription implies that the Samaritans had their own building. This is further supported by the state of preservation and proximity of find of the two inscriptions. Bruneau suggests that they both formed part of the interior ornamentation of the community's building. The conclusion raises the issue of the relationship of this building to other nearby buildings which Bruneau identifies as a synagogue[5] of 'orthodox' Jews (following A. Plassart) and a Jewish habitation of some form (House IIA). Were the 'orthodox' synagogue and Samaritan building contemporaneous? For Bruneau (p.497) the evidence of the inscriptions taken from the gymnasium (a *terminus post quem* of 88 BC) and re-used in the building of the synagogue is inconclusive as they could have formed part of a later addition to the synagogue (ca 50 BC). The synagogue itself may have been older. An earlier date would better suit the fact that a Jewish colony is known to have been resident from the first half of the second century (1 Macc 15.15-24). As Bruneau (p.498) thinks it unlikely that these persons would have waited approx. 100 years to build a synagogue, he prefers to see the buildings of the 'orthodox' Jews and Samaritans as contemporaneous, but he also acknowledges that positive evidence in favour of this position is lacking.[6] If contemporaneous, two explanations are offered for the proximity of the buildings. The Jewish concentration may have been forced on the different groups by the Delian authorities who looked askance at such foreign elements; or again it may have been by the free choice of both parties, who living in a gentile land had loosened their traditional hostilities and chosen one of the few areas free of idolatrous pollution to erect their cultic buildings.

The above inscriptions can be added to other evidence of Samaritans in the diaspora. Communities are attested in Egypt (Josephus, *AJ* 11.345, 12.7, 13.74 and 78, Fl. Vopiscus, *Vita Saturn.* 7.8, and *Cod. Theod.* 13.5.18)[7] and Thessalonica (*IG* X, 2, 1.789; see more recently D. Feissel, *Recueil des inscriptions chrétiennes de Macédoine* [Paris 1983] §291), whilst individual Samaritans are found in Sicily (*IG* XIV 336) and western Iran (Robert, *BE* [1968] §564) and at Delos (*I. Delos* 2616; see also above), Rhodes (*IG* XII, 8. 439; see J and L. Robert, *BE* [1969] 477-8) and Athens (*IG* II (2) 2943, 10219-222).[8] Robert notes that it is a matter of debate whether all the individuals named in the inscriptions were adherents of the Samaritan religion or merely Greek colonists from Samaria. In the case of *I. Delos* 2616 and

---

composition and as such expresses the opinion of the fourth evangelist about the state of the cult. He may have been misled into believing that the cult had ceased by his historical sources.

[5] See Bruneau, *BCH* 106 (1982) 489-95, for arguments in favour of the identification of the building as a synagogue.

[6] Bruneau, *BCH* 106 (1982) 499, reluctantly raises the possibility that the synagogue actually belonged to the Samaritans. Kraabel (p.46) more freely admits the possibility.

[7] A village in the Fayum named Samareia (*CPJ* 22, 28, 128 and *P. Ryl.* 71) further implies the earlier presence of a Samaritan community. For disputes between Jews and Samaritans in Egypt see Josephus, *AJ* 12.10 and 13.74 and 79. For cases of individual Samaritans in Egypt see *CPJ* 513 and 514. References are taken from B. Lifshitz and J. Schiby, 'Une synagogue samaritaine à Thessalonique', *Revue biblique* 75 (1968) 376-7. To these references add *P. Ent.* 62, *P. Herm.* 40, *P. Mich.* IV 224, *P. Mil. Vogl.* IV 212 recto cols 6 and 9, and *P. Strass.* IX 866, though the named individuals may not in all cases be adherents of the Samaritan religion.

[8] References are taken from J. and L. Robert, *BE* (1969) 478.

IG II (2) 2943 it is considered 'certain' that the individuals are Greek colonists, whilst in the other cases they are 'without doubt' Greek colonists.

S.R.L.

§13 The Career of T. Mucius Clemens and its Jewish Connections

Bir el Malik   AD 80s?

Ed. pr. — M. Avi-Yonah, 'The Epitaph of T. Mucius Clemens', *IEJ* 16 (1966) 258-264.

The marble tablet is in five fragments. The left edge is complete but it is broken on the right. Height is 35 cm; the line heights are 2 cm (*ll*.1-9) and 1.5 cm (*ll*.10-11). The width must be estimated on the assumption that the last word (*l*.11) was located on the axis of the inscription. On the basis of the reconstructed reading XAIPE it is estimated that the width was approx. 40 cm or 22-25 letters. However, it must be borne in mind that the final word is reconstructed. Martin's suggested reading ΧΑΡΙΣΤΗΡΙΟΝ would necessitate a different approximation. The text reproduced below is that of Martin, *ZPE* 52 (1983) 204. On the basis of *l*.6 he places a *hedera* ('ivy leaf')between each stage recorded in the *cursus* (*ll*.3 and 4).

Bibliography: *AE* (1967) §525; J. and L. Robert, *BE* 83 (1970) §633; A. Martin, *ZPE* 52 (1983) 203-210, and 60 (1985) 275-6; S. Schwartz, *ZPE* 56 (1984) 240-2, and 58 (1985) 296; and *SEG* XXXIII (1983) §1266.

[Τί]τωι Μουκίωι Μάρκ[ου υἱῶι *tribu*]	To [Ti]tus Mucius, [son of] Marc[us, tribe,]
[Κλ]ήμεντι, ἐπάρχωι στ[ρατευμάτων τοῦ]	[Cl]emens, *praefectus ca[strorum* of the]
βασιλέως μεγάλου Ἀγρίπ[πα (*hedera*) βοηθῶι]	great King Agrip[pa, *adiutor*]
Τιβερίου Ἀλεξάνδρου ἐπάρχ[ου Αἰγύπτου (*hedera*)]	of Ti. Alexander, prefect of Egypt,
5 ἐπάρχωι σπείρης πρώτη[ς Γάλλων Λεπι- (?)]	prefect of *cohors I [Lepi]diana equitata*
διανῆς ἱππικῆς (*hedera*) β[οηθῶι (?) ± 5 letters]	[(recruited) from Gauls], a[*diutor* ...]
Τιβερίου Κλαυδίο[υ *cognomen*]	of T. Claudius [*cognomen*],
ἐπιτρόπου Σε[βαστοῦ Συρίας],	im[perial] procurator [of Syria],
Σιμωνίδης καὶ Ζ[- - - *patronym*]	Simonides and Z[...], sons of [patronym]
10 υἱοὶ τῷ ἑαυτῶν [φίλωι καὶ εὐεργέτηι]	to their [friend and benefactor],
χα[ριστήριον].	a thank-offering.

2. *ed. pr.*: σπ[είρης 3. *ed. pr.*: Ἀγρίπ[πα. Ἐπί; *AE* 1967 §525: βοηθῶι 6. *ed. pr.*: Β[ενεφικιαρίωι; *AE* (1967) §525: βοηθῶι 7. *ed. pr.*: Κλαυδίο[υ Φήλικος 9. *ed. pr.*: καὶ Τ (or Ξ) 9-10. *ed. pr.*: καὶ] υἱοὶ τῶ(ν); *RÉG* 83 (1970) §633, and Schwatz, *ZPE* 56 (1984) 242: οἱ] υἱοὶ τῷ ἑαυτῶν [πατρί 11. *ed. pr.*: Χαῖρε

The text is a dedication by two persons (*l*.9) to the Roman citizen, Titus Mucius Clemens. It is uncertain whether the dedication is funerary.[1] The interpretation of the text has proved troublesome as the inscription is broken along the right side requiring the text to be restored. At critical points details of Clemens's *cursus* are missing or only partially preserved. Avi-Yonah proposed that the *cursus honorum* is shortened and related in reverse or indirect order, i.e. that earlier stages in his military career are omitted and later posts are recorded before earlier ones. According to his reading of the text T. Mucius Clemens was first *beneficarius* to

---

[1] Avi-Yonah, *IEJ* 16 (1966) 258-264, and Robert, *BE* 83 (1970) §633 believe the inscription to be funerary. In view of his reconstruction of *l*.11 to read χα[ριστήριον] Martin, *ZPE* 52 (1983) 210, observes that nothing obliges us to see the inscription as funerary.

Felix,[2] the imperial procurator of Judaea (between AD 52 and 60), then the prefect of an auxiliary cohort under Ti. Iulius Alexander, prefect of Egypt (AD 66), and finally the prefect of an auxiliary cohort in the army of Agrippa II (from AD 66). Avi-Yonah surmises that the occasion of the last transfer, which was intended to strengthen Agrippa's army on the eve of the Jewish revolt, was the visit of the king to Tiberius Alexander in AD 66. It was in this last post that Clemens died (possibly in the 80s) and a dedication was erected by Simonides, his wife and children. From the name Simonides Avi-Yonah further surmises that the dedicator was a Hellenised Jew. On the interpretation of the inscription Avi-Yonah concludes:

> The fact that the epitaph of Clemens was set up by a Jew is but the last link in the chain of evidence which links this Roman soldier with the Hellenized Jewish aristocracy. We observe some elements of this connection in every one of the three posts mentioned in his *cursus honorum*: service under a Roman procurator who had married a Jewish princess, followed by service under the only Jew (by descent) known to have risen high in the Roman army, and finally service under a Jewish king, the brother-in-law of his first patron and friend of his second. Such a concatenation of circumstances cannot be accidental. Obviously Clemens was one of the Gentiles who had associated themselves with the 'Herodian' party mentioned in the New Testament. This party seems not to have been numerous, but must have been influential by its connections with the Roman administration, with the courts of the Herodian dynasts and — as hinted at in the Gospels — with the Pharisees ... The 'Herodians' must have been associated with like-minded gentiles who were favourably inclined towards Judaism: Titus Mucius Clemens might well have been one of those.

AE (1967) §525 made two alterations to the inscription by the suggested reconstructions of βοηθῶι in *ll*.3 and 6. As a result four posts are recorded: (a) command of a cohort in Agrippa's army (*ll*.2-3); (b) *adiutor* of Ti. Iulius Alexander (*ll*.3-4); (c) prefect of the *cohors I Lepidiana equitata* (*ll*.5-6); and (d) *adiutor* of a procurator of Syria (*ll*.6-8).[3] It is further argued that as 'a post of a superior officer in the service of a client king could hardly be occupied at the end of a career after the individual had exercised a function of equivalent rank in the Roman army', the *cursus honorum* must be given in direct order. Clemens first served in Agrippa's army which assisted the Romans during the Jewish rebellion; he became the *adiutor* of Ti. Iulius Alexander who in AD 70 was the Chief-of-Staff (omitting Αἰγύπτου in *l*.4) under Titus; thereafter he became the prefect of a Roman auxiliary cohort; finally he occupied the post of *adiutor* of a financial procurator. The inscription's provenance suggests Syria as the region of this procuratorship.

Martin[4] reasserts against *AE* that the *cursus honorum* is inverted, i.e. in indirect order. The basis for this claim is the new reading of στ[...] at *l*.2, which he completes as στ[ρατευμάτων τοῦ]. Interpreting the terms στρατοπέδων and στρατευμάτων as equivalent, Martin argues that Clemens occupied the post of *praefectus castrorum* (ἔπαρχος στρατοπέδων / στρατευμάτων), a function which usually crowned the career of a *primipilaris*. To counter the objection made in *AE* and to explain Clemens's posting to Agrippa's army, Martin postulates that the move was prompted by exceptional circumstances, namely the Jewish rebellion and the recent blunders of Philippus. The Romans, wishing to control the operations of their allies, assigned to the client king (Agrippa II) a man who was not only tested, but also aware of the local realities and able to act with due care and discretion.

---

[2] The assumption requires that the name of Felix was Ti. Claudius Felix and not M. Antonius Felix.

[3] The interpretation of *AE* (1967) §525 is followed by H. Devijver, *Prosopographia militiarum equestrium quae fuerunt ab Augusto ad Gallienum*, vol.2 (Louvain 1977) 581-2; W. Eck, *PW* suppl. 15 (Munich 1978) s.v. 'Ti. Claudiu[s' and 'T. Mucius [Cl]emens', 89 and 291-2 respectively; H.-G. Pflaum, *Les carrières procuratoriennes équestres sous le Haut-Empire romain*, suppl. (Paris 1982) 130-2; and P.A. Holder, *The Auxilia from Augustus to Trajan* (Oxford 1980) 78.

[4] Martin, *ZPE* 52 (1983) 203-210.

Martin observes: 'I do not think that at the beginning of his career one would have entrusted T. Mucius Clemens with such responsibilities.' His career was thus: (a) *adiutor* of a financial procurator of Syria (in the reign of Nero); (b) prefect of *cohors I Lepidiana equitata*; (c) *adiutor* of the Roman prefect of Egypt, Ti. Iulius Alexander (AD 66-69); and (d) *praefectus castrorum* in Agrippa's army after Ti. Iulius Alexander became chief-of-staff under Titus (AD 70).[5] The last step in Clemens's career indicates to Martin the importance of personal relationship, Ti. Iulius Alexander no doubt nominating his former second-in-charge to the post of *praefectus castrorum*.

In the following year Schwartz, apparently unaware of Martin's article, published an article on the inscription in the same journal.[6] In the article the original identification of Ti. Claudius (*l*.7) as Felix is criticised as both baseless and contrary to the more reliable testimony that the *praenomen* and *nomen* of Felix, like his brother Pallas, was M. Antonius (cf. Tacitus, *Hist.* 5.9, and *CIL* V 34). Schwartz observes: 'we do not know who this procurator was or what position Clemens held under him.' The reading of Martin in *l*.2 is independently confirmed by Schwartz. As the *cursus* is considered to be inverted and the post in Agrippa's army to be Clemens's final one the line is completed ἐπάρχωι στ[ρατεύματος (or στ[ρατοῦ) τοῦ]. Accordingly, it is argued that Clemens occupied the 'important post of commander of Agrippa's army, and not the very modest command of a single cohort'.[7] In a subsequent volume of the journal[8] Schwartz disagrees with the reconstruction and interpretation offered by Martin. He points out that the title ἔπαρχος στρατοπέδων / στρατευμάτων is not equivalent to that of *praefectus castrorum* and again cites Josephus, *AJ* 19.299 and 353, as decisive evidence in favour of his reconstruction of the inscription.[9]

Schwartz[10] also suggests that Clemens himself was Jewish. The suggestion rests on his 'service in the Orient, his burial in Palestine and the name of his son, Simonides'. The argument depends in part on the reading of πατρί in the reconstructed portion of *l*.10. The firmness of the suggestion is later retracted in view of the competing reconstruction φίλωι.[11] Yet he continues to maintain the possibility 'in view of his service under both Ti. Alexander and Agrippa'. Martin[12] rightly questions the assumption that the suggested readings of *l*.10 (i.e. πατρί or φίλωι καὶ εὐεργέτηι) are 'equally possible'. There is, it is argued, no concrete evidence in the extant part of the text indicating a parental relationship; rather, the contrasting onomastic evidence (i.e. T. Mucius Clemens = father of Simonides) provides the best indication against the hypothesis.

---

[5] Martin, *ZPE* 52 (1983) 209, recognises two problems for his interpretation: (a) that Clemens had occupied no military command before his appointment as *adiutor* of the financial procurator of Syria; and (b) a space at the end of *l*.6. If the lost portion of text mentioned the exact domain of Clemens's service, then it must have been in an abbreviated form. Yet the inscription contains no other abbreviation.

[6] Schwartz, *ZPE* 56 (1984) 240-2.

[7] Schwartz, *ZPE* 56 (1984) 242 n.9, also admits the possibility that Clemens was the commander of a division in Agrippa's army.

[8] Schwartz, *ZPE* 58 (1985) 296.

[9] Martin, *ZPE* 60 (1985) 275-6, counters that there is essentially no real difference between his interpretation and that of Schwartz; he had merely sought 'in the usual terminology a formula sufficiently close to the Greek terms which Clemens could have used to describe conveniently his function to a Latin speaker'. He observes: 'Clemens must have played beside Agrippa II the role which Ti. Julius Alexander discharged beside Titus.'

[10] Schwartz, *ZPE* 56 (1984) 242.

[11] Schwartz, *ZPE* 58 [1985] 296.

[12] Martin, *ZPE* 60 (1985) 275.

Avi-Yonah, Martin and Schwartz all stress the Jewish element as a connecting thread throughout the career to T. Mucius Clemens. But how certain is this? Martin notes that the career of T. Mucius Clemens was marked by regional specialisation. The hypothesis is based on an error arising from the changing interpretation of the inscription. Avi-Yonah identified Ti. Claudius as Felix, the brother of M. Antonius Pallas, and restored the end of *l*.7 accordingly. This interpretation in turn justified the suggested reading of 'Ιουδαίας in *l*.8. However, the identification of Ti. Claudius as Felix, the governor of Judaea, is problematic (see above) and the restoration must be surrendered. The editor of *AE* (1967) §525 did just this, leaving the end of *l*.7 blank. However, as the text was now interpreted as a direct *cursus*, it was postulated that the end of *l*.8 should read Συρίας.[13] However, let us not be mistaken. The identification of the region of the procurator's function as Syria is entirely dependent on the provenance of the inscription. Once the inscription is again interpreted as an indirect *cursus*, there is no justification for the identification. The procuratorship might have been in any number of provinces. Yet Martin only considers two possibilities, Syria or Judaea, settling on the former due to the constraint of line length. Once the Jewish connection at this point in the inscription is doubted, there is good reason to question its assumed presence at other stages in the *cursus*. For example, all evidence is lacking for the disposition of the *cohors I Lepidiana equitata* in the period under consideration.[14] Any hypothesis about its location in Palestine is mere speculation. Also, the significance of the Jewish ancestry of Ti. Iulius Alexander may have been merely incidental. How Clemens came to his post is unknown. However, given the way in which the system of patronage operated, any number of connections, not just a Jewish one, might explain his career appointment under Ti. Iulius Alexander. That leaves only Clemens's appointment in the army of Agrippa. If the *cursus* is inverted, then the move is possibly explained by the appointment of Ti. Iulius Alexander as chief-of-staff under Titus and the desire of Rome to place a trusted officer in an influential post in the forces of its ally. If so, this is the only incident of a Jewish connection in the career of T. Mucius Clemens.

S.R.L.

---

[13] Even so, the editor appears to confuse Dora and Dura. See Schwartz, *ZPE* 56 (1984) 240 n.1.

[14] The earliest attestations for the disposition of the auxiliary unit are *CIL* XVI 26 (Pannonia, AD 80), 45 (Moesia Inferior, AD 99) and 58 (Moesia Inferior, AD 114). See further P.A. Holder, *The Auxilia from Augustus to Trajan* 179, 189, 190 and 240.

ECCLESIASTICA

§14 The Christian Symbol ΧΜΓ, an Acrostic or an Isopsephism?

Provenance unknown   5.9 x 15 cm   Byzantine period

Ed. pr. — P.J. Sijpesteijn, 'Wiener Mélange', *ZPE* 40 (1980) 94 and 96 (= *SB* XIV 12658).

There are spaces of 2.5 and 3.6 cm left between *ll.* 1 and 2 and *ll.* 2 and 3 respectively. The papyrus is broken off on the right side and has a *kollesis* on the left. The text appears to be complete and has been written on the back of an earlier papyrus sheet which has been cut to receive the new text. Writing is along the fibres.

    χμγ   (symbol)
    εὐτυχῶς   successfully
    ἀγαθῇ τύχῃ   by good fortune

The editor suggests that the text functioned as a Christian amulet.[1] He cites three other such instances of the use of the Christian symbol χμγ, *PGM* II 3 (p.210, a prophylactic amulet for a house and its inhabitants dated to fourth or fifth century), 8a verso and 24 verso (pp.216 and 232 respectively, both on the back of requests for instruction from God regarding commercial matters and dated to the sixth century). Further support for the apotropaic or protective character of the symbol is provided by inscriptional evidence from Syria. Here a number of examples of χμγ inscribed on lintels can be cited. Mostly the symbol is associated with a request for divine help, e.g. *IGLSyria* IV 1614: χμγ. ὅσα λέγεις καὶ σοὶ τὰ διπλᾶ. Χριστὲ βοήθει τοὺς οἰκοῦντας καὶ τοὺς ἀναγινώσκοντας — 'Whatever you say will be double for you. Christ help the residents and those who read (this)'.[2]

If Sijpesteijn's interpretation is correct, as it most surely seems to be, then the text demonstrates that the symbol possessed a 'magical' character. Whether this was a sense which was later added to a symbol whose meaning had in time been lost or whether it was part of its original function is unclear from a consideration of this text and its function alone. However, a wider analysis of relevant information and possibilities indicates that the symbol's function may well have been 'magical' from its inception. The evidence and arguments are adduced below.

The symbol χμγ is widely attested in antiquity from the fourth to the seventh centuries AD.[3] It is found, for example, in papyrus documents from Egypt, in dedications and epitaphs

---

[1] On the use of ἀγαθῇ τύχῃ at the end or beginning of horoscopes see *P. Köln* V 236 *l.*7 and note (AD 246).

[2] Other examples are *IGLSyria* IV 1452, 1648, 1789, 1812, 1957, and V 2232. Cf. also *IGLSyria* IV 1442, 1443 and 1448.

[3] L. Jalabert and R. Mouterde, *IGLSyria* II, p.154, and L. Robert, *Hellenica* 11-12 (1960) 309-310. M. Guarducci, 'Le acclamazioni a Ursus e a Leo nei sotterranei del battistero lateranese', *Rendiconti della Pont. Accad. Rom. d'Arch.* 46 (1973-4) 181-6, holds that an inscription (dated probably early in Constantine's reign) from the baptistery of the Lateran Church has the prerogative of being the earliest known example in the Christian world. On the basis of *IGLSyria* II 309 (Seleucid year 486 = AD 174/5) and IV 1249 (Seleucid year 522 = AD 211), J.-O. Tjäder, 'Christ, Our Lord, Born of the Virgin Mary (ΧΜΓ and VDN)' *Eranos* 68 (1970) 176 n.10 and 188-9 n.92, tentatively admits the possibility of extending evidence back into the third century. See also H. Leclercq, *DACL* I (Paris 1924) s.v. 'Isopséphie' 182. Jalabert and Mouterde, however, question the reading of year 486 in *IGLSyria* II 309 suggesting 786 (= AD 474/475) instead. In the case of *IGLSyria* IV 1249 they suggest dating from the era of Antioch (year 522 = AD 474). *IGLSyria* V 2179 (Seleucid year 570 =

§14 The Christian Symbol ΧΜΓ, an Acrostic or an Isopsephism?

from Palestine, Syria and Asia Minor, on amphoras from Athens and Egypt, and stamped tiles from Rome. Yet despite the currency of the symbol its key has eluded modern scholarship. This should not, however, be surprising as it would appear that even in antiquity the meaning was uncertain and different interpretations of the symbol were offered.

The letters χμγ have historically been interpreted either as an acrostic, i.e. the first letters of a phrase consisting of three words, or as an isopsephism (or example of gematria), i.e. a number representing a word or expression the sum of whose letters is that number (643 — χ = 600, μ = 40, γ = 3). One of the better known examples of an isopsephism is the number ϙθ (99) which was used to represent the word ἀμήν (α + μ + η + ν = 1+40+8+50 = 99). Words of the same numerical value were associated and the persons, concepts or things to which they pointed were often thought to possess a hidden relationship, e.g. 284 = θεός = ἅγιος = ἀγαθός; 781 = Παῦλος = σοφία; 2443 = Ἰησοῦς ὁ Χρειστός = γένους Δαουίδ, οὐράνιος κλάδος.[4] Be that as it may, under each of the acrostic and isopsephic interpretations there is a preferred solution. For the acrostic interpretation that solution is Χ(ριστὸν) Μ(αρία) γ(εννᾷ).[5] For the isopsephic interpretation the preferred solution is θεὸς βοηθός (θ + ε + ο + ς + β + ο + η + θ + ο + ς = 9+5+70+200+2+70+8+9+70+200 = 643). How is one to decide between the proposed solutions, especially given the growing mood of scepticism over the capacity of present evidence to determine the issue?

Blanchard[6] postulates that two criteria should be satisfied by any acceptable solution: 'd'une part montrer que la formule à laquelle on pense existe réellement et avec une certaine fréquence d'emploi: d'autre part établir un lien authentique entre la formule et le sigle.' He uses these criteria to dismiss the interpretation of χμγ as the isopsephic representation of θεὸς βοηθός. But Lewis[7] points out that under these criteria his own preferred solution (i.e. the acrostic solution) fails. There is no unproblematic attestation of the unabridged expression.

AD 258/9) can also be added to the two examples cited by Tjäder. The last example tends to confirm an earlier appearance of the symbol.

[4] The examples are cited from F. Dornseiff, *Das Alphabet in Mystik und Magie* (Berlin 1925) 96, and F. Dölger, 'Eine christliche Grabinschrift vom Jahre 363 mit exorzistischen Zeichen als Zeilensicherung' in *Antike und Christentum* 1 (Münster 1929, repr. 1974) 301.

[5] The arguments and evidence for resolving the symbol by Χ(ριστὸν) Μ(αρία) γ(εννᾷ) are mustered by J.-O. Tjäder, *Eranos* 68 (1970) 148-190. Other postulated solutions are dismissed by the author, namely the acrostic solutions Χ(ριστὸς) (ὁ ἐκ) Μ(αρίας) γ(εννηθείς); Χ(ριστὸς) Μ(ιχαὴλ) Γ(αβριήλ); and χ(ειρός) μ(ου) γ(ραφή) as well as the isopsephic interpretation. A. Blanchard, 'Sur quelques interprétations de ΧΜΓ', *Proc. XIV (1974) Int. Cong. of Pap.* 20, argues against the solution χειρός μου γραφή by showing that there is no evidence to support it; the ρ in χμγρ is properly read as the chi-rho monogram. More recently A. Gostoli, 'Una nuova ipotesi interpretativa della sigla cristiana ΧΜΓ', *Stud. Pap.* XXII.1 (1983) 9-14, has suggested the solution Χ(ριστὸς) μ(άρτυς) γ(ένηται) or γ(ένοιτο). G. Robinson, 'ΚΜΓ and ΘΜΓ for ΧΜΓ', *Tyche* 1 (1986) 175-7, offers further support for this interpretation on the basis of changes in the symbol's first letter (from Χ to Κ = κύριος, Θ = θεός) and the location of the symbol in the documents. Robinson uses the evidence to dismiss the isopsephic interpretation, but she also concedes that Χ(ριστὸς) μ(άρτυς) γ(ένηται) was probably not the original meaning of the symbol, favouring here instead the solution Χ(ριστὸν) Μ(αρία) γ(εννᾷ). The argument is problematic. The two examples of the Θ substitution (*P. Grenf.* II 100 and *CPR* X 32) are late (seventh century) and confined to the Arsinoite nome. They attest only the interpretation of the symbol by later notaries in that nome and cannot be used to dismiss the possibility of an original isopsephic interpretation. Indeed as Robinson concedes herself, the symbol generated a number of different interpretations.

[6] Blanchard, *Proc. XIV (1974) Int. Cong. of Pap.* 21.

[7] N. Lewis, 'Notationes Legentis', *BASP* 13 (1976) 159.

As evidence in support of the unabridged formula Χριστὸν Μαρία γεννᾷ Tjäder[8] cites two documents:

(a) *P. Grenf.* II 112a (*ca* seventh century), a parchment recording the formula X̄C̄ ΜΑΡΙΑ ΓΕΝΝΑ ΚΑΙ + ΜΑΡΙΑ X̄C̄ ΓΕΝΝΑ Κ(ΑΙ) X̄C̄ ΜΑΡΙΑ ΓΕΝΝΑ before a citation of Psalm 1.3; and

(b) *IEgChr* 663, an epitaph (Nubia?, Byzantine date) for a woman using the formula Χρίστου Μαρία γέννᾳ with ἀμήν on either side. The formula occurs after a prayer for the deceased but before the dating formula.

The difficulty with either document is the case of Χριστός, namely the use of the nominative or genitive cases for the accusative.[9] Of difficulty also is the late date of the attestations. Horsley[10] observes:

> The paucity of texts and the fact that appeal must be made to scribal error in both do not permit a confident association of these wordings with χμγ ... Even if it were to be sustained, the later dates of these texts might cause one to wonder if these wordings were not a subsequent interpretation of the letters.

Other problems also exist. To address the problem posed by the use of the present tense, Tjäder[11] suggests that it should be understood as an expressive (dramatic) present. But if I understand this usage correctly, it makes little sense to employ an expressive present by itself, for a larger linguistic context is needed to provide the necessary temporal point of reference.[12] Another difficulty is posed by the active form of the verb γεννάω. The voice requires Mary to be the subject of the verb, but the expression is unusual. In view of the various credal confessions current in the church one should have expected a passive verb with Χριστός as its subject, i.e. Χριστὸς ἐκ Μαρίας γεννηθείς. Even so the confession is one-sided as it omits any reference to the two natures of Christ, i.e. Χριστὸν ... τὸν ἐκ τοῦ πατρὸς or ἐκ πνεύματος ἁγίου γεννηθέντα and Χριστὸν ... τὸν ἐκ Μαρίας γεννηθέντα. There is also the matter of the unusual word-order in the formula. To explain it Tjäder appeals to the order Χριστὸς – Μαρία – γεννάω in the creeds. The appeal, however, makes little sense as the formula does not follow the form of the creeds within whose linguistic context the order is quite natural. Nor does it explain why the creed should exercise such a constraint, nor why the doctrinal formulation created within a particular Christological controversy gained such wide

---

[8] Tjäder, *Eranos* 68 (1970) 162, also cites as a possible attestation a graffito from Nazareth (second to fourth century ?) which was read XE ΜΑΡΙΑ. See P.B. Bagatti, *Revue Biblique* (1962) 419 and plate XLVIII b, and J. and L. Robert, *BE* (1964) no.513. The inscription is important because of its possible early date. Against the two restorations Χ(αῖρ)ε Μαρία (editor) or Χ(ριστ)ὲ Μαρία (Robert), Tjäder argues instead for ΧΝ ΜΑΡΙΑ Γ[ΕΝΝΑ]. The reading faces two difficulties: (a) E is replaced by N on the basis of an inspection of plate XLVIII b. There is no indication in the ed. pr. that the reading of E is doubtful. On the basis of the printed plate I see no justification for Tjäder's restoration; and (b) Γ[ΕΝΝΑ] is postulated below the M of ΜΑΡΙΑ on the basis of what is perceived to be the upper portion of the letter Γ. Again, I see no justification for reading this letter there.

[9] For Tjäder's explanations of the case endings see Tjäder, *Eranos* 68 (1970) 153 and 160-3. Against Tjäder's explanation of the sigma in *P. Grenf.* II 112a as an indicator of abbreviation see Blanchard, *Proc. XIV (1974) Int. Cong. of Pap.* 22. In agreement with the editors of *P. Grenf.* II the latter author concludes that the sigma was a mistake.

[10] G.H.R. Horsley, *New Docs* 2 (1982) 178.

[11] Tjäder, *Eranos* 68 (1970) 163.

[12] Cf. E. Schwyzer, *Griechische Grammatik*, vol.2 (Munich 1966) 271: Stets geht diesem Präsens ein Augmentumtempus oder eine Temporalbestimmung voraus, die den zeitlichen Rahmen angeben; sie können auch folgen.

§14 The Christian Symbol XMΓ, an Acrostic or an Isopsephism?

and varied acceptance in its acrostic form without multiple and unproblematic attestations of the formula itself. A further question can be raised over the appropriateness of the symbol's context. A. Nobbs observes in a note to me:

> If we turn to consider the motives which may be behind the inclusion of such a formula in an (apparently) unrelated document, it would seem that a reference to — i.e. presumably a request for — God's aid in whatever circumstance is probably more explicable than a simple pious expression or Christological statement.

Tjäder surprisingly tries to make a virtue of some of these weaknesses claiming that they make the solution the *lectio difficilior*. Unfortunately, the analogy with textual criticism seems somewhat forced. Indeed, it is more probable that the difficulties arose from a later attempt to give an interpretation to the symbol which was prompted by its first letter, the 'X' suggesting Χριστός and the remaining letters excluding a passive construction.

Under both interpretations there is a serious methodological problem associated with the use of attestation to validate a solution. Once it is recognized that after its initial usage the symbol took on a number of different interpretations, how is it possible to differentiate between an attestation of the original meaning and an attestation of a subsequent interpretation. Tjäder[13] has offered the somewhat vague criterion that 'the best certified unabbreviated text (or use) must be given preference, if it is generally reasonable and if there is no objection to it'. Factors here include an adequate context, the age of the attestation and its geographical dispersion. Again the preferred solution under the acrostic interpretation appears to fail for the reasons already given above. But there is a more fundamental problem. The criterion might be of help if we knew when the symbol was first used and if we had a number of relevant attestations in close temporal proximity. But the criterion only begs the question as to when the symbol was first used and when exactly it started to be interpreted differently. And to these questions there is no answer.[14] Is there a way forward?

I would argue that simple probability theory may offer assistance. It is noted that the letters are ordered in the usual manner for a number, i.e. hundreds ($\chi = 600$), tens ($\mu = 40$) and units ($\gamma = 3$). How probable is such an ordering of letters in an acrostic? Of the twenty four letters of the Greek alphabet 8 function as units (α through to θ), 8 as tens (ι through to π) and 8 as hundreds (ρ through to ω). The ninth and missing number in each group was supplied from the primitive Greek alphabet, i.e. *vau*, *koppa* and *sampi* respectively. The probability (i.e. p-value) of randomly selecting three letters in the required numerical order is:

$$\text{p-value} = \left(\frac{8}{24}\right)^3 = 0.037^*$$

Under the model there is a 1 in 27 chance that such a sequence might occur randomly. Now, of course, the way in which phonology and syntax work within a language is by no means random. One only has to look at a Greek lexicon to see that words are more likely to commence with some letters than with others. And the lexicon itself is not an adequate indicator as it tells us nothing about the frequency with which words are used in the language. However, none of these objections can be used against the above calculation as the model

---

[13] Tjäder, *Eranos* 68 (1970) 157.

[14] Tjäder, *Eranos* 68 (1970) 168-9, suggests that the phrase Χ(ριστὸν) Μ(αρία) γ(εννᾷ) dates from the second half of the first century in Syria and its symbol χμγ to the end of the first or early second century in Asia Minor. The suggestion is, however, a mere conjecture which at the same time highlights the temporal distance between the creation of the symbol and attestations of its alleged meaning.

maximises the p-value.[15] Indeed, if one were to determine the p-value of actual language samples, it would be found to be less than the figure of 0.037˙ derived above.[16] Indeed, the chance of such a sequence occurring randomly would be closer to 1 in 29 or 30. Those who maintain that the symbol χμγ represents an acrostic must explain why they are satisfied with the risk involved in their decision. I myself find it too high. Moreover, in view of the fact that there is no undisputed nor early attestation of the prevailing acrostic interpretation I am inclined to doubt its feasibility.

The objection might be raised that it was precisely the order of letters in the acrostic which prompted the subsequent isopsephic interpretation of the symbol. This is possible. The objection also shows how arguments in this field, which is little constrained by unambiguous data, can be turned one way and then another. The objection remains, however, something of a smoke screen, for it does not alleviate nor minimise the risk which is taken by those advocating an acrostic interpretation.

There is a more serious objection to the above calculation. As numbers written in alphabetical form were also written backwards (i.e. from lower valued to higher valued letters), it might be thought that the p-value or chance should be doubled,[17] i.e.

$$\text{p-value} = \frac{2}{27}$$

However, I believe that it would be overly cautious to do this. Two reasons can be given by way of justification:

(a) By far the more frequent order of letters in alphabetically written numbers is from higher valued to lower valued letters.
(b) Isopsephisms in Greek are, as far as I am aware, written in the usual descending order.

There is no circularity in appealing to (b), for in seeking the probability of an arrangement of letters in numerical order we are, in view of the two alternative interpretations, really seeking the probability of an isopsephic arrangement.

Those who would argue for the higher p-value must show that in all probability the symbol had its origin in a region or province which used inverted order for numbers. Tentative support for this position is to be found as possibly the earliest attestations of χμγ found in

---

[15] The reason why the model maximises the p-value is that the multiplication of any three positive numbers is always less than or equal to the cube of their mean.

[16] As four examples showing that the p-value of actual language samples is less than the figure derived under the model, the Greek texts of Matthew's Gospel, Acts, Roman and Hebrews have been scanned and the number of words beginning with a letter carrying the value of a unit, ten or hundred counted. The results are given in the table below:

| | Total number of words | Number beginning with letter equivalent to a | | | p-value |
		unit	ten	hundred	
Matthew	18346	7559	6855	3932	0.032996
Acts	18450	7483	6533	4434	0.034514
Romans	7111	3058	2324	1729	0.034172
Hebrews	4953	2021	1778	1154	0.034127

[17] On the order of numerals see M.N. Tod, *BSA* 45 (1950) 129.

§14 The Christian Symbol ΧΜΓ, an Acrostic or an Isopsephism? 161

Syria (i.e. *IGLSyria* II 309, IV 1249 and V 2179) are cited with a date in inverted order. But what the evidence gives on the one hand, it takes away on the other; for the text of *IGLSyria* V 2179 (+ Νικᾷ ΧΜΓ Ι Κ(ύριο)ς βωεθός, AD 258/9) clearly appears to lend support to the isopsephic interpretation of the symbol. Those who argue for the higher p-value must also show that an isopsephism could be written in inverted order. I know of no evidence in support of this. On the contrary there is no instance of ϟθ, for example, written in inverted order in the inscriptions from Syria, Palestine or Arabia.[18]

What then of the isopsephic interpretation? Two points are often alleged in its support: (a) that the use of isopsephisms was common, e.g. τξε = 365 (number of days in the year) = Ἀβρασάξ (supreme Orphic and solar deity) = Νεῖλος (Osiris, solar deity) = Μείθρας (Mithras, solar deity) = ἅγιον ὄνομα;[19] ωπ (used in connection with θεὸν μέγιστον) = 880 = Χάδαδος, Hadad(?);[20] and ωπη (= 888 = Ἰησοῦς);[21] and (b) that numerous cases exist where the symbol is combined with ϟθ = 99 = ἀμήν.[22] On the other hand, Tjäder[23] considers the juxtaposition of χμγ and ϟθ to be merely a later speculation as to the meaning of the symbol. He also argues that the isopsephic interpretation fails to account for the other forms which the formula takes, e.g. χϲμγ (*IGLSyria* IV 1486) and χ^{ν}μγ (*P. Colt* 7 *l*.29 = L. Casson and E.L. Hettich, *Excavations at Nessana*, vol. 2 [Princeton 1950] 147). His arguments, however, carry little weight, for the other forms may themselves be later speculations as to the symbol's meaning. *P. Colt* 7 is dated by its editors to either the sixth or seventh centuries, whilst *IGLSyria* IV 1486 is undated. Furthermore, the fact that the juxtaposition of χμγ and ϟθ actually offers no meaning for the assumed isopsephism makes it difficult to accept its occurrence as 'a later speculation ... concerning the meaning of the group of symbols'.

Blanchard[24] offers a more sustained criticism of the solution, χμγ = θεὸς βοηθός. He attempts to question (i) the alleged attestations of it and (ii) the likelihood of the expression on other grounds.

(i) The resolution of the letters θβ in *CIJ* II 964, 1436-7 (= *CPJ3 Inscr* 1436-7) and *P. Herm. Rees* 64 by θεὸς βοηθός is dismissed in favour of θεῷ βοηθοῦντι.

---

[18] See *IGLSyria* II 310a, IV 1632, 1648, 1814, 1831, *LBW* VI 2145, *Limes de Chalcis* no.206.37, and *DOP* XX 263.10. I find no example of ϟθ written in an inverted order from other regions either.
[19] L. Janssens, 'La datation néronienne de l'isopséphie — Νεῖλος (= Osiris) = Ἀβρασάξ = ἅγιον ὄνομα = Μείθρας', *Aegyptus* 68 (1988) 103-15. The author argues that the isopsephic identification of the three great solar deities was the result of a syncretism operating in the court of Nero.
[20] See *IGLSyria* I 230 (also VI 2916). Dornseiff, *Das Alphabet in Mystik und Magie* 105, suggests Mithras as the referent. This is dismissed by Jalabert and Mouterde. Χάδαδος was suggested by Demircioglu (cited *IGLSyria* VI, p.188).
[21] Irenaeus, *Adv. haer.* 1.15.5. The number 888 (= Ἰησοῦς) was also associated with the letters of the alphabet (8 units, 8 tens and 8 hundreds) and thereby with ΑΩ of Revelation (1.8 and 21.6). See Dornseiff, *Das Alphabet in Mystik und Magie* 131. Other examples can also be cited:
  801 = περιστερά (Matt 3.16 and parallels) = ΑΩ;
  318 = Ἰη(σοῦς) + Τ (cross) = 18 + 300 (*Epistle of Barnabas* 9.8); and
  666 of Revelation (13.18).
[22] See Tjäder, *Eranos* 68 (1970) 155, for the various persons who have argued for an isopsephic interpretation of χμγ using the juxtaposition of this symbol and ϟθ.
[23] Tjäder, *Eranos* 68 (1970) 159.
[24] Blanchard, *Proc. XIV (1974) Int. Cong. of Pap.* 21-2.

Evidence in support of an association between χμγ and θεὸς βοηθός, namely the facts that one instance of θεὸς βοηθός is found on a stamped tile from Rome and that similar tiles carry the letters χμγ, is dismissed as weak.[25]

Comparison of parallel inscriptions is also said to offer no certainty. In regard to the inscriptions Ἐμμανουήλ, μεθ' ἡμῶν <ὁ> θε(ό)ς, χμγ (*IGLSyria* IV 1814B, undated) and Ἐμμανουήλ, μεθ' ἡμῶν ὁ θεός, βοηθός (*IGLSyria* IV 1447, undated) it is noted that χμγ only covers βοηθός and not the whole expression.

It is alleged that there are no other examples of the expression θεὸς βοηθός, and in particular not in inscriptions from Syria or Egypt where the symbol χμγ is so frequently found.

(ii) It is noted that βοηθός is used predicatively of ὁ θεός in the LXX (Psalms 61.9 and 77.35).[26]

It is observed that θεός is more often associated with βοηθῶν.

As a result of the evidence now to hand Blanchard's objections no longer appear convincing. There are a number of examples of θεὸς βοηθός found in both the literary and documentary evidence of antiquity.

(a) Philo, *Moses* 1.174: Moses when faced with the complaints of the Israelites and their unpreparedness to fight the Egyptian pursuers encourages them not to trust in human defences. He states: παρασκευῆς οὐδεμιᾶς ἐστι χρεῖος ὁ θεὸς βοηθός — 'θεὸς βοηθός has no need of armament'. The presence of a preceding predicate (ἐστι χρεῖος) and the position of βοηθός after ὁ θεός indicate that the term has become a fixed epithet of θεός and that the definite article covers the noun and its adjective Of importance also is the military register of the collocation. See the uses in Eusebius below.

(b) θεὸς βοηθός is found at the top of a Jewish inscription recording the names of contributors to a soup-kitchen (*patella*) in Aphrodisias (*IAphrodJud*, third century).[27]

(c) Eusebius in his *Life of Constantine* provides important information concerning the use of θεὸς βοηθός. At the beginning of his account when considering the task ahead Eusebius implores θεὸς βοηθός to help him in the writing of the life (1.11.2). Before defeating Maxentius at the Milvian Bridge Constantine is portrayed as choosing to rely on the one true God, θεὸς βοηθός, rather than on the many gods (1.27.1-2). In the prayer given by Constantine to his soldiers God is called upon as βοηθός (4.20.1).

(d) *Agora* 21 J6 records an amphora (fifth century) bearing the expression θεὸς βοηθός. The association of this amphora with other amphoras (e.g. J 2 and 5) of the same

---

[25] *Römische Quartalschrift* 9 (1895) 509 — cited by Tjäder, *Eranos* 68 (1970) 181 n.48. Tjäder observes: 'There is not necessarily a connection in any way. In this case also, only a large number of instances of a reasonable unabbreviated text encountered in an adequate connection could obviously carry any weight as a fairly certain proof ...'

[26] As another example of βοηθός used predicatively in conjunction with ὁ θεός see the funerary inscription *SB* IV 7432 (Mailnarti, an island near Halfa, AD 1080).

[27] J. Reynolds and R. Tannenbaum, *Jews and Godfearers at Aphrodisias* (Cambridge 1987) 5.

(e) *IEph.* 1285 no.14 (undated) is a Christian graffito from a church in Ephesus:

('Ιησοῦς Χριστός)	(Jesus Christ)
θεὸς βοηθὸς τοῦ δούλου σου	God helper of your slave
Λεοντίου καὶ τῇ δούλῃ σου	Leontios and your slave-woman
Θεο[σεβ]ίᾳ καὶ ['Ι]ουάνου ἀ[πὸ π]α(ν-)	Theosebia and of Ioannes from all
τὸς κακοῦ καὶ ὁ σοὶ καθήκων	evil and he who is meet to you
ευσισιειω[. . . . .]ωκε	[...]

(f) *SEG* XXX 1785 (Cyrene, fourth century) is part of a Christian mosaic from the house of Hesychius:

θεὸς βοηθὸς 'Αλοίπωτι σὺν τέκνοις	God helper of Alypo[29] with children
θεὸς βοηθὸς Λαμπροτυχῇτι σὺν τέκνοις	God helper of Lamprotyches with children
θεὸς βοηθὸς Ἡσυχίῳ διὰ παντός	God helper of Hesychios always
Εὐτυχῶς Ἡσυχίῳ τῷ Λιβυάρχῃ	Successfully for Hesychios the governor of Libya

(g) *SEG* XXVII 1016 (Jerusalem, undated) is an invocation to Poseidon for help. See also L. Robert, *BE* (1978) no. 533. The inscription reads: θεὸς | βοη|θὸς | Ποσι|δῶν | βοήθει — 'God helper, Poseidon help'. In view of its location and the apparent currency of the expression in Jewish and Christian circles, one might think its occurrence here to be a pagan borrowing. But compare the use by Aelius Aristides cited below. See also L. Robert, *BCH* 101 (1977) 105 ff. (esp. n. 84) for the use of βοηθός as an epithet for Apollo, Zeus and Sarapis.

(h) *I. Tyre* I 160bis (undated) is an inscribed stone used to close a *loculus* in the necropolis of Tyre. See L. Robert, *BE* (1978) no. 522 p.117. The text reads:
θεὸς βοη|θός · Βάσ|κανε φεῦγε. | Καλῶς ἶπες (read εἶπες).
God helper. Slanderer flee. You have spoken well.
The text is interpreted by Rey-Coquais in the ed. pr. as a dialogue between the deceased and passer-by. Both this editor and L. Robert note the melding of superstition (i.e. popular belief in the evil eye) and Christian belief, and seek to explain the inscription accordingly. However, on the basis of the use of the expression θεὸς βοηθός alone it cannot be asserted that the text illustrates Christian belief.

As we are interested in establishing a currency for the expression θεὸς βοηθός, occurrences in one of the oblique cases should also be cited. See Epiphanius, *Haereses* 1.267, 2.186, 3.140, 340, 451; Eusebius, *Demonstratio evangelica* 1.1.11, *Commentarii in Psal.* 23.496, 621; Gregorius Nyssenus, *Contra Eunomium* 1.1.338. Aelius Aristides, Πρὸς

---

[28] The editor (p.88) finds confirmation of the acrostic interpretation Χ(ριστὸν) Μ(αρία) γ(εννᾷ) in J 7 and 8 which replace the M in ΧΜΓ with ΘΕ and Θ (θεός) respectively. However, these examples are dated later than those which confirm an association between the letters χμγ and θεὸς βοηθός.

[29] P.M. Fraser and E. Matthews, *A Lexicon of Greek Personal Names*, vol.1 (Oxford 1987) 30.

Πλάτωνα περὶ ῥητορικῆς 109, provides an interesting confirmation for the pagan use of the expression.

In view of the above evidence Blanchard's dismissal of θεὸς βοηθός as a possible interpretation of the letters θβ in *CIJ* II 964 (Ascalon, AD 604), 1436-7 (Alexandria, undated) and *P. Herm. Rees* 64 (fifth century) may be questioned. Two other examples of the letter combination θβ should also be noted. *SEG* XXXI 694 nos 14 and 21 are painted inscriptions on amphoras from Sucidava in Dacia (dated to the sixth century). In the former example (no. 14) the letters are associated with the symbol χμγ. The same symbol is also found on other amphoras listed under *SEG* XXXI 694, i.e. nos 5, 10, 13, 15 and 20. If θεὸς βοηθός is accepted as the correct interpretation, then the use of θβ at the top of *P. Herm. Rees* 64 (an acknowledgement of loan) is significant, for the phenomenon finds parallels in similar types of documents headed instead by the letters χμγ. For example, see *P. Oxy.* VI 995 (fifth century), *Stud. Pal.* XX 167 (fifth century), *P. Wash. Univ.* II 101 (fifth or sixth century), *CPR* VII 49 (sixth century), *P. Batav.* I 22 (sixth century), and *P. Genova* I.50 (sixth or seventh century). An association of the letters χμγ and the expression θεὸς βοηθός has been found in stamped tiles from Rome (see n.25 above) and an Athenian amphora (see d above). If the reading and interpretation of θβ are correct, then *P. Herm. Rees* 64 would supply a third example of the association. However, some caution may be required here. First, there is a slight formal difference. Whereas θβ is located on the first line of *P. Herm. Rees* 64, χμγ was customarily, but not always, placed above the first line of the document. Second, the reading of θ is uncertain. The editor dismisses the possibility of reading ϙθ, but admits that a line may be missing from the top of the document. Could the line have contained the symbol χμγ? A comparison with similar types of documents suggests the possibility. But then again it is unclear whether there actually was a preceding line. In either case what sense can be made of the letter β and what preceded it? There are only a limited number of possibilities due to the laws of Greek phonology. They are that: (a) the β is the end of an abbreviated or elided word; (b) the β is part of a number; or (c) the β is the last letter in a loan word or name. Of these (a) is the most probable explanation and this in turn leads one back to the letters θβ.

The above evidence supporting the formula θεὸς βοηθός also prompts a reconsideration of various pieces of indirect evidence. As noted by Blanchard, a comparison of the parallel inscriptions *IGLSyria* IV 1814B ('Εμμανουήλ, μεθ' ἡμῶν <ὁ> θε(ό)ς, χμγ) and *IGLSyria* IV 1447 ('Εμμανουήλ, μεθ' ἡμῶν ὁ θεός, βοηθός) does not provide a direct example of an association between the symbol χμγ and the formula θεὸς βοηθός, for χμγ only covers βοηθός. However, the omission of θεός in the formula is easily explained as an attempt to avoid an awkward repetition. To return to the point at hand, other pieces of indirect evidence might also be cited. Documents which appeal to God or Christ as helper are numerous and in some of these there is a direct association between this appeal and the symbol χμγ, e.g.

IGLSyria V 2179 (Kneysseh, AD 258/9):
+ Νικᾷ ΧΜΓ Ι Κ(ύριο)ς βωεθός
(Cross) he is victorious χμγ Lord helper

SEG XXXII 1108[30] (Aphrodisias, fifth century):
ΧΜΓ. Θ(ε)ὲ βοήθι
χμγ *God, help*

---

[30] See also C. Roueché, *Aphrodisias in Late Antiquity*, *JRS* monograph 5 (Leeds 1989) no.145.

SEG XXX 1740 (Esna in Egypt, undated):
εἷς θεὸς ὁ βοηθὸς τὰ πάντα· Παύλου, πατὺρ τῆς μουνῆ (read μονῆς) ἐκοιμίθη Φαρμοῦθι κη̄. ΧΜΓ
One God, the helper in all things. Paul, proprietor(?) of the inn has died, Pharmouthi 28. χμγ

IGLSyria IV 1707 (Androna, AD 533/4):
ΧΜΓ. ὦ θε(ὸς) <τ>(οῦ) ἀρχανγέλ(ου), Βοήθι. Ἔτ(ους) ἐμω̄, ἰνδ(ικτιῶνος) αῑ.
χμγ. *Oh God of the archangel, help. Year 845, indiction 11.*

Also relevant here is the use of χμγ in the subscriptions of notaries from the Arsinoite and Herakleopolite nomes in the Byzantine period. In the Hermopolite nome from the second half of the fifth century to the seventh century one finds in these subscriptions the formula κ̄(ύρι)ε βοήθ(ει).[31] As well one can consider those examples where there is an association between the two symbols χμγ and ϙθ as the letters of both ἀμήν and βοήθι have a numerical sum of 99.[32] Now, it can be objected that these examples do not attest the formula θεὸς βοηθός. Indeed, this is why they are designated as indirect evidence. Even so, the examples attest the appropriateness of the symbol's isopsephic interpretation.

The symbol χμγ, it would seem, had its origin before the issuance of the Edict of Milan (AD 313) and thus at a time of possible persecution. However, once it is conceded that the symbol χμγ is more likely to be an isopsephism, it becomes more difficult to hold that the symbol necessarily originated at a time of persecution when the church sought to conceal its confessional allegiance. Another context offers perhaps a better explanation for the use, namely the socio-linguistic context of numerological/cosmological speculation. Such speculation had gained wide currency in antiquity and was variously practised in Pythagorean, Gnostic, Talmudic and Christian circles.[33] It is also apparent in the use of isopsephism (gematria) made by the writer of Revelation. For example, 666 (Rev. 13.18) represented the name of the beast, i.e. the sum of the letters in the name Νέρων Καῖσαρ as well as the sum of the letters in the word θηρίον (beast) when both are transliterated into Hebrew letters. Also the number had the intriguing mathematical property of being doubly triangular. Again, the measure of the wall of the new Jerusalem was 144 cubits 'by human measurement, which is the measurement of an angel' (μέτρον ἀνθρώπου, ὅ ἐστιν ἀγγέλου, Rev. 21.17). Interestingly, the sum of letters in the word ἄγγελος when transliterated into Hebrew is 144.[34] The number, moreover, as the square of 12 was invested with religious significance. Even if Revelation was written at a time of objective persecution (an assumption which is not

---

[31] On the formula κ̄(ύρι)ε βοήθ(ει) see J.M. Diethart, 'Κύριε βοήθει in byzantinischen Notarsunterschriften', *ZPE* 49 (1982) 79-82.

[32] Dölger, 'Eine christliche Grabinschrift ...' 302-3, and L. Robert, *Hellenica* 11-12 (1960) 311 n.1. Other associations could be considered as well, e.g. the symbol χμγ with the quotation of Rom. 8.31, e.g. *IGLSyria* IV 1442 and 1448.

[33] On the phenomenon and its history see Dornseiff, *Das Alphabet in Mystik und Magie* 91-118. H. Leclercq, *DACL* VII (Paris 1927) s.v. 'Isopséphie' 1603, notes that the early Christians 'touchaient de trop près aux Grecs et aux Juifs, participaient trop étroitement à leur état d'esprit et à leurs goûts intellectuels, pour ne pas s'exercer à ces subtilités de la mystique des nombres qui a séduit même des Pères de l'Église'. Eusebius's *De laudibus Const.* 6.5-6 and 10-17 might be cited as a relevant example in which number theory is depicted as underpinning the division of formless matter in the divinely created order.

[34] On the use of gematria (isopsephisms) in Revelation see R. Bauckham, *The Climax of Prophecy. Studies on the Book of Revelation* (Edinburgh 1993) 384-452.

unquestioned[35]), this context by itself fails adequately to explain such examples of isopsephism. Numerological/cosmological speculation appears to offer a better context. As already observed, words of the same numerical value were associated and the persons, constructs or things to which they pointed were thus revealed to possess a hidden connection or relationship, e.g. Nero Caesar = beast. Indeed, the polyvalent nature of the isopsephism formed part of its speculative value. As possible solutions to χμγ the following suggestions have also been offered: 643 = ἄγειος ὁ θεός = νέος Ἥλιος = ἡ ἁγία τριὰς θ(εός).[36] Other words and expressions of equivalent numerical value found in the Greek Bible include, for example, ἄνδρες εἰρηνικοί; εἰς τὰ ἴδια ἦλθεν; ἐκκλησία Ἰσραηλ; ἐποίησέν μοι μεγαλεῖα; ἰδοὺ ἀνήρ; πᾶσα σάρξ; σημεῖον διαθήκης; and τὸ μνημεῖον.[37]

We have already noted above the use of χμγ in association with what may well be a magical amulet (*SB* 12658). In *SB* XIV 12184 (see *New Docs* 8 [1997] §2) this symbol together with the christogram begins what appears to be a curse. In view of these associations we should not overlook the related consideration of the importance of symbols and of their supernatural potency for Constantine and his age.[38] For example, one can cite here the use of the christogram and the sign of the cross. Lactantius narrates that Constantine was ordered in a dream to place the christogram on the shields of his soldiers before the battle against Maxentius in AD 312.[39] No doubt, the symbol had an apotropaic or protective significance.[40] Eusebius,

---

[35] A.Y. Collins, *Crisis and Catharsis. The Power of the Apocalypse* (Philadelphia 1984) 69-73, 84, 98 and 104-7.

[36] See Dornseiff, *Das Alphabet in Mystik und Magie* 111, and Tjäder, *Eranos* 68 (1970) 155-6.

[37] The text of the Greek Bible was scanned for possible solutions. There were 376 possible combinations of words the sum of whose letters was 643. Most were incomplete expressions or otherwise irrelevant. None appeared to offer a particularly suitable solution for the isopsephism. Perhaps in time the practice of reducing a word to the numerical sum of its letters became valid in its own right. In other words, the number took on a significance by itself without being used as a bridge between two words. The practice of writing ϟθ (99) for ἀμήν is a relevant example. Words or expressions in the Greek Bible whose letters have the same numerical sum (e.g. ἀγαθὰ ἡ γῆ ἦν, ἀκοή, Βηθλεεμ, δίκαια καὶ ἀγαθή, ἐμὴ δίκαια, κλῆμα, μεῖγμα, πηγή) do not seem to offer an appropriate complement to our target word. This leads one to doubt whether the writing of ϟθ for amen concealed any other verbal association.

[38] A. Alföldi, *The Conversion of Constantine and Pagan Rome* (Oxford repr. 1969) 21-4. The increase in superstition can also be observed in such areas as the belief that the bodies of saints and martyrs, as well as other holy relics, possessed magical powers. And as A.H.M. Jones, *The Later Roman Empire 284-602*, vol. 2 (Oxford 1964) 958-964, has noted, this belief was not confined to the lower classes but embraced the greatest intellectual figures of the church also.

[39] Lactantius, *De mortibus persecutorum* 44. Two forms of the symbol come into contention:

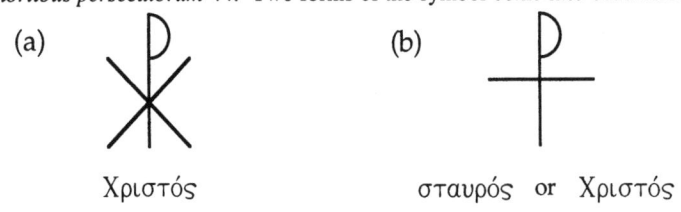

(a) Χριστός   (b) σταυρός or Χριστός

The shape of the symbol is disputed. See H. Leclercq, *DACL* III (Paris 1948) s.v. 'Chrisme' 1481-1534. Both forms of the christogram have pre-Constantinian origins, but the symbol was increasingly used with the official recognition of Christianity. Importantly, Leclercq, *DACL* III 1491 and 1500, argues that it is from the time of the peace of the Church (AD 312) that the christogram lost its value as an abbreviation to become a symbol indicating the religious allegiance of its user. Largely on the evidence of 𝔓66 K. Aland, *NTS* 10 (1964) 75-9, argues that the staurogram (b) was perhaps the original form of the symbol and that it soon evolved into the christogram (a). M. Black, 'The Chi-Rho Sign — Christogram and/or Staurogram?', in W. Ward Gasque and R.P. Martin (edd.), *Apostolic History and the Gospel. Biblical and Historical Essays presented to F.F. Bruce on*

who writes later but credits his report to the emperor himself, offers a different account.[41] The emperor and his army saw a vision of the cross in the heavens bearing the inscription τούτῳ νίκα — 'conquer by this'. The vision was confirmed by a dream in which Constantine was ordered to make a likeness of the heavenly sign. The result was the construction of the *labarum*, the Constantinian standard, which replaced the tradition image of a god, an eagle or some other animal with the christogram (chi-rho) enclosed in a circular wreath.[42] The standard with its christological symbol was to safeguard the emperor and his army against all enemies. The protective significance of the symbol is again evident. Also relevant is the discussion by Dölger[43] of the significance of the cross (both + and x) in ancient cultures. In relation to Christianity he notes that the making of the sign of the cross on the forehead functioned in three principal ways: (i) to consecrate the new believer; (ii) as a confession of belief; and (iii) as a *munimen* or φυλακτήριον. In terms of consecration the making of the sign was associated with prayer and the creed. It was also a sign of admission into Christianity being made by the priest on the forehead of the catechumen at his baptism, e.g. Augustine, *Catech. rud.* 26.50. Cf. also Tertullian, *Carn. res.* 8. But the making of the sign of the cross on one's forehead was also a practice associated with everyday actions, e.g. Tertullian, *De cor.* 3.4. As such it was perceived to protect the individual who made it. The sign was thought to have a protective power and in the case of Hippolytus's *Apostolic Tradition* 42 is described as a breastplate (*lorica*) which protected the believer against temptation and the devil.[44]

---

his 60th Birthday (London 1970) 319-327, disagrees and thinks the contraction in σταυρός to be artificial and secondary (p.327). For him neither form of the symbol is necessarily earlier in Christian practice. Black argues that as the use of the cross (written either as + or x) as a protective sign or talisman is found in ancient Judaism (cf. Ezek. 9.4, Taw - ת meaning both 'sign' and the letter ת which in the ancient script was written as either + or x), the Christian sign may have been influenced by this earlier usage. Originally the sign, either chi or tau, symbolised the Cross with the loop or rho added to mark it as a distinctly Christian talisman, i.e. as the contraction for the name Χριστός. See also F.J. Dölger, 'Beiträge zur Geschichte des Kreuzzeichens III', *JbAC* 3 (1960) 8, who argues that (b) was understood as both the Cross and the monogram of Christ. E. Dinkler, 'Zur Geschichte des Kreuzsymbols', *Zeitscrift für Theologie und Kirche* 48 (1951) 157-162 and 171-2, discusses the use of + or x (Taw) in Jewish circles both in the pre- and post-exilic periods, but he does not believe there to be a direct continuity between this and the use of the sign in Christianity. Rather the relationship is indirect with the Christian symbol representing a new approach.

[40] See J.-R. Palanque, G. Bardy and P. de Labriolle in *Histoire de l'Église depuis les origines jusqu'à nos jours*, edd. A. Fliche and V. Martin, vol. 3 (1950) 31.

[41] Eusebius, *Vita Const.* 1.28-31.

[42] For a pictured reconstruction of the *labarum* see H. Leclercq, *DACL* VIII (Paris 1928) s.v. 'Labarum' 953. Leclercq (940-954) dates the making of the *labarum* before the battle of the Milvian bridge (October AD 312) either earlier in the same year or the previous year. He attempts to reconcile the accounts of Lactantius and Eusebius by making them refer to different events belonging to different times. Later Leclercq, *DACL* III (1948) s.v. 'Chrisme' 1497-98, appears to change his view preferring to date the *labarum* from AD 317.

[43] F.J. Dölger, 'Beiträge zur Geschichte des Kreuzzeichens I - IV', *JbAC* 1 (1958) 5-19, *JbAC* 2 (1959) 15-29, *JbAC* 3 (1960) 5-16, and *JbAC* 40 (1961) 5-17. Dinkler, *Zeitschrift für Theologie und Kirche* 48 (1951) 148-172, also discusses the use of the cross (Taw written as + or x) as a symbol by certain Jewish circles. In his analysis the symbol had both an indicative (marking the person as the property of God and thus subject to the deity and his laws) and an apotropaic (protecting the individual who carried the mark) function. The symbol was originally placed on the person's forehead or hand; however, in the post-exilic period the use of the symbol in eschatological contexts facilitated its transfer to ossuaries, protecting the deceased on the day of resurrection and judgement. The apotropaic function of the symbol is thought by Dinkler (pp.169 and 171) to be magical.

[44] Supernatural power naturally was perceived to extent to the sacraments themselves. Hippolytus, *Apostolic Tradition* 36, states that the believer who partakes of the eucharist is protected against poisoning. On the use of *loricae*, i.e. Latin prayers for protection against harm induced in part by *defixiones* (curse tablets), see

To conclude, the usage of the symbol χμγ, as one would expect, increased with the announcement of official toleration and subsequent embracing of the Christian religion by the state. The interpretation of the symbol as an isopsephism provides a good explanation for this increase. According to the evidence provided by Eusebius in his *Life of Constantine*, it was during the reign of this emperor that the expression θεὸς βοηθός found wider usage.

S.R.L.

J.G. Gager, *Curse Tablets and Binding Spells from the Ancient World* (Oxford 1992) 27-28. On the use of symbols in ancient spells see ibid., 6-11. Such symbols were thought to embody great power.

§15 Christian Letters of Recommendation

Panopolis?   10.5 x 8 cm   Late third or early fourth century

Ed. pr. — K. Treu, 'P. Berol. 8508: Christliches Empfehlungsschreiben aus dem Einband des koptisch-gnostischen Kodex P. 8502', *APF* 28 (1982) 53-54 (= *SB* XVI 12304).

The letter is from the cover of the gnostic Codex P. 8502 (in Coptic). In the cover two sheets of papyrus were glued together. The binding was originally destined for a larger codex but was reformatted for the smaller dimensions of P. 8502. Two to three letters are lost from the right hand side of the papyrus. Writing is across the fibres. The text of the prescript is repeated on the side along the fibres, apparently a first attempt which was abandoned. The *nomen sacrum* is contracted ($\overline{κω}$) and an isospephism (α + μ + η + ν = 1 + 40 + 50 + 8 = 99 = ϙθ) is used for ἀμήν.

Ἡρακλίτης π(α)π(ᾶς) το[ῖς κα-]	Father Heraklites to my
τὰ τόπον συνλιτουργ[οῖς]	local fellow-ministers,
ἀγα‹πη›τοῖς ἀδελφοῖς ἐν [κ(υρί)ῳ]	beloved brothers in the [Lord],
χαίρειν.	greeting.
5 τὸν ἀδελφὸν ἡμῶν Π.[...]	Our brother, (name),
πε παραγινόμενον π[ρὸς]	who is coming [to]
ὑμᾶς προσ‹δέ›ξασθαι ἐν [εἰρή-]	you, receive in peace,
νῃ `δι´´ οὗ ὑμᾶς καὶ τοὺς σὺ[ν ὑ-]	through whom
μῖν ἐγὼ δὲ καὶ οἱ {σ}σὺν [ἐμοὶ]	I and those with [me]
10 ὑμᾶς ἡδέως προσαγ[ορεύ-]	kindly greet you and those with you.
ω. ἐρρῶσθαι ὑμᾶς	I pray you farewell
εὔχομαι ‹ἐν› κ(υρί)ῳ	in the Lord.
$\overline{μνηα}$ ϙθ	99 99
Along the side of the papyrus	
[........]ς π(α)π(ᾶς) τοῖς κατὰ	Father [Heraklites] to my
15 τόπον συνλιτουργοῖς	local fellow-ministers,
ἀγ‹απ›ητοῖς ἀδελφοῖς	beloved brothers
ἐν κ(υρί)ῳ χαίρειν.	in the [Lord], greeting.

Oxyrhynchus   7.5 x 14.5 cm   Fourth century

Ed. pr. — M.G. Sirivianou, *P. Oxy.* LVI 3857 (London 1989) 111-116.

The text is described as 'hastily written, along the fibres, by a practised hand'. Like similar letters of recommendation the back is blank. The letter was apparently folded horizontally six times from the bottom. The papyrus has broken off along the sixth fold resulting in the loss of the name of the writer. *Nomina sacra* are contracted ($\overline{εμλ}$ and $\overline{κω}$) and an isospephism (ϙθ) is used for ἀμήν.

..[.].[	[...]
(vac.)	
τοῖς κατὰ τόπον ἀγαπητοῖς	to the beloved
ἀδελφοῖς καὶ συνλειτουργοῖς.	brothers and local fellow-ministers.
τὴν θυγατέρα ἡμῶν Γερ-	Our daughter,
5 μανίαν, ἐπικουρίας	Germania, who is in need of

	δεομένην, π[αραγι-]	aid, (and) who is
	νομένην πρὸς	coming to
	ὑμᾶς προσδέξασθε	you, receive
	ἐν εἰρήνῃ, δι' ἧς	in peace, through whom
10	ὑμᾶς καὶ τοὺς σὺν	I and those with
	ὑμῖν ἐγώ τε καὶ οἱ σὺν	me greet
	ἐμοὶ προσαγορεύ-	you and those with you.
	ομεν. Ἐμ(μανουή)λ. ϙθ.	Emmanuel. 99.
	ἐρρῶσθαι ὑμᾶς	I pray you farewell
15	ἐν κ(υρί)ῳ εὔχομαι,	in the Lord,
	ἀγαπητοὶ ἀδελφοί.	beloved brothers.

The texts of both papyri are letters of recommendation (introduction) written according to an established formula. In all, the form of the letters is attested by nine papyri (*PSI* III 208, *PSI* IX 1041, *P. Alex.* 29, *P. Oxy.* XXXVI 2785, *SB* X 10255, *SB* III 7269, *P. Oxy.* VIII 1162, *SB* XVI 12304 and *P. Oxy.* LVI 3857). For a list and synopsis of the form of these letters of recommendation see K. Treu, 'Christliche Empfehlungs-Schemabriefe auf Papyrus', in *Zetesis. Album amicorum ... E. de Strijcker* (Antwerp/Utrecht, 1973) 629-36, and Sirivianou, *P. Oxy.* LVI pp.112-4. In his more general discussion of letters of recommendation (introduction) Keyes[1] notes:

> We may conclude that, while the letters of introduction do not slavishly adhere to any single formula, there is abundant evidence that traditional formulae, different from those found in the Τύποι, did exist, and were generally used. As might be expected, a closer adherence to conventional modes of expression is found in the letters of ordinary life than in those attributed to famous men. These formulae were probably contained in handbooks of letter writing which are now lost.

In the nine letters of recommendation cited by Sirivianou one is struck by the degree of formulaic similarity. Although their form is not attested in the handbooks, it is evident that the writers have followed an *exemplum*.

Both of the above letters are written to unnamed clergy who are described as οἱ κατὰ τόπον, i.e. local clergy. Four of the nine letters contain a similar addressee in the prescript. (To the two examples cited above add *SB* III 7269 and *P. Oxy.* VIII 1162.) It would appear that the individuals who are recommended carried the letters with them on their journeys[2] and presented them to the local churches as need demanded, e.g. food and accommodation each night. The purpose of the journeys is not stated.

Four of the letters of recommendation use the imperative χαῖρε in their prescripts (*PSI* III 208, *PSI* IX 1041, *P. Alex.* 29, *P. Oxy.* XXXVI 2785). Four employ the usual infinitive construction (*SB* X 10255, *SB* III 7269, *P. Oxy.* VIII 1162, *SB* XVI 12304). Of interest is the absence of χαίρειν in the prescript of *P. Oxy.* LVI 3857. As already noted in a previous entry, Koskenniemi[3] has observed the overlap of function between the prescript and address of letters, for both gave the particulars of the sender and addressee. He argues that their difference resided in the prescript's use of χαίρειν and that it was only after the prescript ceased to function as a greeting and χαίρειν was dropped that it also began to disappear from

---

[1] C.W. Keyes, *AJP* 56 (1935) 42.
[2] Treu, 'Christliche Empfehlungs-Schemabriefe auf Papyrus' 635, and Sirivianou, *P. Oxy.* LVI p.115.
[3] H. Koskenniemi, *Studien zur Idee und Phraseologie des griechischen Briefes bis 400 n. Chr.* (Helsinki 1956) 155-8.

letters (approximately IV AD). *P. Oxy.* LVI 3857 is an interesting example. The greeting was dropped from the prescript though the the prescript itself was still retained. This may not, however, be a matter of mere chance, for like the other eight letters of recommendation the back of *P. Oxy.* LVI 3857 is blank; the letter does not appear to have had an address. In the case of letters addressed τοῖς κατὰ τόπον κτλ. the absence of an address is not surprising, for such letters had no particular addressee in mind. In the case of letters addressed to particular persons one must assume that the bearer either was given directions by word of mouth or otherwise knew how to find the addressee(s). In either case one must assume that the letters were carried by the persons whom they recommended or introduced.[4]

P. Oxy. LVI 3857 differs from the other letters by designating the recommended traveller as 'our daughter'. Other similar letters of recommendation (introduction) use the terms 'brother', 'sister' or 'catechumen'. Treu understands 'brother'/'sister' to denote a full (i.e. baptised) church-member as distinct from a catechumen. Indeed, the Christian context of the letters themselves, it might be argued, implies an ecclesiastical connotation for the use of such familial titles. Sirivianou takes a somewhat different view. In the case of *P. Oxy.* 3857, Germania is not termed 'sister' but 'daughter'. Considering the use of familial titles to designate various types of non-familial relationship[5] he argues against a Christian connotation here, preferring to see in its use an indication that 'Germania was a person whom most people would describe as young, or at least younger than the sender and the likely recipients'.

In five of the nine formally similar letters of recommendation the addressees are asked to receive their visitors ἐν εἰρήνῃ (to our two texts add *P. Alex.* 29, *P. Oxy.* XXXVI 2785 and *P. Oxy.* VIII 1162). In Sirivianou's view (*P. Oxy.* LVI 3857, p.116), the prepositional phrase serves 'to remind the recipients that it is their duty to give proper hospitality to the recommended person'. On the use of προσδέχομαι in the NT see:

(a) Rom. 16.1-2: Paul recommends Phoebe to the recipients of the letter (αὐτὴν προσδέξησθε ἐν κυρίῳ ἀξίως τῶν ἁγίων). It is of relevance to note that chapter 16 was perhaps originally an independent letter of recommendation to the church at Ephesus which has been joined in error to the end of Paul's letter to the Romans.
(b) Phil. 2.29: On sending Epaphroditus back to Philippi Paul recommends him to the church there (προσδέχεσθε οὖν αὐτὸν ἐν κυρίῳ μετὰ πάσης χαρᾶς).
(c) Luke 15.2: The Pharisees and scribes take exception to Jesus's receiving and eating with tax-collectors and sinners. The use is unusual as one must suppose that it was actually the tax-collectors and sinners who entertained Jesus and not vice versa. Cf. Luke 19.1-10.

Of relevance also is 2 Cor. 3.1-4. In this passage Paul and his co-author, Timothy, describe the church in Corinth as their letter of recommendation known and read by all people. For this reason they do not need to recommend themselves.

Treu discusses the effect which external circumstances had on letters of recommendation. In a time of persecution it was important to prove that the traveller was a *bona fide* Christian. Later when schism arose, it was understandable that a church may not have wished to give assistance to a member of an opposing view. Later still when the number of adherents to Christianity increased a church naturally wished to protect itself against an exploitation of hospitality. Esoteric legitimisation is apparent in a number of features in the letters. Besides the use of *nomina sacra* both letters cited above use an isopsephism, i.e. instead of writing a word or expression the value of its letters are summed and the number written instead

---

[4] See Keyes, *AJP* 56 (1935) 32 and 39-40.
[5] See *New Docs* 6 (1992) 158 n.178.

($\alpha + \mu + \eta + \nu = 1+40+50+8 = 99 = \varqoppa\theta$). We have already discussed isopsephisms with regard to the Christian symbol χμγ (643).[6] Our two letters share the use of ϙθ with one other of the formally parallel letters of recommendation (*P. Oxy.* VIII 1162). Treu (p.634) holds that the numbers were a form of esoteric legitimisation not understood by outsiders. In particular, an association between the use of isopsephisms and letters addressed to unnamed recipients is noted. The number presumably functioned as a guarantee of the *bona fides* of the letter in cases where writers and recipients were unknown to each other. Three of the four letters to unnamed recipients contain the number 99 (*P. Oxy.* VIII 1162, *SB* XVI 12304 and *P. Oxy.* LVI 3857). The one exception is *SB* III 7269.

A fourth letter (*P. Oxy.* XXXVI 2785) uses what appears to be an isopsephism though the recipient is expressly named. Also, the number here (σδ = 204), if read correctly, is unique. In a recent article (*ZPE* 109 [1995] 125-7) I have considered all possible solutions consisting of strings of up to five words generated from a computer reading of the Greek Bible. The most feasible solution was εἰρηνικά (5+10+100+8+50+10+20+1 = 204), a word translating שלום, the usual Hebrew salutation. Cf. the Masoretic text of Deut. 20.11, 23.6, Psalm 34.20 and Jer. 9.7. But the solution was initially rejected as: (a) in none of the passages does εἰρηνικά actually function as a salutation; and (b) the salutation was rendered in the LXX by εἰρήνη σοι, εἰρήνη σοι πληθυνθείη or just simply εἰρήνη.[7] Concurrently with the publication of my article Timothy M. Teeter presented a paper at the 21st International Congress of Papyrology which argues that there were two distinct classes of letter for church travellers of the fourth and fifth centuries. The first was the ἐπιστολὴ συστατική which was issued with episcopal approval to the clergy and to laity of distinction and which concerned admission to communion as well as the provision of material support. The second was the ἐπιστολὴ εἰρηνική. This class of letter was issued to the laity; it did not require episcopal approval and concerned only the provision of material support. Teeter assigns the above nine papyrological letters to this second class. If the identification is correct, then εἰρηνικά may be restored as the solution to the symbol σδ. In this case the number represents not an encoded salutation but an esoteric legitimisation characterizing the class of letter.

S.R.L.

---

[6] *New Docs* 8 (1997) §14.

[7] See Judges 6.23, 19.20, 1 Chron. 12.18, 2 Esdras 4.17, 5.7, Psalms 121.8, 124.5, 127.6, Dan. 3.31 and 4.34. For the use of εἰρήνη in the closing salutation of a letter see 1 Pet. 5.14 and 3 John 15. In *P. Heid.* IV 333 *l*.31 (V AD) εἰρήνη is used in the letter's address.

§16 A Confessional Inscription

Ed. — P. Herrmann, *TAM* V 1, 238 (Vienna 1981) 82.

Sloped stele of white marble ornamented in bas-relief (a horseman supporting a battle-axe on his shoulder). The stone is partly mutilated above and below right. It originated from the village of Kula in Lydia. Dimensions: height = 71 cm; width = 39 cm; thickness = 4 cm. Lettering 16-21 mm.

Ἀντωνία Ἀντωνίου Ἀπόλ- λωνι θεῷ βοζηνῷ διὰ τὸ ἀ- ναβεβηκένε με ἐπὶ τὸν χο- ρὸν ἐν ῥυπαρῷ ἐπενδύτῃ, 5 κολασθῖσα δὲ ἐξωμολο- γησάμην κὲ ἀνέθηκα εὐλο- γίαν, ὅτι ἐγενόμην ὁλόκ[λ-] ηρος.	Antonia, daughter of Antonius, to Apollo, god Bozenos, because I entered the (Temple) area in a dirty garment, being punished I confessed and dedicated (this) eulogy because I became whole.

2-3. ἀναβεβηκέναι   3-4. χωρίον   5. κολασθεῖσα   6. καί

Frisch[1] offers this previously published text as an example of a confessional inscription. In such dedications authors recount how they had offended the god, how as a result they had been punished (e.g. by sickness) and how on confessing the offence they were restored. The dedications were set up as a warning to others to be on guard against the deity's power. Robert[2] observes concerning dedications which were set up after two culprits had been punished, one for having purchased wood grown in a sanctuary and the other for having cut down in ignorance an oak sacred to Zeus Didymeites: 'The recall of these punishments and of the culprit's repentance will be an efficacious protection of the sacred forest'.

Of interest in these dedications is the element of confession (ἐξομολογεῖσθαι), a feature which, Frisch considers, was foreign to the Graeco-Roman world but which was introduced into that world with the coming of Eastern religions. Furthermore, Frisch argues that the practice shows a number of points of contact with Augustine's Confessions:

— the understanding of conversion as a miraculous healing;
— an emphasis on sexual/purity offences;
— the term στηλογραφεῖν/στηλογραφία which not only referred to the composition of a confessional inscription but which was also used as a heading to six psalms (Psalms 15, 55-59), a usage which Augustine repeatedly struggled to explain.

Frisch concludes that it was Augustine who allowed such religious practices of confession to enter into the realm of Christian literature.

The function of confessional inscriptions was to offer direct witness to the powers of the deity. In an article published in 1985 Ameling[3] deals with the function of witnessing in

---

[1] P. Frisch, 'Über die lydisch-phrygischen Sühneinschriften und die "Confessiones" des Augustinus', *EA* 2 (1983) 41-45.
[2] L. Robert, *BCH* 107 (1983) 516. See ibid., 518-523, for the motif of the sceptre placed on the suspected culprit.
[3] W. Ameling, 'Evangelium Johannis 19,35: ein aretalogisches Motiv', *ZPE* 60 (1985) 25-34. See also R. MacMullen, *Enemies of the Roman Order. Treason, Unrest, and Alienation in the Empire* (Cambridge Mass., 1966) 111-3.

aretalogies. Mostly the witness is to some miraculous event and serves to create or increase belief in the deity (ἵνα καὶ ὑμεῖς πιστεύητε). Such testimony guarded each event against being labelled a fraud by unbelievers. As examples of the function of witness in confessional inscriptions Ameling[4] cites a number of examples from Lydia (*TAM* V 1):

No. 317 AD 114/5	ἡ θεὸς οὖν ἔδειξεν τὰς ἰδίας δυνάμις... καὶ νῦν αὐτῇ μαρτυροῦμεν καὶ εὐλογοῦμεν ... *The goddess therefore showed her powers ... and now we witness to her and offer praise ...*
No. 318 AD 156/7	καὶ ἀπὸ νοῖν εὐλογοῦμεν στηλλογραφήσαντες τὰς δυνάμις τοῦ θεοῦ. *And henceforth we offer praise recording on a stele the powers of the god.*
No. 319 AD 196/7	μαρτυροῦντες τὰς δυνάμις τῶν θεῶν ἀπέδωκαν τὴν εὐχήν. *attesting the powers of the gods they discharged their vow.*
No. 464 undated	ὁ θεὸς ἀνέδιξεν τὰς εἰδίας δυνάμις ... ἐστήσαμεν τὴν στήλην καὶ ἐνεγράψομεν τὰς δυνάμις τοῦ θεοῦ καὶ ἀπὸ νῦν εὐλογοῦμεν. *The god showed his powers ... and we erected this stele and recorded the powers of the god and henceforth we offer praise.*

But the motif was very extensive, being found also in other accounts of miracles and healings, as well as in Horace (*Carmen* 2.19), Lucian (*Vera hist.* 1.4) and the Mani-Codex. Furthermore, Ameling notes that the aretalogical function is evident in the Johannine insertion, John 19.34b-35. These verses, which are inserted into the passion narrative, witness to the blood and water which flowed from the side of the crucified Jesus. The witness is given that the hearers might believe (ἵνα καὶ ὑμεῖς πιστεύητε). It is argued that together with other elements in the gospels they share the same aretalogical motif. The following characteristics of the motif are noted:

— The event is termed a δύναμις, e.g Matt. 11.21 and 23; 13.58; 14.2; Mark 6.2, 5 and 14; and Luke 8.46.
— The response of the witness is wonder or fear, e.g. Matt. 9.33; 15.31; Mark 1.27; and Luke 4.36; 5.26.
— Cosmic events (e.g. earthquake or eclipse) are often associated with the event, e.g. Mark 15.33 and 38 with parallels; and Matt. 27.51-53.
— The expression 'I am' is used in the self-revelation of the deity; cf. John 18.6.

The existence of confessional inscriptions and their possible influence on Augustine also raises the interesting question of introspection and the writer's sense of guilt. In an important essay Stendahl[5] has argued that introspection was an essentially Western phenomenon which had its origins in Augustine's Confessions and which led through mediaeval monasticism to Luther's formulation of the doctrine of 'justification by faith'. As such it has influenced the course of Western consciousness and the interpretation of Scripture. Stendahl counters, however, that the interpretation has been imposed on Paul's letters. Paul was not overcome by a sense of guilt and moral depravity before God but rather showed a 'robust conscience'. Passages used to argue for his introspective conscience (e.g. the impossibility of keeping the Law, Rom. 2.17-3.20, Gal. 3.10-12; the struggle with sin, Rom. 7.13-25) really miss the point which Paul was making. The place of the Law and the Jewish/Gentile question, Stendahl

---

[4] Ameling, *ZPE* 60 (1985) 31 n.38.
[5] K. Stendahl, 'The Apostle Paul and the Introspective Conscience of the West', *HTR* 56 (1963) 199-215; reprinted in Stendahl's *Paul among Jews and Gentiles* (Philadelphia 1976) 78-96.

argues, were the issues Paul was addressing. He was not concerned with 'the quest for assurance about man's salvation out of a common predicament'.[6]

In convergence with Stendahl's thesis it is of interest to note that the 'sin' acknowledged in the confessional inscriptions does not imply an introspective conscience. Many 'sins' are committed in ignorance, e.g. the taking of wood from a sacred grove.[7] As in the example cited above, other 'sins' involve the infringement of a purity requirement. Such 'sins' do not imply a stricken conscience. Nor indeed does the fact that the confession is made subsequent to the divine punishment. In other words, it is not events in the inner world of the conscience which prompt the confession, but an external misfortune or illness. It would follow then that if Augustine was influenced by confessional inscriptions, he also transformed their significance.

S.R.L.

---

[6] Stendahl, *Paul among Jews and Gentiles* 86.
[7] Robert, *BCH* 107 (1983) 518.

§17 Baptism and Salvation

Edessa Third century AD

Ed. — D. Feissel, *Recueil des inscriptions chrétiennes de Macédoine* §5 (Paris 1983) 25-27.

The epigram is written in verse, composed of six hexameters over two lines.

ΝΕ ⟨⟩ΦΡΩΨΕΙ[- - - - - - - -]	[...]
δάμαρ τε (vac.)	and (his) wife,
Ἀντιγόνη, Νείκ(α)νδρος ἐπὶ	Antigone, for Nikandros
βιότοιο τελευ[τὴν]	has accepted the end of life,
5 δέξατο, (ἐ)ν νο(ύ)σοις ⏑⏑— (στ)υ-	by wretched (?) illness [...]
γερα(ῖσι ?) δα(μ)ασθε(ί)ς,	subdued,
ψυχὴ(ν) αἰθερείαις α(ἰ)ῶσι(?)	his soul to the ethereal aeons (?)
θέτο, σῶμα δὲ γα(ί)ῃ,	he set and his body to the earth,
εἰσόκαι ἀναστάσεω(ς) εὐ(ά)-	until the glad day
10 γγε(λ)ον ἦμα(ρ) εἴκητε,	of resurrection comes,
ἁγνός, ἐπὶ καὶ (θ)είου ποθῶν	pure since desirously
ἐπετεύξατο λουτροῦ.	he has attained divine washing.

1. [τῷ] νεοφ⟨ρ⟩ω(τ)εί[στῳ]   3. ἐπεί   9. εἰσόκε   10. ἴκηται   11. ἐπεί

The editor notes the early date of the funerary inscription (pre-Constantine) and its dogmatic formulations as points of interest in the text. The mention of resurrection (*l*.9) and baptism (*ll*.11-12) mark it as Christian. The text is composed in verse. Few Christian metrical inscriptions moreover are found before Constantine and, as Pfohl notes, they are much less precise and fine than their pagan counterparts.[1]

The text contains a number of *topoi* which can be paralleled in other Christian inscriptions. These are: (a) the notion that the deceased was subdued by wretched illness (*ll*.5-6); (b) the antithesis of the soul going to heaven and the body to the earth (*ll*.7-8); and (c) the notion of death as sleep[2] until the day of resurrection (*ll*.9-10). The editor considers the mention of aeons (*l*.7) in the context of the second *topos* to be unparalleled, though not surprising. In his assessment it does not imply a heretical angelology, 'since the liturgy cites the aeons among the other categories of the heavenly court'.[3]

The person designated as a 'neophyte' (conjectural reading *l*.1) is probably the deceased. If so, the editor presumes that he had been baptised on his death-bed. A number of examples of epitaphs of adults who had received late baptism are cited.[4] Besides the present example see *ICUR* VII 19820 (Rome), *ILS* 9481 (Salone) and no. 123 in the above edition of Christian inscriptions from Macedonia. Williams[5] notes that 'baptism was often postponed in fully

---

[1] G. Pfohl, 'Grabinschrift I (griechisch)', *Reallexikon für Antike und Christentum* XII (Stuttgart 1983) 504.

[2] On κοιμητήριον in Christian funerary inscriptions see also G. Pfohl, 'Grabinschrift I' 496 and 508.

[3] Feissel, *Recueil des inscriptions chrétiennes de Macédoine* 27. On the use of pagan motifs and their significance in Christian funerary inscriptions see G. Pfohl, 'Grabinschrift I' 495-510 (passim).

[4] Feissel, *Recueil des inscriptions chrétiennes de Macédoine* 120.

[5] H. Williams, 'The sacramental presuppositions of Anselm's *Cur Deus Homo*', *Church History* 26 (1957) 247.

§17 Baptism and Salvation

Christian households until the years of discretion in order to keep its healing and vivifying waters for the cleansing of the fully exfoliated sinfulness of maturity'. Constantine was baptised shortly before his death. As Alföldi[6] notes:

> There (i.e. in Constantinople), as founder of the new Christian Rome, he arranged that he shall be buried, after he had, a short time before his death, been admitted to the Church as a simple believer, and, when death drew nigh, received baptism, following the custom of the age, in order to be freed from his sins by the ceremony of baptism and so enter Paradise.

Baptism was preeminently the rite which absolved the individual from his sins.

Of further interest is the nexus shown in the inscription between baptism and salvation. It must be remembered that the theology of the ancient (i.e. pre-medieval) Church emphasised baptism (not the eucharist) as the sacrament which not only symbolised salvation but was also the means by which one appropriated Christ's redemptive work. Baptism was a once-for-all sacrament[7] of universal significance whereby the catechumen was freed from death and demonic power through the redemptive act of Christ. The theology stressed the significance of the incarnation, for by it the Word became flesh and suffered death. By baptism the catechumen was incorporated into the body of Christ thereby sacramentally participating in his death and thus being freed from liability to it and the power of Satan.[8] In this regard one might compare Feissel, *Recueil des inscriptions chrétiennes de Macédoine* §265, the epitaph of a three-year-old girl. The parents' grief is consoled through Christ who gave her from an eternal font (i.e. baptism) the life of the heavenly beings (ὅς πόρεν ἀφθάρτοιο πηγῆς βίον οὐρανιώνων, *ll*.17-19).[9] Salvation is again tied to the rite of baptism as symbolized by the metaphor of the font.

The development of the rite of baptism can be traced in the literature of the early churches. If one takes the account of Acts 8.37-39 as a starting point, the rite appears quite simple. It follows immediately upon the teaching of Philip and the Ethiopian eunuch's acceptance of his explanation of Scripture. However, by the time of *Didache* 7 it is apparent that a period of preparation preceded baptism. Not only must the catechumens fast one or two days before receiving the sacrament (7.4) but they are also instructed in the teaching of the church.[10]

---

[6] A. Alföldi, *The Conversion of Constantine and Pagan Rome* (Oxford 1948, repr. 1969) 115. The motives of Constantine in delaying baptism are, of course, not transparent and therefore are understood differently depending on the viewpoint of the historian. For example, J.-R. Palanque, G. Bardy and P. de Labriolle in *Histoire de l'Église depuis les origines jusqu'à nos jours*, edd. A. Fliche and V. Martin, vol. 3 (1950) 32, understand the emperor to be motivated by a desire to have a foot in both camps (i.e. Christianity and paganism) thereby safeguarding the independence of the state and his own sovereignty in what was largely a pagan realm.

[7] The understanding of the sacrament of baptism as once-for-all led to the interesting dispute as to whether persons who had been baptised by a schismatic group should be baptised again on admission to the church. See, for example, Tertullian, *De bapt.* 15, Cyprian, *Epist.* 70, and the short description by R.J. De Simone, *Encyclopaedia of the Early Church* vol. 1 (New York 1992) s.v. 'Baptism' 109.

[8] The church used both the Pauline metaphor (death and resurrection in Christ) and the Johannine metaphor (rebirth) to picture the effects of baptism. See E. Dassmann, *Sündenvergebung durch Taufe, Buße und Martyrerfürbitte in den Zeugnissen frühchristlicher Frömmigkeit und Kunst* (Münster 1973) 86.

[9] See further Williams, *Church History* 26 (1957) 245-250. For the role of baptism in Latin inscriptions see G. Sanders, 'L'idée du salut dans les inscriptions latines chrétiennes (350-700)', in *La soteriologia dei culti orientali nell'Impero romano*, edd. U. Bianchi and M.J. Vermaseren (Leiden 1982) 365-71. He describes baptism in these inscriptions as the *signum fidei* (i.e. the most explicit witness of the deceased's being a believer), the source (i.e. *fons*) of salvation and the condition and source of grace.

[10] I understand ταῦτα πάντα προσειπόντας (7.1) to refer to the teaching of the Two Ways (1-6).

The same course of preparation is also apparent in Justin Martyr, *1 Apol.* 61. After the catechumen has accepted the church's teaching and undertaken to live according to it, a period of prayer and fasting precedes his baptism. Tertullian, *De bapt.*, attests further expansion of the rite. The immediacy of the eunuch's baptism at the hands of Philip is an anomaly in need of explanation (8). Indeed, for Tertullian the sacrament should not be given hastily, but delayed until after a period of preparation by prayer, fasting, prostration, a night-long vigil and confession (20). The rite was also preferably to be performed on certain days because of their symbolic significance, i.e. Easter, Pentecost or Sundays (19). Anointing with oil also formed part of the ceremony (7) and the sacramental power of water as a celestial agent was emphasised (3-6).

In the Roman rite of baptism (third century AD) the catechumen had to follow a course of instruction for three years (Hippolytus, *Apost. Trad.* 17).[11] After this the catechumen was separated from the community for a period of prayer, examination and exorcism, followed by bathing (Thursday), fasting (Friday), prayer, prostration, exorcism (Saturday) and a night-long vigil (Saturday night). The period of preparation was followed by baptism on the Sunday. The rite also shows various ceremonial accretions, e.g. the order of persons to be baptised, the use of oils of grace and of exorcism, the signing of the catechumen's forehead and the celebration of the eucharist (21). But all this accretion to the celebration of the sacrament, it has been argued, did not entail a magical view of the rite's effectiveness, for baptism still required faith and continued obedience for santification to be effective (41).[12] Unbelievers are baptised not to redemption but to damnation, e.g. Cyprian, *Epist.* 73.5, and Origen, *In Luc. hom.* 26.[13] Moreover, baptised persons could be expelled from paradise if they did not bear fruit worthy of their baptism, e.g. Cyprian, *Epist.* 73.10.[14] This also explains the requirement that there be a period of instruction and proof. Future members of the community had to know what was to be believed and how they were to live as believers after their acceptance of baptism.

As already stated, baptism was for the church the pre-eminent means for gaining the forgiveness of sins. As such, the infallible effectiveness of the sacrament was often praised. But, as Dassmann argues, with the advent of gnosticism there was a danger that baptism would be misunderstood as a magical initiation into the cosmic process of redemption. The churches met this threat by:

(a) stressing the historical component of redemption, the incarnation, life, death and resurrection of Jesus;

(b) emphasising the need for obedience to the churches' moral teachings; and

---

[11] B. Botte, *Hippolyte de Rome. La tradition apostolique d'après les anciennes versions* (Paris 1968). On the preparation for baptism in the Roman rite see also A.M. Fausone, *Die Taufe in der frühchristlichen Sepulkralkunst* (Rome 1982) 76-81.

[12] Cf. also A. Hamman, *Encyclopaedia of the Early Church* vol. 1 (New York 1992) s.v. 'Baptism' 107, and A. Nocent, *Encyclopaedia of the Early Church* vol. 2 (New York 1992) s.v. 'Sacraments' 749. I do not see how an appeal to the conditions of faith and obedience necessarily obviates the charge that the sacrament was magical, if one was already inclined to view it as such. As J.G. Gager, *Curse Tablets and Binding Spells from the Ancient World* (Oxford 1992) 24-25, argues, the distinction between the terms 'magic' and 'superstition' on the one hand and 'religion' on the other is not absolute but relative. It depends on the position of the observer. In the present instance, to think that faith and obedience remove the rite of baptism from the realm of magic/superstition merely discloses the belief of the observer as to the reality and effectiveness of the sacrament.

[13] References are cited from Dassmann, *Sündenvergebung durch Taufe* 90.

[14] The reference is cited from Dassmann, *Sündenvergebung durch Taufe* 96.

§17 Baptism and Salvation

(c) the careful preparation and instruction of catechumens.[15]

Importantly, Dassmann also contends that because of the significance attached to moral instruction in preparation for baptism, the baptismal event and vow became a recurring point of reference invoked by the church fathers in their attempts to enforce obedience to the moral teachings of the churches. Christians were called to keep alive the baptismal event (τῆρειν τὸ βάπτισμα). The divine demands were conceived to have their basis in the baptismal event described variously by such metaphors as rebirth, new creation, new covenant etc. In this context recalling the baptismal event was a way of keeping persons conscious of their moral obligations. Baptism marked a caesura in the life of the believer. Obedience to the moral teaching of the church was demanded. Failure to keep the baptismal event entailed expulsion and damnation. Dassmann[16] comments:

> People, who in the third century mainly came to baptism as adults and were conscious of their own entanglement in personal sin, experienced the sacrament not as application of a collection of abstract theological content, but in the first place as release from the entanglements and the darknesses of their earlier life, whose sense and purpose through the guilt of their sins had been darkened, at the same time as incorporation into the eucharistic community of the church, the sign of their closeness to God and future hope.

This view of the sacrament explains why some individuals might leave their baptism until later in life. Individuals might by virtue of their office be unable to follow to the letter the moral teachings of their church. Rather than be baptised and risk damnation, such persons might prefer to delay baptism. At the end of their life they could then receive the forgiveness of sins which was the essential gift of baptism. Does this explain the action of Constantine, or for that matter the supposed neophyte of our inscription? If so, by separating the baptismal conditions of faith and obedience and delaying their acceptance of the rite such individuals at least appear to hold a rather cynical, indeed superstitious,[17] view of the sacrament.

S.R.L.

---

[15] Dassmann, *Sündenvergebung durch Taufe* 87-88. Other factors such as the risks posed by syncretism and persecution have also been alleged to explain the developments listed by Dassmann. For example, B. Botte, *Hippolyte de Rome* 29, notes that in a period of syncretism 'the church had nothing to gain in creating half-Christians who would be for it a heavy burden if not a danger'. The danger of persecution and the presence of schismatics also posed a threat. See also Fausone, *Die Taufe in der frühchristlichen Sepulkralkunst* 76.

[16] Dassmann, *Sündenvergebung durch Taufe* 83.

[17] Cf. fn. 12 above.

INDEXES

SUBJECT INDEX

abbrevation	§5 n.25, §14 n.9
abuse	55, 60, 68, 70, 74, 75
acclamation	4-6, §2 n.5
accounting	55, 66
accounts	§4 n.23, 37, 56
annual return	75
archive	64
accusation	143
acquisition of property	141
acrostic	156ff., §14 n.5
act of association	§4 n.23
action against property	§3 n.63
actors	144
address	
letters	123-5, 171, §9 n.8
universal address	127
administrative district	49
adoption	§3 n.21
aeons	176
age	65
agreements	57
agriculture	56
Agrippa	153-5, §13 n.7
Agrippeia	118
Alexandrian court	10
ambassador	110
amphora	157, 162, 164
anachoresis	96, 97ff. §6 n.15
notification	100
angelology	176
anointing	178
apostolic authorship	121
apostolic faith	116
appeal procedure	65
applications for lease	83
aretalogies	174
aristocratic models	108
army	68, 153-5
auxiliary units	§13 n.14
military escort	54, 67
military register	162
post	10
asceticism	104
associates	52, 53, 55, 57, 64, 66, 78, §4 n.23
association of Greeks	19
asylum	10, 14-15, 34-36, 41, 44, §3 n.19-22
athletes	130, 144
privileges	§10 n.2
auction	47, 49-51, 55, 57, 61, §4 n.23
bidding process	53
minimal bid	50
audience	5, 127
Augustine	173, 174
autonomy	110
awarding of a crown	107
banishment	35
bank	48, 50, 55-6, 65, 67, §4 n.11, 19, 21, 23, 28, 36, 92, §5 n.22
bank ledger	67, 99
baptism	167, 176ff.
delaying baptism	§17 n.6
Johannine metaphor	§17 n.8
Latin inscriptions	§17 n.9
magic	§17 n.12
Pauline metaphor	§17 n.8
schismatic group	§17 n.7
signum fidei	§17 n.9
bathing	178
battle of Milvian bridge	§14 n.41
beast	165
beer	§4 n.77
benediction of Amidah	146
benefaction ideology	106ff.
benefaction terminology	113
benefactors	149
bodies of saints and martyrs	§14 n.37
booty	§3 n.22
boulai	§4 n.70
breastplate	167
brigandage	§6 n.22
brothel	39
brother	171
capital	57
catechumen	167, 171, 178-9
catoecic land	47, 66, §4 n.1, 5
Celtic incursion	107
census declaration	37, 73, §3 n.101
census	§4 n.49
central	
administrative control	60
fiscal planning	56
imperial budget	68
centralization of economic power	§6 n.16
centralized and planned economy	57
ceremony	5
chancellery	133
chanting	6
charisma	6
check mark	67
cheirographon	77, §4 n.5
chrematistai	23
Christ's redemptive work	177
Christian	
amulet	156
apologists	120
benefaction ethics	113
funerary inscriptions	§17 n.2
household	116

Christian (continued)		control (continued)	
inscriptions	176	title	§3 n.44
phrases	124	of tax-companies	§4 n.23
rhetoric	121	conversion	173
sign	§14 n.38	copying	141
symbol	§14 n.38	exemplum	137, 170
talisman	§14 n.38	corporate bodies	130-1, 133
Christianity	142, §17 n.6	corporation	58, 74
christological controversy	158	correspondence of	
church	113, 144, 171	strategos	31
circus factions	4-6	corruption	60, 68, 74 (see also abuse)
citizen body	2		
civic		corvée	89, 90, 94
expenditure	60	cosmic events	174
life	120	costs of administration	§4 n.58
modelling	108	court	23, §3 n.55
civic-mindedness	110	created order	§14 n.32
civil appeals	134	credal confessions	158
civil disturbance	36	creeds	158, 167
class and status		criminal appeals	134
attitude to poor	75	criticism of Rome	75
control	§3 n.44	crucifixion	1-2, 35, §1 n.1
decurion class	104	cult	111
elite classes	120	cultic buildings	150
elitist culture	121	cultural smothering	75
elitist ethic	112	curse	4
higher culture	119	custody	46
lower classes	2	custody of books	55
lower strata	67	customary gratuities	§4 n.95
poorer classes	103-4, 121	customs regulations	61
poorer strata	96		
propertied class	26	damnation	178-9
social elite	134	day of resurrection and judgement	§14 n.42
cleansing	177		
cleruchs	88, §5 n.30	day-books	67, 87, 141
coercive power	66-7	death	118-9
collusion	34-5	debtor-prison	67
communion	172	decisions of emperors	137
compensation	15,-6, 35	declaration	
complaints	68-9	of disappearance	102
composition of Philemon and Colossians	45	of guarantor	51
		decline in productivity	§6 n.15
compulsory public service (see liturgy)		deity's power	173
confessional allegiance	165	deliberative exercises	120, §8 n.9
confiscated property	143, §4 n.56	delict of plagium	35
confiscation of Jewish property	146-7	delivery	
		epistulae	§10 n.23
connivance	100, §4 n.90	libelli	§10 n.20
consolation	118	democracy	110
constitutional affairs	111	depopulation	100
constitutional change	55	destitute widows	§7 n.44
contacts and friends	§3 n.17	directors	57
continuity of family	119	disguising of identity	§3 n.9
contract	51	dislocation	
contractors	81	political relationships	59, 104
contributions	149	economic, social	104
control		display of corpse	§1 n.1
government	55-6, 60, §4 n.58	distraint	54, 57,§4 n.19, 23, 33
population	§3 n.103, 109	divorce	143
status	§3 n.44	doctors	144

dogmatic formulations	176
domestic affairs of cities	42
earthquake	174
Easter	178
Eastern religions	173
eclipse	174
economic decline	103
edicts	42, 74
prefects	61
aediles	26
education	
classical curriculum	121
educational system	120
elitist culture	121
epideictic oratory	120
higher culture	119
instruction	178-9
integrity of teachers	§8 n.13
moral teachings	178-9
pragmatikai	120
rhetor	119, 144
rhetoric	118
rhetorical exercise	120
rhetorical training	120
teaching of church	177
efficiency of govt	§3 n.103
embassy	107, 133, §7 n.1
ephebic list	118
equestrian order	57
eschatology	44
esoteric legitimisation	171-2
ethical model	108
eucharist	177-8, §14 n.43
examination	178
of Christians	142
execution	1
exorcism	178
extortion	68, 70, 75
faithfulness of animals	§7 n.55
familial titles	171
family piety	114
family tree	86
fasting	178
favour asked of friend	§3 n.52
Felix	153, 154
financial	
burden	96
liability	57, 68
loss	§4 n.35
period	§4 n.45
procurator	59, 154
fine	54, §4 n.23 (see also penalty)
fiscal	
conceptions	56
domicile	99, 123, §6 n.12
policies	110
risks	56
font	177
foundlings	§3 n.99
free city	§4 n.54
freedman	§3 n.105
freedom	110
funerary inscription	119, 176, §13 n.1
funerary topos	§8 n.5
games	5, 129, 131
gematria	157, 165, §14 n.33
genre of 'lives'	121
gentile benefactors	149
giving evidence	36
gnosticism	178
goldsmiths	§4 n.89
government of Greek city	5
graffiti	6, 163, §7 n.19
grazing rights	§4 n.5
Greek Bible	166, §14 n.36
Greek city-states	74
Greek colonists	150
greeting	123-4
guarantees	51, 56-8, 68, §4 n.23
guarantor	50-51, 53, 56, 57, 66, §4 n.19, 23, 90
guardian	§5 n.30
guilds	69, §2 n.3, §4 n.89
guilt	174
gymnasium	112, §7 n.2
Hadrian's reform	136
harassment	103
Haustafeln	40
healing	173
heavenly sign	167
Hellenisation	§1 n.4
Hellenised Jew	153
herald	50
homily	121, 127
honorific descriptions	108
honorific inscriptions	114, 149
honour of parents	§7 n.56
horoscopes	§14 n.1
horsemanship	§5 n.30
hospitality	171
household relations	114
hyperalla	72 (see also ὑπέραλλα)
hypotheke	§4 n.19
ḥazaqah	142
identification	12
idolatrous pollution	150
ignorance	175
illicit act	122
imitation of meritorious actions	108
imperial	
agents	§4 n.59
archive	136
authority	136

imperial (continued)		Jewish (continued)	
budget	68	schismatics	149
business affairs	59	Jewish/Gentile question	174
coins	113	Johannine dialogue	§12 n.4
constitutions	142	judge	87, 136
court	5	judicial decisions	137
edicts	70	judicial hearing	73
fiscus	(see fiscus)	jurisdiction of local courts	
generosity	§4 n.95	and judges	42
laws	61		
officials	60	king	107
policy	5	kings of Israel	112
post	59, 144 (see also cursus publicus)	kinship relationships	115
		kinship responsibilities	113
privileges	110	koina	§4 n.54
procurator	59, 153, §4 n.56, 59		
provinces	59, §4 n.56, §4 n.58, 60	lamentation	145
respect for law	§10 n.41	language	
revenue	60	antecedents of verb	§3 n.17
rule	58	arrangement of letters	160
scrinium	133, 134	case endings	§14 n.9
subscripts	(see rescripts)	definite article	§3 n.52
whim	§4 n.95	elitist culture	121
impiety towards parents	§7 n.55	epideictic oratory	120
imprisonment	54 (see also prison)	epithet	162
indulgence	41, 132, §10 n.41	expressive present	158
information		fossilization	§5 n.16
laying of	13, 17, 54	generalized audience	127
receipt of	19, 25	Greek alphabet	159
inheritance	§4 n.56	higher culture	119
initiation	178	imperatival infinitive	§3 n.16
instruction	178-9	Johannine metaphor	§17 n.8
intellectuals of church	§14 n.37	Pauline metaphor	§17 n.8
interpolation	128	phonology	159, 164
introspection	174-5	play on words	128
invocation to Poseidon	163	predicative adjective	§14 n.25
irrigated crops	56	protasis	10
isopsephism	171	rhetor	119, 144
666	165	rhetoric	118
888	§14 n.20	rhetorical exercise	120
χμγ	4, 156ff.	stylistic values	120
ϙθ	157, 161, 169, 172, §14 n.17, 21, 36	topos	118-9, 120, 176, §8 n.5
		translation	§10 n.39
iteration	§4 n.75	use of article	§5 n.49
		word-order	158
Jerusalem temple	145	law	174
Jewish		ancestral	42
ancestry	155	force of law	137
colony	149	formulary procedure	134
confiscation of		Hellenistic	42
property	146-7	imperial	61
diaspora	127	imperial respect	§10 n.41
disputes with		Jewish	142
elements	155	revenue	§4 n.11
Hellenised Jew	153	Roman	42, 58, 142
law	142	lease agreement	§3 n.80
names	§4 n.24	lease of animals	§5 n.7
outrage against Jews	146	legal	
revolt	145-6	action	36
Samaritans	§12 n.7	advice	§10 n.12, §10 n.13

legal (continued)	
entity or corporation	58
idiom	139
opinion	42, 133
proceedings	136
protection	§3 n.98
remedies	§10 n.48
service	§10 n.15
terminology	§10 n.1
tradition	135
letters	
condolence	124
introduction	125
pseudepigraphical	§8 n.11
liability	58, §4 n.19, §6 n.2
lintels	156
liquidation of assets	§3 n.33
lists	67, 98-100
liturgy	48, 58, 62, 65, 66, 70, 76, 78, 81, 85, 89, 95, 103-5, 111, 122, 123, 176, §3 n.63, §4 n.81, 84, 86, 100, §5 n.1, 27, 28, §7 n.29, §10 n.2, 3
supervision	48, 64
term	65
local	
bourgeois	75
businessmen	74
churches	170
civic authorities	60
clergy	170
representatives	57
loss of identity	127
magic	156, 178, §14 n.42, §17 n.12
amulet	166
powers	§14 n.37
spells	§14 n.43
magistracy	49, 57, 60, 122
women	§4 n.9
magistrates	54-5, 59, 60
Mani-Codex	174
manumission	39
memorandum-taker	140
messenger	133
methodological problem	159
metrical inscriptions	176
metropoleis of Egypt	§4 n.70
metropolites	§5 n.57
minor	§5 n.30
miraculous event	174
missing persons	§6 n.9
Mithras	§14 n.19
model of Greek city	107
monasticism	104, 174
monetary economy	56
monogram	4, §14 n.38
moral depravity	174
moral teachings	178-9
moral terms	108
mosaic	163
motif	
aretalogical	174
carpe diem	119
death at young age	118-9
death in foreign land	118-9
life as race	§8 n.5
literary	1
pagan motifs in Christian inscriptions	§17 n.3
Mount Gerizim	149
movable property	141
municipal structure	61
musicians	144
names	122
Babylonian	§3 n.36
Egyptian	§4 n.24
Jewish	§4 n.24
nationalistic bias	75
new covenant	179
new creation	179
new Jerusalem	165
nexus between king and city	§7 n.1
nomads	§3 n.17
non-territorial association	144
notice	11, 13, 24
board	111
circular	23
numbers	160
numerological speculation	165-6 (see also isopsephism)
oak	173
oath	50, 101, §4 n.19
offence	173
official toleration	168
officials	53, 55-6, 130
aediles	26
agoranomos	47
antigrapheus	50, 53, 55, 62, §4 n.28
archidikastes	86
basilikogrammateus	37, 50, 61, 65, 91, 98, §4 n.22, §5 n.44
bureau of strategos	11, 23, 28
dekaprotoi	§4 n.13
dioiketes	50, 61
ephodos	53
epistrategos	61, 65, 71, 72, 73
governor	27, 35, 42, 57, 59, 60, 134
gymnasiarch	87, §7 n.2
high official	133
hyperetai	53

officials (continued)		polis-system	§4 n.13
komogrammateus	37, 64, 101, §3 n.63, §5 n.44	political diplomacy	110
		political power	5
logeutai	53	postal system	88, §5 n.4 (see also cursus publicus)
nomarches	65, §4 n.5		
oikonomos	50-1, 53-5, 61-2, §4 n.19, 22, 23, 27, 33	posting	10, 19, 20, 24-5, 30-1, 50, 134-6, 139, 141, §3 n.49, §10 n.9, 31
phylakitai	19, 20, 21, 22, 25		
police officials	11	power of Satan	177
praktor	48, 61-2, 65, 66, 67-9, 70-1, 74, 79, 95, 97-8, 100, §4 n.83, 84, 85, 86	praise	145
		praktoreia	100
		prayer	145-7, 167, 178
prefect	61, §4 n.79	prefectorial prostagmata	61
presbyteros	64, §4 n.86, 100	prescript	122, 170
procurator	59, 153, §4 n.56, 59	demise	§9 n.7
procurator	59, 154	Greek & oriental	127, §9 n.13
proxenoi	119	Hebrews	127
royal functionary	107	intitulations	127
strategos	11-12, 23, 25, 28-31, 37, 61, 66-7, 69, 70, 72-3, 86, 91, 98, 118, 146, §3 n.22, 55, 80, §4 n.79, §5 n.44	James	127
		omission	123
		transmission of NT letters	127
			127
		price of crops	§6 n.15
symbolaphylakes	53	priest	111, 167, §3 n.22, 23, §7 n.4
syntaktikoi	47		
topogrammateus	101	prison	43, 46, 67
xystarches	32-3	private	
oppression	75	debt	77
oracles	104	lawyers	§10 n.12
orphans	§5 n.30	religious celebration	§3 n.52
ossuaries	§14 n.42	private property	
ownership of animals	§5 n.7, 47	ownership of animals	§5 n.13
		ownership of land	§3 n.98
p-value	§14 n.15, 16	ownership of property	§4 n.1, 19, 56-7
paganism	§17 n.6	protection of property	§3 n.61
paradise	178	sanctity of property	26
paraenetic material	127	probability theory	159
parental relationship	154	procuratorship	155 (see also procurator)
partner	58	professional associations	144
patriarchs	112	property of God	§14 n.42
patron	128, §6 n.16	prophetic literature	75
Paul and Seneca	§8 n.11	protective sign	§14 n.38
Paul's imprisonment	44	provision of support	172
payment of expenses	§3 n.17	public	
penalty	2, 15-6, 26, 35, 54, 65-6, 81, 134, §3 n.24-5, §4 n.28	notice	10, 17, 19, 20, 23, 25, 26,19, 25, 64
Pentecost	178	revenue	32
penthemeros	85, 87, 88, 90	service	85
performers	§3 n.52	virtue	109
persecution	143, 165, 171, §17 n.15	publication	135
personal		punishment	1, 2, 4, 40, 41, 54, 173
favour	19	Rabbi Gamaliel II	75
influence	25-6, 57	ransom	§3 n.22
relationship	154	rates of pay	53
petition(er)	133, 144, 145, 147 (see also libellus)	rebirth	179
		receipt	47-8, 53, 61-2, 67, 77, 92
verbal to emperor	§10 n.21		
philosopher	113-4	reciprocity	§7 n.6, 46, 55, 57
piety	§7 n.57	church patronage	§7 n.57

reciprocity (continued)	
ethics	115
ideology	114
motifs	113
norms of	114
parental favour	114
terminology	109, 113-5
recourse and redress	55
regional specialisation	155
registration	78, 81, 90-1, 99
deeds of sale	§3 n.101
minors	§4 n.92
population	39
sheep	§5 n.6
wagons	§5 n.51
regulation of personnel	53
religious disposition	75
remorse	41
repayment	§7 n.55
repentance	41, 173
reports	65-6
republican order	58
requisition	68, §5 n.4
rescript	61, 129ff.
archive	134, §10 n.31
authentication	§10 n.4
authoritative opinions	136
codes	136
composition in Latin	§10 n.39
earliest evidence	§10 n.15
early Church	142
epistulae	§10 n.39
legal status	136-7 141
posting	§10 n.9, 31
private rescript	131
subscripts	37, 73, 101-2, 134-6, §10 n.36, 39
residence of emperor	134, §10 n.9
resurrection	176
retaliatory execution	§1 n.7
revolt	146-7
reward	10, 13, 15-7, 19, 25-6, 31, 45, 51, §3 n.17, 21, 23, 24, §4 n.20, 95
risk	§4 n.19
ritual fund	146-7
robbery	146
Roman	
citizen	152, §5 n.57
citizenship	141
dominium	142
equites	76
generals and dictators	112
influence	2
law	42, 58, 142
legal opinion	42
legal terminology	§10 n.1
legal tradition	135
royal office	§7 n.1
rulers	
gentile	149
Graeco-Roman	132
Hellenistic	132
ideal	111
munificence of	§7 n.29
sacrament	177-9, §14 n.43
sacrifices to gods	142
salary	§4 n.31, 83
salutation	172
Samaritan religion	150
sanctuary	173
Sanhedrin	112
schism	171
scriptures	120
seal	§10 n.4
security	51, 58
self help	25-6
self-revelation of deity	174
senatorial provinces	59, §4 n.56, 58, 60
Serapeum	§3 n.19, 21
serfdom	§6 n.16
sexual/purity offences	173
signing of forehead	178
sins	175
sister	171
slave	
authority to punish	33
branding	§3 n.10
capitation taxes	§5 n.47
collars	§3 n.11
cruelty	36-7, §3 n.20, 98
definition of fugite	41
description of	16, 17, 20, 24, 27, §3 n.101
disease, defect or noxal liability	26
fear of new master	36
fear of punishment	36
financing of escape	34
flight	9ff., 100
flight as remedy	§6 n.2
flight in NT	40
fugitivarius	25-6
fugitive types	18
functions of	§3 n.37, 98
harbouring	16, 28, 33, 35, §3 n.24
hiding place	36, §3 n.109
incidence of escape	39
inclination to flight	26
intention of runaway	41-2
master-slave relationship	1
multiple flight	20, 36, 40
murder of master	1ff., §1 n.7
numbers	§3 n.99
ownership	39, §3 n.11
pursuit	10ff., 26ff.
reasons for flight	36

slave (continued)
 receipt of information 19
 registration §3 n.101
 return of 14
 right of asylum §3 n.19
 rights and interests of
  masters §3 n.44
 sale to another master 14
 seizing §3 n.21
 successful escape §3 n.103
 unclaimed fugitive §3 n.72
 verification of status §3 n.101
 witness §3 n.57
sleep 2
social expectations §7 n.46
social upheaval §3 n.102
solar deities §14 n.18
soup-kitchen 162
status 16, 36, 111, 130, §10 n.39
subcontractor 48, §4 n.22
suit for injury 35
summons 23
Sunday 178
supernatural power §14 n.43
superstition §14 n.37
supervisor 48, 62
symbol 8, 156-7, 159-161, 164-8, 172, 177-8, §5 n.48, 9, §14 n.5, 14, 21, 38, 42-3
 Chi-rho 4, 8, §14 n.5, 38
 christogram 166-7, §14 n.38
 cross §14 n.38, 42
 staurogram §14 n.38
 taw §14 n.38, 42
symbola 50, 51, §4 n.18, 19
synagogue 110, 149, 150, §12 n.5, 6
syncretism §14 n.18, §17 n.15
synhedrion §4 n.102
synod of gymnasts and
 stage-performers §10 n.3
synods 144
syntax 159

talisman §14 n.38
tattoo 11-2
tax
 absconding §4 n.90
 arrears 48, 54, 65, 66, 74, 77, 81, 103, §4 n.84
 assessment 53, 55, §4 n.51, 70, §6 n.6
 assessor §4 n.27
 avoidance 75
 burden 103-5
 burden of tax-farmers §4 n.79
 bureau §4 n.23

tax (continued)
 capitation tax 64, 67-8, 78, 88-9, 96, 98-100, 103, §4 n.90, §5 n.46-7, 52
 checks and balances 55
 chrysargyron §4 n.89
 collection 47ff.
 collectors 47ff., 171
 control of companies §4 n.23
 delinquents 98, 100
 direct taxes 58, 61, 74
 disputed assessment §4 n.27
 economic exploitation 75
 efficiency 68
 enkyklion §4 n.2
 exemption §5 n.44
 farming 47ff., 95
 ferry-tax §6 n.3
 grievances 110
 Hellenistic system 54, 74
 impositions on cities §4 n.51
 increases 68
 indirect taxes 58, 59, 68, 74, 76, §4 n.54
 Jesus's attitude 75
 Judaea 74ff., §4 n.13
 licence-tax 80-2, 94
 lists 92, §6 n.5
 loss 69, §4 n.23
 multiple collecting §4 n.21
 obligations §4 n.35
 personnel 66
 poll-tax 67, 95, 97, 99, 103, §4 n.90, §5 n.47, 57, §6 n.3
 professions §4 n.89
 profit 52, 54-5, 60, 75, §4 n.19, 21, 23, 79
 Ptolemaic Egypt 49ff.
 rates 68, §5 n.57
 recalcitrant taxpayer §4 n.103
 records 61, §4 n.51
 release from §10 n.2
 remission §4 n.95
 Roman Egypt 61ff.
 Roman taxation 95
 sales tax §4 n.20
 salt-tax §6 n.3
 sinners and collectors 75
 tax-debtors 54
 tax-status §5 n.57
 taxable property §4 n.35
 trade-tax 69, 78, 93
 wealth and influence of
  tax-farmers 57
teaching of church 177
temple
 Jerusalem 145
 Mount Gerizim 149
 rivalry §12 n.3

tenant farmers	§6 n.15
testimony	174
theft	13, 16, 34, 36, 40, 41, 138, §3 n.14, 25
Third Syrian War	§3 n.30
Ti. Iulius Alexander	153
tiles	157
tomb	118
trade	§5 n.47
traditional hostilities	150
treason and acts of war	2
treatment of Christianity in courts	142
trials	137
two natures of Christ	158
unfair distribution	103
unlawful possession	147
urbanization	§4 n.51
vigil	178
vote of gratitude	107
wagon	93
wandering charismatics	105
warrant	17, 30, §3 n.49
weavers	69
widow	109, 113, 116, §7 n.57
wild beasts and birds of prey	1
witness	173, 174
woman	48-9, 121, 158, §4 n.9
destitute widows	§7 n.44
gymnasiarchs	49
prisoners of war	§3 n.22
zealots	75
Π^{66}	§14 n.38

GREEK WORDS AND TERMS

ἄγγελος	165
ἀγαθῇ τύχῃ	§14 n.1
ἀγορανομεῖον	§4 n.79
ἀμήν	158, 161, §14 n.36
ἀνακεχωρηκότες	§6 n.6
ἀνάκρισις	§3 n.101
ἀναχώρησις	98, 99, 123
ἀνιππίας	88, §5 n.30
ἀπαιτήσιμα	66
ἀπαιτηταί	78, §4 n.84, §5 n.1
ἀπεργασία	85, §5 n.28
ἀπογραφαί	§5 n.44, 47
ἀπόμοιρα	§4 n.11
ἄποροι	§6 n.6
ἀρχώνης	52, 55, 57, §4 n.58
ἀσχολούμενος	§4 n.2
ἀστυνόμῳ	§3 n.2
ἀτελής	§5 n.59
ἀτιμία	54
ἀφορμή-formula	126
βεβαιωταί	§4 n.19
βιβλιοθήκη δημοσίων λόγων	§4 n.74
βοηθός	53, 66, §14 n.25
βραχεῖα	141
βραχεῖα ἀφορμή	§10 n.49
βύρσης	§5 n.30
γεννάω	158
γραμματεῖς	66
γραφή	54, 55, §4 n.23
γυμνασιαρχίς	49
δαίμων	§8 n.1
δημοσιώνης	§4 n.5
διαλογισμοί	§4 n.19, 23
διάφορον	§3 n.21
δικαία ἀφορμή	§10 n.49
διοίκησις	66
δίπλωμα	(see diploma)
δύναμις	174
δωρεά	§3 n.45
ἔγδεια	52
ἐγκύκλιον	§4 n.19, 20, 79
εἰκών	16
εἰρήνη	§15 n.7
ἕκτον	§5 n.16
ἐλαϊκή	§4 n.11
ἐλεύθερος	§5 n.59
ἐν εἰρήνῃ	171
ἐν τοῖς δεσμοῖς	43
ἐξειληφότες	§5 n.1
ἐξομολογεῖσθαι	173
ἐπιγένημα	51, 52, 55, §4 n.19, 23, 83
ἐπικεφάλαιον	§5 n.47
ἐπίκρισις	§3 n.101
ἐπίσταλμα	33
ἐπιστάτης	§3 n.22
ἐπιτήρησις	64, 65
ἐπιτηρητής	48, 62, 65
ἐσυκοφάντησα	§4 n.103
ἔφορος	55
ζηλωτής	§7 n.2, 4
θβ	164
ἴδιος λόγος	66
ἰδία	99, 100, 103, §6 n.6, 12
Ἰουδαῖοι	149
Ἰσραηλῖται	149
καλοὶ κἀγαθοί	108, 109, 111, 115
κοιμητήριον	§17 n.2
κολάσιμος	7
κτηνοτρόφος	§5 n.36
λογευτήριον	§4 n.23
μερισμός	99-100, §4 n.79, 90, §5 n.7, 47, §6 n.6, 8, 13
μετοχή	§4 n.23

μέτοχοι	52, 64, 66, §4 n.23, 85 (see also associates)	**LATIN WORDS AND TERMS**	
μηνύειν	§3 n.16	a libellis	132, 133, 134, 136, §10 n.4, 15
μήνυτρον	§3 n.17		
μισθός	53	ab epistulis Graecis	132-4
ναύβιον	89	ab epistulis Latinis	132-3
Νέρων Καῖσαρ	165	actio furti	35
οἰκογένεια	§3 n.101	actio servi corrupti	35
ὀνηλάτης	§5 n.36, 46	adaeratio	§5 n.27
ὀψώνιον	51, §4 n.19	adiutor	153, 154, §13 n.5
παράγγελμα	23	aerarium	57
παραζυγὴ ζυγῶν	§5 n.27	aerarium Saturnii	§4 n.58, 60
πεντάδραχμος	§5 n.26	annona militum	48
περιστερά	§14 n.20	apparitor	27
περίζωμα	§3 n.8	assertio in libertatem	§3 n.24
πρακτόρειον	67	beneficarius	152
πρακτορικόν	§4 n.83	bona fides	138, 141, §10 n.49
πράκτωρ	(see praktor)	causa	138
πρόγραμμα	23, 62, 64	censor	57, §4 n.45
προνοεῖν	113	cognitio	35, 134
πρόνοια	109ff.	coloni	104
πρὸς ὥραν	43	coloniae	138
προσαγορεύω	§9 n.9	concilium	§10 n.17
προσδέχομαι	171	conductor	59, §4 n.58, 59
προσφορά	§3 n.59	conquistor	26
σκέπη	122	consilium	142
σταυρός	§14 n.38	corrector	60
στηλογραφεῖν / στηλογραφία	173	crimen capitale	35
		curator	60
στρατοπέδων	153	curator civitatium	60
συκοφαντεία	54	curator rei publicae	§4 n.65
σύμβολον	47	cursus honorum	152, 153, 155
τελῶναι	47	cursus publicus	133 (see also imperial post)
τελώνης	47ff., 78		
τέλος	§5 n.7	decreta	137
τέλους ὠνή	49	decumae	57
ὑϊκή	§5 n.7	decuriones	60
ὑπέραλλα	70, 74	defixiones	§14 n.43
ὑπηρέται	66	diploma	80, 81, 83, 84, 90, 94, §5 n.4, 13, 16, 18, 47, 49, §10 n.2
ὑπογραφή	§10 n.1		
ὑπογραφῆς ἀντίγραφον	102	epistula	131-2, 135-7, 139, 142-4, §10 n.23, 39
ὑπόμνημα	61		
φίλοι	111	fiscus	§3 n.72, §4 n.58, 60
φόρος ἵππων	§5 n.30	fugitivarius	25-6
φόρος νομῶν	§4 n.5	fugitivus	41
φόρος	§5 n.7	furtum	§3 n.25
φυλακίτης	§3 n.52	grammatici	144
φυλακτήριον	167	honestiores	35, §3 n.90
χαῖρε	124, 126, 170, §9 n.6	humiliores	35, §3 n.90
χαίρειν	123, 170	imperium	137
χαίροις	124, 126, §9 n.6	iudicium publicum	35
χειρισταί	66	iuridicus	71, 73
χειρωνάξια	§5 n.46	ius	137
χλαμύς	§3 n.8	ius civile	134, §10 n.48
χμγ	4, 156ff.	ius Italicum	42, 138
χρηματισμοί	61	ius praetorium	§10 n.48
χωματικόν	89, §4 n.90, §5 n.47	iusta causa	138-9, 141, §10 n.49
ϟθ	157, 161, 169, 172, §14 n.17, 21, 36	iustum initium	141
		iustus titulus	§10 n.49

labarum	167, §14 n.41
lex	137
lex censoria	57
lex Fabia	26, 35
lex provinciae	42
libellus	129ff., §10 n.15, 18, 20, 21
loculus	163
longae possessionis praescriptio	139
longi temporis praescriptio	137-8, 141-2, §10 n.48
lorica	167, §14 n.43
lustrum	57
magister privatae	31, §3 n.83
magistri, promagistri	57, 58
manceps	57-8, §4 n.58
mandata	27
memorandum	17, 19, 20, 37, 45
munimen	167
munus	58
nomen sacrum	169, 171
ordo publicanorum	57
pactiones	§4 n.102
patella	162
pilleus	26
pistrinum	46
plagium	35
portoria	§4 n.59
praedes	57
praedia	57
praefectus castrorum	153, 154
praefectus praetorio	35
praefectus urbi	35
praefectus vehiculorum	60
praefectus vigilum	27
praetor urbanus	42
primipilaris	153
procurator	61
procurator Augusti	60
procurators	35
propositio	134
providentia	112
publica custodia 46	
publicani	57-61, 74, 76, §4 n.13, 102
publicum	§4 n.60
quadragesima	§4 n.54
recognovi	132, 133, 135, §10 n.4
relegatio in perpetuum	35
rescripsi	132-3
rescriptio	129ff.
responsa	§10 n.12
scrinium	133, 134
scripsi	135
scriptura	57
senatus consultum	2, 26
senatus consultum Silanianum	§1 n.7
servus publicus	26

signum fidei	§17 n.9
societas publicanorum	58-9, 76, §4 n.58
socii	57 (see also μέτοχοι)
stipendium	74
subscriptio	130-2, 134, 136, §10 n.1, 18, 39
tributum capitis	§4 n.49
tributum soli	§4 n.49
usucapio	138, 141-2, §10 n.48, 49
vectigal	§4 n.58
verba ipsissima	§5 n.59
vicesima hereditatum	59

HEBREW WORDS AND TERMS

פרק	146
הר	149
חרם	147
שלום	172
קרן	147
החרימו קרן	146

GREEK AND LATIN WRITERS

Aelius Aristides, Πρὸς Πλάτωνα περὶ ῥητορικῆς 109	163-4
Aristophanes, Thesm. 1029	§1 n.2
Aristotle, Mag. Mor. 2.12.1	§7 n.50
Augustus, Res Gestae. 1.3	§7 n.41
Cicero, Ad Att. 5.15.3	45
Cicero, Ad Att. 6.1.13	45
Cicero, Ad fam. 5.9.2	26, 45
Cicero, Ad fam. 10.1	26
Cicero, Ad fam. 13.77.3	26, 45, §3 n.14
Cicero, Ad Q. frat. 1.2.14	45
Cod. Theod. 9.40.16	104
Cod. Theod. 12.1.63	104
Cod. Theod. 13.5.18	150
Const. VII Porph., De caer. 318	7
Demosthenes, Contra Theoc. 19-21	§3 n.24
Dig. 1.15.4	27
Dig. 1.4.1.1	137
Dig. 11.4.1.1	26, 27
Dig. 11.4.1.2	26
Dig. 11.4.1.3	27
Dig. 11.4.1.4	27
Dig. 11.4.1.8	27
Dig. 11.4.1.8a	27
Dig. 11.4.3	27
Dig. 21.1.1.1	26
Dig. 21.1.17.1	43
Dig. 21.1.17.12	41, 43
Dig. 21.1.17.4	41
Dig. 21.1.17.5	41
Dig. 21.1.43.1	41
Dig. 28.3.6.9	134

Dig. 29.5.1	2	Pliny, Epist. 9.21	41
Dig. 48.19.28.16	2	Pliny, Epist. 9.24	41
Dig. 48.5.39.10	§10 n.15	Pliny, Epist. 10.96	142
Dig. 49.1.25	134	Pliny, Epist. 10.97	142
Dig. 49.4.1.7, 10	134	Plutarch, Eum. 8.3	§7 n.37
Dio Cassius 57.10.5	68	Plutarch, Mor. 100a	§5 n.30
Dio Cassius 59.6.3	132	Plutarch, Mor. 479F	§7 n.50
Dio Cassius 69.16.2	60	Plutarch, Mor. 802F	§7 n.33
Dio Chrysostom, 3.127	§7 n.32	Plutarch, Poll. 1.210	§5 n.30
Dio Chrysostom, 3.52	§7 n.31	Ps.-Manetho, Apost. 4.198-200	§1 n.2
Dio Chrysostom, 4.44	§7 n.30	Seneca, Ben. 2.11.5	§7 n.50
Dio Chrysostom, 50.3	§7 n.30	Seneca, Ep. 47.5	2
Dio Chrysostom, Or. 3.50	§7 n.30	Seneca, Ep. 73.10	§7 n.42
Dio Chrysostom, Or. 12.42-43	§7 n.50	SHA 13.1	137
Diog. Laert., 7.30	§7 n.37	Stobaeus 3.52	§7 n.52
Fl. Vopiscus, Vita Saturn. 7.8	150	Stobaeus 4.25.52	§7 n.56, 57
Gaius, Instit. 1.5	137	Suetonius, De gramm. 15	45
Gaius, Instit. 2.43	§10 n.49	Tacitus, Ann. 4.6	58
Gaius, Instit. 2.46	138	Tacitus, Ann. 13.32	2
Herodotus, Hist. 2.108	§5 n.30	Tacitus, Ann. 14.42-45	2
Horace, Carmen 2.19	174	Tacitus, Hist. 1.72	5
Iamblichus, Vit. Pyth. 38	§7 n.53	Tacitus, Hist. 2.19	§7 n.39
Josephus, AJ 2.40	§7 n.34	Tacitus, Hist. 5.9	154
Josephus, AJ 11.345	150	Val. Max., Fact. ac dict. mem.	
Josephus, AJ 12.10	§12 n.3	libri IX, 4.8 (ext.) 1	§7 n.40
Josephus, AJ 12.10	§12 n.7	XII Tables 6.3	138
Josephus, AJ 12.160 ff.	§4 n.13		
Josephus, AJ 12.37	§7 n.35		
Josephus, AJ 12.7	150	**PATRISTIC WRITERS**	
Josephus, AJ 13.256	149		
Josephus, AJ 13.74 and 78	150	Augustine, Catech. rud. 26.50	167
Josephus, AJ 13.74 and 79	§12 n.7	Augustine, Epist. 88.2	144
Josephus, AJ 14.10	149	Basil, Epist. ad Libanium 339	§8 n.11
Josephus, AJ 16.23	118	Clement of Alex., Protrepticus 8	§8 n.11
Josephus, AJ 18.85	§12 n.4	Const. apost. 1.6	121
Josephus, AJ 19.213-216	149	Cyprian, Epist. 70	§17 n.7
Josephus, AJ 19.213-216	§12 n.1	Cyprian, Epist. 73.5	178
Josephus, AJ 19.299 and 353	154	Cyprian, Epist. 73.10	178
Josephus, Ap. 2.206	§7 n.55	Didache 7	177
Josephus, BJ 3.307	§12 n.3	Epiphanius, Haereses 1.267,	
Josephus, BJ 3.307	§12 n.4	2.186, 3.140, 340, 451	163
Josephus, Vit. 423	§7 n.42	Epistle of Barnabas 9.8	§14 n.20
Julian, Epist. 36	§8 n.13	Eus., Com. in Psal. 23.496, 621	163
Justinian, Instit. 1.8.1	§3 n.20	Eus., De laud. Const. 6.5-6, 10-17	§14 n.32
Justinian, Instit., 2.6 and 2.6.11	138, §10 n.49	Eus., Demonstr. evang. 1.1.11	163
Libanius, Or. 2.32	104	Eus., HE 7.13	143
Libanius, Or. 30.8-31 and 45.26	104	Eus., Vita Const. 1.11.2	162
Livy, AUC 4.46	§7 n.39	Eus., Vita Const. 1.27.1-2	162
Lucian, Apology 13	§7 n.29	Eus., Vita Const. 1.28-31	§14 n.40
Lucian, Fugitivi 27, 29	10	Eus., Vita Const. 4.20.1	162
Lucian, Vera hist. 1.4	174	Georg. Monach., Chron. 5.795	7
Nikolaos of Damascus, 90 F 134	118	Greg. Nyss., Contra	
Pempelos, Περὶ γονέων	§7 n.56, 57	Eun. 1.1.338	163
Philo, De spec. leg. 3.159-162	68, §6 n.2	Hippolytus, Apost. Trad. 17	178
Philo, Decal. 111-115	§7 n.55	Hippolytus, Apost. Trad. 36	§14 n.43
Philo, Jos. 161	§7 n.37.	Hippolytus, Apost. Trad. 42	167
Philo, Leg. 51	§7 n.29	Irenaeus, Adv. haer. 1.15.5	§14 n.20
Philo, Leg. 253	§7 n.37	Jerome, Epist. 22.30	§8 n.11
Philo, Moses 1.174	162	J. Chrysost., Hom. in Ioan. 2.2	§8 n.11
Pliny the Elder, Nat. Hist. 5.149	118	Justin Martyr, 1 Apol. 61	178

Justin Martyr, Apol. 1.69	143
Justin Martyr, Cohort. ad Gr. 8, 35	§8 n.11
Justin Martyr, Orat. ad Gr. 5	§8 n.11
Lactantius, De mort. persec. 44	§14 n.38
Origen, Contra Cels. 1.62, 7.58-9	§8 n.11
Origen, In Luc. hom. 26	178
Sozomen, H.E. 5.18	121
Tertullian, Carn. res. 8	167
Tertullian, De bapt. 15	§17 n.7
Tertullian, De bapt.	178
Tertullian, De cor. 3.4	167

INSCRIPTIONS

Agora 21 J6	162
AE (1928) 97	61
BE (1968) §564	150
CIJ I 123	§7 n.8
CIJ I 682	§7 n.14
CIJ II 964	161, 164
CIJ II 1436-7	161, 164
CIL III 411	§10 n.31
CIL III 13283	60
CIL V 34	154
CIL XIV 5347	§10 n.15
CIL XVI 26, 45, 58	§13 n.14
Dessau, ILS 6870	104
Dessau, ILS 8858	60
Dessau, ILS 9481	176
Dessau, ILS §8731	§3 n.11
Ditt., Syll.^{3} 736	§3 n.24
I. Delos 2532	149
I. Delos 2616	149, 150
I. Ephesos 555	§7 n.19
I. Ephesos 1285 no.14	163
I. Ephesos 1390	§7 n.15
I. Iasos 150	§7 n.18
I. Kios 16	118
I. Klaudiupolis 70	117, 118
I. Magn. 239	7
I. Nikaia 1005	§2 n.5
I. Tyre I 160bis	163
I. Aphrod. Chr. §181 ii	6
I. Aphrod. Jud.	162
ICUR VII 19820	176
IEgChr 663	158
IG II(2) 1132	§7 n.11
IG II(2) 2943	151
IG II(2) 2943	150
IG II(2) 3449	§7 n.8
IG II(2) 10219-222	150
IG IX(2) 1109	§7 n.22
IG V(1) 1432	§7 n.17
IG VII(2) 2712	§7 n.2
IG VII(2) 4132	§7 n.16
IG X, 2, 1.789	150
IG XII(9) 211	§7 n.21
IG XII(9) 905	§7 n.20
IG XII, 8. 439	150
IG XIV 336	150
IGLSyria I 230	§14 n.19
IGLSyria II 309	161, §14 n.3
IGLSyria II 310a	§14 n.17
IGLSyria IV 1249	161, §14 n.3
IGLSyria IV 1442	§14 n.2, §14 n.31
IGLSyria IV 1443	§14 n.2
IGLSyria IV 1447	162, 164
IGLSyria IV 1448	§14 n.2, §14 n.31
IGLSyria IV 1452	§14 n.2
IGLSyria IV 1486	161
IGLSyria IV 1614	156
IGLSyria IV 1632	§14 n.17
IGLSyria IV 1648	§14 n.2, §14 n.17
IGLSyria IV 1707	165
IGLSyria IV 1789	§14 n.2
IGLSyria IV 1812	§14 n.2
IGLSyria IV 1814	§14 n.17
IGLSyria IV 1814B	162, 164
IGLSyria IV 1831	§14 n.17
IGLSyria IV 1957	§14 n.2
IGLSyria V 2179	161, 164, §14 n.3
IGLSyria V 2232	§14 n.2
IGLSyria VI 2916	§14 n.19
Fouilles d' Amyzon en Carie I 259-263	1
LBW VI 2145	§14 n.17
Limes de Chalcis no.206.37	§14 n.17
Michel 541	§7 n.51
Michel 1011	§7 n.2
OGIS 669 = MChr 102	42, §7 n.12
OGIS 751	§7 n.13
Recueil des inscriptions chrétiennes de Macédoine	
§291	150
§5	176
§265	177
SEG XI 948	114
SEG XVIII 27	§7 n.4
SEG XXII 114	§7 n.23
SEG XXVII 1016	163
SEG XXX 80	§7 n.20
SEG XXX 1740	165
SEG XXX 1785	163
SEG XXXI 694	164
SEG XXXI 1494	5
SEG XXXII 809-810	148
SEG XXXII 1108	164
SEG XXXIII 1266	152
SEG XXXIV 1259	117
SIG3 399	§7 n.11
SIG3 591	§7 n.18
SIG3 618	§7 n.18
SIG3 700	§7 n.9
SIG3 734	§7 n.11
SIG3 740	§7 n.21
SIG3 814	§7 n.19

TAM V 1 238	173	P. Cair. Zen. 59213	§3 n.13
TAM V 1 317	174	P. Cair. Zen. 59537	36, 37, §3 n.95
TAM V 1 318	174	P. Cair. Zen. 59613	17
TAM V 1 319	174	P. Cair. Zen. 59620	15, §3 n.19, 21
TAM V 1 464	174	P. Cair. Zen. 59620-1	36
ZPE 51 (1983) 80-84	145	P. Cair. Zen. 59804	36, 37, §3 n.94
ZPE 51 (1983) 105-114	106	P. Cair. Zen. 59822	45
		P. Cair. Zen. 59837	45
		P. Charite 20	89

PAPYRI

		P. Col. 1 recto 1a-b	67
		P. Col. 1 recto 2	67
BGU 8	67	P. Col. 1 recto 3	67
BGU 77	86, 87	P. Col. 123	133
BGU 136	86, §5 n.36	P. Col. II 1 recto 5	91
BGU 213	81, 82, 84, 85, §5 n.16	P. Col. V 1 verso 1a	85
BGU 267	137, 141	P. Col. Zen. 75	17
BGU 340	61	P. Coll. Youtie 54	125, §9 n.6
BGU 435	§9 n.6	P. Colt 7	161
BGU 515	70	P. Corn. 24	99, 100, §6 n.2
BGU 821	§9 n.6	P. Dura 13	§4 n.101
BGU 908	70	P. Edfou 270	94, §5 n.22
BGU 969	86, 87, §5 n.36	P. Edfou 272	94, §5 n.22
BGU 1073	§10 n.2	P. Edfou 397	94, §5 n.22
BGU 1074	§10 n.2	P. Edfou 446	94
BGU 1565	§4 n.3	P. Ent. 62	§12 n.7
BGU 1730	23	P. Erl. 118	§9 n.9
BGU 1756-1890	23	P. Fam. Tebt. 15	§7 n.24
BGU 1774	22, 23, 30, §3 n.3	P. Fay. 129	125, §9 n.6
BGU 1894	83, 84, 85, §5 n.12	P. Fay. 153	67, §4 n.92
BGU 1993	19-22, 25, 45, §3 n.31, 45	P. Flor. II 140	§9 n.6
		P. Flor. II 345	§9 n.6
BGU 2012	§7 n.26	P. Flor. III 382	70
BGU 2110	§5 n.11	P. Freib. IV 57	25, §9 n.9
BGU 2327	§5 n.28	P. Gen. 5	§3 n.63
BGU 2520	79, 81, 84, §5 n.16, 17	P. Gen. 95	77, 78, 92, §5 n.47
CPH 55 and 70	§10 n.2	P. Gen. 108	§4 n.5
CPJ 22, 28, 128	§12 n.7	P. Genova I 50	164
CPJ 448	§11 n.4	P. Giss. 58	66
CPJ 513, 514	§12 n.7	P. Grenf. 47	36
CPJ3 Inscr 1436-7	161	P. Grenf. II 41	61
CPR VI 4	§4 n.5	P. Grenf. II 100	§14 n.5
CPR VII 49	164	P. Grenf. II 112a	158, §14 n.9
CPR X 32	§14 n.5	P. Gron. 17, 18	§9 n.6
P. Alex. 27	§9 n.6	P. Hamb. 9	81, 82, 84, 85, §5 n.4, 5, 10, 16, 17
P. Alex. 29	170, 171, §9 n.6, 9		
P. Amh. 64	49	P. Hamb. 33	91, §5 n.40
P. Amh. 92	82-84, §5 n.18	P. Hamb. 83	§4 n.5
P. Ant. 32	§4 n.2	P. Hamb. 91	15, 20, 36, §3 n.22
P. Ant. 93	§9 n.9	P. Harr. 62	20, 25, 28-30, 32, 45
P. Bas. 16	§9 n.6, 9	P. Harr. 137	§3 n.80
P. Batav. I 11	§4 n.2	P. Haun II 33	§9 n.6
P. Batav. I 22	164	P. Heid. 212	22, 24, 25, 45, §3 n.3, 76
P. Beatty Panop. 1	31, §3 n.82		
P. Berl. Leihg. 15	20, 37, 39	P. Heid. 333	§15 n.7
P. Brem. 19	§9 n.6	P. Herm. 4	§9 n.9
P. Brem. 56	§9 n.6	P. Herm. 40	§12 n.7
P. Cair. Isidor. 1 and 8	§4 n.70	P. Herm. 45	§9 n.6
P. Cair. Zen. 59015 verso	19, 20, 36, 37, 45, §3 n.17	P. Herm. Rees 64	161, 164
		P. Hib. 29	§4 n.35
P. Cair. Zen. 59070	16	P. Hib. 54	22

P. Hib. 94, 95	§4 n.18	P. Oxy. 1063	§9 n.6
P. Iand II 12, VI 94	§9 n.6	P. Oxy. 1156	§9 n.6
P. Iand. VII 143	92, §5 n.48	P. Oxy. 1162	170, 171, 172
P. Köln III 163	§9 n.6	P. Oxy. 1185	§9 n.5, 6
P. Köln V 219	§4 n.2	P. Oxy. 1189	146, 147
P. Köln V 236	§14 n.1	P. Oxy. 1300	§9 n.10
P. Köln VII 188	§5 n.6	P. Oxy. 1350	§9 n.10
P. Lille I 29	35	P. Oxy. 1409	§5 n.28
P. Lips. 44	131, 132, §10 n.3	P. Oxy. 1422	28, 31, 34
P. Lips. III 105	123	P. Oxy. 1423	32-34, §3 n.13
P. Lond. 1164i	§10 n.2	P. Oxy. 1424	122
P. Lond. 1912	§7 n.28	P. Oxy. 1438	77, 82, 91, 92, §5 n.47
P. Lond. 1917	§9 n.6	P. Oxy. 1457	82, 91, §5 n.49
P. Lond. 1949	16, 22	P. Oxy. 1492	§9 n.6, 10
P. Lond. 1950	16, 22	P. Oxy. 1517	§5 n.46
P. Lond. 2052	17, 20-22, 25, 36, 45, §3 n.3, 30	P. Oxy. 1587	§9 n.5, 6, 10
		P. Oxy. 1643	32, 34
P. Med. Bar. 5	§5 n.30	P. Oxy. 1664	§9 n.6, 10
P. Meyer 21	§9 n.9	P. Oxy. 1667	§9 n.6, 10
P. Mich. 170 and 171	102	P. Oxy. 1675	§9 n.6
P. Mich. 223	82	P. Oxy. 1774	§9 n.10
P. Mich. 224	§12 n.7	P. Oxy. 2150	§9 n.10
P. Mich. 360	85, §5 n.28	P. Oxy. 2193	§9 n.6
P. Mich. 364	§4 n.3	P. Oxy. 2274	§9 n.6
P. Mich. 519	§9 n.9	P. Oxy. 2275	§9 n.10
P. Mich. 529	70	P. Oxy. 2414	91, 92
P. Mich. 580	100, 101, §6 n.14	P. Oxy. 2669	100, §6 n.14
P. Mich. 594	§6 n.2, 4	P. Oxy. 2785	170-72, §9 n.6, 10
P. Mich. 709	78, 83, 84, 91, 92	P. Oxy. 2985	§9 n.6
P. Mich. Michael 27	§9 n.6	P. Oxy. 2986	§9 n.6
P. Michael 29	§9 n.9	P. Oxy. 3094	§9 n.6
P. Mil. Vogl. II 53	83, 84	P. Oxy. 3150	123, §9 n.10
P. Mil. Vogl. IV 212	§12 n.7	P. Oxy. 3469	§9 n.6
P. Nag. Ham. 66	§9 n.9	P. Oxy. 3507	§9 n.6, 10
P. Neph. 12	§9 n.9	P. Oxy. 3556	§4 n.4
P. Oslo III 79	§7 n.27	P. Oxy. 3611	129-132, 144
P. Oxy. 36	54, 61	P. Oxy. 3616	9-10
P. Oxy. 44	61, §4 n.2, 79	P. Oxy. 3617	9-10, §3 n.1
P. Oxy. 112	§9 n.6	P. Oxy. 3645	122
P. Oxy. 122	§9 n.6	P. Oxy. 3819	§9 n.10
P. Oxy. 123	§9 n.10	P. Oxy. 3857	169, 170, 171, 172
P. Oxy. 174	48, 62	P. Oxy. 3863	§9 n.10
P. Oxy. 185	§4 n.2	P. Par. 61	54
P. Oxy. 237	42	P. Par. 62 = UPZ 112	
P. Oxy. 251	100, §6 n.14	P. Petaus 44	86
P. Oxy. 252	100, 101, §6 n.14	P. Petaus 53	§7 n.25
P. Oxy. 253	100, 101, §6 n.14	P. Petrie II 39	§5 n.30
P. Oxy. 283	§3 n.57	P. Petrie III 54b	§5 n.30
P. Oxy. 284, 285	68, 69	P. Petrie III 57 a, b, 58 c, d	§4 n.18
P. Oxy. 298 verso	68	P. Petrie III 110	§5 n.30
P. Oxy. 393	68	P. Phil. 34	§9 n.5, 6
P. Oxy. 394	68	P. Princ. II 50	48
P. Oxy. 472	36	P. Princ. II 71, 74	§9 n.6
P. Oxy. 500	146, 147	P. Princ. III 165	§9 n.6
P. Oxy. 525	123	P. Rainer Cent. 122	§4 n.89
P. Oxy. 526	§9 n.6, 10	P. Rein. 48	§9 n.6
P. Oxy. 705	146, 147	P. Rein. 135	78
P. Oxy. 916	§4 n.5	P. Rev.	49, 53, 54, 61
P. Oxy. 933	§9 n.6	P. Ross. Georg. III 4	§9 n.6
P. Oxy. 995	164		

P. Ryl. 194	65, 81, 84, 85, §5 n.9	SB 11904	70
P. Ryl. 195	86, 89, 90	SB 11974	100-2, §6 n.14
P. Ryl. 595	99, 100, §6 n.2, 9	SB 12015 + 12018	97-99
P. Ryl. 691	§9 n.6, 9	SB 12082	§9 n.6
P. Sarap. 3	91	SB 12087	70
P. Strass. I 37	§9 n.6	SB 12107	§9 n.6
P. Strass. IV 170	123	SB 12176	§9 n.6
P. Strass. IX 866	§12 n.7	SB 12177 (= 36)	§9 n.6, 9
P. Strassb. 22	137, 139, 141	SB 12184	4, 7, 166
P. Tebt. 99	§5 n.30	SB 12260	§4 n.89
P. Tebt. 170	§9 n.6	SB 12304	169, 170, 172
P. Tebt. 360	81, 82, 84, 85, §5 n.4, 16	SB 12504	48, 62, 64
		SB 12506	51, 52
P. Tebt. 417	123, §9 n.6	SB 12590	§9 n.6
P. Tebt. 812	§4 n.19	SB 12658	156, 166
P. Tebt. 1036	§5 n.30	SB 12678	66, 68
P. Tebt. 1061	§5 n.30	Stud. Pal. XX 167	164
P. Turner 19	§4 n.2	Stud. Pal. XXII 177	83, 84, §5 n.18
P. Turner 41	30, 32, 45, §3 n.13	ZPE 61 (1985) 71-3	47
P. Wash. Univ. II 101	164	UPZ 3, 4	15, §3 n.21
P. Wisc. I 36	73	UPZ 112	11, 14-16, 19, 20, 22, 34, 36, 45, 49, 51, 54, 61, §3 n.10, 19, 21, 24, 49, §4 n.23
P. Yale II 105	120		
PBM III 899	§9 n.6		
PGM II 3	156		
PGM II 8a verso	156	WChr 158	§10 n.2
PGM II 24 verso	156		
PIFAO I 3	65, 92, §5 n.20		
PSI 56	66	**OSTRACA**	
PSI 206	§9 n.6		
PSI 208	170, §9 n.6	O. ROM II 160	94
PSI 329	45	O. ROM II 160	§5 n.22
PSI 388	§5 n.30	O. Tait II 1076	§5 n.51
PSI 570	19, 21, 22	O. Tait II 1078	84, 92, 94, §5 n.2
PSI 667	36, 37, §3 n.95	O. Tait II 1079	94
PSI 785	82, 91	O. Tait II 1079-1081	§5 n.22
PSI 787	83, 84	O. Tait II 1080	94
PSI 826	§9 n.9	O. Tait II 1081	94
PSI 871	102	WO 392, 395,	89, 93
PSI 1041	170, §9 n.6, 9	WO 684	89, 93, 94, §5 n.52
PSI 1049	§9 n.6	WO 1054	89, 93, §5 n.51, 52
PSI 1420	§9 n.6	WO 1057, 1261	89, 93, §5 n.51
PSI XI Congr. 11	§9 n.6		
PSI XXI Congr. 13	49		
SB 7243	§9 n.9	**OLD TESTAMENT**	
SB 7269	170, 172		
SB 7432	§14 n.25	Exod. 20.12	115, §7 n.56
SB 7461	67, §6 n.2	Exod. 22.19	147
SB 7462	67, 99, 100, §6 n.2	Exod. 22.22-24	116
SB 8004	§9 n.6		
SB 9050i	§4 n.99	Lev. 27.28, 29	147
SB 9207	70		
SB 9524	§9 n.6	Deut. 2.34	147
SB 9842	92, §5 n.49	Deut. 3.6	147
SB 10255	170	Deut. 5.16	115
SB 10773	§9 n.9	Deut. 7.2	147
SB 11009	§9 n.6	Deut. 10.18	116
SB 11588	§9 n.6	Deut. 20.11	172
SB 11863	70	Deut. 20.17	147
SB 11881	§9 n.9	Deut. 23.6	172
SB 11902	69	Deut. 24.17-21	116

Josh. 8.26	147
Josh. 10.28, 37	147
Judges 6.23, 19.20	§15 n.7
1 Sam. 7	146
1 Sam. 25	§7 n.55
1 Kings 18	146
1 Chron. 12.18	§15 n.7
Psalm 1.3	158
Psalm 15	173
Psalm 34.20	172
Psalms 55-59	173
Psalm 61.9	162
Psalm 68.5	116
Psalm 77.35	162
Psalm 92.1	145
Psalm 121.8	§15 n.7
Psalm 124.5	§15 n.7
Psalm 127.6	§15 n.7
Psalm 132.17	147
Psalm 146.9	116
Prov. 15.25	116
Isa. 22.13	119
Isa. 34.2	147
Jer. 9.7	172
Jer. 25.9	147
Jer. 48.25	147
Jer. 50.21	147
Lam. 2.3	147
Ezek. 9.4	§14 n.38
Ezek. 29.21	147
Dan. 3.31, 4.34	§15 n.7
Obad. 14	146
Mic. 4.13	147
Nah. 3.1	146

APOCRYPHA AND PSEUDEPIGRAPHA

1 Macc. 15.15-24	150
1 Macc. 15.23	149
2 Macc. 4.5	§7 n.37
2 Esdras 4.17, 5.7	§15 n.7
Sir 7.28	§7 n.55

QUMRAN

1QM 1.4	147

RABBINIC LITERATURE

b. Pes. 117a	§11 n.5
m. Ket. 2.2	142
m. Peah 1.1	147
m. Ta'an 2.4	§11 n.3

NEW TESTAMENT

Matt 3.16	§14 n.20
Matt. 5.41	105
Matt. 9.10-11	69
Matt. 9.27	§7 n.19
Matt. 9.33	174
Matt. 11.19	69
Matt. 11.21, 23	174
Matt. 13.58	174
Matt. 14.2	174
Matt. 15.22	§7 n.19
Matt. 15.31	174
Matt. 17.15	§7 n.19
Matt. 17.24-27	95
Matt. 17.26	§5 n.59
Matt. 18.17	69
Matt. 20.1-16	105
Matt. 21.31	69
Matt. 27.32	105
Matt. 27.51-53	174
Mark 1.27	174
Mark 6.2, 5, 14	174
Mark 12.1-12	105
Mark 15.33, 38	174
Mark 15.6-15	5
Luke 3.12-13	74
Luke 3.12-14	69
Luke 3.13	105
Luke 4.36	174
Luke 5.26	174
Luke 8.46	174
Luke 12.19	119
Luke 15.1	69
Luke 15.2	171
Luke 18.9-14	69
Luke 19.1-10	69
Luke 19.8	54, 74, §4 n.103
Luke 19.8	105
John 4.20	§12 n.4
John 5.35	43
John 18.6	174
John 19.34b-35	174

Acts 8.37-39	177	James 4.14	43
Acts 15.23	127		
Acts 19.23-41	5	1 Pet. 1.1-2	127
Acts 23.26	127	1 Pet. 2.18-20	40
Acts 24.2	§7 n.42	1 Pet. 5.14	§15 n.7
Acts 28.16	43		
		2 Pet. 1.1	127
Rom. 2.17-3.20	174		
Rom. 7.13-25	174	3 John 15	§15 n.7
Rom. 8.31	§14 n.31		
Rom. 16.1-2	171	Jude 1	127
1 Cor. 2.4-5	121	Rev. 1.8	§14 n.20
1 Cor. 9.24-27	§8 n.5	Rev. 13.18	165, §14 n.20
1 Cor. 12.13	44	Rev. 21.6	§14 n.20
1 Cor. 15.32	119	Rev. 21.17	165
2 Cor. 7.8	43		
Gal. 2.5	43		
Gal. 3.10-12	174		
Gal. 3.27-28	44		
Eph. 6.5-9	40		
Eph. 6.9	40		
Phil. 2.29	171		
Phil. 4.8	115		
Col. 3.22-4.1	40		
Col. 4.1	40		
Col. 4.12	45		
1Tim 4.8	43		
1Tim. 5.1-8	109, §7 n.6		
1Tim. 5.3	113		
1Tim. 5.3-16	113, §7 n.44		
1Tim. 5.3a	115		
1Tim. 5.4	114, 115, §7 n.46		
1Tim. 5.4b	116		
1Tim. 5.5	116, §7 n.57		
1Tim. 5.8	109, 113, 115, §7 n.38		
1Tim. 5.8a	115		
1Tim. 5.8b	114, 115, 116, §7 n.56		
1Tim. 6.1-2	40		
Philemon	40-45		
Phm. 10	43		
Phm. 10 and 13	43		
Phm. 13-14	43		
Phm. 15	43		
Phm. 16	44		
Phm. 17	41		
Phm. 18	40		
Phm. 18-19	41, 42		
Phm. 19	40		
Phm. 22	45		
Phm. 23	45		
James 1.1	127, 128		

Made in the USA
Monee, IL
15 February 2025